1936

1935

1936

AS RECORDED BY

Introduced and
edited by
Charles Moore and
Christopher Hawtree

MICHAEL JOSEPH

LONDON

First published in Great Britain by Michael Joseph Ltd
44 Bedford Square, London WC1
1986

British Library Cataloguing in Publication Data
1936 as recorded by the Spectator.
1. Great Britain—Politics and government—
1936   2. Great Britain—Politics and
government—1936
I. Moore, Charles   II. Hawtree, Christopher
941.083   DA583

ISBN 0 7181 2672 6

Typeset and printed in Great Britain by
Butler & Tanner Ltd, Frome, Somerset and London

CONTENTS

[Pieces by those authors whose names appear within brackets were printed anonymously.]

ix

INTRODUCTION

'Beginning with a phoney peace and ending with a phoney war,' Malcolm Muggeridge has written, the 1930s had a unity which a decade seldom provides. Within the decade, 1936 has a special unity of its own. 'After I am dead the boy will ruin himself in twelve months,' George V had told his Prime Minister, Baldwin. The King died in January; in December, the new King, Edward VIII, abdicated. Outside Britain, events moved swiftly and horribly towards a crisis, although few were ready to recognise the fact at the time. In 1936, war became inevitable.

'At about this time my own life took a slight turn for the better,' recalled Goronwy Rees, 'as in 1935 I was made assistant editor of *The Spectator*, for which I was paid £500 a year for three days' work a week and was paid, in addition, for reviewing any books I chose. This was a considerable improvement in my affairs, and I also fell in love with a girl with whom, all that summer, I was very happy ... I think I would have been totally happy that year, if it had not been for the shadow of politics which fell increasingly heavily upon anyone who took any interest in such subjects. I had enough money, my job left me a good deal of leisure, I was in love, and I was writing a novel. But also the Germans had occupied the Rhineland, in Germany the concentration camps were full, in 1936 the Spanish Civil War began and several friends of mine joined the International Brigade and some were killed.'

The year opened, like so many in modern British history, with the threat of a coal strike and with an air disaster. These were quickly followed by the death of Rudyard Kipling and of the King.

In the same weeks, a rather less world-shaking death continued to provoke a curious controversy. While motoring along the Kingston by-pass, Lord de Clifford had been involved in an accident in which a pedestrian was killed. De Clifford was charged with manslaughter but insisted on the ancient, somewhat disused, right of a peer to be tried by his peers. He succeeded in his demand and was duly acquitted. *The Spectator* was dragged into the row because Rose Macaulay joked about the case in the paper's Marginal Comments column (see page 131). A libel action followed and out-of-court damages of £500 were agreed. The settlement none the less had to be made in court and the notorious Lord Chief Justice, Viscount Hewart, 'took the opportunity' – as the editor, Wilson Harris, recalled – 'to express in the most caustic language he could command (and he was not incompetent in that sphere) his amazement that a journal of a tradition of *The Spectator* should have been guilty of a piece of defamation so outrageous and so forth'. The fact that *The Spectator*'s Janus column (written by Harris in his lighter vein) had recently questioned the propriety of the Lord Chief Justice's writing in the Sunday newspapers had, of course, nothing to do with Lord Hewart's fierce remarks. It was not a good year for Lord de Clifford: a week later he was named as co-respondent in a divorce case, something on which Rose Macaulay did not venture to comment.

The question of war overshadowed this not very momentous matter.

There had been outrage over the Hoare–Laval Plan of the previous December (a month after the National Government had been returned), which would have left Abyssinia all but a dominion of Italy. 'During my experience of politics,' recalled Duff Cooper, 'I have never witnessed so devastating a wave of public opinion.' In January 1936 Anthony Eden, the new Foreign Secretary, committed the British government to an anti-Italian policy. The commitment again looked rather weak, when the government duly rejected a League of Nations report which recommended that an embargo be made on the supply of oil to Italy. Even so, it did seem that Britain was beginning once more to consider the need to defend herself, although, in his desire for a quiet life, Baldwin was extremely reluctant to have the issue discussed frankly. Early in March, a defence white paper was published which shied away from the question of money but sought a vote in favour of the principle of rearmament. In the course of the two-day debate, Clement Attlee described the white paper as 'unworldly and ambiguous', and Winston Churchill, then all but ostracised, urged speedy rearmament and a minister charged with coordinating defence. Such a post was invented, but Churchill was passed over and it was filled by Sir Thomas Inskip, president of the Lord's Day Observance Society and best known for his vigorous opposition to the Revised Prayer Book of 1928. In March, the Service estimates were considerably increased, the Air Force, in particular, being expanded. The RAF began a search for suitable sites over which to develop bombing techniques, accompanied by explosions of protest – on behalf of wildlife and fishermen – as each successive area was mooted.

The nervousness of these steps towards rearmament at home was matched by teetering, doubting meetings abroad. A naval conference in January failed to get the support of Japan and Italy. In March Eden suggested an air pact to the German Chancellor. Hitler countered by saying that the likelihood of a pact between Russia and France made this impossible. With her own breach of the Locarno Treaty, Germany was hardly in a position to expect that her proposed twenty-five-year non-aggression pact should be taken seriously. Yet, even after the German invasion of the Rhineland in March, Eden continued to believe – or at least to hope – that Germany would be satisfied with this much and no more. A meeting of the other Locarno Treaty members was held in Paris, but, in the face of French eagerness for retaliation, it was deferred to London in the hope of a calmer mood. 'As usual, I think: Oh this will blow over,' wrote as politically indifferent an observer as Virginia Woolf in her diary. 'But it's odd, how near the guns have got to our private life again. I can quite distinctly see and hear a roar.' Public opinion, however, breasted all this equally enough, although it was presently outraged and alarmed by the methods which Italy adopted in Abyssinia. Red Cross units were bombed and poison gas was used against primitively armed Abyssinians.

Just as Germany and Italy were consolidating their gains, civil war brokeout in Spain.

After the initial confusion of the events which followed the election, earlier in the year, of a left-wing coalition and the subsequent rebellion led by the generals, the Spanish war developed into one round which so many of the decade's conflicts polarised. While the French and British governments, eager to avoid a European embroilment, urged non-intervention (duly agreed and flouted by Germany and Italy), intellectual opinion turned it into the central confrontation between the forces of fascism and democracy. A flood of bad verse resulted, and the subject was one of the many to be covered by Victor Gollancz's orange-covered Left Book Club editions which started during the year. One of the better poems, Auden's 1937 'Spain', contained a line – later revised, before Auden disowned the poem altogether – which displays the dubious morality of 'the conscious acceptance

3

of guilt in the necessary murder'. Evelyn Waugh, one of those to take account of the murder of priests at the hands of the Republicans, replied to the same year's famous, somewhat fatuous questionnaire which solicited writers' – rather than, say, greengrocers' – opinions about which side they supported in the conflict. Waugh's reply should be quoted in full rather than as the simple support for Franco (a man he disliked) that it is often claimed to be: 'I know Spain only as a tourist and a reader of the newspapers. I am no more impressed by the "legality" of the Valencia government than are English communists by the legality of the Crown, Lords and Commons. I believe it was a bad government, rapidly deteriorating. If I were a Spaniard I should be fighting for General Franco. As an Englishman I am not in the predicament of choosing between two evils. I am not a Fascist nor shall I become one unless it were the only alternative to Marxism. It is mischievous to suggest that such a choice is imminent.'

Evelyn Waugh's views have been regarded by many – then and now – as perverse. Not only did he veer from the conventional line over Spain, but he had already sided with Italy over the Abyssinian dispute. This was not so much a support of Mussolini's Fascism as a recognition that Italian strength was the only thing that held back Nazi Germany from invading Austria; frustrated in Abyssinia, Mussolini's party might turn in other directions, and even into alliance with Hitler, both of which were duly to happen. Whatever else it might have been, Waugh's stance – his Catholicism in direct opposition to a fear of Communism – derived from a principle, the justification of which would, for all its quirks, be set in a clearer light with the revelation of the full horrors of the Stalin regime, with which Britain was in nominal alliance, and whose evil designs were aided by the treachery of Waugh's more orthodox contemporaries.

One could wish that Goronwy Rees had used these *Spectator* columns to reveal the contents of Guy Burgess's drunken confessions rather than waiting until he prepared his autobiography. In a bid to win Rees over after reading a review by him about a book on the depressed areas, Guy Burgess agreed to give one agent's name, so long as he did not ask for any more. Rees wrote, 'I don't suppose he could have named a person who could have carried more weight with me. He was someone whom I both liked and respected greatly, and with whom I would gladly have joined in any enterprise. Nor was I alone in my admiration; there

4

was no one I knew who did not praise his intelligence, his uprightness, his integrity.' Indeed not: he was *The Spectator*'s art critic at this time, Anthony Blunt.

With such questions of allegiance in the air, one might suppose that the lack of newspaper coverage of royal affairs resulted from the importance of the rest of the news. In fact, it was the consequence of an awkward, unofficial truce between the press and the authorities in the face of a potential constitutional crisis that had caused rival correspondents to lay down that contemporary equivalent of the telephoto lens – the pen and the imagination. As William Deedes explains in his contribution to Part Six, the British press agreed for months to say nothing whatsoever about the affair between the new King and Mrs Wallis Simpson. The foreign press, of course, was not so restrained, and despite censorship of foreign publications by the customs, rumours of what was going on began to seep through. Forbidden to comment, *The Spectator* noted another, equally dramatic destruction of Victorian values – the burning of the Crystal Palace early in December, the loss of 'the last relic of the authentic Victorianism. There it stood for eighty years and more, monument to earnestness and the genuine if limited vision of Albert the Good. All the industry, all the respectability, all the self-complacency of nineteenth-century England were represented by the vast structure that rose before the nation's astonished gaze in Hyde Park on the model of the Chatsworth conservatories. Strange that qualities so solid should be mirrored in a structure in a sense so flimsy.'

The King abdicated on 11 December in order to marry Mrs Simpson. Among prominent politicians, only Winston Churchill opposed the Abdication and tried to take the King's part. The Archbishop of Canterbury, Dr Lang, put the seal of official disapproval on Edward VIII's preference of an American divorcee over his throne and his duty: 'Even more strange and sad it is that he should have sought his happiness in a manner inconsistent with the Christian principles of marriage, and within a social circle whose standards and ways of life are alien to all the best instincts and traditions of his people.'

The strange and sad progress of the year was closely reported and discussed in the pages of *The Spectator*. This was a period when journalists, like politicians, were not often far-sighted about political trends. Osbert Lancaster, for example, records how, in 1938, on his way to London from Portsmouth, he bought

5

a copy of *The Times*: 'In my detached and carefree youth I was no great student of the daily Press and seldom, I am ashamed to say, opened *The Times* and then only to read the dramatic notices and the Court Page; but on this particular morning, having exhausted all else long before the sight of the distant pinnacles of Charterhouse had produced their accustomed *frisson* as we shot past Godalming, was driven by boredom for once to read the leader column. "It might be worth while," hazarded Mr Barrington-Ward, "for the Czecho-Slovak government to consider whether they should exclude altogether the project, which has found favour in some quarters, of making Czecho-Slovakia a more homogeneous state by cession of that fringe of alien population which are contiguous to the nation with which they are united by race." Little attention as I paid to the activities of the Runciman mission and non-existent as was my experience of international negotiation, such an expression of opinion in Printing House Square at this particular moment suggested to me a willingness to capitulate unmatched since the days of Ethelred the Unready. It was of course true that very similar sentiments had been expressed a week before in the *New Statesman* but, being even then aware of the vagaries to which Mr Kingsley Martin's political judgement was occasionally subject, I had neither taken them seriously myself nor expected others to do so.'

The Spectator, however, although sometimes deadened by Wilson Harris's priggish internationalism, was never guilty of the pro-appeasement errors and evasions of Geoffrey Dawson's *The Times*. Reviewing ten years of editorship in 1943, Wilson Harris recorded the 'chastening experience' of re-reading the bound volumes of his paper to discover 'political judgements which subsequent events have found derisory'. But, as time passes, it is heartening to find how successful weekly journalism can be at conveying the flavour and essence of a period. Unlike daily reporting, it does not become entirely immersed in its details. Here, we have a considered view of events, yet with an immediacy which even the best history cannot match.

In 1936, Wilson Harris paid a ten-day visit to Germany, giving a substantially accurate account of the state of the country. He failed to secure an interview with the Führer, and instead one afternoon watched him from a distance in a hotel. 'The scourge of Europe sat, quite quietly, quite unimpressively, consuming sweet cakes and a liquid which I could not at that distance identify, and looking singularly like any other respectable Berlin citizen.' A few days later he went to watch Hitler lay the foundation stone of the new Reichsbank, another event he describes in his autobiography, *Life So Far*, which appeared a year before his death in 1955. 'Everything was tense expectation till, with a blaze of trumpets and a kaleidoscope of banners, Hitler with his SS and SA escort entered the arena at the far end and made his progress to the centre of it, while every arm but mine was lifted in the Nazi salute, and every voice but mine Heil Hitlered till the procession reached the platform, and the proceedings of the day began. I speculated with some apprehension as to what would happen to me as a result of my abstention from the acclamation.'

Nothing at all did in fact happen. It was the one moment in which Wilson Harris diced with danger in his life as a journalist.

At this time (and indeed until the 1970s), *The Spectator*'s home was 99 Gower Street, the title Wilson Harris gave to a collection of his journalism. Unlike the previous premises in Wellington Street, which A.G. Gardiner described as 'a house dressed in a surplice – a house that stands in conscious rebuke of a naughty world', 99 Gower Street had won a more raffish reputation. It had previously been inhabited by 'Angel Anna', the purported daughter of Ludwig of Bavaria and the Spanish dancer Lola Montez, and she ran the establishment as a brothel. Wilson Harris, however, was not the sort of man to be particularly proud of this history.

Born in 1883, he was brought up in a Quaker household, and from Plymouth College went up to St John's College, Cambridge, during all of which time he was strictly teetotal. 'No one, I am certain, is the worse, and a good many people would be much better, for that degree of abstinence,' he wrote. Faced by such virtue, it is refreshing to learn of the story told by James Pope-Hennessy: when Pope-Hennessy was literary editor of *The Spectator* after the war (Harris stayed on until he was eased out in 1953) – he opened a drawer, which the absent Harris had omitted to lock, and found a Bible inside; he was hardly startled by such contents but, on opening the book, was astonished to find it interleaved with pornographic photographs.

After a period as a master at the Leys School, where W.H. Balgarnie, the model for James Hilton's Mr Chips, was his colleague, Harris went on to Leighton Park, and then threw up teaching to read for the Bar. While doing so, he began to dabble

7

in journalism, and in 1908 joined the Liberal/Radical *Daily News* as a sub-editor. Thanks to the Liberal victory of 1906, the paper was enjoying a period of prosperity, and supported a fine cast of the eccentric and the talented on its staff.

One who remains anonymous among Harris's early colleagues in the sub-editors' room was a man with 'an artificial arm, which, as things got hectic towards the end of the evening, he would feverishly detach and thrust between his own back and the back of his chair; whether the relief thus achieved was physical or mental I could never quite determine'. Intact, but scarcely less chaotic, was G.K. Chesterton on his weekly arrival with a brilliant, hastily scribbled essay for the newspaper's assistant editor, E.C. Bentley, a man only a little less immortal for *Trent's Last Case* than for the Clerihew. (Chesterton's death in 1936, mourned by Bentley in *The Spectator* – along with those of Kipling and Housman – marks the end of an era, one which survived for longer than the Modernists generally allow.)

In *Those Days* Bentley recalled that even then Harris was 'well on his way to the front rank of publicists upholding the Liberal idea in world politics, and destined in the fulness of time to breathe new life and soul into *The Spectator*'. That was to be some way off. Harris remained with the *Daily News* for fifteen years, in the course of which he became news editor, leader writer and, after his coverage of the Paris Peace Conference, diplomatic correspondent. As Bentley observed, he was a dedicated internationalist, and was increasingly drawn to the League of Nations Union, which he joined in 1923, and whose journal he edited, as well as delivering numerous speeches on its behalf. 'In the inevitable vote of thanks my address was almost invariably described as "lucid", till I got tired of the sound of the word – though no doubt it is better to be lucid than unintelligible.'

Lucidity was a quality that he brought to his editorship of *The Spectator* in 1932.

Harris was only the sixth editor in the 104 years since the journal had been founded in 1828 by Robert Stephen Rintoul, who remained editor for thirty years until, after a brief gap, he was succeeded by Meredith Townsend and R.H. Hutton – a partnership of almost forty years which was, as John Gross has written, 'one of the success stories of Victorian journalism ... the new *Spectator* quickly established a reputation for blameless sobriety. For thousands of readers it was *the* respectable weekly – a fact resented by the *Saturday Review*, which scoffed at its public as one sheltering from the boisterous realities of life in leafy rectories and somnolent villas'. The association with the country's rectories continued into the editorship of St Loe Strachey in 1897. By the beginning of this century the journal was 'in fact something of a laughing-stock among the intelligentsia of the period, and, indeed, among the younger members of our own family, who applied the term "spectatorial" to any particularly pompous and respectable pronouncement', recalled the editor's cousin, James, whose brother Lytton, ten years away from *Eminent Victorians* and fame, was grateful enough to suppress his natural instincts in his reviews for the journal.

In 1925, two years before St Loe Strachey's death, *The Spectator* was acquired by Evelyn Wrench, for it had become clear that Strachey's son, John, the future author of *The Coming Struggle For Power*, was going to break with family political tradition. Wrench, 'whose name,' Duff Hart-Davis has written, 'might have come out of Waugh and whose manner out of Wodehouse,' was editor for seven years, although for part of that time it was very much under the control of two bright young men, who can be said to have set in motion that sense of elegant anarchy which has often characterised the journal over the past fifty years.

Peter Fleming, brother of Ian, whose various adventurous expeditions must have been more than welcomed by Wrench and Harris, was joined in this rejuvenation of the journal by a beguiling, erratic character, Derek Verschoyle, who in 1936 was literary editor. Verschoyle's blithe good spirits, continual wishful thinking and cheerful assurances that all was going well meant that his career, with each fresh start – such as a post-war publishing company – never fulfilled all that it promised: he ended up as editor of the *Grower* magazine, of all things, after another wife had wearied of the way in which he spent her money to so little effect. (His path again crossed that of Goronwy Rees during the war, when he told him that he had a remarkable source of information in Italy, one that involved considerable danger, for which his contact would require sufficient recompense. Rees was able to secure this from his masters in the intelligence services and, in due course, Verschoyle passed on translations of his contact's reports. So astonishing and authoritative did these appear that MI6 soon became eager for closer liaison, something that proved awkward to arrange, for, fuelled by an evening's drinking and with the prospect of the next payment to spur him on when his energies flagged, Verschoyle had contrived the reports himself.)

The first book in which Peter Fleming appeared was a 1933 anthology of *Spectator* pieces, *Spectator's Gallery*, which he and Verschoyle edited for Jonathan Cape, a book of whose existence Wilson Harris only became aware when he saw it for sale in a shop.

Part of *The Spectator*'s strength in the Thirties derived from a distinct difference between its 'front' and 'back' halves, with the preponderance of fun coming in the back. Harris broadened the religious coverage, and secured copious advertising for the financial section – as he also did for a peculiar health supplement, in which was placed an advertisement for a lunatic asylum in Northamptonshire 'strictly for the upper and middle classes', whom it attempted to entice with the offer of trout-fishing. Harris tended to run rather worthy series about the state of the world by such men as H.G. Wells and Aldous Huxley. Often more obsorbing are the pieces which we include by the now all-but-forgotten journalists whom Harris had known earlier in his career. The 'back' half introduced the world to the talents of Anthony Blunt, A.L. Rowse (now *The Spectator*'s longest-standing contributor) and Graham Greene, who in 1936 was the paper's film critic.

This book tries to give the flavour of 1936 as it seemed to *The Spectator* and its contributors then. In order not to impair that flavour, the editors have not intruded, but they have been very lucky to secure the services of four distinguished writers – William Deedes, Sir Hugh Greene, Peter Quennell and A.L. Rowse – who were 'there' then, and are with us still. Their short reminiscences do much to deepen the reader's perspective on the events of fifty years ago. Both their writing and the extracts themselves recapture for us an age extraordinarily different from our own, and yet as weakened by doubt, uncertainty and division.

CHARLES MOORE
CHRISTOPHER HAWTREE

Part One: The King Is Dead . . .

THE KING WE SALUTE
[R. C. K. ENSOR]

In the person of a new King there ascends the Throne an unknown quantity. That must nearly always be so, for kingship is
a unique office. In other capacities Edward VIII has, as Prince
of Wales, been very much in the public eye. Millions have seen
him personally, and everyone in the Empire knows his photographs. His doings have filled a considerable space in the newspapers for twenty years. For all that, anyone trying to estimate
his qualities for his new task has little to go upon.

Some formal facts must, of course, be brought into account.
As Prince, he has travelled widely, visited nearly every corner of
the Empire, and in some – especially in Western Canada – spent
considerable time. He has likewise visited the United States and
South America. On the European Continent he has been in the
habit of sojourning (unofficially) about as much as – not conspicuously more or less than – is usual with young men of means
and leisure. Adding it all together, he is one of the world's most
travelled personages, if mileage be the test. But is it? Does it
add much to equip the wearer of the Crown, that he has chased
steers in Alberta, shot elephants in tropical Africa, played polo
and squash rackets all over the world, or ridden point-to-point
races on a great variety of occasions? Yet these, apart from the
performance of ceremonial functions, are the kinds of activity
chiefly reported of the Prince of Wales during the post-War
years. Blameless indeed, but irrelevant to his new career. What
one would really have liked to know, was how far upon his
rounds in the Empire he had used the opportunities given him
for studying how it was governed – its vast, bewildering, yet
absorbing variety of constitutions, political outlooks, traditional
methods, and leading statesmen. That is the harvest of travel
which, if he has it, will be an asset to him now. We have little
means of judging whether he has it or not. The daily newspapers,
that have talked so much gossip about him, have on these really
important topics – perhaps necessarily – been silent.

It is the same with his earlier upbringing. We know that during the War he was attached to the Staff at G.H.Q.; that he
previously spent some terms at Magdalen College, Oxford; that

earlier still he was a cadet at Dartmouth. We need not suppose any of these experiences valueless, but we can be quite certain that the Prince could not undergo them in the sense and in the way that any ordinary person would. The inferences that might be drawn from them about anybody else, cannot be drawn in his case. That is no fault of his, but it is the fact. In one way his father was more fortunate; he did not become Heir Presumptive till he was twenty-six, and his experience of the Navy before that was genuinely professional. Edward VIII has been in the direct succession to the Crown since his birth.

What then is known of him? Chiefly, perhaps, that he has 'personality.' And what, in a Royal personage, does personality mean? It means that in sustaining his part he has been more than a lay figure; that when people come into touch with him, they find him individual and arresting; when they converse with him, he has something of interest to say. Here has been the secret of his world-wide popularity. It is not an easy accomplishment for persons so placed, nor is it at all common among them. His grandfather, Edward VII, had it in a conspicuous degree; and there is no doubt that in this and some other characteristics the new King recalls his ever-popular namesake. It is a gift that will advance a King a very long way along the path of duties which pertain to the modern Head of the British Empire. But, like most gifts, it carries a risk – the temptation to rely on it too exclusively. It was a risk that Edward VII did not escape. Few criticised what he did or left undone, while he lived; for his charm disabled criticism. But after his reign was over it was noted that the prerogatives and effective personal influence of the Monarch had diminished and not increased during its course. If Edward VIII – who has the advantage over his grandfather of ascending the throne much younger – is to profit fully by the lesson of his career, he will seek to combine with the qualities of that brilliant monarch some others that were more conspicuously displayed by Queen Victoria and by George V.

We have faith that he will rise to the height of his great calling. The last fault that anyone has ever charged him with hitherto is inertia. On the contrary he has given at times – especially in the physical sphere – an impression of over-activity, of resting too little, of taking too incessant a toll of his nerves. But that, if it be so, is the defect of a warm and spirited, not of a weak or commonplace nature. And of kingship this is certain – that, if great qualities of character are there, it will find openings for them and call them out. Nothing could be further from the truth than to suppose the position of a British constitutional monarch a sort of gilded captivity. His opportunities and responsibilities are alike magnificent, and should make unfailing appeal to all the best that is in him. If this was the case before the passing of the Statute of Westminster, it is now doubly so. The theory whereby the King, as the sole formal element of unity in the British Commonwealth of Nations, is separately 'advised' by six separate Governments, each for the sphere of the nation that they govern, may be accurately described as a fiction. But it is not necessarily the worse for that; fictions honestly and ably adhered to have played a great part in the history of past progress. Nobody supposes that Edward VIII, any more than George V, will be able to keep himself acquainted in detail with the inner politics of five other nations besides Great Britain. But he may none the less make his moral headship a felt reality in each, and set an example of public spirit and adherence to duty that will not be lost on any of them.

Corresponding to the impartiality with which he must be King of 'all the Britains,' and not of Great Britain merely, is his duty to be King of all classes, rich and poor, brain-workers and hand-workers alike. Here his course can never be easy; but if he follows in his father's footsteps – as in his Accession statement he declared he would – it will be clear. We see no reason to doubt that he will, and that the special lustre with which history will on this account crown George V's name, may in due course rest equally upon his son's name also.

24 January

A SPECTATOR'S NOTEBOOK
JANUS

It has fallen to *The Spectator* in the course of its history to record the deaths of five British sovereigns. A study of the verdicts passed in its columns on the two earliest of them, King George IV and his successor, is an instructive revelation of the strangely low repute in which the throne was in those days held, or of the candour by which Press criticism was in those days marked, or – more probably – of both. What, it may be asked with some curiosity, would the elegist find to say of George IV? He found this, among other things:

15

'A very nice attention to the rigidities of moral observance can hardly be asked from one who, to the vigour of youth and an eminently handsome person, unites a complete command of fortune, and whose will every man who surrounds him is more anxious to flatter than to regulate. The King at a very early period of his life gave evidence of his fondness for female society; a failing of all others the most excusable, but it not unfrequently brings down on its possessor a degree of censure that the colder and darker vices of a disposition inherently evil do not provoke.'

There follows a list of the principal successive objects of His Majesty's amours, and the quarrel between him and Queen Caroline is summed up heavily against the Queen.

* * * *

Rather strangely William IV evokes distinctly stronger criticism, prefaced with the remark that the strictures

'are the dispassionate convictions of a calm retrospect having no regard to aught but the plain truth.'

The plain truth thus commended is that

'on the throne, as in private life, William IV appears to have been a good-hearted man with frank impulses and kindly feelings; willing to do right but not unfrequently doing wrong from want of knowledge and strength of mind. He had little information and strong prejudices. Though sufficiently conceited and self-willed, he was easily imposed upon and led by the designing.'

Or, if you will:

'His late Majesty, though at times a jovial and, for a king, an honest man, was a weak, ignorant, commonplace sort of person. ... Notwithstanding his feebleness of purpose and littleness of mind, his ignorance and his prejudices, William IV was to the last a popular sovereign, but his very popularity was acquired at the price of something like public contempt.'

* * * *

When it is considered that these appreciations appeared in each case within some four days of the late King's death the changes that a century has brought in journalistic method are sufficiently demonstrated. The change indeed was effected in much less time than that. When Queen Victoria died in 1901 no word was spoken of her in these columns but in praise, though of her son

16

as he ascended the throne a certain subtle criticism is implied, in the suggestion that

> 'as to the past we believe that the nation will not and ought not to think. Their attention must be fixed on the King that is and will be and not on the Prince of Wales. The King will be judged and ought to be judged solely by his life and actions as King.'

*   *   *   *

The Order of Service followed by the great gathering in St Paul's Cathedral on Tuesday had necessarily to be compiled in haste, and any word of captious criticism would be ungenerous, the more so since the service was, I believe, that used after Queen Victoria's death. But the one prayer in which King George was mentioned was taken from the Order for the Burial of the Dead in the Book of Common Prayer, and the whole service found its centre in the words:

> 'We give Thee hearty thanks for that it hath pleased Thee to deliver Thy servant KING GEORGE out of the miseries of this sinful world.'

What does this mean? That if the King had died at sixty instead of seventy, and so been spared ten years of the miseries of this sinful world, our cause for thanksgiving would have been by so much the greater? Does such a doctrine deserve to be perpetuated? And could no word of thanks have been uttered for the King's life, what he did, what he gave, what he was? Very different was the note sounded at the outset of the Prime Minister's broadcast address on Tuesday night, 'After he had served his own generation by the will of God he fell on sleep.'

*   *   *   *

What did Mr Masefield, in the sonnet he cabled from Los Angeles, mean by the quatrain:

> 'And when the War was ended, when the thought
> Of revolution took its hideous place,
> His courage and his kindness and his grace
> Scattered or charmed its ministers to naught'?

What revolution, where? The whole sonnet deals with England (the Poet Laureate should surely have said Britain) but the threat of revolution here after the War is surely a new discovery.

24 January

17

... LONG LIVE THE KING
PHILIP GUEDALLA

It is not easy for a young man to be King of England.

Even if he is not quite so young as he appears to be, the fact is slow to penetrate; and nothing will prevent men of half his experience from viewing him with the indulgent eyes of age. True, their travels may not have taken them further than a few Continental health-resorts, and their conversation rarely moves beyond the groove of their profession, whilst he is equally accustomed to ships at sea, railway-trains in Africa, and aeroplanes above the Andes and has listened in his time to almost every kind of specialist talking shop. But there is nothing to prevent his elders from feeling comfortably certain that they must know more about it all because they happen to be older.

Yet if experience is to count for anything, it is not easy to say just how many years of average experience have been crowded into that short lifetime. Men of twice his age are lucky if they have seen half as much. The years slide past them, and they will reach the honourable end of their professional careers without touching life at more than a quarter of the points where he has made contact with it. His life has been a swift training in the elements of commerce, several professions, war and diplomacy, with illustrations on the spot from men who know their business well enough to be at the head of it. An education of that order is a fair substitute for greying hair. For it ages a man rapidly, and he can hardly help being a trifle older than his years. So possibly the King of England is not quite so young as he may seem to all his subjects.

But it is not easy for a man of any age to be the King of England in 1936. Even if England were all that he has to be king of, it would be anything but easy. For modern England is a bewildering affair, a shifting complex of politics, economics, public services and private enterprise, consisting in unequal parts of agriculture, trade returns, sport, unemployment, national defence, and the West End of London; and a true king must make himself at home in all of them. The old simplicities have vanished. The happy days when a mild interest in good works and a moderate familiarity with the armed forces of the Crown sufficed for royalty are more than half a century away. It was so easy to be charming when life held little more than a few guards of honour to inspect and a few wards in hospitals to walk through.

But modern royalty has far more than that to think of – the heavy industries, afforestation, shipyards, the stricken coalfields, salesmanship, the grind of poverty, the good name of Britain in foreign countries, welfare work, the cost of living, and a whole sea of problems that are more generally to be found on the agenda of Board meetings than in the thinner air of Courts and camps. (One sees King Edward somewhere in the picture with almost all of them.) Contemporary life has grown almost intolerably civilian; and even on its higher levels it cannot be conducted without a wider range of knowledge than is customary among Field-Marshals.

Full recognition has been given to that fact in the range and diversity of the new King's training. For, admirably lacking in routine, it has effectually multiplied his contacts with almost every drab activity that goes to make up the common round of England. He has heard engineers talk shop, listened to experts planning assaults on foreign markets, and watched the slow alleviation of maladjustments in the workers' lives. The higher salesmanship, group migration, and the mysterious processes by which frozen credits may be thawed have all passed before him; and few men have been vouchsafed a more commanding survey of the whole roaring, creaking, smoky rattle-trap of affairs and industry which goes by the name of England. If it is the business of a modern king to hear and know about such things as that, there is not a more modern king in Europe.

But, happily or not, England is not the only place of which he has to be king; and in the wider field he has rare advantages, since he has been a persevering traveller. If it is an advantage to have seen the world as very few have seen it, he enjoys it to the full. A sight (and he has had more than one) of North and South America, Africa, India, and the Dominions is a generous education in quite a number of things that we are not customarily taught at home, and he has had the chance to learn them all. That is another means by which his years have been augmented in the same process which enabled him to serve his country overseas in foreign markets and the Dominions.

What is the sum of it? A modern king with a far wider range of contacts than any of his subjects and a complete awareness of their real occupations and the problems which confront their country; a sharp questioner and a shrewd listener of wide experience; a busy mind that finds its own solutions and prefers to say the things that it has thought of for itself; a man of innumerable and diverse friendships; and the last man in England to desire to hear smooth things on serious affairs.

Small wonder that, if there were no monarchy, he would be the uncrowned King of England.

24 January

MONDAY NIGHT IN FLEET STREET
R. J. CRUIKSHANK

The death of the King presented Fleet Street with a series of difficult problems. The official bulletin did not appear on the tape machines until 12.12 a.m. Tuesday. Yet within a few minutes there were streaming from the presses newspapers which not only announced the King's death on their front pages but contained eight, nine or ten pages of letterpress and pictures connected with the event. Not all the London newspapers 'caught the first editions,' but two, at least, achieved the miracle. It was a combined triumph of human ingenuity and mechanical skill.

When King Edward died the newspapers had no rivals in the dissemination of the news. But on the night of George the Fifth's passing Fleet Street was acutely conscious that the nation would first learn the news from the B.B.C. This meant that the first sharp impact of the shock would have passed long before the papers had issued from the machines. For the first time many of us felt that our actions were conditioned by a new medium outside our own. The public, whose hopes and fears had hung suspended for hours and were finally resolved that evening by the broadcast announcer, would expect from their morning newspapers something more than a repetition of what they knew already.

That is why Fleet Street strained its resources to produce newspapers that would contain the fullest possible accounts of the dead King's life, the scenes outside the Palace, in the London streets and at Sandringham itself, and of the impression made by the announcement throughout the Empire and in foreign lands.

Competition induces miracles, and the production on Tuesday morning of newspapers embodying ten pages of letterpress and pictures about the dead King and his successor was one of them. The feat of legerdemain apparently impressed the public, because newspaper sales next day were enormous, and this was particularly true of those papers which announced special supplements. I think this result suggests that broadcasting may be an ally as well as a rival to the popular Press.

The experience on Monday night of one Fleet Street office may be taken as typical of all. When the first intimation of the King's illness reached us on Friday afternoon we began to prepare for the worst. Four pages of special articles and pictures composing a panorama of the reign were produced in advance. Then we set to work on an alternative front page announcing his Majesty's death and describing the procedure consequent upon the accession of the new Sovereign. A substitute editorial page consisting of a leading article on the King and a personal appreciation of him was also assembled. These provisional pages were cast and held in waiting for transference to the machines immediately the signal of release was given. I should add, however, that the front page was revised from time to time by the inclusion of the latest bulletins from Sandringham, so that the full story of the King's illness would appear.

Meanwhile we went on with the task of preparing the normal paper, fully aware that when the tape machine whirred again all our efforts might be nullified. This would be part of that waste of human talent and costly mechanism which is inseparable from the production of a newspaper. No reader can ever guess how much patient labour of how many hands may be sacrificed on such an occasion as this.

From the time of the first announcement, most of us had a depressing intuition that the King would not recover. As Monday lengthened, the statements from Sandringham, coupled with private intelligence, strengthened these fears. When, at twenty-five minutes past nine, came the bulletin, 'The King's life is moving peacefully to its close,' we were certain that this night would see the end. (Incidentally, that message touched us by the startling beauty and dignity of its phrasing, and we attributed it to the good taste of Lord Dawson.)

The effect of this grave bulletin was almost uncanny. At a time of night when a newspaper office is usually at its busiest ours was curiously hushed. Our men turned listlessly proofs and pages that we now felt sure would never appear: articles on the Coal dispute, on the co-ordination of National Defence, on Oil Sanctions. The meeting of the League Council, which he had thought so important, would be relegated to a back page. The troubles of M. Laval no longer seemed significant. We took steps to excise the Wireless programmes, for we had learned that the B.B.C. was proposing to suspend its activities for twenty-four hours. The Stock Exchange and commodity markets, sports, the theatres – all these normal parts of the nation's life and the day's news would be modified when the final word came from Sandringham.

The tardy moments crawled past. A crowd clustered around the tape machines. Men stared at the clock or marched nervously across the sub-editorial room. Old hands recalled waiting for the death of King Edward. It had come, they said, at 11.45 p.m. Telephones rang incessantly. These were inquiries from the outside world. New arrivals crowded around the Night Editor's desk. Almost every department of the newspaper office was represented. All were waiting the signal.

On an ordinary night our first edition – the papers that chiefly serve the West of England – goes to press at 10.35. Tonight the circulation manager had arranged with Paddington to hold back the newspaper trains. We could make the change if the news came before twelve. The hands of the clock drew perilously near that hour. Then, at last, a man standing near the tape machine cried, 'Flash.' Doors swung open. Messengers stood poised for running. 'We understand the King is dead.' But we dared not take that as authentic. The presses had begun to turn. We were printing an edition announcing that the King was dying.

A few minutes later the tape assured us that the statement of death was correct though not yet officially confirmed. But still we held our hands. Then at last the instrument tapped out the official announcement, 'Death came peacefully to the King at 11.55 p.m.' At once the machine we had laboriously constructed began to function. The presses were stopped. A van loaded with papers was halted at the top of the street and brought back. The alternative front page was slipped into place, the new editorial page substituted for the old, and the four additional pages describing the late King's life inserted. All this was done with incredible speed and without a single slip. The co-ordination between the sub-editorial room, the composing room, the machine room and the distribution department was military in its precision. One felt a boyish pride and at the same time an adult regret that journalism, once the most casual of all man's occupations, could be so perfectly regimented. The vans sped away. The Western trains were waiting for us. And every paper that went out from our building recorded the King's death.

Immediately after the presses started thundering the staff of sub-editors began recasting the paper for the next edition. There was a strange pause after the brief announcement that George the Fifth had passed into history. Then news came in a spate. From the four corners of the world flowed expressions of regret. Telephone calls came from Paris, Berlin, Geneva, Washington. The calling of Parliament, the new King's message to the Lord Mayor, the effect in the provinces, the curtailing of London's multifarious activities – all these descended rapidly upon us. Far into the morning hours we worked, preparing edition after edition. In every other office in the Street our actions must have been repeated as in a series of mirrors.

It seems oddly old-fashioned nowadays to talk of the romance of journalism. Our satisfaction was that of a duty accomplished in the face of apparently insuperable difficulties. It was a task that could be lightened by no other satisfaction, because Fleet Street was deeply sincere in its regrets at the death of a monarch whom it respected and admired. It remembered the many occasions when it had seen him performing the functions of his great office with dignity, with graciousness, with kindliness. Despite the printed words, it seemed impossible that so familiar and so well-loved a figure had passed forever from the scene.

24 January

A SPECTATOR'S NOTEBOOK
JANUS

Like many other people I know, I have been a good deal exercised in the past week regarding methods of showing respect for King George. Of the depth of feeling that has pervaded the whole nation there can be no question. Never perhaps has a great people so expressed itself. No mournful trappings could add anything to the demonstration of sorrow and affection which the queues in Westminster Hall and the multitudinous homage of last Tuesday provided. But King Edward was right when he decided that Tuesday should not be officially declared a day of national mourning. The nation made it so, but the nation was not necessarily right. The day could not be a holiday, and no one wanted to make it that. And a lengthened midday stoppage, covering the period of the funeral at Windsor, would have been more effective in many ways than the conversion of a week-day into a Sunday. For a man to leave his job for an hour or two because of King George, and then go back and do it a little better because of King George, would be the best all proofs of respect.

31 January

Part Two: Foreign Affairs

The Encroaching Nightmare

A. L. ROWSE

The year 1936 was decisive in that Hitler's Germany learned that there would be no effective opposition to his long-planned programme of aggression announced in *Mein Kampf*, for anyone intelligent enough to read the message. In March he remilitarised the Rhineland, tearing up the Locarno Treaty Germany had signed. Twice the British government refused the urgent request of France and Belgium to put economic and financial pressure upon Germany. Twice Baldwin's nerveless government refused our allies: 'It might seem to be closing the door in the face of Germany, and so rendering European appeasement even more difficult.'

Geoffrey Dawson, as editor of *The Times*, was the most influential appeaser outside the government, and consistently used the immense influence of his paper then to urge Germany's case. At All Souls he held forth: 'It is their own backdoor.' This was the regular cliché with which the Conservative Party, the City and the appeasers let Germany get away with it, and renew the war for *Weltmacht* (world power) she had begun in 1914. Most politicians did not know enough history to realise that this was the beginning of the second round of the German attempt, as their best historian, Franz Fischer, has shown in his books.

Hitler's instinct that there would be no opposition was confirmed by Britain's total failure to deal with Italy's aggression against Abyssinia – never applying oil sanctions which would have stopped it (actually selling Italy the oil by which to fight the war). When Sir John Simon was asked at All Souls why a ship could not be sunk to block the Suez Canal, then under British control, he said, 'It would mean that Mussolini would fall!'

This betrays the motive behind Britain's attitude all through these years: anti-Communism. Anti-Communism was a perfectly understandable and proper attitude. What these would not realise was that Soviet Russia, weak as she then was, was no danger to Britain: the immediate and growing danger was from Germany. The Foreign Office and a few Conservatives like Churchill, Duff Cooper and the Cecils were intelligent enough to see that.

Actually, Dawson and *The Times* came out strongly, if only

rhetorically, against Italy's war. When I argued with him that Italy was only a secondary power, the real danger was from Germany, he replied, 'I'm not accepting your argument; but if it is the case that Germany is so strong, ought we not to go in with her?' I was staggered by the short-sightedness and historical ignorance. The Foreign Office knew better. But here was the mental confusion that sacrificed Britain's interests, undermined our friends and helped forward our enemies.

France had been discouraged the year before by the Anglo-German Naval Agreement with Hitler, which gave him a great boost and which he never meant to keep, building the *Bismarck*, a more powerful battleship than any of Britain's – which sank our most powerful *Hood* in the event. The short-sighted folly of this agreement was doubled in 1936 by our scrapping five cruisers which were still serviceable and of which we were in deadly need when the war came.

Meanwhile, the civil war in Spain distracted attention from what Germany was up to. Having drawn their conclusions that they could go ahead, both Germany and Italy used the Spanish battleground to test out new weapons, aerial bombing, tactics, etc. It must be remembered that in 1936 the democratic government of the Spanish Republic was not Socialist, but Liberal. Soviet Russia gradually intervened to counter Hitler and Mussolini, but ineffectively, from too far away.

What was the British government's attitude? Britain was a democracy, and should have given support to a friendly democracy, in spite of its shortcomings; France would have followed suit, and Hitler and Mussolini been checked in time. Together we were in a far more favourable strategic position.

Instead of that, Britain initiated the policy of non-intervention, which refused to allow the democratic government of Spain to purchase arms from this country. This contributed handsomely to the defeat of the Spanish Republic. No wonder the teeth of the younger generation we were then were set on edge, and we would not accept anything that came from Baldwin and Co., even when they were right.

At All Souls Dawson described the blameless Sir Arthur Salter as 'that rabble-rouser', for sympathising with the Spanish Republic. Salter did immeasurable service to the country, in both German wars, in the Allied Shipping Control, later in the great American effort. This, as against the immeasurable disservice Geoffrey Dawson did to his country. But Salter was completely in keeping with his party and class. The impersonal *Annual Register* registers 'the unconcealed sympathy of the bulk of the Tory Party' for Franco.

I had no illusions about the Spanish Left, their idiot internecine conflict, killing each other as they killed priests and burned churches. I left these adolescent illusions to my friends, like Spender and Auden (who came back *dis*illusioned). Actually, my Communist friend, Ralph Fox, did not want to go but was deliberately sent by the CP to be a martyr.

For the historian it was more a matter of the interests of our country, and I saw these being sacrificed all round for the class interests of Baldwin's Conservative Party. It kept me on the Left, when I had ceased to have much hope of it either – utterly ineffective as it was. I had a private word for my own feverish activities: the Biblical phrase, 'making bricks without straw'. And I used to inveigh against the ineffectiveness of all the good liberal-minded everywhere in Europe, against the all-too-effective evil types, who knew very well what idiots the masses were. (And didn't the masses follow them to the death!) It wasn't at all good for a duodenal ulcer – by which I was increasingly ravaged.

The increasing danger to Britain called for clear leadership, alerting people to the threat, and the right policy to deal with it. There were people in the Foreign Office who understood well what was necessary: Wigram did, but was felled by a stroke; Eric Beckett did – the anxiety of it all gave him a duodenal ulcer. Vansittart was right about the Germans all along, and ultimately victimised for being so. It needs no argument, it can be proved. Chamberlain kicked him out to replace him by Cadogan, who confessed in 1939, 'It has all worked out as Van said it would, *and I never believed it.*' QED. That is, these people never believed what was obvious to anyone of historical judgement or political foresight.

The right policy was the traditional one of an alliance of all the European nations threatened by an overmighty aggressor: France under Louis XIV and Napoleon, Bismarck's Germany under the Kaiser and Hitler. This had been the sheet-anchor of Britain's security and the source of her greatness in the past two centuries. That was the essence of 'collective security' under the League of Nations, what it meant to me and Hugh Dalton, who knew Europe and the German record.

I urged this in a *Times* correspondence – to be answered by Lord Lothian, who devoted his persuasive talents to appeasement. (In the war that inevitably followed his great friend, Lionel Curtis, said that Lothian died 'in the knowledge that he had been wrong'. What was the good of that?)

Another of them, Sam Hoare, had the hardihood to defend this course, of conceding every demand that Hitler made – militarising the Rhineland, annexation of Austria, part of Czecho-Slovakia and the Polish Corridor – in the hope of Germany keeping the peace. Couldn't he see that this process of concession would build up a Germany so powerful as to dominate the whole of Europe, and threaten Britain's very existence?

In 1914–18, in Germany's first attempt, Britain confronted the almighty danger with France, Russia, Italy, Belgium, Rumania, Greece for allies – even then it was not enough without the United States from 1917. In 1940 Britain confronted a German-dominated Europe plus Italy – alone.

This was the end result of fifteen years of Tory government, under Baldwin, the front figure on the political stage in all that time. A nice man personally, a skilful party leader, he took no interest in Europe beyond the Channel, upon which Britain's very existence depended. In this year 1936 he dismayed Parliament by admitting that he had not warned the country of the danger of German rearmament because then he might have lost the election in 1935 – which he had cannily fixed, as in 1931.

The effect on the Labour Party was disastrous: only fifty-five MPs in 1931, with an old pacifist sheep, George Lansbury, as leader; only 155 MPs in 1935. There was no effective opposition. The irresponsibility of the party and its endemic confusion of mind was redoubled. Baldwin's government was in a position to do whatever was necessary to alert and prepare the country.

Here the historian must in justice say a word for Neville Chamberlain. At last, in this year, he announced a programme of rearmament. This was only common sense. While in Germany the workers were working, under direction, all hours in rearming, in Paris under a Socialist government Léon Blum had to go to the happy workers to plead with them to finish the Paris Exhibition in time. In vain, of course: they did not. This was Socialism in action or, rather, in inaction.

In Britain the Labour Party was at sixes and sevens, still

suffering from the trauma of 1931 and the loss of its old leaders, filled with distrust at the fraudulent elections of 1931 and 1935. Leo Amery, the Churchillian Tory whom Baldwin kept out, admitted to me that the Tories perpetrated a fraud in 1935. The result was that we would accept nothing from them.

The Labour Party Conference that year opposed the government's programme of rearmament. This was crazy in the circumstances; Attlee gave no lead – and admitted years after that he had been wrong. The interesting thing is that Ernest Bevin, though not in Parliament nor yet a political figure, stood out in seeing that rearmament was necessary, and argued that – in spite of everything – the government should be trusted to carry it out. Actually he had Hugh Dalton with him, who knew what the Germans were good for.

But Baldwin refused to implement rearmament with the necessary Ministry of Supply, which Churchill constantly urged. Nobody would listen to him, and Baldwin typically fobbed him off by appointing a tame old lawyer, Sir Thomas Inskip, with a staff of two or three, to co-ordinate defence! And of course, the Old Men would never recruit Churchill to their government – the only thing, the German generals told us, that would warn Hitler that Britain meant business. But she did not: rudderless, without leadership, she meant to appease Hitler.

This helped to discourage and confuse France too: it is hardly surprising that France deserted us in 1940 – Britain had frustrated French policy towards Germany all along, when the French were roughly right. (De Gaulle made Britain pay for that in the end – and I don't blame him.)

Again the *Annual Register* notes the increasing dissatisfaction with Baldwin's 'leadership', and rumours of moves to displace him – which Churchill longed to do. At All Souls, at this time, he privately described Baldwin, who kept him out, as 'a whited sepulchre'. Then in December came the bombshell of the King's Abdication. This saved Baldwin, who handled it with his usual skill – the kind of thing he was good at, rather than thinking of the security of the country. In cabinet he would say, when foreign affairs were under discussion, 'Wake me up when that is over.' But he manoeuvred Edward VIII off the pitch with practised skill, and that was to the great benefit of the country – for the King was a pro-German, and even pro-Hitler.

I am bound to own that we of the younger generation were

wrong about this, Baldwin and even the Labour leaders right. Speaking for myself, it was all politics to me: I didn't care tuppence for the pipsqueak of a monarch and his divorcée girlfriend – I was on edge to get rid of Baldwin in time. This was undoubtedly a prime motive in Churchill's mind too.

But the consequences in party politics were disastrous. At that moment there was a prospect of Churchill bringing together all the various elements opposed to the spineless government of the Old Men: not only the Labour opposition and half the Liberals, but those Tories who saw the danger and put their country before class. Over the Abdication Churchill put himself wrong with the public, and the prospect of bringing together an alliance against the government vanished; Baldwin was able to make his bow gracefully and retire – as I always thought, with dishonour. He had forfeited the country's safety for party advantage, and that was unforgivable.

When I stated this in an article, he admitted peaceably to his old friend, Warden Pember at All Souls, that he had been 'holding down' a job that he was physically incapable of running. (I rather think he had had a slight stroke – but he was always an easy-going, indolent man.) His place was taken by the orderly, methodical Neville Chamberlain, who was bent on methodically coming to terms with Hitler (*and* Mussolini).

Well, of course you could come to terms with Hitler, *on his terms*. There swiftly followed the annexation of Austria; Chamberlain actually helped him to dismember Czecho-Slovakia, then take over the big Czech armaments industry. A business man, Neville Chamberlain really believed he could do business with Hitler: rather than the Czech President, Beneš, 'I prefer to trust Herr Hitler's word.' With Hitler's attack on Poland, the Foreign Office at last got its way – not Chamberlain – and called a halt.

It meant war, the renewal of the German war after twenty years, and in the worst possible circumstances – brought down upon us by the fumbling confusion, and the collusion, of the governing classes, I have always thought, to the ruin of the country. Britain ended its historic career in flames of glory in 1940–5; but it should never have been necessary, Churchill considered – if an effete governing class had been worthy of its ancestors who had made her great. 'Britain is either great,' Canning said, 'or she is nothing at all.' And today ... look round! I think in his terms.

* * * *

32

All through that decade I was an active Labour candidate fighting an uphill constituency in Cornwall. Though well read in Marxism intellectually, I was not a fellow-traveller like so many of the Left intellectuals, but a solid, middle-of-the-road follower of Ernest Bevin and Morrison. I did not go off to Spain to vaporise about the Spanish Civil War, publicise myself by writing books about it, Odes to Spain, and whatnot. I watched the hopelessness of it all with despair, the two sections of the poor, suffering, idiot working-class killing each other off to give Franco the victory. They got the Franco they deserved.

I gave up all my vacations from Oxford, and sometimes had to dash down in term-time, to meetings and party work in Cornwall – where I had started and wrote for the *Cornish Labour News* – as well as elsewhere. I was feverishly busy, trying to run three careers. Teaching at Oxford took ten or twelve hours a week; as a Research Fellow I was restricted to that number, most of my academic time being devoted to historical research and writing. After years of research at the Public Record Office and in the British Museum, I was now writing my first research work, *Sir Richard Grenville of the 'Revenge'* (published in 1937), and I had amassed a lot of material for *Tudor Cornwall* later. I was reviewing regularly for the *Spectator, Economist, Listener, Political Quarterly*, and broadcasting quite a bit from the BBC in London and at Plymouth.

To all these activities I gave up keeping my journals, which I had kept for years before and was to resume after the war. But from my calendar I can reconstruct what I was doing. At New Year a fortnight's meetings all over the china-clay area – Ugh! 'January 15: walked home from St Stephens [some 5 miles] in biting cold and wind.' Next day: 'sick, unable to go to St Austell Labour New Year party.' At regular intervals are these entries: 'sick at night,' 'sick after train.' This was the ulcer encroaching on me, I now realise, with the encroaching nightmare. Still, nothing would induce me to give up, or even let up, determined to go on.

Speaking with Attlee down in Cornwall in September; League of Nations Union protest meetings against Britain's knuckling under to Mussolini; WEA lectures, Historical Association lectures, WETUC lectures at Cambridge. There I was friends with Maurice Dobb, Communist mentor over generations, who would gladly have recruited me to the CP – which I had too much working-class horse-sense to join, unlike the middle-class intellectuals. Then at Cambridge again to speak to the Democratic Front. I was all over the place, it seems.

In London a debate with the nefarious William Joyce, the later notorious Lord Haw-Haw, a Fascist brute with a duelling scar on his ugly face. It was under the auspices of the dear Fabian Society; when I had got the audience thoroughly aroused against him, the lily-livered chairman stopped me in mid-career, saying that we ought to hold the balance in favour of our guest, since our sympathies were the other way. I reflected: the bloody fool, just like the ineffectiveness of the good and right-thinking – it is the thugs who are all too effective. Intellectually, in articles, I campaigned against the 'Rationalist Fallacy', the ignorant middle-class assumption that the masses were reasonable, rational beings. Hitler and Mussolini, Lenin and Stalin knew better. So did I; the poor fools didn't know what one meant, some called me a Fascist for being familiar with the facts of life.

In London too I was meeting with Sir Francis Acland, Liberal MP for North Cornwall. I was trying to arrange an understanding between Liberals and Labour in Cornwall, not to fight each other and let the Tories everywhere in. (In 1945, after my decade of work, my constituency, Penryn–Falmouth, went Labour.) Isaac Foot – Acland described him as 'a pure party-man' – would not agree: Liberals and Labour continued to fight each other, Baldwin and Chamberlain were free to go on and have their way with us.

When I asked Hugh Dalton if the Labour Party in Parliament couldn't co-operate with Churchill, he answered, sensible man, that he was not opposed to it, but how many Tories would support Churchill? Out of 450 – only 20 or 25 at most. One of them was Harold Macmillan, who was also right all through that nightmare decade: both against appeasement and for economic expansion – so they kept him out. No wonder I came to call that Parliament 'the unspeakable assembly'.

I find another meeting with E. D. Simon of Manchester, another Liberal I tried to draw into co-operation with Labour, as I was always trying to do with Keynes. My pamphlet on *Mr Keynes and Socialism* came out this year.* Why couldn't he see the point, the urgent necessity of it?

All this left little time for my other writing – even though my head was in politics and the present, my heart in poetry and the past. I wrote very few poems, and those political: 'Vox clamantis

* For my dealings with him *v. Glimpses of the Great.*

in deserto', for instance, very suitably entitled, for nobody would listen. Very well, then, I wrote – unlike the optimistic illusions of the Poets of the Left about the people they did not know:

> A day will come when there shall descend on them
> From the skies they do not observe, some stratagem
>
> Of fate to search and sear their flesh with fire ...
>
> Liquid fire will rain down from the air,
> Will suddenly arrive upon them there
>
> And lick their bodies up and burn their bones,
> No one at hand to hear their mutual groans:
>
> For these are they who, warned of what's to come,
> Walk blindly on to their appointed doom.

Not much time was left for literature, though I did take time off to see Auden's not very good play, *The Dog beneath the Skin*, and Eliot's *Murder in the Cathedral*, for which I had provided the reading. He had asked me what he should read for the story of Thomas Becket; I told him Dean Stanley's *Memorials of Canterbury Cathedral*, and it comes mostly out of that. Once only I attended a *Criterion* dinner, to which Eliot was always bidding me; but, though I regularly wrote for it, I had not much time for literary or social life, and never have had.

My friends were mostly on the Left; there they occur in the book: Douglas Jay, the Pakenhams, J. G. Crowther, Frank Hardie, Nicholas Davenport; then there is Stephen Spender for the night, Vivian Phillips, chief organiser of the Labour Party; lunches and dinners with my scholar friends, Veronica Wedgwood, David Cecil, Charles Singer, Carr-Saunders, David and Gervase Mathew, Martin D'Arcy at Campion Hall. Ka Arnold-Forster turns up, famous as Ka Cox, lover of Rupert Brooke. Among German refugees, scholarly J. P. Mayer, authority on Marx and Tocqueville.

I kept in touch with Germany. There was handsome Fritz Caspari, whose doctoral thesis on Renaissance Humanism I had to examine. Then, omen of what was to come – I had helped to get Adam von Trott a Rhodes Scholarship to Balliol; I now had to talk to Geoffrey Dawson, a Rhodes Trustee, to get Adam renewed for a third year. I have told part of the story of my close relations with him – he was my window into the German soul – in *A Cornishman Abroad*. He was hanged on a butcher's hook in Plötzensee prison in 1944.

35

THE REAL HITLER?
R. H. S. CROSSMAN

The English tourist who crosses the German frontier moves at
once into an entirely strange world. But he does not know it.
The railways, the hotels and the museums – the only parts of
Germany which he really sees – are just as they were in the days
of the Republic. But under this superstructure of international
respectability lives a nation whose economy, morality and religion have been completely transformed. So complete is this
transformation that anyone who is initiated into it soon begins
to believe that England is an unreal fantasy. Imperceptibly he
accommodates himself to the new standards: imperceptibly he
accepts the life of Nazi Germany as the normal life of the modern
State. When he returns to England the reverse process occurs.
Again he feels himself in a dream world, a world of law and order
where you can speak without fear of spies, where truth is attainable and where decent people do not always go in fear of their
lives. Gradually he accommodates himself to the change, and
Nazi Germany in its turn becomes a nightmare, something which
you read about in the penny papers but which cannot really
exist.

Anyone who has lived in both England and Germany will
recognise this feeling of hallucination which overcomes the
traveller as he moves from one country to the other. He cannot
simultaneously believe both worlds to be real. In reading Dr
Olden's new book* I had a similar sensation. For the first fifty
pages I felt, 'This cannot be true: it is grotesquely one-sided, a
malicious parody of the facts.' As I read on, I began to settle
down again in Nazi Germany. The feeling of nightmare passed:
this was the sober truth, the German truth which no one who
has not experienced a little of it can possibly believe. This far-
rago of sadism, idealism and cunning is the biography of the
Founder of the Third Reich. It is interesting to observe how Dr
Olden has achieved this effect. He has added very few facts to
the data already gathered by Conrad Heiden in his *History of
National Socialism*, and by Arthur Rosenberg in his *History of
the German Republic*. Apart from some sordid details about Hitler's family, and some recollections of his Vienna days furnished
by a fellow-vagrant, there is little new material in this book. As

---

* *Hitler*, Rudolf Olden. (Querido Verlag: N.V. Amsterdam)

history it is sketchy and disjointed: no solid framework of economic or political causation is attempted. Instead, Dr Olden has immersed himself in the turgid waters of *Mein Kampf*. His biography is indeed a brilliant commentary upon Hitler's own autobiography, with parallel passages from Goebbels' reminiscences.

Dr Olden's commentary makes one fact incontestably clear – the consistency of the Leader's policy. *Mein Kampf* was published ten years ago. Hitler has never swerved from the principles there enunciated. In it he laid all his cards upon the tables – his objective, the destruction of the weak, the triumph of the strong: his methods of propaganda, the repetition of simple slogans until they are believed: his tactics, to side with the influential people and to use every means to power available; his panacea for social evils, the annihilation of the Jews; his political programme, to maintain capitalism, to increase armaments and to win the war of revenge. Everything was to be read in *Mein Kampf* by anyone bold enough to brave its style.

From the day of the Munich Putsch, when the Reichswehr fired on the SA, Hitler decided to keep on the safe side of the Law and of the Army. His revolutionary supporters said to themselves that the Leader was a clever man to talk in that way. But he meant it, as those revolutionaries found to their cost on June 30th. Equally clearly he maintained his intention, at whatever cost, of exterminating the Jews. His conservative backers thought it excellent election chatter. But he meant that too. He has been completely open and outspoken; but friend and foe alike have heard only what they wished to hear. Will he have the same miraculous success in foreign affairs? Here too *Mein Kampf* is unequivocal. And yet, charmed by the magic of his personality and their own wishes, the foreign Powers too seem inclined to say 'He cannot really mean it: after all he must be a normal, intelligent man.' Nothing has contributed more to his success than this belief that, when it came to a pinch, Hitler would behave in the normal way. But Hitler is not a normal man.

What is it that makes him the prodigy that he is? Dr Olden rightly points to the fact that his complete philosophy of life, apart from the finishing touches added by Alfred Rosenberg, was conditioned by his vagrant years in pre-War Vienna. His pan-Germanism, anti-Semitism, anti-Socialism, anti-Liberalism are all resultants of that dreary period when he slept in doss-houses and tinted picture postcards for a living. There has been no

37

development since then, only adaptation to circumstance. For close on twenty-five years he has had no intellectual cares: in an epoch of doubt and uncertainty his adolescent fixations have suffered no change. Secondly, his conception of politics is peculiar. Denying the importance of economics, despising the working-classes as fools for whose intelligence no lie can be too stupid, he has remained unscathed by the worries which attack the normal politician, and has felt no impulse to attack injustice or inequality. Profoundly respectful to the army, the capitalist and the junker, he has longed only to abolish the system which deliberately gives to the weak and the oppressed weapons with which they can defend themselves against the strong. Rejecting the fundamental principle of democratic civilisation, he has longed to restore the pristine glory of a Germany where the strong ruled and the weak were subject.

These are qualities which belong to many of us singly. Bestow them all upon one man and add the gift of illimitable rhetoric: you have created a national portent. Herr Hitler has been the supreme dissolvent of political parties. By substituting the *Weltanschauung* for the principle as the bond of unity, he has transformed the party into the amorphous mass. As Dr Olden says, there is no Left or Right under National Socialism. For Left and Right imply differences of principle, whereas National Socialism is the denial of principle. Stripped of the political, personal and religious loyalties of common, democratic humanity, the nation becomes an obedient herd. In charge of the herd are a few discordant herdsmen, and behind the herdsmen dimly discerned stand the owners of the cattle. The owners are perhaps a little uneasy. They have paid the herdsmen well, but they realise that only one among them knows the word of command to which the cattle answer. If he should fail... But a kindly providence has arranged that Herr Hitler's respect for the powers that be is beyond question.

So Dr Olden. Such ideas will seem fantastic to most English readers. I found them fantastic too, as I put Dr Olden's book aside and returned to the routine of English life. And yet the suspicion haunts me that his fantasy happens to be the sober truth.

10 January

FIFTEEN WEEKS OF WAR
MAJOR L. I. ATHILL

When the Italian high command began to plan its Abyssinian campaign much of its work had already been done for it by the nature of things. The absence of nerve centres through which Ethiopian resistance might be paralysed, and of vital arteries by the severance of which it might be bled to death, left no scheme of conquest available other than by the methods of the steam-roller; or, perhaps more correctly, of the mower, since recrudescence of opposition in the wake of the machine had inevitably to be provided for. In one direction only was there a clear-cut objective – the cutting of the railway. There, indeed, lay an artery on which Abyssinia depended not for the circulation of her life-blood, but for the infusion of new energy from the outer world. So, on broad lines, General de Bono had little choice of methods.

There were, however, certain important points on which he had to come to a decision. From what direction or directions should his operations be launched, and how wide a swathe should he attempt to cut? Along the whole of her northern frontier, for 250 miles, Abyssinia marched with the Italian colony of Eritrea. Geographically there was no insuperable obstacle to an attack along the whole front. Early in its career the wave of invasion would, it is true, have been split by the almost impenetrable massif of Samien, but it could still sweep forward over Tigré on the left and Amhara on the right and later over Wollo and Gojjam, where, perhaps, the true heart of Abyssinia lies. This would involve the parallel advance of at least four if not five main columns and a colossal programme of road construction. It must be slow. But it would have the great advantage of leaving no vulnerable flank to guard.

Again, the coastal arm of Eritrea for 250 miles separated Abyssinia from the sea. It, too, was separated from the Abyssinian highlands by an obstacle almost as formidable as the sea – the Danakil desert; but at its South-Western extremity, near Mount Musa Ali, it approached to within 100 miles, as the crow flies, of the railway. To the south-east 450 miles of debatable frontier, already deeply transgressed by 'peaceful penetration,' separated the Abyssinian and Italian Somali territories. The choice was a wide one.

General de Bono decided to have three simultaneous bites at his cherry. He did what all Italy was clamouring for him to do, and occupied Adowa within a few days of the first shot being fired. Probably quite rightly, he put aside the project of an advance along the whole Northern Front as being beyond his powers in view of the other tasks he had in mind. Perhaps with less wisdom, he continued his advance southward through Tigré on a narrow front. From Musa Ali he threatened the railway line with a concentration which has so far proved abortive. General Graziani, by a well-planned and methodically conducted drive through the Ogaden, menaced the Harrar plateau and the railway from the south.

It was a promising and well-thought-out plan of campaign, but it involved dispersal and, in the long run, dissipation of force. It was based on an underestimate of the physical difficulties to be overcome, and probably on an optimistic belief that the Abyssinians would exhaust themselves in massed attacks. In its over-confidence it neglected to make sure of the only thing that really mattered – the early cutting of the railway. The Musa Ali venture petered out, defeated by the desert. It may be revived. General Graziani's impressive progress suddenly and rather unaccountably faded away, and has left him after fifteen precious weeks little more advanced than when he started. It will no doubt be resumed, but nothing can recapture those fifteen weeks. In the north the inevitable result of an advance on one sector only of a wide front soon became apparent, and the invading forces had to turn to the right from the narrow front of their advance to protect a flank which, with every mile of their progress, became longer and more vulnerable. From Amhara, which the plan of campaign left untouched, and from the mountains of Tembien, in spite of the combing-out process reported in the Italian *communiqués*, bands of enterprising Abyssinians, quite undismayed, effected not only infiltration but attacks of considerable importance crowned with no small measure of success; and rain, a full month before its time, began to fall. Such is the situation which now faces Marshal Badoglio.

Of heavy fighting there has been little enough to justify the Italian claim that this is a singularly bloodless war. The little that has taken place, of which the Italian native troops have borne the brunt, has demonstrated some rather significant facts. The first, which does not come altogether as a surprise, is the comparative ineffectiveness of aircraft. As used by General

Graziani in preparation for, and support of, infantry assault they served their purpose admirably. As an independent arm unconnected with simultaneous ground action they have scattered a vast tonnage of metal and explosive over the Abyssinian hills and plains to singularly little purpose. That their bombing of Red Cross camps was due to anything more deliberate than the deplorable indiscretion of a subordinate commander suffering from prolonged strain all who know and admire the Italian airman will be loath to believe; but, whatever the explanation may be, air action so far has done more to alienate the sympathy of the outside world than it has to shatter Abyssinian *morale*.

What, however, is more astonishing, is the vulnerability of the light tank. Even if the Abyssinians are exaggerating when they claim to have captured twenty of these – and there is no reason to think that they are – the fact of their being able to capture any, except as the result of mechanical breakdown, is an astonishing proof of their enterprise and ability to adapt themselves to unfamiliar forms of warfare. That the Abyssinian warrior is a most formidable opponent in wooded or broken country has been abundantly confirmed.

What does remain an almost entirely unknown quantity is the Abyssinian supply position. The Emperor has declared himself satisfied with it. No war correspondent is in a position to report on it with authority; and there is always the possibility that Abyssinian resistance may suddenly melt away as the hungry warriors scatter in search of the food which the theatre of war and accumulated provision can no longer supply. In this possibility lies the main chance of a sudden swing of the pendulum in Italy's favour.

It is, however, very unlikely that Marshal Badoglio will be content to await such a development or that he is blind to the lessons of the past fifteen weeks. He does not seem to contemplate – for the present at all events – an extension of the Northern front. He may even think fit to draw in his horns there, and not improbably regrets the advance which took his predecessor to Makalle. But everything points to reinforcements having been sent to General Graziani and to a resumption of the advance on Harrar to the exclusion of less vital issues. In the south nothing more than temporary interruption by rain need be expected till well on in May, and in the four campaigning months that remain General Graziani may well achieve the result which he looked like achieving in the first ten weeks of the war. If he does so, and reaches the railway before the rains break, his problem will become one of food rather than of munitions, since active fighting will be in suspense.

If this situation arises, the key to it will pass into French hands and the policy of sanctions may be put to a test perhaps not generally foreseen. The port of Jibuti and the French section of the railway have never been closed to food supplies for belligerent Ethiopia. Will they remain open to food supplies for belligerent Italy? If they do not, the maintenance of a large force at Harrar during the rains will be extraordinarily difficult. If they do, Italy will start the new campaigning season – if she survives economically to start it at all – with solid achievement behind her and greatly improved prospects of success. On the answer to this question the whole issue of the war may hang.

17 January

CLOUDS OVER EUROPE
[R. C. K. ENSOR]

No informed person can ignore the menace of the European outlook. It is a gathering, not an immediately impending, storm. There may have been moments last year when Italy seriously thought of capping her adventure in Abyssinia with a war in the Mediterranean. But the whole Italo-Abyssinian episode lies in a sense outside the main drama. It has complicated, not created, the situation that is raising the spectre of international tragedy. A far more decisive factor is the re-armament of Germany, already prodigious, but by no means complete. Unless some fundamental change intervenes to save peace, those immense preparations must eventually be utilised. But not yet. Even when they are relatively complete, the German authorities will desire a few more years, if they can get them, to perfect the process of mesmerising their nation and to end the risk of having to deal with an 'internal enemy.'

So there is still probability of a respite, short or long. How can we best use it? That is to-day's instant problem. Three broad alternatives confront Great Britain. One is Lord Beaverbrook's idea – that she should stand aside and let the tragedy develop for others, trusting that she herself will be immune. Another is that she should strengthen the collective system to a point where it will overawe any aggressor. A third is that she should promote and support such 'revisionist' policies as may lessen the motives for aggression. The first is agreed by most persons outside Lord Beaverbrook's personal following to be wholly impracticable. The second and third are not. Nor are they incompatible with one another. But each presents serious difficulties.

Let us glance at the more constructive first. It is in the long view perhaps the more indispensable. For no system of mere coercion, however 'collective,' would be capable ultimately of holding down great nations like Germany and Italy in conditions of economic privation, where they could feel sentenced in perpetuity to rank among the 'have-nots' of the earth. It is worth stressing here the word 'economic.' Other pleas may from time to time be put forward; *e.g.*, the prestige-argument that it is beneath the dignity of a Great Power to be without colonies – an argument not heard before 1914, when nobody suggested that Austria-Hungary need feel humble beside Portugal. Even the Hitler of *Mein Kampf* dismissed the colony claim summarily. War being the terror that it now is, what people would embrace it for an artificial reason like that? But economic motives are real – the most real in the post-War world. And a great community, where all classes find themselves kept poor and workless and hopeless in comparison with their fellows in neighbouring countries, may feel driven in the end to fight to reverse the position.

The moral is that a question like that of the ex-German colonies, whose economic importance is small, is only very secondary. It may be desirable to alter their status, but to do so will not avert war, because at most it can only put bread in an insignificant number of German mouths. To restore Germany's economic well-being peacefully means facing a totally different problem – that of lowering the barriers of economic nationalism, the 26 economic partition-walls in Europe, the host of quotas and currency restrictions and tariffs elsewhere. The same is true for Italy and for Japan. It may be answered, no doubt, that this is not within Great Britain's power to effect. But at least she might throw her influence much more strongly and publicly on that side. Were her Government really convinced about it and prepared not only to give leads, but to follow them up pertinaciously on all suitable occasions, a great deal might be effected. That is what the Government has never done. The chief defence for our resorting to a tariff in 1932 was that it would arm us to negotiate for the demolition of other nations' barriers. How half-hearted our demolition campaign has since been! Sir Samuel Hoare's 'revisionist' observations in his famous Geneva speech would have had far more practical value had they stressed this issue.

Let us turn to the other side – the support of the collective system. Here the country must face an obvious and pressing need for adequate measures of British re-armament. We cannot expect the collective system to function if we ourselves are too weak to uphold it. The Italo-Abyssinian affair, though extraneous, as has been said above, to the main course of European events, offered, nevertheless, a rare opportunity for strengthening the League system in a way calculated to give that main course a very powerful direction. Why was the opportunity not seized, as it would have been had the Government followed the advice, say, of the Archbishop of York? There is only one natural explanation; which is that, on the advice tendered to it by the responsible heads of the armed forces, it concluded that the nation lacked the armed strength to face an Italian threat in the Mediterranean with confidence, and that the support of other League States in that area could not at the time be counted on with certainty. Thus, partly for want of adequate power in its own hand it missed an invaluable chance of building up a far greater power in the hand of the League collectively. The essence of the Covenant of the League of Nations in one of its aspects is the doctrine that the collective strength at the disposal of the League must be overwhelmingly greater than the strength of the strongest possible aggressor. We cannot refuse to frame our armament policy in the light of that principle.

But if some measure of re-armament must be accepted, at least let Parliament insist that it be done on rational lines. The present situation, with Navy, Army, and Air Service still presenting what in substance are uncorrelated demands, is indefensible at all times; and if it led to a vast new capital expenditure (the figure of £280,000,000 has been mentioned) arrived at by mere bargaining between their chiefs on the sub-committee of the Committee of Imperial Defence, not only economy, but efficiency, too, must suffer. At the present stage the whole problem of the relative uses and capacities of aeroplanes, battleships, and tank squadrons within a thought-out scheme of British strategy needs to be worked out as far as possible from a central standpoint. Frankly, that can never be done under a system whereby each Force separately estimates its separate

44

demands, and then on a principle of mutual obligation all arrange how far each will back up the others' proposals. In these columns on January 10th last Sir Frederick Maurice made some suggestions for improving the working of the system – their essence being the appointment of a civilian Minister to act as chairman of a sub-committee of the Chiefs of Staff of the three Services, and at the same time as deputy-chairman of the Committee of Imperial Defence. They were conservative, and must be considered as a bare minimum. Few, unless obsessed by the interests of a particular Service, would be content with anything less. The House of Commons will have a first chance of re-discussing the question on the day when these words appear. It is to be hoped that it will push its probes deep enough.

14 February

SPAIN'S LEFTWARD MOVE
[GORONWY REES]

It is tempting and easy to think that what happens in Spain is of no account to the rest of Europe. Isolated by the sea and mountain, Spain only too often seems a park of history, romance and culture. Only those who know its poverty, and the present efforts of the Spaniards to conquer it, become aware that Spain, like every European nation, is engaged in a passionate and sometimes tragic struggle for progress and for liberty. Further, the struggle is, though under different conditions, that which is being fought in every other country in Europe, but in Spain with an intensity that must interest every European. Not only this: in other countries the same political and economic struggle has tended to favour forces which are a danger to Europe and the world, while in Spain, it has, for the moment, given success to these causes which every good European must approve. If any testimony were needed to the vigour and vitality of the Spanish people, it would be found in the swift recovery of the progressive forces in Spain from the sufferings of the 1934 revolt. But the elections of this week show that the revolt was, in fact, not a defeat but a victory for the Left. The elections register a setback to the forces of reaction, as the revolt put an end to their advance. If the Left had lost, Fascism would have had another ally on the shores of the Mediterranean.

The results of the election are not yet complete; but the

45

success of the Popular Front has been decisive enough to drive aristocrats and Conservative politicians out of the country in a flight characterised by the Right leader, Gil Robles, as cowardly and treacherous. The explanation of their panic lies in the sense of guilt which infects the Right after the merciless suppression of the 1934 revolt. The same cruelty largely explains the success of the Popular Front, whose most urgent demand is for the release and amnesty of the thousands of political prisoners, among them Don Luis Companys, ex-President of the Generalidad of Catalonia, and for the restoration of the municipal councils. In Catalonia itself the success of the Left has been overwhelming. The cruelties of the suppression came with a shock to Spain because they were revealed only after eighteen months had passed, when the censorship was raised immediately before the elections, and the popular sympathy with its victims infected even the Catholic women, who in the last election voted for the Right parties. Those parties have, since the election, put themselves decisively in the wrong by a last-minute attempt at a military and Fascist *coup d'état* under General Franco. Nothing could show more clearly the force of popular feeling than the refusal of the troops to obey their orders to charge the demonstrators in the Puerta del Sol in Madrid on Monday evening. The same temper is shown by the failure of Gil Robles, on whom popular hatred is concentrated, to obtain re-election in Madrid.

These indications seem to suggest that the strength of the Left is even greater than its electoral successes. Señor Robles' party, the reactionary C.E.D.A., will still be the strongest party in the Cortes. But the C.E.D.A., despite its leader's powers of organisation, is not a single force; like the Right in general, it is a conglomeration of those who, on whatever grounds, cling to Catholic and authoritarian conservatism. The Right is, save in its admiration of Fascist methods, a negative force; the proof of this is to be found in the wasted years since 1933, when the Right in power has been able to do nothing which can be of use to Spain. The Left, the successful Popular Front, is, equally, a coalition, including Radicals, Socialists, Communists and Anarchists, differing both in purpose and methods. But though the union may only be temporary, it is a union for precise and positive ends; and Señor Azaña has already shown that he can exercise a severe control over extremist allies. Briefly, the Republican demands are six: the amnesty of political prisoners, defence of the Republic and its constitution, religious emancipation, land reform, educational reform, satisfaction of Catalonian aspirations. This is a formidable but not Utopian programme. Land reform requires the modernisation of agriculture and the reconstruction, on a popular basis, of the system of land ownership; educational reform requires the building of State schools to replace the Church schools abolished at the Revolution. Religious emancipation involves the destruction of the political and economic power of the Catholic Church, whose legitimate influence has been gravely compromised by the support given by the Vatican to the Right in the last election. The solution of the Catalonian problem, which is one not of separatism but of decentralisation, can be achieved by the restoration of the Statute of Autonomy, which was suspended after the 1934 revolt.

The strength of the Popular Front lies in its concrete programme. Its danger is that it may break on internal questions before they are achieved. The first aim of Señor Azaña must be to hold his coalition together until the fundamental reforms are effected. Señor Azaña, Don Martinez Barrios and Señor Caballero are men of ability and determination, and schooled by now by grim political experience. But the Popular Front must realise its responsibilities. 'Catalans are not children but men,' said Señor Sunyer, head of the restored municipal council of Barcelona on Monday. 'We have once more come into our own with a full sense of responsibility.' These are words which every Spaniard, and every member of the Popular Front, should applaud. But Señor Azaña, the new Prime Minister, will have grave problems to face between now and March 16th, when the Cortes meets.

21 February

MR ROOSEVELT AND THE WHITE HOUSE
S. K. RATCLIFFE in Washington

It can be hardly less curious to Americans, I think, than to the English observer to find at this early stage of the presidential campaign the name of Herbert Hoover again in the headlines. If ever a party and national leader met with a final overthrow, that would seem to have been the case with Mr Hoover in 1932. And yet at the moment of writing, three weeks after Al Smith opened fire upon the President, it is a speech by the only living ex-President which is being most widely quoted. Not because it was an important utterance – except for the reference to government spending, his words gave no hint of an alternative Republican policy – but because it was rather more apt to the occasion than some other speeches which, perhaps to the surprise of newspaper readers, are printed verbatim.

The presidential candidates will be nominated four months hence. The election falls on November 3rd. The interval is long enough for almost anything to happen, and no one who considers the last national poll will be disposed to underestimate the element of chance in this year's contest. In 1934 Mr Roosevelt's popular victory was greater than in 1932. In 1936 any inquirer who should make the mistake of confining himself to the Press of the great cities and the associations of business men could easily be led to infer that the President is already defeated. The political climate, east of Chicago and St Louis at all events, has changed during the past twelve months to an extraordinary degree, and the change, of course, is the more noticeable because of the President's unique position during the first 18 months of his term. Congress turned against Calvin Coolidge, Congress and the country turned against Mr Hoover. But neither of those Presidents ever approached the popularity enjoyed by Mr Roosevelt in 1933–4. The harshness and violence of the feeling against the President throughout the business world today is not unlike that poured out against Woodrow Wilson in 1920. And yet three years ago, Franklin Roosevelt saved American business, with the banks, and investment houses, from utter disaster. His friends in that world would seem now to be no more than a scattered remnant. The newspapers of the Eastern States steadily encourage the view that the tide of public sentiment is mounting against the Democratic Administration. The Republicans then, you would conclude, must be cheerful, while the President's supporters are increasingly anxious.

But that is certainly not what one finds between New York and Washington. The political campaign has opened at a far too early date. Al Smith's speech in Washington on January 25th was broadcast over the whole country. It made a greater stir than any speech within living memory delivered against a reigning President in advance of the campaign proper. It was followed immediately by four or five others of similar length, by aspirants to the Presidency, all heard on the air, and all alike being accorded the dubious advantage of verbatim publication in the daily papers. Over here, of course, is publication on a scale such as the great political orators of the past could not have imagined. These speeches before the battle, we may certainly assume, are listened to by a vast multitude; they are even read by great numbers. But what can they be said to amount to, several months before the presidential candidates are chosen and the party platforms take shape?

It is interesting to note that so far the firing is almost all from one side. Mr Roosevelt does not answer, and evidently has no intention of being drawn in. He knows that his opponents, especially if they are thinking of office, must keep to a negative line of attack; or else that if, like Governor Landon of Kansas, they are courageous enough to hint at a social policy, a general likeness to the New Deal must be apparent. Although Al Smith declared that there was only one man who should or could reply to him, the President made no sign, and no one can suppose that he is under any temptation to do so. Al himself, the former Democratic champion, is not a candidate, and it has been universally remarked that his present associates, the opulent supporters of the non-party Liberty League, make strange companions for the man who as Governor of New York and opponent of Mr Hoover came nearer to being what we in England should recognise as a radical progressive than any other head of a great American party. Mr Roosevelt knows that this opponent is most effectively answered by the Al Smith of seven years ago. The deadly parallel, said a conspicuous Washington correspondent the other day, is a game that is going to be played this year against every man in the field; but no one has more cause to fear it than Al Smith, once the most formidable fighter on the President's own side.

As for the Republicans who have thrown themselves thus early into the fray, there is no need to treat their speeches as of any account, for reasons that are perfectly well understood. The one important figure among them, Senator Borah, will not be considered when the nominating convention meets in Cleveland. He is over 70, and is the lone wolf of Washington; he has never led even the smallest group. And if any one of the others now aiming at the Republican nomination should secure it – for this year almost anything in the Grand Old Party is imaginable – the choice will have been made for one reason and one alone: because the managers of the party have agreed upon their man. And yet the Supreme Court is making the greatest of constitutional issues a reality. What an extraordinary opportunity for fighting the

49

1936 election on American fundamentals! The central point to note at the present stage is this: that within the party opposed to the Rooseveltian Administration there is going on a terrific struggle for the control of the party machine. The general assumption among Republican politicians is still that in November the New Deal will win and Mr Roosevelt be re-elected. What matters in 1936 is the fight for the mastery of the machine.

28 February

WHERE JAPAN AND RUSSIA CLASH
WILLIAM HENRY CHAMBERLIN in Tokyo

It is not an accidental coincidence that some of the severest clashes on the uneasy northern frontier of Manchoukuo have taken place along the ill-defined boundary between Manchoukuo and Outer Mongolia. Skirmishing started on this border shortly before Christmas and has never entirely died down. The highly contradictory communiqués that were issued from Japanese and Soviet sources when more serious fighting broke out in the middle of February agreed on only one point: that larger forces were steadily becoming involved and that more formidable weapons than the rifles and machine-guns with which a frontier post would normally be equipped were being used. The Japanese Press reported the fact that two Soviet aeroplanes participated in an engagement at Olahodka on February 12th, where eight Japanese were killed and eleven Japanese and Manchoukuo soldiers were wounded. Several Soviet statements have mentioned the appearance of armoured cars and trucks on the Japanese-Manchoukuo side.

Mongolia is a pivotal problem for Japanese and for Soviet strategy. Until and unless the present state of armed tension between Japan and the Soviet Union gives way to some kind of understanding and appeasement the frontiers of the Mongolian areas which are under the direct or indirect control of the two Powers are likely to be especially disturbed. Vast in area, sparse in population and natural resources, the lands occupied by the Mongols lie directly across the pathways which seem marked out for Japanese and for Soviet expansion. At the present time these lands are divided. It is probably inevitable that the more ambitious spirits both on the Soviet and on the Japanese sides of the dimly-indicated line of demarcation should try to exploit their

50

own Mongols as a nucleus for propaganda and perhaps eventual advance into the Mongolian territory held by the other Power.

A number of officers of the Kwantung Army (Japan's military force in Manchoukuo), notably Lieutenant-Colonel Terada, have become specialists in the Mongolian question, learning the language, becoming familiar with the religion and customs of the Mongols. There can be little doubt that some of these officers cherish dreams of a Pan-Mongolian State, protected by Japan, purged of any Bolshevik influence and based on the ancestral tribal customs and the lamaism (a kind of corrupted Buddhism) which has long been the dominant religion in Mongolia. Outer Mongolia would be an integral part of any such State; and it is quite conceivable that the Japanese military authorities would be willing to consent to an administrative detachment from Manchoukuo of the Mongolian provinces which lie to the west of the Hsingan Mountains, provided, of course, that Japanese influence on the hypothetical new Mongolian State was assured and unchallenged.

The Soviet Union, on the other hand, regards Outer Mongolia, where a puppet state, under Soviet influence, was set up with the aid of the Red Army in 1921 as a valuable outpost in the Far East, which it does not propose to abandon. Outer Mongolia, so long as it preserves its Soviet orientation, is a potentially useful military corridor, through which Soviet cavalry and motorised units could strike into the western part of Manchoukuo, threatening the communications of the Japanese armies on the Amur, Ussuri and Argun rivers on the northern boundary of Manchoukuo.

The loss of Outer Mongolia would lay bare a thousand miles of Siberian frontier and make more difficult the already complicated task of defending the Soviet Far Eastern provinces, which lie thousands of miles away from the country's main centres of industry and population. A Japanese air base in Ulanbator, the capital of Outer Mongolia, might even threaten the large iron, steel and machine building works which have grown up in Novosibirsk and Kuznetzk, in Central Siberia, and which would certainly be turned to military uses in the event of war.

There has been an appreciable growth of Japanese influence in Inner Mongolia during the last months. A pro-Japanese *régime*, apparently headed by Manchoukuo Mongols, has been set up in southern Chahar. The Mongolian Autonomous Political Council, under the leadership of Prince Teh, has moved further in the direction of snapping the tenuous ties which bind it to Nanking. Inner Mongolia has been under a curious kind of dual government, with Chinese military and civil authorities and Mongolian princes ruling side by side, for some time. It is extremely difficult, on the basis of meagre, irregular and contradictory reports, to know the precise balance of power at any given moment. But it seems to be a reasonable prediction that Japanese military power and influence will grow, rather than diminish, in Inner Mongolia with the passing of time. A substantial increase in Japan's North China garrison is planned; and Japanese military leaders, both in Manchoukuo and in North China, attach very great importance to Inner Mongolia, because it is through this region that Soviet aid in propaganda, arms and money might reach the peripatetic Chinese Communists.

By contrast with Inner Mongolia, where distance and lack of means of communication are the main obstacles to effective Japanese penetration, Outer Mongolia is a distinctly harder nut to crack. Two prolonged conferences which were held at the Manchoukuo border town of Manchouli last year failed to lead to any agreement between Manchoukuo and Outer Mongolia on such questions as frontier delimitation and exchange of diplomatic representatives. I was present in Manchouli for a short time during one of these conferences and found the Outer Mongolian delegates surrounded by Russian 'advisers' and as inaccessible as a Tibetan Grand Lama. The moving spirit in the Manchoukuo delegation was a Japanese diplomat attached to the Hsinking Foreign Office.

The conference broke down because the Outer Mongolians, obviously under Soviet prompting, stubbornly refused to admit a Manchoukuo mission to their capital, Ulanbator. Trouble was freely predicted in Hsinking (the capital of Manchoukuo) after the failure of the conference; and trouble there has been since the latter part of December. Inasmuch as there are no foreign observers within hundreds of miles of the obscure scenes of conflict and since the Soviet and Japanese accounts of the circumstances of each clash are invariably and violently contradictory, it is impossible to assess the responsibility for these frontier skirmishes.

It is significant, however, that the Outer Mongolians are putting up a stiff fight, which would scarcely be possible without Russian support and technical aid with more complicated weapons. While it would still perhaps be premature to say that the Soviet Union would regard a serious Japanese drive against Outer Mongolia as a *casus belli** there seems to be no doubt that the Soviet Far Eastern military authorities will help the Mongols to offer vigorous resistance. Since Outer Mongolia is carefully isolated from the outside world (with the exception of the Soviet Union) it is difficult to say how much internal disaffection, promoted by the drastic innovating policies of the new Mongolian *régime* in the fields of property and religion, exists and might come to the surface in the event of a major attack from without.

The Mongolian problem is, of course, closely bound up with the larger problem of Russo-Japanese relations. These are now much worse than at any time in recent years. Soviet self-confidence has visibly grown and finds expression in a stiff unyielding attitude on such questions as border demarcation, the settlement of the chronic fishing rights dispute and the establishment of Manchoukuo consulates in Siberia. Should the often predicted Russo-Japanese clash occur the Mongols will doubtless be drawn in on both sides; and Mongol horsemen, mounted on their shaggy ponies, will be active in scouting and skirmishing in the prospective western theatre of hostilities.

13 March

DOES GERMANY MEAN PEACE?
[WILSON HARRIS]

When the international crisis was dealt with in these columns a week ago the dominating question was whether Herr Hitler's word, after his flagrant violation of the Locarno Treaty, could be relied on. It is the dominating question still. Much has happened in the intervening week. The Locarno Powers and the League Council have met in London. Herr Hitler himself has made public pronouncements on the situation at Karlsruhe and Frankfurt. And Herr Ribbentrop, supported by a strong German delegation, has come to London to take a seat at the League Council table. That in itself marks some advance. *Les absents ont toujours tort*, and nothing could be much worse than negotiation by public speeches. But over every conversation and discussion is still written the question, Does Germany want peace? And if

---

* [No longer premature. In an interview with an American journalist, M. Stalin stated categorically on March 5th that a Japanese attempt on the Outer Mongolian capital, Ulanbator, would make 'positive action' by Russia a necessity. – ED. *The Spectator*.]

so on what terms? There are, of course, other questions of less importance to be answered first, questions of procedure which, however anxious the impatient may be to brush them aside, are too nearly questions of substance for that. The French are perfectly right in refusing merely to condemn Germany's action formally and then forget it and pass on to the discussion of Herr Hitler's new peace programme. If bridges are to be built they must be begun from both sides, and Herr Hitler may still be expected to take some step to diminish the suspicion his *fait accompli* has provoked.

But assume that done – and the skilful handling of the situation by Mr Eden has gone far to make the impossible possible – how are Herr Hitler's peace proposals, when the ground is cleared for the discussion of them, to be approached? Not, certainly, in a spirit of sceptical mistrust that will make agreement hopeless. But not, equally, in a spirit of credulous confidence that would produce precisely the kind of agreement that suited Germany's policy. If it were clear what that policy was the outlook would be a great deal clearer. In M. Litvinoff's view its keynote is hatred of his country and all it stands for, and it is impossible to read the bitter speech he delivered at the League Council meeting on Monday and not admit that there is justification for almost everything he said.

Nothing in Herr Hitler's peace proposals, except his suggestion of Germany's return to the League of Nations, is inconsistent with the theory that Germany wants peace in the west with a view to freeing her for action in the east. Herr Hitler proposes a non-aggression pact with France which would immobilise France if Germany were at war with Russia. He offers no non-aggression pact to Russia. In his speech at Karlsruhe, made since his peace programme was framed, he again launched violent attacks on Bolshevism and the country where Bolshevism prevails. If Germany does return to Geneva her representative will have to sit side by side with Russia's, and it is not unreasonable, in view of the interpretations to which Herr Hitler's proposals lend themselves, and the attacks he has directed against Russia since, that Russia should, with general support, ask for very explicit assurances that Germany not only means peace but means it everywhere.

So much it is necessary to say, for it is inevitable that in negotiations opened on the morrow of the violation of a treaty the treaty-breaker should be required to put his good faith in the matter of future engagements so far as possible beyond question. Herr Hitler's public speeches have been both satisfactory and the reverse in that respect. He has declared, no doubt with sincerity, his desire to live at peace with France, and a huge audience at Frankfurt acclaimed the declaration. But in his Karlsruhe speech two days earlier he had affirmed just as emphatically Germany's right to be judge in her own cause and her refusal to be 'haled before international courts, ... particularly when Germany is in the right.' Such declarations cannot be dismissed as matters of indifference. The choice in international affairs is between anarchy and a loyal observance of freely contracted agreements, coupled with readiness to submit to impartial arbitrament questions about which genuine dispute arises. Herr Hitler appears to take the position, fatal to constructive international understandings, that only Germany can decide whether Germany is right. Immensely desirable as full co-operation with Germany, and her return to membership of the League of Nations is, no co-operation is possible unless she honestly undertakes the same obligations as any other State member of the League. The first test will be the submission to the Permanent Court at the Hague of Germany's claim that the Franco-Soviet Pact is itself a violation of the Locarno Treaty. German consent to that course is not needed, but the reception by Germany of the verdict of the Court, whatever it may be, on a question she herself has raised, will throw valuable light on her good faith.

It is well that these aspects of the situation should be frankly faced. The Hitler proposals open up possibilities that have justly raised hopes high. But it is essential to build on sound foundations, and to test the foundations before the building is begun. Meanwhile the immediate problems have still to be solved. France is in some quarters being unjustly criticised. It is true that her policy has been largely responsible for Herr Hitler's rise to power, and it was she who rejected successive offers of mutual disarmament. But what is under discussion today is the immediate, not the remoter, past, and the possibilities of both the immediate and the more distant future. The task of reconciling France's just stipulations with the necessary exploration of the German proposals is delicate to the last degree. Mr Eden has shown great ability in devising formulas which have secured the presence of a German delegate at the League Council table, but he will still have the most formidable obstacle before him if, as there seems some reason to apprehend, condemnation by the League Council is treated by Germany as an inevitable and meaningless formality to which she need have no regard. The French Government, with an election campaign before it very different from the staged plebiscite in Germany, where only one party can nominate candidates, is in a doubly delicate position. The immediate crisis, no doubt, is past. There can be no question of League-imposed sanctions where there has been no resort to war. And this country could not join in military measures where there has been no such action by Germany as would in itself endanger peace, though for that very reason it is the more necessary to make it clear that Germany's violation in no way relieves the other signatories of the Locarno Treaty of their obligations to one another. If that, and the resolve to maintain and strengthen collective security through the League (to which a relaxation of the sanctions imposed on Italy would directly give the lie) can be demonstrated to France's satisfaction the way may yet be cleared for the conversion of the German proposals into the basis for a more stable peace.

20 March

THE HOLLOW MAN
GORONWY REES

Hitler, Konrad Heiden. (Constable)

Herr Heiden has already written the best history of the National Socialist movement. He has now written the best biography of its Führer. It is not a perfect or a final account of the man, for Hitler must remain a nightmare figure, so long as Europe endures the bad dream caused by its undigested and unwholesome meals of the post-War period. We cannot say what Herr Hitler will look like in the light of common day; the dream is not yet over, but Herr Heiden has almost succeeded in piercing the illusion. He throws a sharp light upon Herr Hitler's character, of which the most important qualities are these.

He is essentially uncivilised. The son of a petty anti-Semite civil servant of poor stock, a failure as an art student, an unskilled labourer in Vienna, a corporal in the War, an agent of the Reichswehr, a political adventurer, he has experienced nothing which could teach him what civilisation is. What he knows of it he has learned from books, from Wagner and from such authorities as Goebbels, Rosenberg and Hanfstaengl. His knowledge is secondhand and fits him like a cheap suit. It remains outside him, and when he speaks of civilisation it is with the mingled cunning and ignorance of the ambitious grocer who talks of charity but practises putting sand in the sugar for his poorer customers. Therefore the values of civilised men are unreal to him; what is real are the instincts of brutality and barbarism whose effects can be seen, touched, smelt, and easily understood.

He is an uneducated man, and is too lazy to educate himself. He is ignorant of facts and does not understand theories. One idea is to him very much like any other, and for him words have no meaning but only an emotional propriety. When he says Peace he might as well say War, for all the meaning his words and actions have; what is significant is the emotion with which he charges them.

He is a treacherous man. He has, in the past, made many promises and broken many. Those who believed him are dead, tortured or defeated. For he understands promises, not as obligations to be kept but as instruments for deceiving people.

He is a superb actor. His real personality is expressed only by his instincts. They are violent and intense, but can only be sustained for short moments of brutal ecstasy. Soon exhausted, they leave him empty, and, being sensitive as an octopus, he takes on any character, which suits the circumstances and pleases the observer. His instincts assuaged, the murderer of Röhm, torturer of Ossietsky, becomes to the timid middle-aged *Hausfrau* a gentle celibate, stooping with dim eyes over the perambulator to kiss the baby that can never be his.

He is a lucky man, because he is a representative man. He rose to power at a time when the pressure of starvation, bad nerves and unemployment broke the fabric of German society, and reduced men to the state of nature. To Herr Hitler that state is natural and he has never known any other, and in it his qualities have a survival value superior to that of men who were born for better things. It was this pressure which reduced Germany to his level. When it was relieved, he sank into insignificance: when it was intensified, he was again the man of the day.

He has many qualities which are less than human, but one which raises him, as a politician, above the ordinary. He has an unerring sense of power, without minding what it is used for. Other politicians are handicapped by the double task of seeking power and trying to use it for some end. Herr Hitler has only

57

the one preoccupation: to seek power. He does not mind how it is used; he lets it use him and passively enjoys it. And for him power has always meant – the Reichswehr, and nothing is better or more valuable in Herr Heiden's book than his long and detailed analysis of Herr Hitler's extraordinarily shrewd career of intrigue with the Reichswehr and dependence upon it. So Herr Heiden, and though his estimate may be exaggerated it is certainly not baseless. Many people should read this book, and especially those politicians now engaged in the perilous task of negotiating with Herr Hitler. That is not a reason for not negotiating, but it is a reason for hedging any agreement about with any conceivable safeguard.

20 March

YOUNG GERMANY AND *MEIN KAMPF*
R. C. K. ENSOR

Nobody who wants to understand the policy of Nazi Germany can afford to neglect its Bible – Herr Hitler's *Mein Kampf*. In England it remains little known, and the only English translation omits many of its most significant passages. Were it otherwise, the extraordinary spectacle of English left-wing organs on March 9th welcoming the recent Hitler *coup* as a great new starting-point for world-peace would scarcely have been witnessed.

Mein Kampf's conception of German foreign policy is one of the most coherent things in a book not everywhere coherent. The principal expositions of it are in Vol. I chapter 4, and Vol. II, chapters 13 and 14. The strictures that the Führer there passes on Germany's pre-War foreign policy, and the goals that he indicates for the future, are alike determined by a perfectly clear-cut view.

Certain presuppositions need not delay us here – as that the German race is the finest in the world, that its political integration ought to be the object of every German, and that the arch-foe of this race-ideal is Jewry. But the root problem for Nazi foreign policy is the fact (as Herr Hitler regards it) that the Germans, a rapidly expanding race, have not enough land to live upon. Four possible solutions are propounded: (1) to diminish population by birth-control, as in France; (2) to increase the productivity of the already available land; (3) to annex new land; (4) to expand factory production for foreign markets. The first the Führer rejects; the second he considers incapable of meeting the need; the fourth he deprecates, because he wants Germany to feed herself and be self-sufficient. There remains the third, and that governs the whole programme. Germany is to increase her area. She is to make it large enough to contain not merely present but future population, and to contain it sufficiently spaced out for industry and agriculture to be interdependent and the need of foreign markets to be reduced to a minimum. A widely spaced population is also recommended for 'military-geographical' reasons, because it is less vulnerable to an enemy.

The scale of the new territory which *Mein Kampf* contemplates annexing is indicated on p. 767, where we are told that, whereas today there are 80 million Germans in Europe, the right policy must look forward a century, and provide land 'on this continent' where 250 million Germans can live – 'not squeezed together as factory-coolies for the rest of the world, but as peasants and workmen, who through their production assure a livelihood to each other.' Where is this vast area to be found? Herr Hitler does not beat about the bush. It could only be found, he says quite frankly (p. 154, p. 742), at the expense of Russia. And Providence has opportunely brought Russia into a state propitious for the enterprise (p. 742). Such a policy, he adds, cannot be pursued by halves. It would be – and before the War it was – a great mistake to quarrel with other Powers about oversea colonies, which in any case could not afford settlement for a large white population. Germany's future lies not on the water, but on the land. *Bodenpolitik* is the slogan.

The implications are all quite clearly drawn. How are the Germans to obtain this Russian land? By the sword, by fighting for it, as their fathers fought for the soil that is now Germany. And the morality of such aggression? 'State frontiers are man-made, and men may alter them ... The right to land and soil may be turned into duty, if without an extension of its soil a great people appears doomed to destruction.' Germany 'will either exist as a World Power or not exist at all'; but for the *rôle* of a World Power this enlarged area is proclaimed essential to her. Therefore National Socialist policy will concentrate on the one aim. It will discard the colonial policy and the oversea-trade policy of pre-War Germany, and it will make every friend that it can in the West in order to secure Germany's rear when her trek eastward begins. The obvious ally is Great Britain, and Italy is also possible. France, at the time when he wrote, Herr Hitler dismissed as hopeless. She was for him always 'the mortal enemy' (*Todfeind*); her age-long plans to keep Germany weak and disunited could only be defeated by crushing her. The Führer has lately told a French journalist that he does not feel like that now; that he considers a Franco-German agreement possible. But this does not imply any change of principle. He never wanted, for its own sake, to fight any Western Power; he would only fight France to guard his rear during his attack on Russia. If instead he could buy her off without bloodshed, so much the better for him.

These doctrines, the statement of which is publicly sold today by the hundred thousand in Germany and inculcated as a sort of Holy Writ, are in close conformity with what their author's Government has since done and proposed. It has violently resented the Franco-Soviet Treaty – why? Because the treaty was the Soviet's answering precaution against the attack to come. It has hastily re-occupied the demilitarised zone – why? Because, while the zone remained defenceless, Germany could not parry a French counterstroke at her rear; even Essen lay exposed. It has offered a 25-year peace pact to all the States bordering it both west and east – why? Because Russia is not a State bordering Germany, and such a pact would leave her out in the cold, for Germany to pick a quarrel with while the hands of the rest of Europe were tied. No one who had read *Mein Kampf* could miss the anti-Russian point of Herr Hitler's peace-note on March 7th.

Surely a perfectly plain question may be put to the Führer. Does he stand by *Mein Kampf*'s programme of a predatory war against Russia, or does he not? If he does not, why does he not withdraw *Mein Kampf* from circulation, or issue a revised edition with the *Bodenpolitik* left out? The last course, one must admit, would be scarcely practicable; you might as well excise Hamlet from *Hamlet*. For Herr Hitler climbed to power on the economic crisis, and to make good eventually he must provide bread and work for his countrymen. Temporarily he has done so by a policy of rearmament. But his permanent policy is the *Bodenpolitik*, and he has no other. More, he has denounced most of the obvious alternatives in scathing terms. He is, in truth, tied to his programme, nor is there anything to show that he regrets it. His one weakness is that he cannot wholly choose his own time; for, if Japan attacks Russia, he must follow suit. And it may be that recent signs of precipitance on Japan's side had as much to do with dating the events of February 29th as the Franco-Soviet Pact.

Meanwhile, whether or not *Mein Kampf* represents Herr Hitler's latest thoughts, the fact remains that the youth of Germany have been brought up on it for half a dozen – in many cases a dozen – years. And they still continue to be. What must be the result? Can it conceivably be consistent with twenty-five years of European peace?

3 April

THE POISON-GAS CAMPAIGN
[WILSON HARRIS]

That Marshal Badoglio has been using poison-gas in his Abyssinian campaign must now be regarded as established beyond all possibility of repudiation. In these columns the ascription to Italy of an action abhorrent on grounds of humanity and constituting yet one more flagrant and deliberate breach of treaty has been scrupulously avoided so long as the evidence was anything short of what an impartial tribunal would pronounce conclusive. But the evidence is now decisive. The Foreign Office is understood to have received from Europeans in Abyssinia statements that leave no room for any shadow of doubt. And, among independent testimonies, an article of great importance in Saturday's *Times* gave detailed accounts by an eye-witness of constant gas-attacks from March 1st onwards. In many cases mustard-gas was sprayed from aeroplanes and fell indiscriminately on soldiers and civilians, men and women and children, many, according to the account in question, receiving ghastly wounds on the head and shoulders. The facts, then, must be taken to be no longer in question.

What is to be said of them? The unspeakable brutality of the use against defenceless negroes of an instrument diabolical in its capacity for inflicting agony and disablement is in one sense the least part of Italy's crime. The citizens of this and other countries have read for six months and more with sickened disgust of Italian military successes owed to the aeroplanes which detect every movement of an enemy 'blind' himself, and drop tons of bombs on his camps and concentrations while he has hardly a machine that can attempt a response. But that is in a sense legitimate warfare, except when the objectives of the attentions from the air are Red Cross units or open towns like Harrar. It was the memory of gas-war in Europe from 1915 onwards that led to the treaty of 1925, whose signatories, including Britain and France and Italy and Abyssinia, bound themselves to abjure absolutely and for ever the use in war 'of asphyxiating, poisonous and the other gases, and of all analogous liquids, materials or devices.' That was in 1925. This is 1936. For so long and no longer has Italy's signature been honoured. She has broken her pledge without even the hollow excuse of military exigency. She did not need gas to win the war. Her aeroplanes and tanks and heavy guns were blasting from her path an enemy devoid of all such weapons. Her assumption of the badge of barbarism is gratuitous and deliberate.

So much for Italy and her civilising mission. The matter passes now into other hands. Far larger questions have to be decided. When the 1925 convention is torn up by Italy is it torn up for all its signatories? Technically, of course, it is not. Every other country that signed remains as completely bound as ever. But what confidence can be placed in future in an agreement which any signatory can break at any moment with impunity? What, in the light of events in Abyssinia, is the value of any treaty designed to mitigate the most hideous horrors of warfare? Those are questions which particularly concern Herr Hitler, for he has repeatedly expressed his belief in the possibility of humanising warfare, and the document he addressed to the Locarno Powers last week proposed specifically, under the head of disarmament, prohibition of the dropping of gas, poisonous or incendiary bombs, and various other forms of bombardment from the air or the ground. All that is admirable if there is reasonable hope that the prohibition will be observed, or, failing observation, enforced. But it has always been insisted that the one point at which an aggressor can be checked is at the outset, and that when once he has broken treaties which bind him not to begin war at all it is highly unlikely that he will observe others which purport to regulate his conduct of war. Italy has the distinction of demonstrating conclusively the soundness of that argument.

The League of Nations is now presented with a challenge which there would seem to be no possibility of evading but for the capacity for evasion which that body has displayed in the last six months. That is not said in disparagement of the League as conceived in 1919, or of the Covenant then drafted. Full and complete provision was made in the Covenant for such a contingency as has arisen in Africa. If the Covenant had been carried out all intercourse of any kind whatever between League States and Italy would have been severed within a week of her aggression – the more so since she had been patently preparing it for months before – and material assistance of various kinds would have been given to Abyssinia. If squadrons of aeroplanes from League countries had been sent to help in the defence of Abyssinia's frontiers Italy could have had no just cause for complaint, and she could have been left to carry the war into Europe at her peril if she chose. Instead of that, financial and economic sanctions were not put into operation till the war had been in progress for close on seven weeks, and the essential petrol sanction is not even decided on today, after six months of conflict. Conciliation has been proposed to, and accepted by, both sides, and Italy has used the interval to smother with mustard-gas the regions which Latin civilisation is designed to bring to blossom.

That is the situation today. Italy has gone to war in violation of the Covenant and the Kellogg Pact, with relative impunity. She has deliberately broken the poison-gas convention (for the despatch of gas to Africa began months ago) with complete impunity. If that ends the matter, if an aggressor is left to profit not merely by his aggression but by the devilry with which he supplements it, then the hope of basing civilisation on treaties having for their signatories the effect of law vanishes like a puff of smoke. The world has been profoundly disturbed by Herr Hitler's treatment of an obligation freely and solemnly contracted. But his action is venial compared with Signor Mussolini's. His own proposals, moreover, will be futile if agreements such as he himself proposes, whether bilateral, regional or more widely collective, can be broken at will by any signatory which finds their observance inconvenient. The Committee of Thirteen, which is in effect the Council of the League, is assembling as these words are being written. The future of the League of Nations may be in its hands. It can record some solemn protest for the derision of the Italian Press, or it can signalise its view of treaty violation by deciding forthwith on measures it ought to have taken months ago, such as the withdrawal of Ambassadors from Rome and the genuine severance of all communications of every kind with Italy. If the League had dealt with Italy's treaty-breaking as the Covenant prescribed, it would not

63

have had to deal with treaty-breaking by Germany at all. If it condones the latest Italian outrage Germany can well afford to ignore it altogether.

10 April

WHAT FRANCE IS THINKING
GASTON ARCHAMBAULT in Paris

In most letters from England two questions recur: What does the ordinary Frenchman think of the international situation? How will he vote in the general election at the end of the month?

To forecast the reactions of the ordinary Frenchman you must first consider his environment, for in this drama the setting dominates the players. Above all you must remember that the French Revolution is not quite 150 years distant. To the ordinary Frenchman it seems even closer, because more familiar than many subsequent decades, Robespierre and Danton still live in his mind, whereas he has forgotten Cavaignac and possibly Guizot. Allusions to the 'Immortal Principles' and to the 'Great Ancestors' are understood in any gathering. Jacobinism remains a yardstick to measure political tendencies.

And into those 150 years have been crowded experiments with every possible form of government, every possible political or economic nostrum, accompanied by every possible calamity – regicide, dictatorships, empires, kingdoms (by divine right as well as by the will of the people), republics; inflation, devaluation, managed economy, forced labour, unemployments; new calendars, new weights and measures, new systems of administration, justice and religion; socialism, communism, anarchism; plebiscites, insurrections, blood purges, civil war; a Mexican adventure, a Dreyfus Affair; several foreign wars and three invasions of the national territory. France has been surfeited with events. Most ordinary Frenchmen suffer from the same complaint – ill-digested French Revolution.

The life of the ordinary Frenchman has been affected by so many unheavals that he is not yet sure of his ground. Although he asserts that he has become a free man, there are moments when he fears that it may all be a dream and that he will awaken to find himself still a serf in revolt. To convince himself of his emancipation he addresses his fellows as 'Citizens,' he inscribes 'Liberty, Equality, Fraternity,' on his monuments, he discourses

64

on Rights of Man and Federation of Peoples, he names his battle-ships *Democracy* or *Justice*. Politically he progresses from liberal to radical, from radical to socialist, from socialist to communist. It is a token of emancipation to go ever to the Left, ever farther from old shibboleths. It is a token of emancipation for some to deny the existence of the Deity.

But these are outward manifestations. At heart the ordinary Frenchman feels that the true token of freedom is the right to possess. He yearns to own something, land for preference, for generally he is of peasant stock; something to which he can cling and which may survive in the event of more cataclysms. He does not yearn for very much, because small possessions are easier to preserve, and he has remained modest in his needs. So that the general ambition is to become a 'small proprietor.' The French Socialist himself is a bourgeois in embryo. The simile of the Dutch cheese has become hackneyed but remains apposite; The ordinary Frenchman is red outwardly but quite white within.

Everything conspires to make the ordinary Frenchman 'small' – his tastes, his inheritance laws, his innate thrift, his moderate ambition. Therefore *petit* is the typical French qualificative. The mass of the population consists of small landholders, small arti-sans, small tradesmen, who aspire to become small investors or small pensioners, reading self-titled *petit* newspapers, living with a small family in a small house with a small garden.

Jean-Jacques Rousseau's conception of the general interest as merely the sum of individual interests suits the ordinary French-man perfectly. He is satisfied to consider the nation as a feder-ation of private interests, each necessarily small. As a conse-quence, in any national emergency his reaction is twofold, the collective and the personal – and they may be contradictory. Inevitably, his outlook, too, is small, nationally and even more internationally. He is timorous to venture, to risk his all. On principle, he is a pacific opportunist.

Since in his view the general interest is but the sum of all individual interests, the ordinary Frenchman has come to con-sider that the main function of government is to further these interests. His logical mind would deny this in the abstract, but he is content to accept it in the concrete. At public meetings it is proper that candidates should expound doctrines and develop programmes. But once the candidate is elected, the ordinary Frenchman sees in him only an intermediary between himself and the authority that dispenses grants, subsidies and bounties,

65

and protects trade, industry and agriculture. In the broad stream of individual interests that make up the general interest, the ordinary Frenchman has mentally tinted his modest rivulet a special colour so that it may never be lost to him.

The Revolution and Napoleon left him another heritage – centralisation, codification and classification, with all their attendant documents. The ordinary Frenchman accumulates 'papers' from birth to death. His every act is regulated by ordinances and instructions. The walls throughout the land are placarded with them. They may be disregarded or forgotten, but they exist and can be produced, either to support or to refute.

On this point the ordinary Frenchman cannot be understood by the ordinary Englishman, who knew no 'papers' until passports came back with the War. Poincaré, an ordinary Frenchman with extraordinary talents, could not be appreciated in England; his insistence on documents savoured too much of the pettifogging attorney.

In the present contingency the ordinary Frenchman cannot conceive English repugnance to commitments in writing. He argues thus: 'If France should be attacked and invaded, England will be in grave danger. So if only for self-protection England will not allow France to be attacked wantonly. But she will not sign a paper binding herself in advance. Why?' He does not doubt England's word, but there arise inevitable memories of the Revolution – Pitt and Quiberon and *la cavalerie de Saint-Georges*. And his mind would be easier if he had a document to file away.

Yet he prefers a neighbour who will not sign to one who repudiates his signature. He recalls that after 1870 he took his beating and paid his debt, with enemy occupation so long as a sou was still owing, Thiers having vainly turned to Europe for mitigation of Bismarck's terms. He had signed and he honoured his signature. Whereas now ... The ordinary Frenchman would prefer to treat Germany on the principle of live and let live. But he is afraid of her, especially of Hitler. Where he sees small, Hitler sees big. And he is uneasy, for he is very inferior numerically. He seeks support among his neighbours or in Geneva, but he finds few willing to enter into commitments and collective security seems to remain a pious hope.

The coming election is likely to result in a Chamber much like the last. Considerations of individual interests will play the major part. For the rest, those who fear war and have no faith

66

in collective security will switch to the Right as more likely to press military measures. Those who fear war but have faith in the possibility of organising collective security will switch to the Left as more likely to achieve it.

Further than that, the ordinary Frenchman feels that his fate is on the knees of the gods. He will not attack; but if his small possessions are menaced he will fight to preserve them. And he believes that he has proved to the world that he can fight.

10 April

A SPECTATOR'S NOTEBOOK
JANUS

Every bridal couple in Germany in future is to be presented with *Mein Kampf*, an ordinance which further justifies the description of that volume as the Bible of the German people. Family life, therefore, is to be nurtured from the first on the idea that France is the eternal enemy and Russian territory the ordained field for German expansion. It seems almost tragically ironical that Germany, if she utters conciliatory words in one breath, must invariably provide an antidote to them in the next.

24 April

EVOLVING RUSSIA
[GORONWY REES]

In a series of articles in this journal, Sir Bernard Pares has given his impressions of Moscow revisited after an absence of nearly twenty years, and those who remember him as a severe critic and opponent of Communism may have been surprised at the admiration which, with reservations, he expressed for the Moscow of today. It would be more surprising if one with so great a knowledge and love of Russia as Sir Bernard Pares could visit Moscow, at whatever time, without pleasure and admiration, for the Russians, though Communists, remain Russians, and there is much in their manner of life, in their characters, in their cultural achievements which must always astonish and delight a Western visitor. But it is the specific achievements of the Communists which interested and impressed Sir Bernard in Moscow, and on them he bases his conclusion that between Russia

67

of today and the Western democracies there exists a 'common ground' for sympathy and understanding. This conclusion is the more interesting because it arises not from a theoretical belief in Communism but from an inspection of its works, and, especially, from an awareness of the 'wholesale' changes which have taken place in the Soviet Union in the last two years.

It is indeed doubtful whether, unless for political or theoretical reasons, anyone would have come to the same conclusion two or three years ago. A visitor then was impressed by the sense of need, of strain, of an insufficiency of food and clothing, and even an awareness of the great industrial plants and factories arising under the Five Year Plan could not overpower the impression of fatigue and exhaustion which he thought he noticed in the faces of the workers of Moscow or Leningrad. He saw little of the good clothes and plentiful food of which Sir Bernard speaks; the shops seemed empty of all save unsatisfied customers; and he saw even less of the spirit of wellbeing and happiness of which recent visitors have spoken. The Five Year Plan was almost more of an effort than the nation could bear. To carry it out meant a continuation of the political methods which characterised the Communism of the intervention and the civil war. And a visitor who was aware of this unrelenting discipline and intolerance had his impression confirmed by the defences of political terrorism made by Communist propagandists. But it was the success of the Five Year Plan, the material progress it achieved, which has made possible the evolution of Russia in the last few years, and that evolution has given considerable justification to the Communists' claim that ideals of personal or political freedom, of justice, of culture, of peace, can only be realised when the material and economic basis for them have been properly prepared. It is the realisation that these ideals have prospered with the success of the Five Year Plan which has lately made Western observers anxious to secure the co-operation of Russia in the reconstruction of Europe, and even to suspect that Western democracies may have something to learn from the Soviet Union.

In foreign affairs, certainly, that co-operation has been given to an extent which could never have been expected before the victory of National Socialism in Germany. That disastrous event brought the Soviet Union into the League of Nations, and has made of it a determined and unwavering supporter of collective security, willing to put the whole of her resources behind the defence of the rule of law in international relations. It is not the fault of the Soviet Union if other countries have not been so unwavering. By now the Soviet Union certainly attaches greater value to the hopes of peace inspired by a collective system of security than to any hopes of world revolution to be expected from the activities of the Comintern, and it has tried to dissociate itself as much as possible from those activities. And not only in the League of Nations has Russia shown herself pacific. To a series of violent provocations by Japan she has replied, through the mouth of M. Voroshiloff, the Commissar for War, with an offer to settle all their differences by amicable means.

But to this change in foreign policy has corresponded a change also in domestic policy. Indeed, Russia would not be so anxious for world peace rather than world revolution if the progress of her own society was not such that she thinks it worth while to make every sacrifice rather than have it interrupted or destroyed. The evidence of that progress is by now considerable, and indeed the more striking because it appears at numerous and apparently unconnected points. M. Stalin has promised the reform and democratisation of the political system, with the introduction of universal, direct, and secret suffrage. He has opened the schools and universities to the children of the hitherto oppressed classes of the kulaks and the bourgeois. It is a sign that the period of internal tension and fear is over; and a similar sign is to be seen in the reconciliation of the Cossacks to the *régime* and the formation of two new regiments of Cossack cavalry, under the names of Voroshiloff and Budenny. In slighter ways also the same spirit is seen. Education has become less orthodox and rigid: in history the place of personality is not to be ignored but explained. And artists will be glad that M. Stalin himself has now done justice to the memory of the persecuted poet, Mayakovsky. But it is not only greater freedom and tolerance that Soviet society wants, but greater stability: and many will find the impulse to freedom more genuine because it is accompanied by such a desire for more orderly, more permanent, and more productive relationships as is shown in the recent reform of the divorce and marriage laws. That desire is indeed evidence of the change which may now make possible a closer and more spontaneous understanding between Russia and Western Europe. For it begins to be possible to believe that the course of Russia's development is towards the realisation of ideals to which Western democracies have clung and still cling, though daily it becomes more difficult: and in Russia they may yet find a powerful ally in their defence.

1 May

THE QUESTION OF COLONIES
[WILSON HARRIS]

The colonial question is making increasing demands on public attention. Ministers have for the last ten days been bombarded with questions in the House of Commons on their intentions regarding British colonies and mandated territories. Mr Eden is engaged in evolving a discreet interrogation to Herr Hitler as to the meaning of his reference to clearing up 'the question of colonial equality of rights.' Dr Schnee, the former Governor of German East Africa, stated Germany's demands in explicit terms last week in a speech in which he expressed confidence that the said equality of rights – *Gleichberechtigung* – would in fact be conceded. And, much more important, Mr Baldwin, in a considered statement in the House last Monday, explained the conditions under which mandated territories were held and those under which they might conceivably be transferred, adding with some emphasis that the Government had not considered and was not considering the transfer of any British mandated territory to another Power. That assurance, it will be observed, covers the past and present, but not the future. Regarding that the Prime Minister stated that if the question were raised by another country no decision would be taken by the Government without a full discussion in the House of Commons. Mr Baldwin could say no less, and at the moment there is no reason why he should say more.

But before long more, perhaps much more, will have to be said. There is every sign that Germany intends to press her claim for colonies, though to what point remains to be discovered. Dr Schnee's demands need not be taken too seriously. An ex-colonial governor naturally thinks there is nothing like colonies. But when Herr Hitler puts them in his March 7th programme it is another matter. That programme is being taken up seriously by Mr Eden, as it should be, and colonies will have to be discussed like everything else. But before there is discussion there must be elucidation. What does Germany actually want, and why does she want it? The second question is less important than the first, though much more ink and argument have been lavished on it. It may be perfectly true that neither Germany nor Italy nor Japan has ever used colonies as an outlet for its surplus populations. (The white inhabitants of all the German colonies in 1913 numbered 20,000; the Italian inhabitants of Eritrea and Italian

Somaliland in 1931 numbered just over 6,000, and of Libya about 30,000.) It may be equally true that the colonial dependencies of the various European Powers, and particularly the mandated territories, are by no means rich in raw materials, except rubber and tin, and that so far from there being any difficulty about access to such raw materials as there are, the real difficulty is for the producers to find markets. The facts regarding that, and they are highly important, will be found clearly and objectively set out in a booklet on Raw Materials and the Colonies just published (at half-a-crown) by the Royal Institute of International Affairs.

All that may be regarded as established, but none of it alters the fact that Germany does insistently demand what Herr Hitler at any rate is content so far to term 'colonial equality of rights.' He has not as yet gone further than that, and he asks no more than that after Germany has entered the League the matter shall be cleared up by friendly negotiations. That, if that is all, does not portend deadlock. But equality of rights regarding colonies may mean many things. It may mean, to begin with, equality of trade in the colonies of other Powers. That is not a demand that can be rejected unless colonies are to be regarded, as this country refuses to regard them, as preserves to be exploited for the benefit of the possessing Power. Over a great part of Africa, thanks to the Convention of St Germain (embodying, with revisions, the Berlin and Brussels Acts) and the terms of the various mandates, the open door does prevail. But in other British colonies varying measures of Imperial Preference exist, and many French colonies enjoy reciprocal free trade with the mother-country. If Germany claims that on re-entering the League of Nations she and every other League member should find the door open to trade in the colonies of every League Power she is asking something perfectly reasonable. The doors of British colonies in Africa are almost completely open. We should be prepared to open them quite completely, and – a necessary accompaniment – fix them open by spontaneously applying to the colonies the provisions that already govern a territory under B Mandate, *e.g.,* Tanganyika, including the presentation to the League of an annual report on administration to the League. That would in fact impose no trammels and set no standards that are not being observed already. But it would be a convincing proof to the world of British good faith.

Mandated territories are another matter. They consist, in

71

Africa, of former German colonies, and men like Dr Schnee demand the return to Germany of all of them. There is no evidence that that is the official policy. Herr Hitler's March 7th declaration suggests something quite different. What Germany does protest against, and intelligibly, is the implication that she is morally unfit to hold colonies or administer mandated territories. The so-called colonial guilt clauses of the Treaty of Versailles are as repugnant to her as the so-called war-guilt clause. That can be understood. The demand for 'equality of colonial right' by a country in Germany's present temper is inevitable. But, once more, what does the demand imply? Not, obviously, equality of colonial area with Britain or France or any other Power. Not necessarily restoration of German sovereignty over the former German colonies. But, quite definitely, recognition of the right of Germany to administer colonial territories no less than other European Powers. So far as only a recognition of principle is called for it can be accorded at once. But suppose Germany wants something more, wants an actual territory to administer, as proof that equality of colonial right has been made a reality? That obviously raises very difficult questions. Nothing can be worse for native populations than their transfer from one *régime* to another, and the fact that such a transfer took place, for better or worse, in 1919 is reason in itself why it should not take place again twenty years or less later. Nevertheless, in such a matter the world's loss must be measured against the world's gain. If Germany's equality of right could be established to her satisfaction by the transference to her of the mandate for a territory where the change of *régime* would be least unsettling, *e.g.*, Togoland or the Cameroons, that solution should not be ruled out. At the same time the open-door principle might be gradually introduced in the recruitment of personnel for the administration of the different mandated territories, and an international colonial service thus be slowly built up. That is essentially in the spirit of the mandate system, and it would give Germany, when a League member, an increasing approach to equality in mandate areas. If Herr Hitler's aspirations run along these lines, the colonial question need not be insoluble. To discover whether they do is Mr Eden's immediate task.

1 May

THE DESTROYER
[WILSON HARRIS]

Signor Mussolini has succeeded to admiration in piling destruction on destruction. He has destroyed an ancient African Empire and the only independent native kingdom on that great continent. He has destroyed the rule of an enlightened monarch who was beginning to bring order and prosperity to his wide and disparate domain, and had sought the assistance of the League of Nations in his task. He has destroyed all faith in an Italian signature. He has destroyed the hope of replacing force by law. He has destroyed Anglo-Italian friendship for a generation. He may quite well have destroyed the League of Nations. One thing only he has signally failed to destroy – the impression of dignity and courage and fortitude in distress that has won honour for the Ethiopian Emperor wherever men can recognise the existence of higher virtues than the worship of brute force. It is brute force alone, interpreted in terms of modern invention, that has carried the Italian troops to Addis Ababa. Their aeroplanes, operating daily unopposed, have watched every movement of the opposing armies, and Italian aviators in perfect security have dropped their bombs indiscriminately on military concentrations, peaceful villages and Red Cross stations. And when the destructive efforts of those engines failed to satisfy, poison-gas was invoked as a new destroyer. As a climax the troops from Italy, screened in every previous engagement by black Askaris, moved into the front line on Tuesday for the bloodless entry into Addis Ababa.

What is celebrated as a day of jubilation in Italy is a day of humiliation for the world – of humiliation for the League of Nations, of humiliation for this country. Mr Anthony Eden on Saturday claimed that we had played our part to the full as signatories of the Covenant and had nothing to reproach ourselves with. Such complacency ill befits the Foreign Secretary. The League of Nations has hardly begun to carry out its Covenant obligations, and the British representative at Geneva has never attempted to urge it further. Half-hearted sanctions have been imposed on Italy, but there has been no withdrawal of Ambassadors, no stoppage of postal and telegraphic communications, no stoppage of exports to Italy, except of particular commodities; above all, no prohibition of the export of petrol. Not one of those measures, all obviously called for under the

Covenant and all stopping short of military action, has been proposed by a British delegate at Geneva. If Mr Eden finds satisfaction in the reflection that we have been no worse defaulters than other States in the discharge of our Covenant obligations – we were, at any rate, less hesitant than France – he is entitled to it. We owe very much to Mr Eden, but this particular claim is irreconcilable with fact. What happened, bluntly, was that when measures that might have seriously impeded the prosecution of the Abyssinian war, and should therefore have been taken, were mooted, Signor Mussolini was allowed to veto them by the threat of military reprisals. We acquiesced, and now we are left with gravely impaired prestige to deal with a Dictator flushed by his spectacular if hollow victory.

The Foreign Secretary is not to be envied the task that faces him next week at Geneva. Italy is in possession of half Abyssinia. The Emperor and his Ministers have fled. Most of Addis Ababa is in ruins. A war openly prepared for nine months by a Great Power in the face of the world against an unarmed and unoffending African people has run its inevitable course, and Abyssinia has appealed to the League for effective help in vain. Italy, having made a desolation and called it peace, will no doubt urge plausibly that the past be treated as past, Abyssinia be left to the civilising care of Marshal Badoglio or General Graziani, and the number of League States be quietly reduced by one. That would be the final humiliation, and there is no ground for believing that either this country or the League of Nations is prepared to drink that cup yet. The League stands committed to certain principles which it cannot abandon and survive. It has declared formally – what was of course blazoned in any case across the sky – that Italy was guilty of an unprovoked attack on Abyssinia. A League committee drew up a scheme for the reform of Abyssinian administration which, while it never came up for formal approval, was generally accepted as the maximum limitation that could in justice be laid on the sovereignty of Abyssinia. Justice has not become a different thing because Italian aeroplanes and gas have shown themselves more effective weapons than Abyssinian rifles. And the question once more poses itself, whether the aggressor is to be allowed to profit by his perjury and aggression and retain his place in a covenant-keeping society of nations.

The decision on that will determine whether the League of Nations is for the future to be a philanthropic society or a political force. The first problem that arises is whether any recognition can be given to an Italian annexation, open or veiled, of Abyssinia. The answer to that can hardly be in doubt. No League State – with the momentous exception of Salvador – has yet recognised the achievement of Japan in Manchukuo. Sanctions, moreover, are, of course, still in force. To remove them at this moment would be a plain condonation of Italy's crime; the case for extending them is strong. Can the League go so far as to insist that Italy shall not profit by her aggression? Or is it with its fifty members, three of them Great Powers, incapable of doing what groups of States, or even single States, have done repeatedly in the past? When a Great Bulgaria was constituted under the aegis of Russia in 1877, the Conference of Berlin was summoned, and Russia and her *protégé* gave way. When Japan conquered China in 1895 and annexed the Liao-Tung peninsula, three European States, Russia, Germany and France, compelled her to relinquish her booty. When a French force set foot in the Nile Valley in 1898 this country, single-handed, forced its withdrawal. It is still not too late for the League to insist on the establishment in Abyssinia of a *régime* consonant with justice, without Italian domination, though the difficulties of its task are immensely aggravated by Signor Mussolini's faculty for destruction, which has substituted anarchy and chaos for the cohesive influence of a wise and strong personality. But whatever the League may be able to achieve, there is no question what the League ought to attempt. Of Mr Eden no one will ask the impossible. This country cannot and should not take individual action; it remains to be discovered what the attitude of the new Government in France will be. But it would be unjust to charge other States with hanging back till they have been challenged to go forward. If Mr Eden presents the challenge and finds no response, then and only then will he be entitled to claim that Great Britain has done all it could. In that event our whole relation to the League will be called in question.

8 May

PRESIDENT ROOSEVELT OR MR LANDON?
[S. K. RATCLIFFE]

The American political scene has undergone notable changes during the past month. When the first of the great party conventions met, in Cleveland, the result of the November elections was being taken for granted. Republican politicians and their newspapers had accepted their opponents' view that a second term for Mr Roosevelt was certain, and that this year's campaign was therefore not important. The Old Guard of the party, being without a candidate of their own, had no serious objection to Governor Landon. They assumed that he must be dependent upon them for campaign funds, that they would as usual dictate the platform, and that they could retain full control during the next four years and so be ready to recapture the Presidency in 1940. The easy Landon victory in the Convention upset these calculations. The relative Progressivism of the platform did not accord with Mr Hoover's attack on the New Deal. The emergence of new managers showed that the Westerners had their own plans for running the campaign, plans which were not based upon the defeatism of the Atlantic States. The Landon forces will fight independently of the Eastern bosses, and their commanders will be fresher men.

That is the first important new fact in the election. The second was almost unforeseen, but may prove more important in the November polls. In the interval between the two main conventions a fourth presidential candidate (Mr Norman Thomas of New York is again the choice of the Socialist Party) appeared in the person of Mr William Lemke of North Dakota. Under his fantastic standard – of complete national self-sufficiency, wage-scales on a national basis, and monetary inflation – will be gathered probably some millions of the hopeless and discontented who respond to Father Coughlin and Dr Townsend of the lavish old-age pensions, and to whom, had he not been removed, Senator Huey Long would have appealed as an inspired champion. Mr Lemke is extensively unknown and as a politician is a complete nonentity. But if he remains in the field Father Coughlin will win adherents for him and we may assume that the bulk of his supporters will have to be subtracted from the Roosevelt total. For the Democrats the fight will be much harder than they were expecting a month ago.

To say this, however, is not to say that Mr Roosevelt is a less dominant figure than he has been hitherto. The election will turn upon him, and upon the character of his leadership rather than upon his policy, since the Republican platform parallels a good part of the revised New Deal. Mr Roosevelt had the last word on the Democratic platform, and it is most characteristic of him that in shaping his speech of acceptance he should have ignored the demands of the local party leaders for an explosion of personal invective and made his appeal to the American people on a lofty prophetic note. The President's phrases are new. He did not repeat the language of his inaugural address, nor did he go back to an earlier Roosevelt's denunciation of 'certain malefactors of great wealth.' With greater accuracy and skill he spoke of the economic monarchs of America who have built their kingdoms upon 'concentration of control over material things.' He recognised that it was natural and human that 'privileged princes of these new economic dynasties' should reach out for control over the Government itself, creating a new despotism and 'wrapping it in the robes of economic sanction.' To these privileged interests, Mr Roosevelt pointed out, had fallen the control of hours and wages and the conditions of their labour – that is to say, the exercise of an authority which, under the Constitution as now interpreted, the Federal Government did not now possess. America was fighting, Mr Roosevelt concluded, to save (he should rather have said to regain) 'a great and precious form of government' for itself and for the world.

The President was unusually impassioned; his party platform is as cautious as that of the Republicans, although he was in a position to dictate its provisions while his opponents were condemned to a long haggle in committee. The central political issue of this year's contest is, inevitably, the Supreme Court and its power to nullify the work of Congress. The Republicans, or at least Governor Landon, are committed to the principle of amendment, if necessary, in order to make possible the regulation of industry and the operation of social services by the State Governments. The Democrats, knowing well that in touching the Constitution and the Court they are playing with explosives, have fallen back upon the formula of 'legislation within the Constitution.' They promise to seek such a clarifying amendment as will assure to the State Legislatures and to Congress, 'each within its proper jurisdiction,' the right to 'regulate commerce, protect public health and safety, and safeguard economic security.' That is as far as the Democrats could dare to go, and the careful language will not suffice to guard the President and his party against attack and misrepresentation in the contest as it grows in bitterness.

Two extraordinary features of the June assemblies have been widely commented upon – first, their avoidance of debate on all the urgent American issues, such as unemployment, taxation,

77

public works, and the Supreme Court; and secondly, the complete silence maintained over international relations. The greater themes can never be dealt with at a nominating convention: that is an unalterable rule of American politics. But this year the platforms of the two great parties omit all mention of foreign affairs, except for the Republican repudiation of Geneva and the Supreme Court, and the reference (doubtless put in for Senator Borah's benefit) to renewed efforts for the collection of war debts. Isolationism in America is once again rampant, and never before have the framers of party platforms bowed so completely to the force of a popular sentiment. The Republicans would have done this in any event. With the Governor of Kansas as their candidate they were impelled to give unqualified form to the isolationist doctrine, and the Democrats, thinking only of winning the election, decided to keep silence even on the World Court. This is a full reflection of the popular mind. In its complete and despairing negation, it is the Western democracy's judgement upon the action of the League Powers.

In the situation as now modified we have a number of facts and tendencies which seem to be indisputable. Many prominent Democrats have been driven from the fold by the President and the New Deal, but the party will not be materially weakened thereby. Throughout the employer class and the professions there is a ferocious hostility to Mr Roosevelt which he cannot hope to overcome. Governor Landon as the plain American candidate will be able to mobilise a great force of Republican opinion, though he will find the support of the Hearst Press a heavy handicap. The new Lemke 'Union' party, despite the absurdity of its basis, will attract large numbers of small-town voters, men and women, and may take several States out of the Democratic column. But on the other hand, the advent of a new wild party puts the President in the centre; industrial Labour is for him, the farm vote is mainly secure, the many millions who are dependent upon public relief will not go against the Administration. And Mr Roosevelt is a great campaigner.

3 July

THE LEAGUE'S FRESH START
[E. H. CARR]

There is little to be said about the session of the Assembly which ended on Saturday save that it was the most painful in the history of the League. The first call on our sympathy is for the Emperor. He had to listen to what one of his Delegation described as 'a sentence of death on Abyssinia'; and he suffered with dignity the worst humiliation of all – the humiliation of realising that even his few supporters at Geneva, with the honourable exception of Mr Te Water, the Delegate of South Africa, were less interested in the fate of his country than in the fate of the League. There was a certain stubborn heroism in the last futile gesture of compelling twenty-three members of the League to vote against granting financial assistance to Abyssinia, while twenty-five others were too ashamed to vote at all. Sympathy may also be felt for Mr Eden, whose reputation only a few months ago stood so high with friends of the League, and who has become, by force of circumstances, one of the principal agents of its defeat; and finally for M. van Zeeland, who per formed the uncomfortable task of presiding over the Assembly, and of offering to Abyssinia, in his final speech, the grim consolation that fifty of her fellow-members of the League had at least tried to help her. The resolution which closed the Assembly does not mention Abyssinia, and its substantive paragraphs do not allude to the past at all. The discussion behind the scenes which held up the last scene for more than twenty-four hours turned on the question whether States should be invited to submit before September 1st proposals designed to 'strengthen' the League or merely to reform it. Compromise was reached on the non-committal word 'improve.'

In honest truth, there is and can be no question of 'strengthening' the League. The crisis is too grave to be disguised in terms of conventional optimism. The League is in retreat; and the question at issue is whether it shall abandon its territory or abandon its weapons. Both opinions are held in this country as well as at Geneva. There are those who would like to see the maximum of universality, and a Covenant representing the maximum of international co-operation attainable on that basis – in other words, the abolition of sanctions and a consultative League which would draw in Germany and, some day, the United States. There are others who would see the League not only retain, but strengthen, its weapons, at the cost of restricting its field of action to the area where its available weapons are likely to be effective – in practice, to Europe, and perhaps not even the whole European Continent. It is true that M. Delbos appeared to contemplate 'regional pacts' in other continents. But where are the prospective guarantors of China, or Nicaragua, or Liberia?

Precedent is clearly on the side of the regionalists. In the Covenant itself, the League accepted a self-denying ordinance for the American continents. In 1931, it pleaded that the Far East was too remote a region for effective action. In 1936, Africa has been thrown to the wolves. Retirement into Europe with its weapons so far as possible intact seems therefore the predestined course; and Mr Eden's very guarded words at Geneva may perhaps be taken to indicate that this is what the British Government, like the French Government, have in mind. Nevertheless, the course is full of difficulties for a country in the situation of Great Britain. A European League in which non-members, including the British Dominions, pay their subscriptions and play the *rôle* of supers is not the League which has become, irrespective of party, an article of faith for so many of the most progressive minds in the British Commonwealth of Nations. The Central and South American Delegates are already restive; and other more important resignations can scarcely be avoided if the League is to proclaim that its effective interests are limited to Europe.

The regional solution presents other obvious pitfalls for a Government whose traditional policy in Europe is one of peace and conciliation. Public opinion in this country will share the determination of the Norwegian and Netherlands delegates to the Assembly that the League should not allow itself to be transformed into a 'grand military alliance.' The apprehension that French and Soviet policy may be working in this direction is increased by the apparent anxiety in certain quarters to bring Italy back into the League scheme – an anxiety which evidently inspired the refusal of France to embody in the Assembly resolution any direct declaration of non-recognition of the Italian conquest of Abyssinia, though the resolutions passed by the Council and Assembly in the Manchukuo dispute are couched in general terms and are, in theory, applicable to the present case. Co-operation with Italy in European affairs cannot be based on faith in Italy's word or belief in Italy's desire to keep the peace or to discourage aggression. It can only be based on common self-interest in the containment of Germany; and a scheme under which sanctions are designed to operate against Germany, and against nobody else, will square ill with the policy of a Government whose 'strongest desire,' as reiterated by Mr Baldwin in his speech last week to the City of London Conservative Association, is 'to bring together France and Germany, without whose collaboration no peace in Europe is possible.'

These are some of the problems which will have to be considered by the Government during the next two months – and not only by the Government, but by public opinion. For public opinion, in the last resort, will have to decide whether sanctions – which imply, as we now know, readiness to run the risk of war – are to be applied in any given case. The present crisis is due not to any defect in the paper guarantees provided by the Covenant, but in the eagerness of some of the principal members of the League to seize any pretext for not putting those guarantees into effect; and it is disquieting to observe how easily a good many people appear to assume that the remedy for this state of affairs is to strengthen and make more precise the paper guarantees. If, in Mr Eden's words, 'the lessons of the past few months must be embodied in our practice,' the crying need of the revived League is for certainty, not guesswork, about what its members are prepared in the last resort to stand for. It is the duty of the Government, before setting the signature of Great Britain to any new commitments, to know beyond a peradventure that public opinion will allow it to honour them. It is the duty of public opinion, which has plenty of means of self-expression when the issue is clearly put to it, to make itself heard before, not after, such commitments have been assumed. No sincere and right-minded person will blame the League for not being able to do everything. But the League gives a justifiable handle to its enemies when it fails to perform what it has solemnly undertaken That must not, so far as it depends on the British Government and on British public opinion, happen again.

10 July

THE DICTATORS' BARGAIN
[E. H. CARR]

Herr Hitler has the art of the dramatic gesture. On four occasions during the past three years he has, by a process as apparently simple as the pressing of a button, not merely fluttered the Chancelleries, but substantially altered the balance of forces in Europe. Two of these gestures have been minatory: the repudiation of the military clauses of a Treaty and the reoccupation of the Rhineland. The other two have been just as signally pacific: the German-Polish Agreement of January, 1934, and the German-Austrian Agreement which was announced last Saturday. The secret had been well kept – except from Signor Mussolini, who hastened to explain that everything had been done with his approval. Nobody had really expected that Herr Hitler would do exactly what the Powers had been asking of him, and exactly what had been proposed in the Protocol signed on the occasion of M. Laval's famous visit to Rome. He has undertaken to respect the full sovereignty of Austria and to 'exert neither direct nor indirect influence' on internal political conditions in that country. Austria remains a totalitarian State in which the Nazi party is banned. In return, Herr Hitler has obtained a reference in the agreed *communiqué* to Germany and Austria as 'the two German States' and the appointment of two additional members of the Austrian Government, who may be taken to represent the German (though not necessarily the Nazi) point of view. The agreement, translated from the terms of diplomacy into those of *Realpolitik*, means that Austria, from being an Italian dominion, has become a German-Italian *condominium*.

There is no reason for Great Britain not to welcome this agreement. Even if Herr Hitler's calculation is that the closer embrace of the 'two German States' must ultimately lead to the absorption of the weaker by the stronger, and even if one suspects that this calculation will justify itself, there is no reason to alter the verdict. The seizure of Austria by force would have provoked deep-seated hostility in this country; and though Mr Lloyd George may have been right the other day in saying that Great Britain would never fight for Austria, such a step would have caused a grave setback to Anglo-German relations. But no such objection can be felt to the peaceful and gradual assimilation of Austria by Germany, if such is the will of the Austrian people. Public opinion in this country has never been altogether happy about the treaty prohibition on the union between the two countries, so incompatible with the declared principles of the Peace Settlement; and it has often been asked in the last two or three years whether this prohibition has not been in part responsible for Herr Hitler on one side of the frontier and for Prince Starhemberg on the other. The brutal *coup* against the Viennese

Socialists in February, 1934, destroyed the only circumstance which identified the independence of Austria with the cause of democracy. The Austrian refusal last autumn to associate herself with the sanctions front revealed to the world at large what had long been known to those on the spot – that Austrian independence was already a myth. Since that time it has been difficult to resist the impression that if Austria had to live under a totalitarian *régime*, kinship and common speech must in the long run determine the *régime* towards which she would gravitate. The present agreement, whatever its other implications, seems clearly to mark a step in that direction.

In France, the reception of the Agreement has been cool and frankly suspicious. This, too, was inevitable. Austrian independence has become for France a symbol of resistance to Germany and has acquired as such an importance incommensurate with its intrinsic value. Above all, it was regarded as a bone of contention providentially provided to keep Germany and Italy at loggerheads and to secure Italy for the French alliance. It is not possible for the French politician of any party to reflect without bitterness on the course of Franco-Italian relations since the Mussolini-Laval agreement. The cessions of territory made to Italy in Africa did not, perhaps, in French eyes amount to much. The fate of Abyssinia counted for still less. But it cannot be forgotten that France sacrificed to Signor Mussolini her friendship with Jugoslavia, her loyalty to the League, and, last of all, something of her good name in Great Britain. For Italy the Rome Agreement and the Stresa Front have meant nothing but lip service to French policy, paid to secure a free hand in Abyssinia. It has cost Signor Mussolini nothing, and with a wave of the hand the pretence has been dismissed as soon as its purpose was served. Nor can Signor Mussolini's present attitude give much satisfaction to those circles in this country which were prepared to sacrifice so much to retain the friendship and co-operation of Italy.

Comment in the Little Entente countries has up to the present been slender. Jugoslavia has contented herself with welcoming the Agreement on the ground that it rules out the probability of a Hapsburg restoration. M. Titulesco, who enjoyed himself last week at Montreux trouncing the inconsistencies of British policy, has returned to Bucharest to carry on a private campaign against the Fascist front in Roumanian politics. Czechoslovakia, the country most directly affected of all by the new development, has also remained silent. It is regrettable that, at this crucial moment, the Czechoslovak Government and the large and well-organised German minority in Bohemia should be waging a bitter struggle, in which the faults are certainly not all on one side. It would be an act of prudent statesmanship on the part of M. Benes to take the initiative, so far as it rests with the Government, in composing these differences and thereby remove from the path what may yet prove a serious stumbling block to the pacification of Central Europe. Such a step would be the best of all possible replies to the German-Austrian Agreement.

The motives of Herr Hitler seem sufficiently clear. Apart from the tangible advantages which he has secured in Austria and the satisfaction of his rather naïve anxiety to make a good impression in this country, he has destroyed, apparently for good, the bogey of the Stresa Front. Like everyone else, he had underestimated Italian prospects of victory in Abyssinia. Like many other people, he may now, by a process of reaction, be exaggerating the accession of strength which that victory has brought to Italy. There is, however, no sign that he is prepared to trust Italy far. Germany has not forgotten that Italy let her down both in 1914 and in 1933. This time Herr Hitler has demanded payment down. The *quid pro quo* for Herr Hitler's renunciation of an active policy in Austria is the announcement that Italy will not attend the forthcoming Locarno conversations unless Germany is invited to participate in them. A certain loss of pride both for Great Britain and for France may be involved in inviting Germany to the conference at the dictation of Italy. But this is now so plainly the right and inevitable course that neither the British nor the French Government can long hesitate about it. The German-Austrian Agreement has removed what was, by common consent, one of the principal obstacles in the way of an agreement with Germany. It is time to see whether other obstacles cannot now be removed. A conference without Germany at the present juncture would be an empty, and perhaps dangerous, demonstration.

17 July

THE ROOTS OF THE SPANISH REVOLT
BASIL BUNTING

The Communist post-master of Orotava was not too pleased with the election: the Centre looked like winning. He had on his desk two batches of returns from outlying polling-stations, certain to be Centre or even Right, waiting to be sent to Santa Cruz to complete the voting. He addressed the bundles to 'Don Fulan Fulano, La Coruña: to be left till called for.' Before they could be retrieved the Communist candidate had taken his seat in the Cortes, there was a Left majority, and no chance of the 'error' being adjusted.

The majority in February was small, but its first action was to purge Parliament by annulling the election of many Catholics and Monarchists and arbitrarily appointing their defeated opponents to sit instead. The process is traditional in Spain, but apt to mislead foreign observers who judge the state of parties in the country by their representation in Parliament.

No one doubts that the popular vote was neither for Socialism nor against the Catholics, but for an amnesty. 'Why,' asked our valued washerwoman, in tears, the day the prisoners returned, 'Why did they lock up So-and-so? Poor fellow, he never did any harm! He only threw a bomb into a tank' – destroying the water-supply of some hundreds of people and putting some scores of irrigation peones permanently out of work. Spain is always against prisons and police.

The enthusiasm for the red flag developed *after* the election, when the UGT promised immediate work for everybody. A few months later, with rising prices and no great amount of work after all, enthusiasm was abating.

At first the Right was merely cowed. The worst oppressors – landlords and a few politicians – fled to escape the vengeance inevitable after every change of government in Spain. Thousands whose consciences were not quite bad enough to drive them into exile were imprisoned illegally, but without rousing much indignation. An uncertain large number were killed. But real trouble began with the Reinstatement decree.

Azaña ordained that everyone who had been dismissed for 'political reasons' during the past two years should be immediately reinstated and compensated for a part, sometimes for all, the wages he had missed. As with the amnesty, it proved impossible to distinguish political from other reasons. In practice everyone

85

had to be reinstated: even those who had been dismissed for fraud or ceased work of their own accord or been evicted by governmental decree had to be compensated at the employer's expense. Many businesses went bankrupt, creating a new and rapidly growing unemployed, or were confiscated by the State or seized illegally by the workmen. Those who failed to pay were imprisoned.

Small employers who had voted Left – for the amnesty – were annoyed when they found themselves, in effect, fined large sums merely for being employers. At the same time many workmen engaged after the Asturian rebellion had to be dismissed to make room for the reinstated.

When at last the Cortes had purged itself sufficiently it was expected to legislate the definite programme of the Popular Front, to which the Government was pledged. Unfortunately Azaña betrayed an unsuspected hankering for splendour. The president was deposed – on the absurd legal ground that the election had been unnecessary – in favour of the, for the moment, omnipotent leader, who moved into the palace at once and set about redecorating it. The astonished Press hurriedly discovered the need for pomp, to give prestige to the Republic. President Alcalà had been content to live as a private citizen in his own house, remitting a large part of his salary in aid of taxes. Azaña announced his intention to live in state, occupied the ex-Queen's suite, reorganised the Guards, reopened the summer-palace in the mountains, and shook the respect many people had begun to feel for the Presidency.

Still the Cortes did nothing but take revenge on obnoxious individuals. Up to the end of June not only the decrees of Señor Casares but many of Azaña's own had not been legalised. No progress had been made with the programme, unless a few purely destructive decrees be reckoned as progress: for instance, abolishing the remains of catholic education without offering any substitute. Hundreds of new schools were promised, none opened and no funds provided. No new teachers were being licensed, many old ones suspected of lack of enthusiasm for the Popular Front were dismissed.

Meanwhile it was understood that the Socialist and Communist militias might do pretty much as they pleased – and two years of Right government had left them plenty of heavy scores to pay off. Even before the election Azaña said that after a popular victory the Government must shut its eyes for a period. The period lengthened until it was too late for his successor, Casares, to intervene. The extreme Left, armed, was crying daily for abolition of police and army. The Right, disarmed, found its local leaders in gaol or exile. To avoid punishing transgressions of the Left, the Government attributed every outrage to *agents provocateurs*. More than once the priest of a gutted church was accused of having burned it himself 'to discredit the *régime.*'

Casares spent his time in the War Office juggling the Commands, trying to find a combination that should be powerless to act. The officers, never very hearty republicans, were unnecessarily irritated. After the mutiny at Alcalà de Henares it was easy to foresee the outcome.

Fascism was negligible in Spain before the election. After a month of Señor Casares's rule Gil Robles complained that great numbers of his Catholic Youth had gone over to Falange Español. It is impossible to say what strength the forbidden organisation may have gained in the past few months, but the present revolt is not a Fascist one.

General Franco, who is believed to be a moderate republican may be forced into the arms of the Monarchists, or driven to disguise a purely military dictatorship as Fascism. His manifesto commits him to nothing. Every government for a decade has feared him and sought to keep him as far from the centre, and from reliable troops, as possible. His brother was one of the founders of the Republic. He is not likely to bring Don Alfonso home if he can help it.

In February there was a small majority for the Left. In March or April it would have been enormous, but much has been lost by governmental incompetence, by the feud of the Socialist leaders, Prieto and Largo Caballero, and by the unwillingness of Anarchist syndicates to co-operate with Socialist trade unions. They strike alternately, not together, and fight each other almost as much as the enemy. There is still a substantial Left majority, the extremer section armed. Against it, the disarmed Right, the officers and the few regular troops, foreign legion, guards. Their discipline counts. Their union, if they can avoid jealousies between the generals, counts. On the whole the forces seem balanced. There may be a long war.

For even if Franco triumphs for the moment he can neither conciliate nor disarm half the nation, and the murder of Calvo Sotelo which precipitated the revolt has deprived the Right of its only able civilian. There would be constantly new Asturias, and the moderate men, friends of ex-president Alcalà Zamora, are not likely to support a military usurper.

If the Popular Front triumphs, it must fall wholly into the hands of the professed Marxists. The Right cannot be kept from arming itself in a country as chaotic as Spain since the Republic. The Civil War will be renewed many times. In my opinion, the Left has the better chance in the long run, for it has, in Spain, the better cause. You cannot starve a nation forever. But the long run may be a Marathon of blood.

The problem of government in Spain is to feed the people. The peasants are half-starved and half-clothed, yet it has always been impossible to get a quorum in the Cortes for any economic debate. Spanish Socialism is independent of economics. Could Franco, could Largo Caballero, give the Canary peones, the Andalucian cowboys, enough to eat and a few coppers for the cinema? There is no reason to suppose that either of them has the slightest idea how to set about it.

24 July

OLYMPIC BERLIN
[E. A. MONTAGUE in Berlin]

The Olympic Games have taken possession of Berlin, and the whole thought and conversation of the inhabitants are absorbed by them. It is the result, of course, of a long process. For many months the Berliners have seen rising on the edge of the Grünewald the huge walls of the Olympic stadium. They have been preparing flags and decorations, going without eggs so that there should be enough for the Olympic visitors, and learning by constant instruction from above that Germany's conduct of the Games will demonstrate the excellence of Nazism to the world. German enthusiasm rose to a climax on a Saturday when the Olympic Games were formally opened by Herr Hitler, and it was crowned on Sunday by the rapture of seeing Germany win her first Olympic victory in a men's event – putting the weight – in the presence of the Führer.

The city is packed with visitors, both German and foreign, and every evening the streets are filled with slowly moving crowds. The whole city is beflagged. The most prominent points on the route from Berlin to the Reich Sports Field, such as the Rathaus, the Knie and the Adolf Hitler Platz, as well as the stadium itself, are adorned with flags of all the 53 competing nations, but in side streets and on private houses, except those of foreign residents, one sees only two flags, the red German flag with the swastika and the white Olympic banner with its device of five interlocked rings in different colours, pale blue, yellow, black, green and red. The Olympic rings are to be seen everywhere, on flags, on houses, on buttonhole badges or women's scarves, on railway engines (one commonly sees a swastika painted on the engine and the Olympic rings on the tender), and even on the side of the Zeppelin 'Hindenburg,' which was flying over the Reich Sports Field on the morning of the opening day.

The various competing teams are housed fifteen miles away in the Olympic village of Doeberitz, but the city itself is full of foreign athletic officials, most of them wearing coats or blazers with their national flags on the pockets, and the native Berliner goes about with a chart of flags of all nations, which he pulls out of his pocket when he sees a flag which he cannot identify; it is interesting to see how many people need to consult the chart when they see a Union Jack. Everybody is friendly and helpful, and one has only to wear a foreign blazer and look helpless on an underground platform to collect in no time a small crowd of willing, even if generally incomprehensible, advisers. A whole corps of interpreters is scattered through the city, mainly in the big railway stations; they wear small national flags on their brilliant uniforms to indicate the languages that they speak, and even if the flag sometimes promises more than the wearer can perform, they will go to endless trouble to help the foreigner. Everywhere there are soldiers and SS or SA men with various armlets, showing that they have one or other of the myriad jobs that the Olympic organisation has created.

It has to be recognised that this is not an Olympic festival as that has been understood in the past. The feeling one gets constantly is that Germany has taken the Olympic Games under her patronage. Competent foreign residents here say that the German Government and people really do desire peace, in spite of appearances, and one has seen several things in this festival which suggest that Germany wants to impress her Olympic visitors not only with her efficiency – this wish is inescapably obvious – but also with her desire to be friendly. There was something deeply moving in the passionate response of the German crowd at the opening ceremony to the Olympic salute of the French team, which the Germans apparently took as a Nazi salute given in token of courtesy and friendship to themselves. But it has also been made clear again and again that they regard this as essentially a German festival at which the other nations are honoured guests, but still only guests.

There was much evidence of this at the opening ceremony, which incidentally was conducted with extraordinary efficiency. When the teams marched round the track the crowd, though it did not show unfriendliness to anybody, applauded with much the greatest fervour those teams which appeared to be giving the Nazi salute. A considerable though unintentional slight was given to the American team, which marched next in front of the Germans, through the fact that, when the German team appeared, everybody stood in silence while the two German anthems were played, and the Americans were thus deprived of the applause which the other teams received. No other team was honoured by the playing of its national anthem, and such a thing has never been done at any recent Games. Another new and not very desirable departure is the endowment of Herr Hitler with the title of patron of the Olympic Games. And there was a noticeable little incident when a German athlete, taking the Olympic oath on behalf of the competitors of all nations, grasped in his hand a fold of the German instead of the Olympic flag. All these are trifles, but they seem to indicate an attitude of mind which, though well-meaning, is instinctively too national to be truly Olympic. A journalist may also cite with some annoyance the fact that all the athletic results and times are given out exclusively in German; the usual Olympic practice is to give them in several languages.

There has been nothing approaching the 'incidents' beloved of sensational newspapers, nor does one expect any. Not only would they be impolitic, but the German public is feeling much too happy and friendly to suffer from such temptations. The applause at the stadium during the first day's contest was generous and reasonably impartial, and the German spectators, like all others, have fallen completely under the spell of the American negro, Jesse Owens, who is already the hero of these Games. Fortunately Owens is a charmingly courteous and modest person, or the adulation that he is receiving here would turn his head. In his two races yesterday, in which he first equalled and then beat the world's record for 100 metres, he made his opponents look almost ridiculous, not only by his speed but by the sheer beauty of his running. No athletic art has ever been so perfectly concealed. When other great runners are straining and contorting themselves in a supreme effort Owens is gliding majestically away from them; he too is making his supreme effort, but there is not the slightest trace of angularity or strain. One only realises his speed by noticing how long it takes him to pull up afterwards. The Germans, with their strong aesthetic sense and their present adoration of physical skill, are enraptured by his running. His name is cheered as soon as it is announced before a race, and when he is going back to the dressing-room afterwards the spectators all along the track shout to him to stop so that they can photograph him. Whatever the currents beneath the smooth surface of this festival, we are all one people when Owens is on the track.

7 August

EUROPE AND SPAIN
[GORONWY REES]

The civil war in Spain has lasted for over a fortnight, and there is as yet no prospect of a final victory for either side. Before the Government's authority can be restored the rebels must be expelled from Navarre, Burgos, Saragossa, Cordova, Seville, Granada and Spanish Morocco, and, even when that has been done, further conflicts may break out between the Government's supporters. Before the rebels, on their side, can establish a new Government, they must capture Madrid, Barcelona and the whole of the west of Spain, and defeat the entire Spanish working class, now armed and ready to fight to the death for the Popular Front. Neither side, at the moment, is able to achieve its object, but in the long run the balance of forces is on the side of the Government. But this war of attrition already tempts, and will continue to tempt, other nations to intervene and decide the issue to their own advantage. Indeed, attempts at intervention have already been made. Italian army aeroplanes, loaded with munitions for the rebels, have crashed in French Morocco; Germany is suspected of sending supplies and ammunition, and the battleship 'Deutschland' at Ceuta has been welcomed by the rebels; the Russian trades unions have voted £1,000,000 for the support of the Spanish Government; M. Blum is being pressed by his supporters to send help to the Frente Popular. In ordinary times the civil war might have raged in isolation behind the

Pyrenees, as in some African province of Europe, but in the troubled circumstances of today it threatens to divide Europe into hostile camps and cause a war of intervention in the style of earlier centuries.

It is not difficult to find motives for intervention. A protracted civil war in Europe is in itself a disaster, especially when conducted by both sides with such merciless ferocity as in Spain. Though newspapers always exaggerate, there is no need to doubt the reports of the atrocities. In a civil war, which is also a class war, they are inevitable, and in this civil war they have been committed equally by either side. But some more material motives than a desire to prevent violence have been needed to attract the attention of foreign Governments. It is especially the military position in the Mediterranean which concerns them. A rebel victory resulting in a Fascist pro-Italian Spain would threaten Gibraltar and the route to India: and General Franco is reported to be willing, in return for Italian help, to cede Ceuta and the Balearic Isles to Signor Mussolini and make the Mediterranean an Italian lake. Further, a Fascist Spain would be yet another enemy on the French frontier, and, with Italy, a means of cutting her communications with French Morocco. These military and naval advantages would mean an immense accession of strength to the Fascist countries. But the civil war also invites intervention on grounds of political and intellectual sympathy. The revolt has so far intensified the political struggle in Spain that the defeat of the rebels would, in all probability, be followed, not by a relatively Liberal Government, such as the present one, but by an administration of the extreme Left, such as has been formed in Barcelona, containing Socialists, Communists and anarchists, and resting on the armed support of the workers. General Franco has presented Europe with the choice between a Fascist or a Communist Spain: a Europe 'red at both ends' is as attractive to the U.S.S.R. and the French Popular Front as it is repugnant to Germany and Italy.

The only possible policy for this country is to work for the isolation of the conflict. We should be perfectly entitled to license arms-exports to a constitutional and regularly-elected Government, locked in a death-struggle with desperate rebels. But we are under no obligation to do that, and as M. Blum sees, it would be folly to do it at the risk of provoking Italy and Germany to counter-measures. M. Blum, with the wisdom we have come to expect from him, has resisted the temptation to intervene. His policy was well expressed in a speech by M. Delbos, the French Foreign Minister, at Sarlat on Monday: 'There must be no crusade of ideals in Europe, a crusade which would inevitably lead to war.' Europe cannot afford that mad plunge; and M. Blum has chosen the wisest course open to him by inviting the British and Italian Governments to collaborate with France in negotiating an agreement of non-intervention in the Spanish conflict. The agreement does not exclude Germany; to be effective it must include the U.S.S.R. It must provide not only for refusal to lend assistance to either side, but a means of ensuring the proper observance of treaties regulating the position in the western Mediterranean, the port of Tangier, and in French and Spanish Morocco. If such an agreement can be negotiated, and if it prevents any assistance being given to the rebels from Germany or Italy, M. Blum will have given the Spanish Government indirectly all the help it is possible to give in the present condition of Europe.

More than that neither France nor this country can do. Callous as it may seem, the great issues which hang on the Spanish conflict must be entrusted to the courage and endurance of the Spanish people themselves. It is fortunate for us that they have shown they have enough of these qualities to win the victory. Our task is to persuade Germany, Italy and Russia to observe the abstention which France has so wisely urged. That Germany desires international harmony during the Olympic Games, Italy desires rehabilitation and a *rapprochement* with Britain and France, and Russia desires peace above all things, are favourable factors. But the situation will be full of menace till a firm understanding between the Great Powers is reached.

7 August

THE DEFENCE OF DEMOCRACY
[WILSON HARRIS]

That the Spanish Civil War has raised far graver issues outside Spain than inside it is a commonplace. Fortunately the immediate dangers have been exorcised by the agreement at last reached by the Great Powers to refrain from intervention direct or indirect on behalf of either party in the Spanish conflict – an achievement for which great credit is due to the French Prime Minister, M. Léon Blum, and hardly less to our own Government, which has supported the French initiative strenuously and

93

single-mindedly in every capital in Europe. The agreement is belated. Both sides, the rebels much more than the Government, have profited considerably already by external assistance, and it still remains to be seen how loyally the agreement, when it is finally and formally concluded, will be honoured by the various contracting Powers; there is obviously a case for some kind of international supervision. But the first necessary step has been taken. It is legitimate to hope that the Spaniards will now be left to fight out their own battles in their own way. Disastrous and deplorable as the fate of the unhappy country is, the fate of Europe would be tenfold more deplorable if the attempt to isolate the Spanish war failed.

At this juncture it is profitable and necessary to point out one danger which sympathisers in this country with the respective combatants are gratuitously creating – the danger of dividing the country when it was never more essential to unite it. Democracy and Fascism, we are told, are at grips in Spain, and sections of the British Press (since public men are widely scattered at this season the Press becomes more than ever the stimulant of opinion) are extolling the Government or the insurgents, as the case may be, as the potential saviours not only of Spain but of Europe, if not the world. That, it may be said, is inevitable. The answer is that it is not inevitable at all, except within the narrowest limits. There is no doubt a Right and a Left in every country, and it may be natural that the Right in this country should tend to sympathise with the Spanish rebels and the Left with the Government. But that such sympathy should lead, as it is leading, to the distortion of truth, the suppression of facts, the fomenting of domestic antagonisms and a blind subservience to misleading appellations is neither natural nor rational nor pardonable. Neutrality of spirit, such as President Wilson asked of his countrymen in the early days of the Great War, may be neither attainable nor desirable, but at least confusion of thought can be abjured, and some restraint on inflammatory impulses achieved before they translate themselves into inflammatory words.

That appeal will be addressed in vain to organs whose attitude is the fruit of blind and dishonest bigotry and nothing else. But there are others – the persons and papers in particular whose conviction that the battle for democracy will be won or lost in Spain is reiterated daily. That doctrine is both dangerous and false. It is dangerous because it implies that the business of the

94

democratic countries is to support Spanish democracy by all means legitimately possible, notably by supplying the Government with all the aeroplanes, munitions and weapons it needs for defence against the rebels, in spite of the certainty that the dictatorship countries would continue to arm the rebels on an equal and more extensive scale, that the result would be to sever more fatally than ever the democratic from the 'Fascist' Powers of Europe, and that the inevitable end would be a European war. And it is false, because it rests on a veneration not merely for labels but for spurious labels.

Consider these labels. In Spain, it is said, democracy is pitted against Fascism. What Fascism is we need not here stop to enquire. The State structure in Italy is certainly not the same thing as the State structure in Germany, and what the State structure in Spain would be if General Franco's military rebellion succeeded neither General Franco nor anyone else knows. Spanish democracy deserves closer study, for in the name of that the democrats of this country and France and Russia – the democratic Russia of Tuesday's shooting-squads – are being urged to intervene. The plain fact is that in Spain there is no democracy, as democracy is understood in Great Britain and France; there never has been; and there is no shadow of possibility of the establishment of a democratic *régime* after this war, whichever side wins it. There has for the last five years been a Parliamentary system which spasmodically and for brief intervals has functioned as a Parliamentary system should, and every adherent of Parliamentary institutions anywhere must wish it well, deplore its failures and hope for its survival and ultimate success. But to call the system that has existed in Spain since Primo de Rivera fell a democracy is either affectation or ignorance.

What are the essential elements of Parliamentary democracy? These at least; that there shall be freedom of speech and writing; that the executive shall be responsible to a legislature elected by the free vote of men and women sufficiently educated to know what they are voting for; that laws shall be enacted only by a majority vote of the legislature; and that no man shall be punished for breaking them except after a fair trial in public. It is notorious that hardly one of those conditions has been fulfilled in Spain in recent years, or indeed ever. An illiterate electorate has been exposed to every kind of influence, from the priests, the landowners, the labour unions, the village bosses (*caciques*), the mayors (*alcaldes*); local authority, regular or irregular, has

95

always been more effective than the writ of the central government; no administration, not even that elected last February, has been strong enough to maintain order and suppress rioting; not the most constitutional government, such as that elected in 1931, could govern for more than a few weeks without abandoning constitutional methods and resorting (in breach of the constitution) to special legislation providing for the suspension of newspapers, imprisonment without trial, internment or deportation, and all the familiar expedients of arbitrary governments in Moscow and Rome and many other lesser capitals. This is distressing, but it is true, and profound as our sympathy with the Spanish Government in its struggle may be, it is plain folly, and dangerous folly, to label that Government democratic and declare that by its success or failure the cause of democracy everywhere stands or falls.

The Spanish war, lamentable as it is, is a civil war, and it must be kept a civil war – as there is now good reason to hope that it will. If, and only if, the Government is victorious, there may ultimately be an advance to something like a democratic *régime*, though certainly not for years to come. Meanwhile democracy elsewhere has plenty to do at home in its own defence. In this country we need to guard jealously against encroachments on individual liberty and any tendency to subordinate the authority of Parliament to the will of the executive. The best way to defend democracy is to make democracy work, and work better than any dictatorship system can. That is a duty which devolves on Conservatives, Labour and Liberals alike – for belief in democracy is not a virtue peculiar to the two latter.

28 August

AMERICA THANKS GOD
D. W. BROGAN in Washington

It was at an interval in an all-in wrestling show that I heard the standard American verdict on the European situation. 'When you look at Spain you're grateful you're an American.' 'Yes, and all these European countries are going to try to get us in again.' What the wrestling fans said millions, it is safe to guess, are thinking. Europe is more than ever the incorrigible continent; doomed to flounder, perhaps to drown in its own blood, and America, or so the average American is resolved, will add neither blood nor money to the mess. Not blood, for that has already been spilled to no purpose 'to make the world safe for democracy'; not money, for it is firmly believed that it was at least as much to rescue the financial commitments of Wall Street as to save democracy or civilisation that the American troops were sent overseas.

It is from this standpoint that the American man in the street is contemplating the gathering storm in Europe. He is a spectator at an all-in wrestling match who is firmly resolved not to be provoked, even if one of the combatants is thrown into the ringside seats. The professional diplomats and the professional students of world affairs may have their doubts about the possibility of preserving this calm in the face of an increasingly complex situation, but the plain man has no doubts. Going to war is a thing that is willed; it does not merely happen. It will not be willed and so will not happen.

In Washington the atmosphere is less detached, for here the problems of neutrality are more keenly felt than in the run of American towns, here the connexions with Europe are constantly being renewed, and here the European visitor is asked his opinion of the situation with much less detached curiosity than even in New York. The Spanish civil war, in the ten days I have been here, has ceased to be a contest in which only a sporting interest is being taken, and has become a problem. When the President hinted that already there was arising the problem of supplying munitions to the belligerents, a shudder ran through official and newspaper circles, for it was the first sign that the ghost that many thought laid for good was walking again. The neutrality legislation of last year does not provide for a civil war like this; there is no legal obstacle to supplying either side with arms if it can pay for them.

The American view of the general European situation is not encouraging to the British visitor. With varying degrees of politeness it is conveyed to him that the possibility of a definite and courageous policy being carried out by the British Government is a contingency hardly worth considering. The impression of feebleness left by the Abyssinian *débâcle* has not been erased by any subsequent action, and it is taken for granted, even in very Anglophile circles, that there will be no real resistance to the demands of the Fascist Powers until Britain is pushed into a corner. She is not quite in that corner yet, but if the Fascists win in Spain it is assumed that an isolated Britain and a defeated

France will be in no position to resist the next drive of the dictators. Apart from British interests in stability in Portugal, it seemed evident to most of the Americans with whom I talked that British interests are bound up with the triumph of the Left in Spain, but there is also a widespread belief that British policy will not necessarily follow its best interests, firstly because of sympathy with Fascism in high quarters and secondly, because of timidity.

The conviction that Britain has moved or is moving over to the German camp is held very widely by men who are far from credulous. As far as this shift is based on prudence (a harsher word is often used) it is regarded with some tolerance; beggars can't be choosers, and in the present situation, Britain is a beggar. But as far as it is based on sympathy for the Nazis it is regarded with a much less tolerant eye. It may seem at first sight paradoxical that in a country with its own ugly record in race questions, with a great deal of barely concealed anti-semitism permanently festering, Hitler should be looked at with less toleration than he is in England. One easy explanation is, of course, the great number of American Jews, the millions of poor Jews, the hundreds of powerful Jews. But their influence, in a sense, works against the Jewish community, for it makes suspect the criticism of Nazi theories and practices that marks the New York newspapers.

The American mistrust of Nazi achievements goes far deeper than Jewish influence can account for. For one thing, the official religion of America is democracy. All American children learn the creed of that religion, 'The Declaration of Independence,' and though it may mean little in practice, the words of Jefferson fight against the theories of Rosenberg. Equally important is the easy American realisation that a great national movement, drawing on the sincere devotion of millions, may yet be led by madmen, crooks, charlatans. The simple-minded British visitor who can't believe that a movement which has such nice boys and girls in it, so obviously full of loyalty and decency, may yet be poisonous to the soul, may be the instrument of mean revenge or monomaniacal folly, has few American counterparts. The American knows better; he has had the Ku Klux Klan; he has the Black Legion.

The suspicion of the new Germany has been reinforced by the triumphs of negroes in the Olympic Games. Whatever reasons induced the Führer to avoid receiving Jesse Owens, the American public put them all down to chagrin at the defeat of the Aryan runners by the black pride of Ohio. Even southern papers and southern individuals who might be expected to 'have no use for a nigger' enjoyed the discomfiture of the maker of modern Germany, and the widespread belief that Herr Hitler can 'dish it out but can't take it' has not added to the small stock of respect with which he is regarded here. Yet it is believed that Britain is now giving way to Herr Hitler, perhaps consenting to follow in his wake. The only hope of saving what is left of democracy in Europe lies, I am constantly being told, in a close alliance of France and Britain, but few believe it possible. The weakness of the French Government in the Spanish question, in face of what Americans take to be open aid from Italy and Germany for the rebels, is taken as an ominous sign that in France democracy will collapse in face of Fascist pressure from within and without, unless a French Left government can show achievements in foreign policy that will reassure the timid.

Such a reassurance can only come from Britain, but Britain having shown that her bluff can be called by Mussolini, is in no position to reassure France or intimidate Germany. In the next year or two there must be a showdown, or a more or less graceful recognition of the fact that the countries whose leaders can use threats of war with a chance of being believed will always be able to coerce countries whose bite is not better than their bark. A Fascist Europe with Britain in uneasy isolation on its edge, or a Europe divided into two armed camps – one united in policy and ruthless in execution, one timid and vacillating – that is the picture many well-informed Americans paint for themselves.

Either way, the resolution to leave Europe alone is a fierce passion. Sympathies may waver a little, but that is all. No politician dare use vague words that might be twisted by an opponent into an advocacy or condonation of 'entanglement.' The Republican platform, with its denunciation of adherence to the World Court, marks another stage in the retreat from Europe that began in 1919. The promises of Governor Landon that he will try to collect the War debts, as far as they have any meaning at all, are a gesture of repudiation of a past policy that allowed these debts to be contracted. If isolation is really possible it will be tried out fully, and most Americans are convinced that it is possible. Only a few note that each step away from Europe brings America nearer Japan – and in another sense, Russia; only a few remember the maxim of Mr Dooley that you can

99

refuse to like a man or to lend him money, but if he wants a fight you have got to oblige him.

28 August

SPAIN AND THE FUTURE
V. S. PRITCHETT

Spain has been called the country of the unforeseen, where the imponderables in a clash of movements have an importance which they reach in no other European country. This romantic view of Spain is unpopular among those determinists who see the whole of Europe in clear-cut Fascist and anti-Fascist black and red, and who forget that the erratic tradition of Bakunin is far more powerful on the Spanish Left than the teaching of Marx, but it can find considerable justification. And any attempt to say what is going to happen during the present struggle and after it must bear the romantic elements in mind. First of these is the fact that there is no such country as Spain. There is a collection of highly diverse regions, nations in miniature, some with their own languages, all with very different climates and physical characteristics, cut off from close knowledge of each other by bad transport and differing economic conditions, and all of them in varying degrees as much concerned with their own interests and their independence as with a Spain united under this political doctrine or the other.

Today the large, popular forces of the Anarchist federation aim at a complete disintegration of government, while the Syndicalists want no more unity and government than would be provided by innumerable local trade unions. Such a theory of government must seem to us fantastic, yet its appeal to a very large number of the Spanish working classes is immense because it is fantastic; and the Army garrisons, whose history is nothing but a long series of risings against the central authority, are possessed by the same anarchism. The anarchist temperament is as much General Franco's as anyone else's; and its spiritual exaltation, its stress on honour and the individual light, finds inevitably and naturally its chief sanction in physical force. Force alone can bring liberation from the cruel oppression of centuries; force alone can save us from anarchy. Such is the theory. As the Spanish poetaster has said:

'Free thought I now proclaim to all
And death to him who does not think as I do.'

The hope of Spain was and is its Socialist movement, because
at last, from the 70's when it began to grow, there was a united
organised movement which believed in authority as firmly as the
Roman Catholic church. In Socialism and, latterly, in the very
small Communist party, there were signs of a genuine political
education which provided the progressive elements in the country with some stable defence against the Roman Catholic reac-
tionaries – and one must distinguish among devout Catholics
between clericals and anti-clericals – and against the anarchy of
soldiers and Syndicalists alike. In the present struggle the Socialists, in spite of their divisions, alone have a political programme.
General Franco has none. The Liberal Government in Madrid, at
present the prisoner of the mixed revolutionary committees, has
none beyond a hurried, anxious throwing of meat to appease the
lions. And if General Franco wins he will, like his nineteenth-
century predecessors, merely be an executioner, until inevitably
the struggle for economic and social justice breaks out again.

The difficulties of the victors – if there is such a thing as a
clear-cut victory – which seems very doubtful – on either side
will be immense. Unity is easy enough in battle. A rapid victory
is essential to General Franco, but although he has trained
troops, the Moors, Italian and German bombers and so forth,
and may even capture Madrid, one does not see him easily con-
quering Catalonia and the East. His failure so far to capture
Irun may be decisive; the successful resistance of Irun decided
the Carlist War. The longer time he takes, the more promises he
has to make to the Moors. A curious report, which sounds untrue
but which is curiously reminiscent of the first Moorish invasion
of Spain in 700, says that he has offered the Moors land and
mosques in the South. The point is, he has had to promise them
something. He has already weakened Spanish Morocco; he will
have to weaken it even more, and it would not be surprising to
hear that, although he is said to be a first class organiser and
has left everything in good order in Morocco, his fate was decided
there. He planned a *coup d'état* and has plunged Spain into the
bloodiest civil war it has known; even supposing he gets a superficial victory, the guerilla fight will go on, and it is that kind
of disorder which will bring disunity in his own ranks quite apart
from his lack of programme.

Moreover, he is likely to be seriously affected by international intervention sooner or later, as (I think) any future Spanish government will be. The weakness of Spain is congenial to English policy, but not the incapacity of Spain to hold her own. One cannot see how, after a long and exhausting conflict, Spain will be able to hold Morocco if the two Fascist dictators think her weak enough to make a bid for it. From the patriotic and the social points of view Franco seems to be a disaster, and all the worse for being an anachronism. His victory portends, not only the death of the attempt of the masses to liberate themselves, but the paralysis of that quiet, diligent liberal movement which, despite its failures, has done immense work in fitting the Spanish mind for the changes the modern world was inexorably bringing about in the country.

A victory for the Government will mean first of all that General Franco has set in motion the social revolution which he pretended he had risen to suppress. It will be a victory of democracy only in the sense that every defeat of Fascism is this. But who is going to run the revolution? Fighting should have completely united the two powerful Socialist groups, but has it taught the Syndicalists and Anarchists anything? One does not see them so quickly renouncing their beliefs, for in characteristic Spanish fashion it has been the *religious or moral fervour* of anarchism which has risen against the materialism of the Marxists. Will Anarchists of this kind abandon the faith any more readily than the out-and-out Catholics of Franco's kind will abandon theirs? Will the Anarchists fight the rest of the Left? Or will they suddenly drop out and refuse to co-operate? Moral fervours make civil wars, if economies make revolutions, and the question is whether the Anarchists will permit a revolution any more than General Franco would. One does not imagine Azaña being more effective a teacher than the bookish leaders of the First Republic were. If the Left, after a victory – which would be brought about by disaffection among the Moors and half-hearted conscripts – are not united, one foresees more Generals beginning with liberal intentions and becoming more and more reactionary, and the country dragging along like a recalcitrant mule team on the Castilian roads.

It depends upon how much the Left has learned. The tactics and necessities of revolution, with the Russian revolution so near, ought to have become clear. From the revolutionary point of view the growth of a middle class and its steady, if precarious, enrichment, springing from neutrality in the Great War, has made an awkward obstacle. The revolutionaries deny the intellectuals this class has produced, though these have been in the forefront of the struggle for education and justice; and, having thrown them overboard, are left to face the unweakened and tenacious middle-class Fascists who in the cafés of Cordoba and Seville last year were exultant because 30,000 workers were in gaol and were still having peasants arrested because they were rude to bailiffs. No Great War had weakened these people; the neutrality made them; but the poor are always hungry. And not all the hungry are on the Left. The wretched peasant proprietor of Burgos, eking out his few acres in the bleached treeless plateau, is Right to the marrow. He is the classical Spanish reactionary.

And the Left, too, will have to face the problem of Morocco. Many would gladly let it go. But that presumably would not suit England or France. A Left Government has much to fear from the Powers if Spain is too weak to hold Morocco, more if France drifts into Fascism. Any government will have much to fear from famine also; for if Spanish peasants follow their habit of abandoning revolt for their cattle and crops, what becomes of a general rising? If the war goes on, what becomes of the cattle and crops? Can even the towns, traditionally the decisive factors in Spain, go on on empty stomachs? And what will happen to the Moorish mind if Franco's Moors go back to tell of the Spaniards they have conquered?

Once more Spain has become Europe's vicarious battleground. The defeat or victory of General Franco, though he may not have bought his shirt off the Fascist peg, will have a deep effect upon his fellow irrationalists, who have introduced anarchy into Europe. For us what happens in Spain is important for the effect it has on Europe; but if Madrid wins there is some reason to hope that Spain will eventually create a new political cast of thought as refreshing and re-vitalising to Europe as the Spanish personality is already. The anarchist of today, transformed by fire, may become the builder of some curious decentralised State of tomorrow.

4 September

THE SHADOW OF DESTRUCTION
[WILSON HARRIS]

Europe today, and this country as part of Europe, is living under the dominion of fear. It is not the same fear everywhere. In France there is fear of Germany. In Germany there is fear, genuine or artificially fomented, of Russia. The fear that oppresses us here is not the fear of any particular country, but the fear of war, and of a war that we shall have had no part in provoking. That prospect overshadows every beneficent activity. Life goes on; trade slowly but consistently expands; stock-exchange values mount; unemployment diminishes; slums are cleared and houses built. But through it all penetrates ceaselessly the recurrent thought that all our building is for destruction, all our wealth is being amassed only to be destroyed in the work of destroying, all the wise expenditure of the nation on the education and health of its children and the support of its unemployed, its sick and aged, will be checked or disastrously contracted by the need for laying on ourselves and future generations insupportable burdens in preparation for a new war, before the business of paying for the old one has come within the range of human vision.

On the whole we are a resilient people, and a little fatalist. War must come? Then come it must. When it does we shall suffer whatever may be in store for us, praying that it may be obliteration, not the torturing survival of maimed and crippled bodies. Meanwhile we go about our business and our pleasures as we may – and rightly, for we know not the day nor the hour when the destruction may break upon us, and we cannot stultify ourselves by waiting paralysed for the blow to fall. But all the time the preparations for war continue. In every country, in Russia and Germany, in Italy and France, in Britain and Poland and Rumania and Belgium, military service is being lengthened or new taxes are being levied and new inroads made on the finance of every social service, that munition-factories may be built, guns cast, new keels laid down, new squadrons of aeroplanes constructed and bombs and shells turned out by the million for the destruction of open cities no less than fortresses, of peaceful citizens (if ever again there are peaceful citizens in war-time) no less than armies, of zealots of peace, no less than apostles of war.

These are no mere literary elaborations. They are the inevitable reflections of every man who ever gives serious thought to the world in which he lives. He cannot compute his investments without realising that in a week or a day they may be reduced to a quarter of their value. He cannot fill up his Income Tax returns without being reminded that a war may leave him without any income at all. He cannot look from his window without recognising that the houses he sees from it, and his own as well, may in a night be reduced to shattered ruins, and such inmates as have escaped destruction by explosion or concussion or fire be left to choke their lives out in a welter of poison-gas. And for what? There are causes for which the vast majority of men and women in this country would resolutely, though with unutterable reluctance, decide to fight. They have been discussed in recent articles in *The Spectator* – the defence of these shores, defence of the Empire, defence of the principles for which the League of Nations stands. But the prospect is that if war comes it will be on no such clear and immediate issue as even the defence of the League of Nations. Moreover, defence of the League remains a questionable *casus belli* till it appears what the League of the future is to be. A society that cannot count on its members even to impose resolute economic sanctions cannot call on them to shed their blood for it.

War in Europe, if it comes, will be the fruit of a clash between two schools of political thought and practice, neither of which is ours and from whose doctrines we only ask to keep our country free. We have witnessed in the past two months the massing of the storm-clouds in the rival partisanships over Spain, and more noisily in the competition in invective, written and spoken, between Berlin and Moscow. The carnival of oratory at Nuremberg need not in itself arouse undue alarm. Nuremberg oratory is an affliction which Europe has to live through every year. But more than oratory is involved. Hitler at Nuremberg has been reviewing his army and his air force. Stalin has simultaneously been reviewing his army and his air force on the steppes. And at a moment when Europe needs beyond all things a spirit of appeasement and restraint it is regarded as the highest public service in Germany and Russia to foam at the mouth or the pen in the emission of sentiments denunciatory of the national enemy. That is the way war comes, difficult though war will be in this case geographically. And if war does come France, through her treaty with Soviet Russia, will inevitably be involved. Poland and Czechoslovakia, placed as they are, could not remain aloof. Nor could the other members of the Little Entente. All Europe would be at war, and, Locarno or no Locarno, it would be as hard for Great Britain to remain at peace as it was in 1914 – particularly if Belgium had been drawn in with France.

But black as that prospect is, we are not yet compelled to resign ourselves to the inevitability of war and our own implication in it. For all his fulminations against Boshevism, Herr Hitler confined himself at Nuremberg to threats of how he would repel the foul thing from the German frontiers if it ever tried to cross them – which it shows no signs of doing. Germany may refuse to sit at a council-table with Russia (though in fact she is doing it in London today), but her self-imposed encirclement in itself makes war more remote, if France and Russia, Poland, restored to amity with France, and the Little Entente stand on the defensive around her. Nor is it to be regarded as axiomatic that if war does come in Europe we shall be swept with the rest into the pit. We well may be. To stay out may be harder than to go in. To advertise that in no circumstances would we fight would be impossible, and inadvisable even if it were possible, for it would encourage one side or the other materially by reducing the odds against it. But this country will never go to war again without compelling cause, and a conflict between Fascism and Bolshevism is, so far as we are concerned, no cause at all. An atmosphere of war is being engendered no less on the Russian side than on the German, and the fact that France has decided to identify herself with Russia is no reason why we should let ourselves be entangled too. To Germany's obvious design to free herself by peace treaties in the west for adventure and aggression in the east we cannot lend ourselves, but so long as Russia is matching invective with invective she forfeits all claim on us if trouble follows. Arm we must in an arming world, but more with a view to enabling us to remain at peace than to enabling us to fight – even if to fight were to win. Our highest task is to preserve within these islands traditions of democracy and liberty which another war would go far to submerge in the general destruction.

18 September

MR ROOSEVELT AND THE FUTURE
[D. W. BROGAN]

The United States goes to the polls next Tuesday, and unless every omen is fallacious it will elect Mr Franklin D. Roosevelt President for a further four years. Whatever lingering doubts there may be as to the result of the election, there can be none of its character. It is a plebiscite for or against Mr Roosevelt, and a re-election of the President would be a victory for him, not for his party, and a victory for his personality and attitude rather than for any defined policy. Such a victory would have its special significance in these days when the prospects for democracy seem so gloomy. So many commentators, from Mr Lloyd George downwards, have stressed the claims of the dictatorial governments to be able to work with a speed and decision apparently impossible to democracies, that the decision of the most powerful nation in the world to entrust its destinies again to Mr Roosevelt would have more than ordinary significance. For the President, whatever his faults, has not diplayed either undue caution or a fondness for the time-wasting and point-evading devices attributed to democratic statesmen. The American election is a demonstration that there is a demand for resolute and bold government – and a sign that it can be provided by other means than the sacrifice of liberty to the totalitarian state.

It is true that the noisiest, if not most convincing critics of Mr Roosevelt have done all in their power to identify him with dictatorship, but the allegation is palpably absurd. It is idle to compare the President to Hitler or Mussolini or Stalin. Denunciations of presidential absolutism ring curiously false in a world in which real tyranny is so abundantly represented, and in which the incompatibility of dictatorship and free criticism has been made manifest by so many striking examples. Mr Frank Knox, for instance, after his months of campaigning as Republican Vice-Presidential candidate, will be able to return to his editorial chair without any serious fears that the *Chicago Daily News* will have to suffer the fate of the *Berliner Tageblatt* or the *Corriere della Sera*. Mr Alfred Smith and Mr John W. Davis will wake up on Wednesday with no anticipations that they may share the fate of such party dissidents as Herr Gregor Strasser or Comrades Zinoviev and Kamenev.

If Mr Roosevelt has done nothing else, he has shown that the naïve demand of the average man for action can be satisfied without either an Ogpu or a Gestapo, without the stifling of criticism or the murder, exile or terrorisation of his opponents. But this lesson is not all that the triumph of the administration teaches. It has seemed an axiom of American politics, since the defeat of Wilson, that it was always safe to adopt the most intransigent attitude to any dealings with foreign States. In the first part of his administration Mr Roosevelt showed no desire to imitate even such timid advances as Mr Hoover made towards international action. But the nature of things proved highly educative and the patience of Mr Cordell Hull and the courage of the American Treasury have been rewarded, not merely by substantial achievements like the trade treaties or the currency truce, but by political advantages.

If the administration has learned a good deal, has dared to act on its acquired wisdom and has gained by its boldness, the Republican Party has shown a dogged stubbornness in error and a determination to avoid thought and candour that has been the despair of some of its more enlightened members and has driven back to the Democratic camp such bitter and able critics of the administration as Mr James Warburg. It was thought (or hoped) that the Republicans' declared determination to collect the War debts and thereby impede international trade even further was only a piece of political window-dressing, put in to salve the consciences of the veterans who had contributed the Smoot-Hawley tariff to the troubles of a sufficiently distracted world. But as the campaign progressed, and, from the Republican point of view, from bad to worse, the temptation to appeal for easy votes to the assumed vast reservoir of permanent xenophobia, proved too much, and it is hardly excessive to say that if Mr Landon is elected he will have been committed by some of his more noisy allies (one can hardly call them supporters) to an economic policy far more to the taste of the Nazi apostles of autarky than to that of Dr Schacht. Even if he saw the light and threw his supporters over, he would have to face a Senate in which no Republican triumph could overthrow the present Democratic majority, and in which the temptation to bedevil President Landon, as Senator Lodge and his allies did Wilson, would almost certainly be too much for political human nature.

One other aspect of the election, while it concerns the United States primarily rather than Europe, is yet of considerable interest to Europe. Had Mr Landon been allowed to follow his own bent, it is probable that he would have offered, in internal affairs, an alternative to the New Deal that would have been near enough to it in spirit to win many voters from Mr Roosevelt. But the old disharmony in the Republican Party proved too much for him. His eastern supporters wanted no compromise. They had opposed nearly every social achievement of the administration, not only as badly planned or as badly executed, but as wrong and needless from beginning to end. There has been in Wall Street, and in other centres where the Wall Street outlook prevails, an obstinate refusal to understand the moral damage done to the prestige of the business rulers of America by the collapse of 1929. The belief that there was nothing seriously wrong with the system that ended in the dreadful years from 1929 to 1933, and the further belief that the average man could be made to see this, ruined the Republicans' chances of success at the Congressional elections of 1934. The eastern leaders of the Republican Party have been at least as much a liability as an asset to it, for their attitude intensified the inclination of the Middle-West farmers to support the President who had saved them from disaster. Mr Roosevelt, with the election pending, has had to pick his way warily in the last eighteen months. If he wins his hands will be free, for a third term is as unattainable an ambition as it ever was. That may mean a great deal.

30 October

IS GERMANY PREPARING WAR?
COUNT WLADIMIR D'ORMESSON

Is Germany preparing war? This question haunts most men's minds, and envelops Europe with a paralysing uneasiness. We know, of course, that Germans themselves jib at the question, and certainly the great mass of the German people is in no way desirous of war, and remains convinced that the actions of its Führer are entirely pacific. Nevertheless, two points force themselves on our consideration. The first is the fact that Germany is the only Power of whom the question can possibly be asked – is this country preparing war? It is, in fact, self-evident that neither British nor French democracy can be suspected of harbouring any such lurking intention. In the nature of the case, their foreign policy is 'conservative.' If the temper of France had been bellicose, she could readily have proved it on March 8th of this year. Italy, for her part, despite her preenings, is certainly not in a position deliberately to provoke a war *in Europe*. The most she could do would be to intervene on one side or the other when the conflict was already under way. Meanwhile, and for 20 years at least, she has Abyssinia on her hands. As for the U.S.S.R., her policy during the last three years is proof enough of how much she is afraid of war: burning what she adored and adoring what she had burned (including the League of Nations, the French bourgeoisie and British capitalism!), she too has been working to become on the diplomatic plane a 'conservative' Power of the established order in Europe. Would she have made advances to everything she hated, if it were not to obtain better safeguards of security? No. The idea of a possible European war was reintroduced, and the atmosphere of the Old Continent was charged with this sinister electricity, because – it must be said plainly – German militarism reappeared in the heart of Europe, upheld by an inflexible dictatorship and the intensified rearmament carried out by the Third Reich.

Here one essential point should be noted. All things considered, it was natural that Germany should not endure beyond a certain period the disarmament clauses of the Treaty of Versailles. A day was bound to come when the German army would be built up anew. But it is one thing for a country to maintain a military force proportionate to its importance, and quite another for it to sacrifice everything in order to have the most formidable army in the world. There is a point beyond which any military machine ceases to be a legitimately defensive organism and becomes an aggressive weapon. And there is every ground to believe that Germany is in process of passing beyond that point, if she has not already done so. Already she has in her hands an *active* army of about 900,000 men. She has in addition a specialised and mechanised army, styled the Hitler Militia, which comprises another 200,000. At the present moment she has six mechanised shock divisions, doubtless capable of passing any obstacle and opening a breach for invading forces: and nobody knows precisely what her aerial power amounts to. If we remember, too, that her youth in the Labour Camps is likewise submitted to military discipline, and imbued with ultra-nationalistic mysticism, we cannot but ask ourselves why all these preparations are made unless it be for war, and why Dr Goebbels declares that Germany needs guns more than butter, unless it be to use the guns.

In the second place – and it is all of a piece – it cannot be forgotten that the present master of Germany is the very man who, in a famous book which has become the Bible of contemporary Germany, made it plain that, in his view, war was the only means whereby the German people could attain the objectives to which they were entitled, and that the greatness of these aims would justify the horror of the means. It may be argued that an irresponsible author has nothing in common with the responsible ruler of a great nation. Possibly. The fact remains that the Führer, since attaining power, has with logical persistence put into practice the programme formerly laid down by Adolf Hitler. To read the closing chapters of *Mein Kampf* is in this respect very illuminating. The Führer's general political conceptions here link up with the special concerns of the army chiefs, who have themselves, for years past, been constantly and methodically pursuing the same objectives under cover. The result is that at the present time, behind the social screen of the Nazi *régime*, there is an unprecedentedly close agreement between the civil and the military leaders; and we may well wonder whether the former, planning only to build up an unrivalled National-Socialist Reich, and the latter, filled only with thoughts of their 'revenge,' may not both be uniting in the selfsame preparations, although impelled by different motives.

These observations, therefore, entitle us to ask the question – is the Third Reich preparing war? Let us be clear, however: for in such matters nothing is ever categoric. It cannot be taken for certain that, in the minds of Germany's rulers, the intention of a European war is here and now settled. Probably they live from day to day to a greater extent than they are believed to do. Probably they are even sincere in declaring themselves to be 'human beings' first and foremost, and in their condemnation of fratricidal strife. But by a contradiction characteristic of the German mind, and especially of the Hitlerian mind, 'human' considerations can quite readily exist in it alongside of a contempt for death, the cult of violence, and the certainty that there exist certain 'sacrifices' which are paramount over certain 'scruples.' Furthermore, although it is not certain that the Hitlerian leaders are here and now resolved upon war, it is quite certain that they have decided to pursue a policy *which involves the risk of war*; it is certain too that they are preparing a weapon of war which they hope to be invincible, in order at least to be able to set it up as a bogy in discussion (which always leads to one inevitable result); *and it is, above all, certain that, if ever the European chessboard displayed such a position as to make them think that Germany would clearly stand to emerge victorious from a swift intervention, abruptly carried out at one point or another, they would decide within a few hours to strike, and strike hard, without even giving Europe time to turn round.*

For the rest, the Führer himself has been at pains to give us warning – and it is known that if he does not always honour his pledges, he always honours his threats! 'I shall not act like Mussolini,' he said last year at the Nuremberg Congress, 'I shall not warn my adversary by preparations and discussions. If I attack, I shall act as I have always acted, striking like lightning, in the night.' Here also, and here only, is the explanation of the recent 'two years' law in Germany. The Reich leaders intend to have at their disposal an active army large enough *to be able to dispense with a process of mobilisation*, and between one day and the next to hurl hundreds of thousands of well-trained men on the foe.

It may be objected, I know, that the Führer has made several offers for peaceful understanding. But it should not be forgotten that these offers *always* coincided with challenges, so that it was virtually certain that they could not be given consideration. The German tactics, in fact, consist of sugaring the bitter pill. But the taste of the pill is over in a moment! It will also be said that the Third Reich has no quarrel with France, or Britain, or Belgium, but that it fears Russia and the activities of the Soviets, and that since the conclusion of the Franco-Russian pact Germany feels herself threatened by a vice and driven to react. 'Give a dog a bad name and hang him,' says the proverb. That is more or less what Germany's attitude towards the Soviets amounts to. It is ridiculous to claim that Russia is threatening Germany. Between the two countries lies the mattress of Poland, three or four hundred miles thick. The Poles would never permit the passage of an army of Soviet aggression. Furthermore, they have a treaty of friendship with Germany. But Czechoslovakia? What of her? Is it conceivable that a small country like Czechoslovakia would take the initiative of provoking the German colossus? Besides, she has no common frontier with Russia, and an invading Russian army would have to pass through Poland (which is out of the question) or through Rumania. What a march! Lastly, no Russian voice has ever been raised to covet the smallest shred of German territory, whereas only the other day at Nuremberg the Führer was talking openly of the Ukraine as a Promised Land – once again true to what he had written in *Mein Kampf*.

One may be hostile to the Soviet system, one may be opposed to their doctrines and ideals, but one is forced to admit that of these two countries, Germany and Russia, the one which presses a definite threat to peace is not the second. As for the Franco-Russian pact – a pact open to all, and primarily to Germany –

it would lose the whole of its *raison d'être* if only Germany spoke one word or made one gesture *in favour of the consolidation of European peace in its entirety*. France has only one aim in view. It is that the peace of Europe as a whole be safeguarded. She is convinced, in fact, that Europe has become too small to be divided into hostile *blocs*, and convinced too that no conflict between great Continental Powers could be localised.

The troubling fact is that the leaders of Germany always shrink from any such word or gesture. What is alarming, is that the German masses do not appreciate the double policy of their rulers, do not see where they are being led, and that, deprived of all methods of instruction and control, they run the risk, if the present drift continues, of being plunged into catastrophe in a night. What is overwhelming, is the fact that they will be sincere when, with moans, they then protest: 'No, we did not want this ...'

30 October

IS GERMANY PREPARING WAR?
DR RUDOLF KIRCHER (Editor of the *Frankfurter Zeitung*)

When I read Count d'Ormesson's article in the last issue of *The Spectator* on the question whether Germany means war, and was asked to reply to it from the German point of view, I found myself in something of a dilemma, because, frankly, I found much to take exception to in Count d'Ormesson's article. First of all, I do not like insinuations when proofs are lacking, nor do I like inaccurate figures when figures are given. Secondly, I do not think it helpful, when what is needed is not one-sided accusations but arguments, to pass judgement on a political situation without any regard to its origin. Thirdly, however useful a discussion between a French and a German publicist in a well-known British journal may be, it is questionable whether the average British reader should be encouraged to assume that he can fitly adopt the *rôle* of referee. British policy is in my view very largely responsible for the creation of the situation which Count d'Ormesson discusses without a hint of the possibility that anyone but Germany may be responsible – least of all France.

As I am firmly convinced that a real and lasting understanding is never possible till on all sides feelings are relieved and the fundamental facts revealed, I shall take leave to speak perfectly frankly. In one way my French colleague takes the same line, when he ends his grave accusations against Germany with the pathetic declaration that a single word, a single gesture from Germany 'in favour of the consolidation of European peace as a whole' would be sufficient to take the wind out of the sails of that ill-starred Franco-Soviet Pact.

Count d'Ormesson goes fundamentally wrong at the outset in suggesting that Germany should buy off that pact. Germany, I am convinced, would go a long way to come to an honest understanding with France, because there exists in Germany no hatred against the French people, nor is there any serious Franco-German problem which could not quite well be solved once it was removed from the present atmosphere of suspicion or fear. But, on the other hand, there will be no solution so long as the old-fashioned game is played: intimidate or bluff your neighbour, and then invite him to buy off the cause of his fear, and thereby strike as favourable a bargain as you can. There is nothing in the Franco-Russian pact in itself to induce Germany to pay anything at all for its abrogation, nor, as I have already said, would this be a right method for creating sound European co-operation. It is not so much the pact as the policy hitherto underlying it which must disappear before prospects in Europe can be improved.

I doubt whether British readers realise how far that part of French policy which we call the policy of alliances was, and still is, connected with the famous 'No' pronounced by M. Barthou when a military convention of great value was well in sight some eighteen months ago. Indeed, the very reason which prompted the French Government of that day to refuse the conclusion of the military agreement was M. Barthou's hope of achieving much greater security for France by some new political and military pacts in Eastern Europe than by a military convention with Germany, Italy and Britain. Today everyone knows that this 'no' was one of the most unfortunate of the many errors committed in recent years. Barthou's 'No' prevented the limitation of armaments on a level which today would seem surprisingly low, whereas the eastern commitments of France met with growing criticism and scepticism both in France itself and elsewhere.

Why then, I shall be asked, if you consider France's policy of alliances is a failure, do you insist on making a fuss about it? The answer to that is that Germany, while very unfavourably impressed by the Franco-Russian pact, abstained from 'making a fuss about it' up to the time when Czechoslovakia was included in it, and this rather short-sighted country thus became a prospective starting-point for Bolshevist aeroplanes. Look at the map, and you will see at once what I mean. In little more than half an hour Berlin could be reached easily by aeroplanes starting from Czechoslovakia. It may be replied that so long as Germany behaves as she should there will be no fear of that. But why, I rejoin, should we Germans trust other people more than other people trust us? Your comforting assurance 'as long as you behave you have nothing to fear' – is true either for everybody or nobody. And this at the same time is my answer to Count d'Ormesson's accusation, or rather insinuation: I and all of us resent utterly the hypocritical state of mind which permits other people to think and say 'We alone are peace-loving, we alone can be trusted. Even if we arm to the teeth, even if we conclude the most objectionable pacts, even if our ally is the only proposer and propagator of a world-wide revolution, we alone are right and righteous. You Germans are not and never will be.'

I said I should speak plainly, and I hope I may be forgiven if I have. The opportunity for a complete change of European policy is once more so great that it would be inexcusable to shrink from exposing the fundamental facts. When Count d'Ormesson (like many others) asks whether Germany is preparing for war, the German answer can only be: after what has happened, Germany is bound to make herself as strong as possible in order to face any situation she may be placed in by those who have not yet abandoned the hope of imprisoning Germany in a new cage – the old one, made in Versailles, being destroyed and done with. Barthou's 'No' in connexion with the policy of alliances was one more attempt, perhaps the last, to avoid a square deal with Germany on the basis of full equality. France's eastern policy was one more attempt, perhaps the last, to negotiate with Germany after submitting her to the pressure not of common sense and goodwill but of force. Add to this the detestable slogan about 'preventive war,' add to this the poisonous propaganda of the Comintern, which British readers are certainly not fully aware of, since they do not listen in and understand when the Moscow wireless descants in German on the Red Army, 'which is ready to invade Germany' and turn her Communist – I say, add to this all that is and must be in the minds of Germans as long as they are thus threatened, and you will begin to understand that Germany is making her preparations not in order to *attack* anyone, but to ensure that no one shall be able to attack or bully our country again.

But one thing is certain. If the contributors to public discussion do not refrain from giving erroneous facts and inaccurate figures, both of them rather objectionable in themselves, the aim of all who really desire to be helpful will hardly be furthered. How is it possible to speak of a German army of a strength of 900,000 in addition to several tens of thousands enrolled in 'a special mechanised army styled the Hitler Militia'? Count d'Ormesson might at least have read *The Times* on the subject, or asked the French military *attachés*. How is it possible for a distinguished writer like Count d'Ormesson to quote from a speech of the Führer of the Reich a passage taken apparently from a grossly misleading newspaper cutting, but certainly not from the speech Adolf Hitler actually delivered? How, moreover, can Count d'Ormesson, without a word of proof, simply state on his own authority that Germany will not hesitate to invade her neighbours suddenly and with overwhelming force once she feels certain of victory?

How can a German be expected to embark seriously on the discussion of theories and misinterpretations of an article of this kind when he finds that even the cheapest propaganda stuff is not excluded from its arguments? What I am referring to is this: the Führer, in comparing the achievements and possibilities of National Socialism and Bolshevism, exclaimed in Nuremberg 'what would Germany, who cultivates with infinite care every single inch of her soil, have achieved if her territory and resources were as vast as those, for instance, of the Ural district or the Ukraine, while Bolshevism, in spite of all these advantages, seems unable even to keep its peasants from starvation?' Instead of accepting the true meaning of Adolf Hitler's speech, Count d'Ormesson misuses it as a new proof 'of Hitler's desire for imperialist expansion.' How can we possibly discuss the means and prospects of attaining peace and friendship in Europe with any hope of success if a single word like 'Ukraine' is sufficient to destroy the very basis of any honest discussion, fairness and goodwill?

Count d'Ormesson, like others, will not understand my resentment. He will reply, as he has already in anticipation, 'Don't forget that book, *Mein Kampf*!' There is only *one* authoritative comment on this volume – Adolf Hitler's actions, that is to say, the actual programme and the deeds of the man who was defeated and imprisoned when he wrote his book, but is now the Führer and responsible Chancellor of the Reich. Be fair to Germany and you will be rewarded. The absence of fairness and broadmindedness on the part of those who now raise offensive questions was responsible for most of what has happened in the past. That, at least, is the German contention.

6 November

SEMI-FASCIST JAPAN
WILLIAM HENRY CHAMBERLIN in Tokyo

The recurrent outbursts of Army radicalism in Japan, of which those of May 15th, 1932, and of February 26th, 1936, were the most striking and far-reaching, naturally suggest the question whether it is Japan's destiny to join the ranks of the world's Fascist States. Curious as it may seem, the semi-Fascist character of the present Japanese *régime* is perhaps the best guarantee against the emergence of a full-fledged Fascist State, of the German or Italian type.

Japan's constitutional position today is difficult to define. It is not a dictatorship in the familiar sense of that term. There is no permanent, irreplaceable, dominant 'leader' of the type of Stalin, Hitler and Mussolini. Power in taking vital decisions of internal and foreign policy is diffused and divided in a baffling way between the senior statesmen who are close to the Throne, of whom the most eminent is the venerable Prince Saionji, the military and naval authorities, the bureaucracy and the representatives of the big business and financial interests.

The Army is credited with playing, and does play, an important part in shaping decisions on many questions of foreign and internal policy. Yet the Army lacks personification in the form of an outstanding, unmistakable chief. War Ministers change as rapidly as occupants of other Ministerial posts in Japan. General Sadao Araki, who during his term of office as War Minister three or four years ago attracted world-wide attention by his not infrequent utterances of flamboyant nationalism, is living today in quiet retirement and, in the judgement of most Japanese, has lost almost all his former influence.

If Japan is not a dictatorship it is even more obviously not a democracy. The powers of the Diet, always more circumscribed than those of a Western parliament, have become more and more shadowy since the occupation of Manchuria, which was a signal for an outbreak of political reaction in Japan itself. The Press is muzzled, not so absolutely as in Germany, Italy or the Soviet

Union, but still quite effectively. Even the 'Asahi,' long a bulwark of liberalism in the Japanese Press, has become tame and lifeless since the rebellious officers directed a special assault against its premises on February 26th. There is just enough freedom of speech left in Japan for an unusually bold editor to announce occasionally that there is no freedom of speech. Labour demonstrations, when allowed at all, are accompanied by almost as many policemen as marchers.. Since February 26th the police has enjoyed a freer hand in its favourite occupation of spy-hunting, and the atmosphere of secrecy which surrounds all State affairs and decisions in dictator-ruled lands is definitely increasing in Japan.

Some features of the Fascist Corporative State already exist in Japan. Discipline and regimentation are ensured as a result of the extraordinary powers and wide functions exercised by the police. The duties of the Japanese police go far beyond detecting and apprehending criminals and regulating traffic. They intervene in paternal fashion in the everyday lives of the people, telling the residents of a given district just when they are to carry out the annual compulsory housecleaning, offering advice, warnings and reprimands in domestic quarrels. They are apt to be the final court of compulsory arbitration in protracted labour disputes. They are constantly on the look-out for what a Japanese bureaucrat once, with agreeable although unconscious humour, described as 'dangerous thoughts.' 'Police bans' are the bane of the Japanese newspaper editor, who is often told by the police, under penalty of fine and confiscation, to print nothing on some forbidden subject. Censorship of foreign publications has become markedly more severe in recent months.

Voluntary or enforced subordination of the individual for the supposed benefit of the general welfare is a characteristic of the post-War dictatorships which is fully shared by Japan. In contrast to the Chinese, who, with few exceptions, place the family ties and obligations above everything else, the Japanese are prepared to make a second sacrifice of the individual personality on the altar of the nation. The cult of militant patriotism is very strong in Japan. Every schoolboy knows the story of the three 'human bombs,' Japanese soldiers who rushed forward to certain death in order to blow up barbed-wire entanglements which were holding up the Japanese advance during the fighting at Shanghai.

This propaganda for intense nationalism, fusing with the cult of profound reverence for the Emperor, which is especially stressed during the present period, is quite in harmony with Western Fascism. So is the tendency of the State to take an active part in the economic development of the country. Modern capitalism developed late in Japan, and naturally grew up more dependent on State aid and co-operation than the same system in other countries. Partnerships between the Government and private enterprise, such as the great South Manchuria Railway system, where the Government supplies part of the capital, guarantees a dividend, has a voice in the nomination of the directors, but allows private business methods to prevail in the management, are symbolic of Japan's State-aided capitalism.

Fondness for long-term planning is another characteristic which Japan shares with Communist and Fascist *régimes*. The portfolios of Japanese officials are fairly bursting with blueprints for the future, among which may be mentioned a five-year plan for the rehabilitation of the chronically depressed Tohoku (the north-eastern section of the Main Island), a fifteen-year plan for the development of South Sakhalin, a twenty-year plan for Hokkaido, laying down specifications for the future of that northern island, from the number of peasant households which are to be settled to the number of horses which are to be bred, all reminiscent of the famous five-year plans of the Soviet Union.

But, while Japan possesses many features of the Corporative State and has certainly been influenced by the rise and spread of Fascism in recent years, just as its intelligentsia was strongly influenced by Russia during the 'twenties, several important elements in the Fascist scheme of things are still lacking. There is no omnipotent and infallible leader, no single ruling party: and Japan's achievements in mass propaganda and mass terrorism, while not altogether lacking, are considerably less impressive than those of the Soviet Union, Germany and Italy.

And it is just the semi-fascist character of the Japanese political, economic and social order that seems to set up barriers against the coming of Fascism of the standard European type. In super-policed Japan a Hitler or a Mussolini could not go very far in the direction of building up a mass party and personal following. The tradition, especially cherished by nationalist and military circles, that Japan must always be an empire ruled over by a line of Emperors, 'unbroken through ages eternal,' to quote a famous phrase in the Japanese Constitution, also militates against the emergence of an individual leader who would concentrate popular adulation on himself.

But, while a precise duplication of the European Fascist pattern seems out of the question, a gradual evolutionary trend in the direction of greater State control over national economic life, especially where strategic considerations are involved, and still more rigorous curbing of the feeble remnants of liberalism and individualism, are by no means unlikely. One can already see indications of such an evolution in the draft project for State control of the electrical power industry, which is now a subject of bitter discussion; in the military insistence on greater autarky and more provision for military and naval needs through such measures as the extraction of oil from coal, regardless of cost; in the growing tendency to see a spy in the travelling foreigner and a deep military secret in some commonplace bit of industrial or commercial information.

6 November

OBJECTIVE CRITICISM
E. E. KELLETT

A recent trial in Germany has aroused widespread interest. It will be remembered that some ten days ago, Dr Goebbels, the Minister for National Enlightenment and Propaganda, announced that *criticism* of works of art was forbidden; it could not be tolerated that writers should be allowed to pass *judgements* on actors, dramatists, musicians, or poets. Unless the critic could do better in the art than the man he presumed to appraise, he had better be silent, or at most confine himself to an objective and impersonal description of the work under consideration.

In flagrant contempt of this decree, a contributor to the *Schachspieler* had the audacity to pass a subjective judgement on the play of Dr Euwe in the recent Nottingham tourney. His actual words were as follows: 'At this point Dr Euwe was guilty of a gross oversight. After playing remarkably well during the first part of the game, he carelessly moved his Bishop into a loose and undefended position. His opponent, Dr Lasker, taking prompt advantage of the error, moved his Pawn, and shortly afterwards gained a piece. Continuing to play with great skill, he compelled Dr Euwe to resign in half a dozen more moves.'

The speech of the Public Prosecutor began by pointing out

how often a critic of a work of art had, under the transparent veil of aesthetic appraisals, conveyed a covert censure of the Nazi *régime*. If such a crime was possible with the drama or with poetry, how much easier was it in connexion with the game of chess, which, it was well known, had repeatedly been treated as a political allegory. A check to the king might, with no great dexterity, be so spoken of as to denote an attack on the Führer; and the Government was determined to put down such disguised treason with the utmost rigour of the law.

'But,' went on the Prosecutor, 'to leave that point and to proceed to the crime now before us. It will be seen that this Hans Schmidt has contravened every one of Dr Goebbels's injunctions in the most open and unabashed fashion; and there will, on that account, be no need for me to inquire whether he has not, in addition, been guilty of allegorical or symbolical treason. I have no doubt that, were I to investigate the point, I should find, lurking beneath the surface of his words, an inveterate antagonism to our system. But I will not insist on that; I merely ask you to bear it in mind. His overt act is enough to condemn him. To quote the words of our great Nazi poet, his offence is rank and smells to heaven.

'First, he has dared to criticise art; for that chess is an art needs no proof. Who can deny that its combinations often show an almost lyrical beauty? Its moves are rhythmical, like those of a dance; its revelations surprising; and the chess-player's eye, like the poet's, often rolls in a fine frenzy, glances from earth to heaven, and almost literally bodies forth the forms of things unknown. Chess is poetry, and it has been the theme of poets. Long ago Vida made the "Art of Chess" the subject of some elegant cantos – Vida, who, had he lived today, would have been a devoted adherent of Signor Mussolini, and thus a friend of our Führer.

'Chess being an art, then, this "know-better" Hans Schmidt had no business to criticise it at all. For, as Dr Goebbels has shown, criticism discourages the artist, and prevents him from putting forth of his best. How can we expect Nordic chess-players to gain the supremacy which is their due if they are to be subject to the carping strictures of lookers-on? Justly has our Minister forbidden this presumption. The utmost Schmidt had a right to do was to record the moves, and that in our noble Nordic notation, and not in the effete anti-Nazi style of England and America.

'Think again. No one has a right to judge an artist unless he is a better performer than that artist. Is Schmidt a better player than Dr Euwe? I have looked into his record, and I believe that Dr Euwe could give him a pawn, a move, and a beating. Let him wait awhile before he accuses an Euwe of error! Was there ever a greater piece of insolence than that a third or fourth-rate chess-player should dare to use an expression like "carelessness" about a man of such world-wide repute, such universally acknowledged eminence, as the champion?

'Incidentally, in attacking Dr Euwe, he is insulting our Aryan race. For, though Dr Euwe is a Dutchman, he belongs to the outer fringe of Germanism, which we shall not long permit to remain the fringe. Nor is it necessary to point out that, even were biological and genealogical evidence not available, Dr Euwe's great ability would by itself prove his Germanic origin, as a similar argument would show that Philidor, Labourdonnais, and Morphy all belonged to our unique and noble race. Schmidt, therefore, must beware!

'But to return. The decree, as I said, lays down that criticism – if I must use the word – should be impersonal and objective. It must describe the work, and say nothing about the author. Why then, I ask, did not Schmidt, when telling us that Lasker took instant advantage of Dr Euwe's error – why did Schmidt not add that Lasker is a Jew, a member of the most detestable of races, the most grasping, the most insidious? This is the Lasker who, during a quarter of a century, by dint of a low cunning, maintained himself as chess-champion of the world, thus, in true Liberalistic-Semitic fashion, depriving Nordic players of their legitimate rights. Nay, in his early youth, by similar devices, he managed to take the highest mathematical honours in his University, thus here also preventing some member of a nobler stock from achieving that distinction. And now we find Schmidt describing him as "prompt," and as showing skill. Why, I ask, did he not use other terms? Why did he not speak of indecent haste and underhand craft? Why, further, did he conceal Lasker's sinister origin? Where is that impersonality and objectivity which Dr Goebbels so rightly demands from criticism? To slur over a man's Judaic descent is to forget that you cannot appraise a man's work duly until you know whether his grandmother was a Jewess or a Gentile: then only can you be truly objective. But the explanation is only too plain. Schmidt himself is a Jew. He has not the Hebraic features – there is his cunning. And his very name betrays him. It is so common in Germany that it is constantly adopted as an alias by those who, for one reason or another, wish their true one not to be known. Beyond doubt Schmidt is an Israel, an Abraham, or even a Marx. When our Führer determined to change *his* family designation, how differently he acted! Do we say Heil Schmidt? A thousand times No! Gentlemen, deal out fearless and impartial justice; cleanse the State of its dangerous taint; remove its persistent and subtle adversaries; say with me Heil Hitler, and give this crafty intriguer the punishment he has earned.'

After a short deliberation, the jury found Schmidt guilty, and he was sentenced to three years' detention in a concentration-camp, no chess-board being allowed him.

18 December

'Dear Mumma': Berlin 1936

HUGH GREENE

On the evening of 10 February 1936 I sat in the *Daily Telegraph* office on Unter den Linden (now the British Embassy to East Germany) feeling rather bored. I wrote to my mother, beginning as always 'Dear Mumma', that things were very quiet. By Hitler's standards nothing much had happened for several months. Though the process of brutal repression continued inexorably inside Germany, his last coup of international importance had been the repudiation of the disarmament clauses of the Treaty of Versailles in March 1935. All the same, there were rumours and rumblings. The ratification debate on the Franco-Soviet Treaty was due to begin in the French Chamber of Deputies on 11 February. That Hitler would react in some way if ratification was approved was obvious. But how and when?

It was some time before I wrote to my mother again. Then, on 8 April, my letter began: 'I'm sorry I haven't written for so long but life has been very crowded. In the last six weeks I've had only two free days and about half a dozen free nights and have been alone in the office for about half the time.'

Early on 7 March Hitler had sent his troops into the demilitarised Rhineland. As usual he had chosen a Saturday for his coup: Hitler knew everything about the English weekend. The year which had begun so quietly was to be one of the most 30itical of the interwar period, the last year when vigorous action by Great Britain and France could have halted the march of war without a shot being fired and damaged Hitler's aura of infallibility, which had not yet mesmerised the German generals, beyond repair.

On the morning of 7 March I was in the Reichstag to report Hitler's speech. Since the Reichstag fire in February 1933 the Reichstag had met, when Hitler had chosen to call it together, at the Kroll Opera House in the Tiergarten, a building of which no trace remains today. As usual Hitler's speech began with a long and boring preamble about world politics and National Socialist philosophy and, of course, the peaceful nature of the German people. All the same one had to keep awake. No advance copies of his speeches were made available to the press. At any moment he might switch from long-winded generalities to the most exciting and vitally important particulars.

When Hitler came to his announcement that the Franco-Soviet Treaty had annulled the Treaty of Locarno and that he had sent his troops into the Rhineland, I kept my eye on General Werner von Fritsch, the commander-in-chief of the German army, only two years later to be dismissed by Hitler on trumped-up charges of sexual relations with a male prostitute. The general, I noticed, was not on this occasion the very model of a calm poker-faced Prussian officer. He fidgeted, he sweated, he kept polishing his monocle.

General von Fritsch had every reason to be nervous. Only three battalions had moved across the Rhine, to Aachen, Trier and Saarbrücken. Their orders were that if only one French battalion was set in motion they were to withdraw behind the Rhine without offering any resistance. The German high command, then in the early stages of rearmament and building up the strength of the Reichswehr, had the greatest respect for the French army. Hitler, with his extraordinary instinct for political and military realities, had no respect for the French political and military leaders or, for that matter, for their British counterparts. He *knew*.

After half a century the blindness, weakness and cowardice of the French and British governments seem just as astonishing as they did then. I think that most journalistic and some diplomatic observers in Berlin understood with complete clarity that this was probably the last chance to stop Hitler in his tracks. Britain and France had every right to take military action. They should have known of the weakness at that date of the German army and realised that the risk of war was slight. Instead they grasped eagerly at the peace offers with which Hitler, as always, accompanied his belligerent actions.

Geoffrey Dawson's *Times*, with its usual fatuity, ignored its excellent correspondent in Berlin and produced a leading article with the headline 'A Chance to Rebuild'. Even *The Spectator* seemed to think that the real danger of war came from the French, who at first demanded that a withdrawal from the Rhineland must precede negotiations.

Eustace Wareing, who was then my boss in Berlin, and I put our heads together and composed an article in which we said that the Rhineland would now be fortified: France would thereby be prevented from coming to the aid of her allies in Eastern

Europe; Austria would be swallowed up; Czechoslovakia's powerful defences would be outflanked and she would have no means of resisting German threats; finally, demands would be made on Poland for the surrender of Danzig and the Polish corridor with war as the alternative. I only wish that I still had a copy. Neither Wareing nor I, after the failure to do anything about the Rhineland, expected any action by Britain and France at any point to interfere with Hitler's plans.

This article did not require an extraordinary degree of farsightedness. That is what is so tragic about the whole thing. Anybody who had read Hitler's *Mein Kampf* and studied his speeches with care could have written a similar article. I dare say that some people did.

The article was not used. This was uncharacteristic of the *Daily Telegraph*. Unlike *The Times*, it had an excellent record in its policy towards Hitler and in what came to be known as the policy of appeasement. Our Berlin dispatches were not censored evening by evening, as were those of our *Times* colleagues, to avoid irritating Herr Hitler.

What happened was this. Ribbentrop, later to be ambassador in London, had been sent to London by Hitler on a special mission to assure British ministers, only too eager to listen, of his peaceful intentions. Lord Camrose, the proprietor of the *Daily Telegraph*, saw Ribbentrop and either showed him or told him about our article. Ribbentrop, of course, said that it was all a lot of nonsense – and Ribbentrop was believed.

On his return to Berlin, Ribbentrop invited me to lunch to try to impress me with the error of our ways. In fact he spent most of the lunch drinking in the remarks of his other guest, an egregious character called Conwell Evans, a supporter of Mosley, who delighted him with an account of the pro-German sentiments of the new monarch, Edward VIII, who had succeeded his father a few weeks earlier.

Incidentally the death of the old King in the middle of the night had given me an opportunity, which I described with glee to 'Dear Mumma', to haul out of their beds the Nazi officials I disliked most to obtain their reactions to the sad event. When I spoke to them with due solemnity, they had on such an occasion to be polite and pretend to sympathise with the British nation in its sorrow. In those days the *Daily Telegraph* had an insatiable appetite for 'reactions' from its foreign correspondents.

Even in Berlin in 1936 life was not all the tramp of armies and

126

the death of kings. Sometimes one had a glimpse of the technology of the future. On 5 March, only two days before the march into the Rhineland, I wrote to my mother: 'Dear Mumma, I had quite a nice little scoop last Sunday, when I managed to be the first Englishman ever to talk on the long-distance visual telephone. A service has been opened between Berlin and Leipzig. It's all rather disconcerting. The image is like a very early film – very flickering and jerky – but quite recognisable. As in the early talkies one didn't feel that the mouthing creature on the screen had anything to do with the words one heard on the telephone. I was quite unable to imagine that the person at the other end was seeing me. Other people, though, seemed to be taken differently. An American correspondent who was with me carefully combed his hair and straightened his tie before going to the booth. It's expected to be ten years before it will be possible to have this arrangement in private houses. But as it's got no particular practical use I should think it will remain a stunt.'

At the end of March Hitler, the Peacemaker, called on the German people to endorse his policies which, of course, they did. According to the official figures, 99 per cent of the electorate cast their votes and 98.8 per cent of these voted 'Yes'. There was enormous psychological pressure: people believed that the vote was not secret, even if it was. Perhaps it is remarkable that 540,211 people had the courage to vote against or spoil their papers. On polling day I wandered around the streets of Wedding and Neukoelln, former communist strongholds in the east end of Berlin. I reported to the *Daily Telegraph* that there were more streets unflagged than in other parts of the city but no real sign of defiance. The main impression was one of apathy.

On 4 May I wrote to my mother, 'Depressing times, but there'll be worse soon.' What came next meant the beginning of the end for Austria. On 11 July Germany and Austria signed a pact. Two Austrian Nazis entered the cabinet headed by Dr Schuschnigg and, among other provisions, all critical articles about Nazi Germany in the Austrian press were to cease. The Trojan horse was inside the gates of Vienna, and in Germany the preparations for the eventual absorption of Austria were continued. At about this time I visited the 'secret' headquarters of the Austrian legion in Bad Godesberg on the Rhine. There in an anteroom stood Nazi banners inscribed with the names of all the main cities and towns in Austria, all ready for the takeover.

127

The pace quickened. On 17 July civil war broke out in Spain. Hitler did not hesitate for a moment. Within hours he had ordered arrangements to be made for the supply to the Spanish rebels under Franco of aid in the shape of war supplies, money and men, including what was to become the Condor Air Legion. Hitler did not send enough help to ensure victory, just enough to prolong the war and provide a training ground for aircraft and tanks. In August the period of conscription in Germany was extended to two years.

Also in August Hitler enjoyed a personal triumph at the Olympic Games in Berlin. I do not believe for a moment that a boycott of the Olympic Games would have changed the course of history in the slightest. But one would have been spared the disgusting and humiliating spectacle of Hitler basking in the admiration of his foreign visitors, a sight which deeply depressed the opposition to Hitler inside Germany and encouraged him in his increasing megalomania.

At Nuremberg in September came a party rally, exceeding all its predecessors in splendour, at which Hitler announced that Goering would be in charge of a four-year plan with 'no limit on rearmament'. 'The next war,' I wrote to my mother on 16 September, 'has been brought a stage nearer.' Throughout the autumn there were exchanges of visits between Germany and Italy, and on 1 November Mussolini in a speech in Milan for the first time used the term 'axis'. The same month Germany and Japan signed the Anti-Comintern pact and the alignment of the major allies for the coming war was complete.

The emphasis on rearmament at all costs, the policy of guns before butter, began as the winter of 1936 drew near to have its effect on German standards of living. In September I wrote to 'Dear Mumma' that I expected food ration cards would soon be introduced. 'Already there's no pork or beef and there'll soon be no eggs or butter.' I was not exaggerating.

December brought the expulsion from Germany of my close friend Norman Ebbutt, the correspondent of *The Times*. 'I wonder who will be the next little nigger boy,' I wrote to my mother on 16 December. My turn was to come two and a half years later, in May 1939.

1936. That was the year that was . . .

Part Three: Home Affairs

MARGINAL COMMENTS
ROSE MACAULAY

A verdict of interest to motorists was given, by direction of the judge, at the Old Bailey the other day, when Lord de Clifford was declared not guilty of dangerous driving. As was admitted at the manslaughter trial which had preceded this, two cars had collided on the Kingston by-pass owing to one of them being driven on the wrong side of the road. The other car was on its right side of the road. and according to a police witness who had seen it pass earlier, was being driven in perfect control. The driver of this car was killed; that of the other acquitted not only of manslaughter but of dangerous driving. After a parade of mummery and pantomimery, which seems to be the fault of no one but the law of the land, and in reporting which the newspapers seem to have noticed every detail but the tragic one that an innocent man had lost his life, the defendant is acquitted on both charges, without even a suspended or an endorsed licence.

It would appear that driving on the wrong side of the road is considered by the law less dangerous than other motoring crimes for which drivers are fined, endorsed or imprisoned; less so, for example, than taking a corner too fast, for which a woman last year received a sentence of nine months. It is to be hoped that this will not encourage the practice, already far too common, of off-side driving. Selfish drivers continually drive on the crown, or over the crown, of the road; perhaps they like to feel in a position to overtake anything ahead, or to keep cars behind from overtaking them, or simply feel more comfortable there. Anyhow, as everyone knows, it is a common sin. Lord de Clifford's counsel said, at the House of Lords trial, that it was no evidence of negligence; possibly it is more often evidence of reckless selfishness, stupidity and bad manners. It seems a pity that Mr Justice Charles uttered no word of warning or disapproval of this bad habit at the Old Bailey trial. Instead, he reserved his reproof for those who had caused Lord de Clifford 'annoyance' by writing him anonymous letters. There certainly seems no reason why such letters should not be signed; but the fact that a little annoyance has been caused to a defendant otherwise so fortunate, and who has been the cause of so tragic a misfortune to others, scarcely seems worth his counsel's public complaint. In any case, Lord de Clifford, photographed walking out of court, had the air of a thoroughly happy man; perhaps a graver expression of face might have been more suitable to the circumstances but one supposes that acquitted persons do feel cheerful, whatever tragedy may have led to their trial.

The laws by which motoring offences are tried certainly seem to be in a state of confusion only matched by the traffic chaos itself. One driver may be fined and endorsed for driving at thirty-two miles an hour through a built-up area, but regularly does forty through the Parks with impunity; another for leaving his car about too long or in the wrong place, though a whole queue of unsummonsed cars surround him; another for smelling of drink; another, who runs down someone on a pedestrian crossing or drives against the traffic lights, is let off altogether. I am not sure myself (I speak as a motorist) that motoring on the public highways should not be in itself a punishable offence, and that, in a better world, it would not be so. So the confusion of our legislature in the matter is excusable. Still, it does seem clear that to drive on the wrong side of the road cannot be right.

17 January

LORD DE CLIFFORD

We understand that Lord de Clifford takes exception to certain references to him in 'Marginal Comments,' by Rose Macaulay in *The Spectator* of January 17th. The article was concerned primarily with inconsistencies in the administration of the laws affecting motorists. We regret that Lord de Clifford should regard it as directed against him personally and tender him a sincere apology for any inconvenience he may have been caused so far as that interpretation has been put on it. It is clear that Lord de Clifford was completely vindicated by his acquittal by the House of Lords and in the subsequent proceedings. Miss Macaulay associates herself unreservedly with this expression of regret.

31 January

AIR-POWER AND SEA-POWER: A NAVAL VIEW
[CAPTAIN A. C. DEWAR]

In his article in last week's *Spectator* Mr E.N.B. Bentley stated
the case for the aeroplane as against the battleship. That, however, is only a particular aspect of the general issue between
air-power and sea-power. And even on this single question the
writer of the article referred to omits quite a number of relevant
facts. For instance, in the case of the bombing of the old German
battleship 'Ostfriesland' off Virginia Capes, in July, 1921, he
slurs over some by no means minor points. First of all the 'Ostfriesland' was at anchor. Secondly, it was not a question of one
single bomb; fifty bombs of 230 to 600 lbs had already been
dropped round her, of which thirteen hit without doing vital
damage. Five big bombers then dropped four 1,000 lb bombs, of
which three hit, but failed to sink her. Finally, she was attacked
by six bigger bombers with 2,000 lb bombs, of which two ex-
ploded close to her port side. She listed to port and sank in
twenty-five minutes. It should further be noted that the 'Ostfriesland' was built about 1909, and that a modern 'blistered'
ship would not have succumbed so easily.

Nor is this the first time that the knell of the battleship has
been sounded. The torpedo boat when it appeared in 1880 was
to make an end of the battleship. It did nothing of the kind –
indeed, far less, as a Gael would say. Then about 1905 came the
submarine which Sir Percy Scott said would drive the battleship
off the sea. Once again the scurvy trade of prophecy proved
wrong. The submarine drove the battleship out to sea but could
not drive it off the seas. And more – not one single Dreadnought
battleship was sunk or even hit by a submarine in the whole
course of the late War. And even if a bomber can hit a battleship,
that does not necessarily abolish the battleship. In the late War
fourteen destroyers were sunk by mines, but that did not
diminish the utility of the destroyer, nor lead to its abolition.

Again, it is quite incorrect to say that a bomb exploding close
to a ship 'below the level of her keel' is going to break its back.
A ship's 'back' could only be broken by a charge exploding
directly under the keel, which an air-bomb obviously cannot do.
Nor is there any reason to believe that a bomb will be one bit
more destructive than a 15-inch shell. If twenty-four big shells
and one torpedo were not enough to sink the 'Seydlitz' at Jut-

land, why should one suppose that a couple of bombs are going to sink a modern 'bulged' ship? Again it is all very well to talk of swoop-dives at 350 miles per hour, but can a big bomber with two 1,000 lb bombs do gymnastics of this sort?

But, after all, these are technical points which do not affect the real issue. The real issue is not between battle-ships and bombs but between air-power and sea-power. They both have on the water a common aim – to control communications. Aircraft can exercise a potent influence in narrow seas and coastal waters. Invasion (in the old sense of the word) has become much more difficult and in face of a strong air force almost impracticable. In fact it may be said that a coastline adequately defended by aircraft is invulnerable to an attempt at landing. But air-power is limited in range and endurance. In wider and more distant waters the control of communications will depend on sea-power. The instruments of sea-power are ships of war which require bases, both for anchorage and for docking and repair.

Aircraft can attack these bases which are an adjunct of sea-power, or they can attack the warships which exercise control or the merchant ships which are the means of communication and supply. These questions all boil down to one word – geography.

Could aircraft do much against a squadron like Von Spee's in the South Atlantic? Could they have done the work of the Tenth Cruiser Squadron in the Blockade? Aircraft are strong in the vicinity of their own main bases of repair and supply, but parted from them they grow weak, for they cannot, like a ship, stop anywhere to effect repairs. On the other hand, it may be admitted that a naval base within easy air-range of an enemy would be untenable. Let us suppose the highly improbable case of hostilities between Great Britain and France. What is to become of Portsmouth, Cherbourg, Plymouth and Brest? Even if bombs did not actually hit the docks and ships, the dislocation of work caused by a constant menace would greatly reduce the utility of the base.

Three centuries of sea-power have left us with a heritage of bases whose protection used to be insured by the fleet that they served. But we must not rush to the conclusion that Portsmouth is useless. It might be untenable in the case of a war with France, but it would still retain a high degree of utility in the case of a war with, say, Patagonia. Of course, anyone who kept thinking of a war with France would be bound to think of shifting our naval bases to Ireland or Canada or the North of Scotland. There is, however, another and more economical course – not to go to war with France. Malta and Gibraltar come into the same category. Malta is some seventy miles from Italy and Gibraltar is only a few miles from Spain. But this proximity does not necessarily mean the abolition of the battleship, for the battleship would not be there. In different areas the conditions would be different. Each area must be governed by its own circumstances. The fleet would exercise control over oceanic areas and in areas not accessible to aircraft, and its control would be strengthened by means of aircraft-carriers.

The advent of air-power, then, tends to accentuate what may be called the geographical aspect of sea-power. Thirty years ago there was a tendency to regard the sea as one, but the late War showed that the North Sea was one sea and the Baltic another. There can be little doubt that a naval base within 500 miles of a big force of aircraft would tend to be unsafe for ships and the question affecting any harbour or particular area would be whether aircraft could render it untenable by ships. This will depend on the continuity of the bombing and the air-force available. To keep a port 500 miles away constantly bombed by squadrons of four 'planes would require something like 40 'planes. Again there is the wastage not only in 'planes, but men. One of the causes of the breakdown of the German submarine campaign was the loss of skilled commanders. A loss of two 'planes a day would soon reduce the bombing force to zero. On the other hand, one must remember that Dunkirk and Ostend were constantly being bombed in the late War with no decisive military effect. And even if air-power could render a particular base untenable, it must not be at once concluded that it has wiped out sea-power. The Straits of Malta is one place and the Red Sea is another.

The question of big battleships is not so much a question of bombs as of docks. There are very few docks that can take ships of 35,000 tons. Given equal constructional skill, size undoubtedly means power, but there comes a point where it also means great inconvenience and great expense. There can be little doubt that it would be very much to everyone's advantage to keep the size of battleships down to 26,000 tons, but France has already laid down two ships of 35,000 tons. War is largely a matter of competition, and this element of competition can only be eliminated by goodwill and common sense. It is very desirable to place a limit on the size of instruments of war, but this is really to place a limit on war, in which case it would be infinitely preferable to abolish it altogether, which would mean the abolition of both bombs and battleships.

24 January

MR KEYNES'S ATTACK ON ECONOMISTS
H. D. HENDERSON

The General Theory of Employment, Interest and Money, John Maynard Keynes. (Macmillan)

Mr Keynes's new book presents the reviewer with an almost insoluble problem. It is avowedly a technical book, addressed, as Mr Keynes tells us in the Preface, to his fellow-economists. Moreover, it is a very difficult technical book, involving much novel terminology, a considerable use of mathematical symbols, and above all an elaborate abstract argument which is sustained as a connected whole through more than 332 of the 384 pages. It is a book, in short, for specialists, not for the general reader. None the less the general reader will wish to know much more *about* this book than he was content to know about, say, Mr Keynes's own *Treatise on Probability*. For here is the most famous of living economists claiming to have demolished a large part of the classical theory of economics which he has himself taught for most of his life; and this classical theory, as he is careful to insist, is no esoteric affair but 'dominates the economic thought, both practical and theoretical, of the governing and academic classes of this generation, as it has for a hundred years past.' What, then, the general reader will ask, is the gist of Mr Keynes's argument and is he right or is he wrong, or is it a matter on which opinions may legitimately differ? What is the issue and on what does it turn? To answer these questions, however crudely, in a review of tolerable length, is a difficult, and perhaps a hopeless, task.

Mr Keynes accuses classical economic theory of proceeding on the assumption that the resources of production are, subject to certain qualifications, fully employed. It recognises, of course, that there may be a considerable amount of unemployment due to 'various inexactnesses of adjustment,' *e.g.*, demand may shift from the products of one set of industries to those of another, and the shifting of labour required as a consequence may be a slow and painful process. Moreover, certain modern economists, notably Professor Pigou, have argued that there may be an additional element of unemployment, if the level of wages is maintained at an unduly high level. Subject to the foregoing, classical economic theory asserts that economic forces will work so as to bring the demand for labour into equilibrium with its supply. Mr Keynes denies this, and maintains that unemployment may exist on a large scale, over and above 'frictional unemployment' and any 'voluntary unemployment,' as the result of a general deficiency of 'effective demand.' Not only may unemployment occur for this reason; it is in fact likely to occur, remedial policy apart, as the normal rule; and its scale is likely to be larger the wealthier society becomes.

To elucidate the issue, we must turn to the mysteries of savings, investment, and the rate of interest. Mr Keynes founds his argument on the 'fundamental psychological law' that the wealthier a man becomes the larger is the proportion of his income which he will seek to save. As society becomes more prosperous accordingly, the members of it will spend a diminishing proportion of their incomes on current consumption. If investment increases correspondingly, no harm is done; full employment may still be maintained. But, argues Mr Keynes, there is no reason why investment should increase correspondingly; and, if it does not, unemployment will result, the productive powers of society will not be fully employed, and its aggregate income will be diminished.

What has the classical theory to say to this? It admits, of course, that this may happen for a period, as the phenomenon of a trade depression. But it asserts that such a state of affairs is not a 'position of equilibrium,' and that there are corrective forces, which, however slowly and clumsily they may work, would prevent its indefinite continuance. It argues that, on the assumptions made, the supply of capital would exceed the demand for it in the capital market, that this would lead to a fall in the rate of interest, and that a lower rate of interest would check saving and stimulate investment until equilibrium were restored. Mr Keynes does not dispute that a lower rate of interest would stimulate investment, and that it might check saving. On the contrary, he is emphatic that a reduction in the rate of interest is, in principle, the right and essential remedy. But he denies absolutely that natural economic forces would do anything whatever to bring about a fall in the rate of interest. He denies indeed that there would be any tendency for the supply of capital to

137

exceed the demand. What would happen in the circumstances supposed is that employment would be deficient, so that aggregate incomes would decline, and the capacity to save would be diminished. It is anathema now to Mr Keynes to suggest that savings may exceed investment. *That* he insists is impossible, if the terms are correctly employed; and the point seems to have for him a more than terminological importance. The rate of interest has become for him an 'independent variable.' It is not determined, as orthodox theory argues, by the relations between the demand for and the supply of capital, but by quite different influences, namely the quantity of money 'in conjunction with liquidity preference,' *i.e.*, the extent to which people choose to keep their resources in cash or some other liquid form.

Mr Keynes has much to say about the important part that may be played by variations in 'liquidity preference,' as, for instance, by the spreading in an atmosphere of distrust of a disposition to hoard idle bank-balances; and his analysis of this matter forms in my opinion a valuable section of his book. But the possibility of such variations represents essentially a qualification of his main argument, the practical moral to which they point being the uncongenial one of the importance of maintaining 'confidence.' Subject to possible changes in this factor, it is Mr Keynes's view that the rate of interest is determined by the quantity of money made available by the Central Bank, and not in the least by whether we are a thrifty or an extravagant people. If we are unduly thrifty we shall have heavy unemployment as a normal state of affairs; if we are sufficiently extravagant, we may maintain 'full employment'; but it will make no difference in either case to the rate of interest. This is the real crux of the controversy; and it is here, in my judgement, that Mr Keynes fails to make out his case.

I should formulate as follows the answer of the classical school. They would agree that over a short-period monetary conditions exercise an important influence on the rate of interest and a dominating influence upon short-term rates. They would point out that depression and heavy unemployment will serve (subject to 'liquidity' complications) to bring about conditions of abundant bank-money, so that the natural corrective forces, though they may work far less smoothly than used to be supposed, are none the less really there. On the other hand, they would insist, the influence of changes in the quantity of money on the rate of interest is purely transitional. Other things (including the state of 'liquidity preference') being equal, an increase in the quantity of money, operating through the medium of lower interest-rates, will be set in motion a tendency towards higher commodity prices, this will involve an increased use of money, and when prices have reached a level appropriate to the increased quantity of money, the complicating influence, so to speak, of money will be removed, and the more fundamental factors of the supply of capital, arising from the capacity and propensity to save, and the demand for capital, arising from the opportunities for investment, will resume their sway as the determinants of the rate of interest. There is nothing that Mr Keynes has to say in his chapters on prices and wages which seems to me in any way destructive of this explanation; and though it may seem to the general reader in some respects remote from reality, this is due to the great short-term importance of those complications about changes in 'liquidity preference' which qualify Mr Keynes's main assertions as much as those of the classical school.

Much of what Mr Keynes has written in this book is a real and much-needed contribution to short-term economic analysis. But, as I have indicated, the practical implications of what he has to contribute in this field are of a conservative nature which is distasteful to him; and I suspect that it is largely a conflict between his desires and his intellectual apprehensions in the short-term sphere that has led him to undertake so fierce an offensive against classical long-term theory. It is true, in my judgement, that the long-term morals of the economic troubles of recent years are different (and decidedly less conservative) from the short-term ones. But it is unnecessary, in order to establish them, to discard the classical theory of economics for a brand-new system of thought.

14 February

THE FUTURE OF THE B.B.C.
[GORONWY REES]

The Report of the Ullswater Committee on Broadcasting is as complimentary as the B.B.C. could have wished; and the Committee's recommendations are intended not to criticise but to strengthen the policy which the B.B.C. has followed in the past, with a success that everyone must recognise. The Committee proposes that the Charter should be prolonged for a further ten years; that Parliamentary control should be exercised through a Cabinet Minister free from heavy Departmental duties; that the B.B.C. should receive a larger share of licensing revenues; that relay exchanges should be controlled by the Post Office; that the staff should be as free as possible from interference in their private lives; and that 'sponsored' items should continue to be excluded from the programmes. Somewhat irrationally, the Committee also recommends that, in the early stages of television broadcasting, 'sponsored' items should be admitted. The Governors of the B.B.C. have noted 'with gratification' the compliments paid to their administration and finance, and to their News and Empire Services, and the 'absence of valid criticism of programme policy.' They emphasise the Committee's flattering phrases on their wisdom, independence, idealism, prudence and 'intellectual and ethical integrity.' Thus the Governors, and the Committee, like everyone else, are satisfied that the B.B.C.'s monopoly of broadcasting has fully justified itself and must be continued in the future.

There is no need to praise again the virtues of the B.B.C.; they are too well known. But is the note of self-satisfaction not a little too strong? The News Service, for instance, and especially the Second News, does not fulfil its function of giving a clear and simple summary of the events of the day. It is confused with commentaries and interludes which are presumably meant to give entertainment value to news which is itself, unfortunately, already exciting enough. Again, that $33\frac{1}{3}$ per cent of the B.B.C.'s programme time is taken up with 'light music' of low quality suggests that there may be, after all, 'valid criticism of programme policy,' and it is surprising that the B.B.C. does not relieve us of this surfeit, either by devoting the time of only one station to 'light music,' or by always offering an alternative form of education or entertainment in other programmes. The Committee urges an extension and development of regional broadcasting and especially the establishment of a Welsh station. The Governors reply that a Welsh station would have already been established, 'if it were technically possible.' Does this mean that the technical difficulties cannot be overcome and that the Welsh will never have their station, so much desired? Lastly, the Committee makes the excellent recommendation that, to avoid political distortion, all material coming from Government sources should be announced as such, and it is to be hoped that this recommendation will be applied in its widest sense, and not merely, as the Governors assume, to announcements made at the Government's request.

It is a tribute to the B.B.C. that these criticisms apply only to points of detail; but that is perhaps because the Committee's Report does not raise any fundamental questions. It may be unfortunate, considering the extension of the Charter and the extension and development of the Corporation's services which are recommended for the future, that the Committee has not attempted a closer analysis of the Corporation's policy and position. The Committee, like everyone else, is agreed that the Corporation's independence and impartiality must be maintained. But, like the Governors, it assumes too easily that impartiality is an ideal which can be realised by human beings. It is, strictly, impossible that the B.B.C. should approach impartially the problems it must face. Like everyone else, they must make decisions of policy and of attitude. Equally, it is impossible that, in fifteen years, so strong and decided a character as the Controller-General should not have impressed a certain attitude and personality upon the Corporation under his control. Indeed, unless he had, he could not have succeeded so well.

The B.B.C. has a personality of its own, pervasive and unmistakable, and it affects it reactions to public events, to education, to entertainment, and to the arts: it is the foundation of its policy. Yet, while criticism of that policy is made in detail, its general trend, its objective, is not discussed or made public. It is not sufficient to answer that the B.B.C. aims to preserve 'intellectual and ethical integrity,' or to 'raise' public taste or to 'educate' or 'entertain' its audience. 'Education' or 'entertainment' are terms which can have as many senses as there are ideals to aim at. The B.B.C. has formed, if only vaguely, its ideal, it has a mission, but we do not know what it is, though we may guess. If the ideal were known, subsidiary issues, such as, for instance, the problem of Sunday programmes, would resolve themselves: certainly both appreciation and criticism would be easier. And the B.B.C. cannot merely respond to public demand, for it is agreed that the Corporation must educate as well as entertain. The Corporation is empowered, and the Committee approves, to extend its educational activities in the schools as well as the home. In the next ten years the B.B.C., with its influence increased by television, will be, as it has been, perhaps the most powerful single influence upon the minds of men, women, and children. Neither the Report of the Ullswater

141

Committee, excellent as it is in detail, nor the observations of the Governors enable us to control that influence properly, because they do not tell us what it is, what it intends to be, or what ideal or objective it aims at.

20 March

MARGINAL COMMENTS
ROSE MACAULAY

Continuing my investigations into entertaining human activities, I attended last Sunday evening a 'Rally' of British Fascists at the Albert Hall, only to reflect again and as usual, what a piece of work is man, and what an odder piece still is a crowd. The floor of the hall had apparently been reserved for impassioned Fascists, and very obediently these did their stuff. We began with some songs (or hymns, perhaps, is the word) about vested powers, Marxian lies, Moscow-rented agitators, Red Front, and the massed ranks of reaction. One line stated that 'the streets are still,' which was, at the moment, not noticeably the case. After the songs, THE LEADER ENTERS, said the programme. And Enter he did, heralded by a procession of banners, rolling drums, and blasting trumpets, and lackeyed by an attendant beam of spot-light (mauve). Between massed ranks of his frenzied approvers, the Leader proceeded up the hall to the platform, wearing an air of exalted uplift which he maintained despite a sudden derisive laugh which broke out from somewhere in the hall. The whole business had a comically histrionic air.

Then (said the programme) THE LEADER SPEAKS. And Speak the Leader did, for two solid hours. It was the old familiar fascery and tushery, such stuff as Blackshirt dreams are made on: how, when We come into power, we shall stop all this talking at Westminster, ally, on highly advantageous terms, with the other Fascist States and with Japan, and break and exile British communists and Jews. At every reference to British Jews, Sir Oswald appeared to experience a considerable and painful excitement; he cried out, he gestured, he pointed. The affair became more and more like a violent revivalist meeting of Holy Rollers, Shakers, or what not. The Fascist part of the audience, answering hysteria with hysteria, responded with frenzied applause. Crowds are like that. If anyone shouts to them with enough repetition, vehemence, and spot-light that any section of persons, such as

Jews, Christians, landlords, lawyers, soldiers, pacifists, witches, Germans, French, or Portuguese, are the cause of all their troubles and must be punished, it seems that they will believe and applaud. Thus are set afoot hunts after old women, spies, aliens, Protestants, Roman Catholics, and those who differ from the huntsmen in politics or race. Crowds have the half-ludicrous, half-sinister suggestibility of the pack, who may be sent by the huntsman's word after any quarry. One felt, woe to any Jew who should that night cross the path of that applauding mob. And yet, taken singly, most of them were probably the ordinary, stupid, kindly Briton, who can be persuaded of anything.

Those who had come to see disturbances were rewarded by several somewhat violent ejections. Heckling by political opponents is obviously not part of what We mean to allow. Definitely, We do not believe in free speech. This is one of the great differences between Us and the old effete constitutional parties. At the end of the meeting, the audience were invited to send up questions to be answered. Many did so; but only a few were answered. Like other examination candidates, Sir Oswald apparently selected the easy ones. People near me sent up questions about freedom, British tolerance, and so on: these were overlooked. The reply I liked best, following as it did the diatribe against Jews was, We believe in complete tolerance of all religious sects.

Certainly an odd meeting. I suggested lately that we might go to it for entertainment. But I was wrong. It was too like a meeting in a mental home for that.

27 March

FOOD STORAGE AND DEFENCE
FRANCIS GOWER

At a time when, unhappily, defence considerations are necessarily occupying so prominent a place in the public mind, it is imperative that food supplies in relation to defence should be closely considered. There may be doubts as to the value of the 35,000-ton battleship, controversy may rage over the relative claims upon the public purse of the three fighting services, but after the experience of the Great War there can be no hesitation in placing the question of food supplies high upon the list of defence factors. Since the War science may have greatly improved our methods for combating the submarine, but in any future war hostile aircraft may prove as serious a threat upon the sea-lanes converging upon British ports as did the submarine in 1916 and 1917.

It is sometimes claimed that these islands produce half the food required by the population, but this is an estimate based on values and not on quantities, and the high relative value of milk, eggs, home-killed meat, vegetables and the soft fruits distorts the picture. The United Kingdom has to import over 70 per cent of its wheat, about 50 per cent of its meat and cheese, over 80 per cent of its butter, and the great bulk of its sugar and animal feeding-stuffs.

To obtain greater security in time of war, two courses of action, apart from direct defence measures, are possible. One is to decrease the urgency of the punctual arrival of food-laden ships by having recourse to food storage, the other to increase national food production. Both methods can be adopted, but the first has the advantage of being relatively simple, in that the increase of the actual stocks of the non-perishable foods within the country would be rapidly achieved.

The Board of Trade returns show that of the foods imported for men and animals (and both are almost equally important) wheat, maize and sugar are far and away the most considerable in terms of quantity. In 1935 we imported 101,000,000 cwts of wheat, 59,000,000 cwts of maize and 38,000,000 cwts of sugar. These three commodities taken together represented six times the weight of all imported meats, including bacon, and ten times the weight of imported dairy products.

It is fortunately unnecessary for our defence authorities to contemplate the complete stoppage of sea-borne trade, but constant interruption involving the loss of many cargoes of food must be guarded against. If stocks of wheat, maize and sugar could be raised to a level guaranteeing supplies for the entire country for a considerable period, it is clear that the whole defence position would be immensely improved. Fortunately, wheat, maize and sugar are all capable of being stored for relatively long periods without deterioration. Since wheat is the most important of the three, it is as well to consider the position in relation to that. Recent answers to Parliamentary questions have indicated that existing accommodation for wheat storage at the ports is sufficient for 1,500,000 tons, but that at the present time only some 215,000 tons of wheat are actually in store. On the other hand, it has been estimated that over the last three years the total stocks of wheat and flour in the country have on August 1st (the end of the crop year) varied between 900,000 and 1,000,000 tons. The difference is probably due to stocks held by millers at country mills and possibly also to flour at bakers.

The total annual consumption of wheat and flour is roughly 7,000,000 tons. It therefore appears that if port stores were filled and internal stocks maintained at their average levels the country would secure between three and four months supply without having to build new elevators.

Reasonable security, however, demands that the stocks in the country should be sufficient for longer than that – say six months. To achieve this increased storage facilities would be necessary, but the cost would not be high in comparison with the freedom from anxiety and the strategical elasticity which the possession of such stocks would confer upon the Admiralty and the Air Ministry. It has been estimated in Canada that with wheat at its present level of prices the cost of storing wheat is about 10 per cent of its cost per annum. If it is asumed that the normal stocks of wheat and flour carried in this country are 1,000,000 tons, then the annual cost of increasing this figure to 3,500,000 tons would be in the region of £1,150,000, apart from the capital cost of erecting new elevators. When this figure is contrasted with the cost of new naval construction it will be realised at once how comparatively cheap it would be to provide sufficiently adequate storage facilities to relieve the defence authorities from overwhelming anxiety on this score.

The selection of the grain for this purpose is important. Wheats differ considerably in their behaviour in storage. The main factor is dryness. English or Continental wheats harvested in the normal weather of a European August contain too much moisture to store well. The hard Canadian or the dry Australian wheats are much more suitable. It would, of course, be necessary to arrange a constant turning over of the stocks in store. Millers would need to draw their supplies from the wheat in stock, and the newly arrived wheat would be used to take the place of the quantities thus removed. The machinery for such arrangements need present little difficulty, since the milling industry is in few hands, three organisations now buying about 70 per cent of the wheat sold for milling purposes.

Although English wheat is not well suited for long storage yet one method of increasing available stocks would be to arrange that Government assistance to the wheat farmer should be modified so as to give an inducement to the farmer to hold his wheat in stock for a longer period than at present, thus spreading the marketing of the home-grown crop over the whole year. The arrangements for maize and sugar need present no greater difficulties than for wheat. To maintain six months' supply of these three commodities would not cost more than the price of a single modern cruiser, while the existence of the stocks might well prove equivalent to a dozen cruisers in time of war.

There is another method of increasing the country's food supplies which must not be overlooked. The public conscience has recently been stirred over the question of adequate nutrition. There is general agreement that public health would be greatly improved if the consumption of the protective foods, particularly of milk, could be greatly increased. To raise milk consumption in the United Kingdom to the levels regarded as desirable by modern science would demand an increase in dairy herds of some 1,500,000 cows. Apart from the desirability of such a development from a health standpoint, the defence aspects should not be overlooked. An addition of 1,500,000 cows would mean that in the event of war the country would have an additional 450,000 tons of beef available on the hoof, a quantity almost equal to the total annual imports of chilled beef.

Under present international conditions the case for increasing national food supplies is overwhelmingly strong, and if, as appears probable, this defensive policy could be made to promote the peace-time interests of Great Britain and of the Empire the case for its adoption is unanswerable.

17 April

OCCASIONAL BIOGRAPHIES: MR CHAMBERLAIN
[ROBERT BERNAYS]

'A good Mayor of Birmingham in a lean year' – that is said to have been Mr Lloyd George's summary of the capacities of the Chancellor of the Exchequer, who introduced his fifth consecutive Budget in the House of Commons on Tuesday. How far is such an estimate accurate? The answer is of considerable importance, for Mr Neville Chamberlain is not merely this year's Chancellor of the Exchequer but may quite well be next year's Prime Minister. There is now little doubt that if Mr Baldwin resigns after the Coronation it will be Mr Neville Chamberlain whom he will recommend the King to summon to Downing Street in his place. Sir Samuel Hoare's chance disappeared in the Hoare-Laval fiasco and Mr Runciman's hopes, always slender, vanished altogether when his father accepted a peerage at the age of eighty-six. Mr Neville Chamberlain has now no rivals in the field.

Mr Lloyd George's gibe has at any rate this basis in fact, that Mr Neville Chamberlain came, like his father, into political life from the Council House in Birmingham. Joseph Chamberlain made two great contributions in his political life – to his native city and to the Empire. It was therefore not unnatural that he should set his two sons on those paths. Austen, the elder, came into Parliament to work for the Empire's unity at the age of twenty-seven, and Neville the younger remained in Birmingham. Neville Chamberlain had, it is true, a brief apprenticeship to business life in the West Indies, but he was soon back in the Midland city managing the great screw business on which the Chamberlain fortune was built and throwing himself with all his father's energy into municipal affairs. He became in turn chairman of the Town Planning Committee, Alderman, and in 1915 Lord Mayor. In all of these positions he proved himself a competent administrator, but in none of them did he display such talents as would make men say that what Birmingham had gained, the British nation and the Empire had lost. At the age of forty-five he was chief citizen of Birmingham but nothing more.

His chance came in 1916 when he was made Director-General of National Service. But he was not a success there. His powers, like those of Lord Eustace Percy lately, were ill-defined, and like Lord Eustace he developed no talent for making his job important. A year later he resigned. He was not included in the Coalition Government of 1918, and for four years he remained a diffident and quite undistinguished figure on the back benches. In 1922 came his second chance. The Coalition Government was struck down by Mr Baldwin, and with it went the elder Chamberlain and Mr Lloyd George, Lord Birkenhead, Sir Robert Horne, in fact all who had dominated politics in the critical post-War years. Mr Bonar Law formed a Government which was described irreverently by Lord Birkenhead as that of 'the second class brains.' It was considered at the time peculiarly appropriate that in that Government, in which Austen Chamberlain had no place, should be included as Postmaster-General his still obscure younger brother.

147

But it was the turning point in Neville Chamberlain's political life. His political career was now really launched. The following year Mr Bonar Law died, and was succeeded by Mr Baldwin. Immediately there sprang up a close political friendship between these two business men from the Midlands. It soon had far-reaching repercussions. In the autumn of 1923 Mr Baldwin went to Plymouth to address the annual Conference of the Conservative Party, and announced to a bewildered but delighted assembly that he could not, as Prime Minister, face another winter of unemployment without a mandate from the electorate to protect the home market. Many reasons have been adduced for this startling decision. It has been suggested that Mr Baldwin made his announcement without consultation with his Cabinet colleagues, that he was indulging in his familiar habit of thinking aloud, that he had no idea that his statement would precipitate an election.

It was in fact no accidental or happy-go-lucky decision. It had been deliberately planned, and its real author was not Baldwin but Neville Chamberlain. The moment that the Conservative Government had been formed, Chamberlain had made it his one consuming object to unite the Party forces still shattered by the wreck of the Coalition. He realised that no strong Government could be formed which did not include the two great Conservative figures of the Coalition, then in isolation. He conceived that one bold act would bring them together – an appeal to the country on tariffs. Secret gatherings took place at Chequers. Baldwin was won over to the Chamberlain view and an election was decreed.

It proved disastrous, for the Conservative Party was fairly and squarely beaten. But the following year Mr Baldwin was back in office again and Neville Chamberlain's dream was achieved, for the new Government included Mr Churchill as Chancellor of the Exchequer, Lord Birkenhead as Secretary of State for India, and Sir Austen Chamberlain went to the Foreign Office. Neville Chamberlain himself became Minister of Health, and began to show for the first time his supreme competence as an administrator. With consummate skill he piloted the far-reaching but highly complicated and controversial De-rating Bill on to the statute-book. For better or for worse it has changed the whole face of Local Government. He began to develop, too, a trenchant style. Old Parliamentary hands noted with delight that 'Neville had something of "Joe" about him' in the way that, on occasion, he could castigate the Socialist Opposition. He was, in fact, one of the outstanding successes of that rather unimpressive and dreary administration.

In the National Government he has gone from strength to strength. His administration of the Treasury has been accompanied by the slow but steady progress of the national credit from the edge of the abyss. His budgets have reflected his essential character. There has been nothing showy or startling about them. They have been one and all cautious, capable and reassuring. Neville Chamberlain has his severe limitations. His name is associated with no great stroke of statesmanship nor one single original idea. Undoubtedly he got the worst of the bargain at Ottawa, and one of the urgent tasks of the Imperial Conference which will meet in 1937 will be to revise much of the work to which he set his seal four years ago. At the World Economic Conference he propounded no plan of action. The world waited in vain for a gesture of leadership. On currency issues he sheltered behind Roosevelt and the American crisis, and though he announced that 'the root of our present economic ills lies in the decline of our export trade' he propounded no policy to improve the situation.

He is not in any sense a platform man. In public he seems cold and unsympathetic, more like the chairman of a municipal committee anxious to keep down the rates than a leader of the nation. Even in the House of Commons he appears aloof and slightly magisterial. Apart from Mr Baldwin he has few friends even among his colleagues, and the back-benchers hardly know him at all, for he is not easily approachable in the Lobby and seldom, if ever, visits the smoking-room. He jokes with difficulty. I recall a dreadful occasion when in his Budget statement in 1932 he referred to the longevity of men with great fortunes that would one day fall into the maw of the Treasury by means of Death Duties, and addressed them in the rather brutal words of the Duke of Wellington to his troops: 'Come on, you rascals, you cannot live for ever.' His humour on the rare occasion that he employs it is self-conscious and studied and rather tasteless, like that of a man striving to be the life and soul of a funeral party.

Yet with all these drawbacks he is the one man on the Government Front Bench today who could take charge in a crisis. He has a real relish for the cut-and-thrust of debate. I have watched him through a stormy all-night sitting calm, unruffled, a slightly contemptuous smile on his face, while the steady stream of insult and invective flowed upon him from the Socialist benches, and then rising to speak equipped with the succinct and smashing answer. He is quite fearless. No Parliamentary attack can daunt him, and I am certain that the international situation, however much it may worsen, will never unnerve him. He will never bend to pressure or play for cheap applause. If the country has to be told further unpalatable truths and required to shoulder in the future fresh burdens to pay for increased armaments he will not shirk his task. He has that vital quality in modern statesmen – the courage to tell democracy the truth. Neville Chamberlain is no Gladstone or Disraeli, nor even an Asquith, but he is far more than 'a good Lord Mayor of Birmingham in a lean year.' He is, in fact, the model of the middle-class business man – capable, diligent, upright, and with a high sense of public duty. It may well be that he is just the type of man that the country needs in these sombre days when the clouds darken and the storms approach.

24 April

THE CASE FOR MR BALDWIN
[ROBERT BERNAYS]

There is a widespread feeling, to judge by the Popular Press, that Mr Baldwin has exhausted his usefulness to the State, that he has lost his grip on National affairs, that he has no longer the power to make decisions, that in the few months since his triumphs at the Election he has suddenly become an old man, and that his retirement to his Worcestershire orchards, for which he so frequently and so engagingly sighs, is already overdue. What is the truth of it all?

Mr Baldwin is certainly very tired. It is not surprising. He has been in office now since the August of 1931. Though he has only held the Premiership for a year of that time, he has had the ultimate responsibility for the direction of affairs during the whole of the period as leader of the Conservative Party which controlled the Government. He has piloted the country through the financial crisis; it has been his task to meet and beat the formidable opposition of the Diehards on the India Bill; he has made himself responsible for drastic measures of rearmament, and he has led his followers twice to overwhelming victory at the polls.

He has certainly earned his rest. Ought he to take it? If he goes the only man who could possibly take his place is Mr Neville Chamberlain. By the law of compensations, Mr Chamberlain has every right to the Premiership. His father never held supreme office, though next to Gladstone he was probably the most outstanding Parliamentary figure of his generation; and his half-brother, Sir Austen, has on at least two occasions through adventitious circumstances missed the prize. There is no doubt that sooner or later Mr Chamberlain is bound to succeed to 10 Downing Street, but there is in my opinion no justification for hastening the event.

For with Mr Baldwin will go much more than a successful Prime Minister. For more than a dozen years Mr Baldwin has fought with remarkable success against those influences in Conservatism which would make of it a class party, narrow in outlook and wedded to the support of indefensible vested interests. He has made it his object on almost every occasion to represent the Left Wing tendencies of his followers and to fight for them against all the powerful influences of the Right. The result has been that the Party under his direction has always inclined to the Left Centre and his Governments on the whole have maintained themselves in the middle of the road. He has given to his countrymen that stability combined with social progress without which Great Britain might well be enduring today some of the internal disturbances and convulsions of her neighbours.

He has always succeeded in securing a broad-bottomed administration which, though it has never excited the country, has never driven it to seek refuge in extreme Socialism with its inevitable concomitant, a swing back to bleak reaction. Like Halifax in Queen Anne's day, he has 'kept the country on an even keel.'

Even his most resolute opponents would probably agree with these tributes, but they would go on to argue that he is now a spent force. I can see very little evidence of this in the House of Commons. There is no truth, for instance, in the suggestion, openly made now, that Mr Baldwin is deaf. It was only necessary to watch him last week, in the absence of Mr Eden at Geneva, answering fifty questions and as many supplementaries from all parts of the House to expose its absurdity. He has shown once again both in his manner in the House of Commons and his speech at the Albert Hall that the reserves of strength that he can always count upon in an emergency are not by any means exhausted. The mere sight of him calms a storm. He stands at the despatch-box in the House of Commons or at the flag-draped table of a public meeting with that air of quiet and confident authority that impresses his followers with the conviction that he is still, however slack and easy-going he may seem when times are good, master of a situation in a crisis.

He is criticised for being slow to appreciate the peril in which Great Britain's relative state of disarmament had placed her and to have been dilatory in taking the necessary measures to meet it. I do not believe that the country would have consented to rearmament a moment before it was finally taken in hand. It had to be convinced beyond a shadow of a doubt by the stark logic of events that all hope of an agreement for a general reduction of armaments must be abandoned and that the only hope of security lay in repairing, at whatever cost, the gaps in our defences. Had a man of the calibre and outlook of Mr Churchill been in charge of the Government, the electors would have recoiled in horror and indignation at the very idea of building up a vast air force. But no man or woman in their senses would regard Mr Baldwin as a man of war. When he at length announced that rearmament on a large scale was imperative, and disclosed in his attractive fireside manner on the wireless the processes of thought that had led him to this irresistible conclusion, the country realised that the issue could no longer be burked and gave him the largest majority ever accorded to a Prime Minister asking for a second reign of office for a Government that had already enjoyed a long period of power.

Mr Baldwin has not half the intellectual equipment of Asquith, but he does possess the power that Asquith exhibited in the zenith of his strength of commanding national confidence. He has too, in a remarkable degree, softened the asperities of political life. There was truth in Lord Winterton's recent observation, though it was said in jest, that in comparison with the pre-War debates the fiercest political scene in our own time is 'a pleasant Sunday afternoon, with the dear Vicar in the chair.' 'Give peace in our time, O Lord,' Mr Baldwin said on a famous occasion when in his second premiership he was seeking to hold back his followers from an unwarranted and vindictive attack on the Trades Unions. He may not always have been faithful to that vision. To translate fine dreams into realities requires an energy and a drive and a constructive statesmanship that not even Mr Baldwin's firmest friends could say were his essential characteristics. But though he has not had the power to fashion a world nearer the heart's desire, he has had the will to do it and when all his failures have been taken into account, his Party under his leadership has carried out more social reforms than at any period in our history since Disraeli. The result has been that the gulf of parties, instead of widening as seemed likely in the first tumultuous post-War years, has lessened. Again and again I have seen in the House of Commons the Trade Union Members nodding their heads, no doubt unconsciously, in agreement with Mr Baldwin as he makes one of his broad surveys of international or industrial affairs.

Such a man with all his shortcomings can ill be spared at this time. Admittedly he has made mistakes which would have made resignation for a lesser man inevitable. He misinformed the House on the grave issue of the extent of German rearmament in the air. The original acceptance of the Hoare-Laval proposals within a month of an election fought on the maintenance of the Covenant of the League was a lamentable affair. He must have had a very uncomfortable half-hour when Sir Austen Chamberlain, almost the synonym of political loyalty, upbraided him for these blunders. But he remains on the Front Bench as permanent-looking as one of his Worcestershire oaks, and few but those who would benefit by his removal would have him uprooted.

Napoleon, when the qualifications of one of his Generals were submitted to him, used to reply: 'But is he lucky?' Mr Baldwin is essentially a lucky politician. Political parties do not easily dispense with such a man. Above all, men realise that he means more abroad than any man who might take his place. I remember Mr Eden telling me once that there was no surer way of convincing French statesmen that the British Government was opposed to a certain course of action than to say that Mr Baldwin would not stand for it. He has seldom extended his travels beyond Aix-les-Bains and has therefore all the fascination of a legendary figure. To Germany, too, he represents the solid, sturdy Englishman, the embodiment of all our traditions of independence and age-long security. They realise there that in him is represented all that is fine and most formidable in the English character. He remains the great pillar of decency and democracy in a reeling world. His countrymen would do well to keep him as long as he feels able to do them service.

22 May

DICTATORSHIP IN ULSTER
[R. C. K. ENSOR]

The official reply which the Government of Northern Ireland has made to the report of a commission appointed by the National Council for Civil Liberties, to enquire into the nature and working of the Special Powers Acts in Northern Ireland, increases rather than diminishes the force of the commission's findings, for it leaves the principal strictures undiscussed. The report, it is true, discloses a state of things very difficult for anyone to defend. When the Government of Northern Ireland set up house originally, it was confronted, of course, with the terrorism of the Irish Republican Army, a body which organised murder and called it war. The rest of Ireland had for years been convulsed by it, and remained so for some years after. In such circumstances the Protestant community of Northern Ireland, fighting with its back to the wall, was constrained to take, through its Government, strong emergency measures to secure life and property and crush the murder-clubs. It may be that the Special Powers Act of 1922 did not at the time go beyond what the circumstances warranted; at any rate one would be chary of criticising men who had the formidable responsibility of keeping the peace in a great city like Belfast, and who did, against vast obstacles, win through. The gravamen of the charge in the report is different. It is that an emergency system has been retained in force long after the emergency has ended; and that temporary despotic controls over the lives and rights of citizens, justifiable, perhaps, during a state of siege, have been allowed to ossify into a permanent tyranny exercised by faction-leaders over the rest of the community.

The decisive step in the transformation was taken in 1933. From 1922 to 1928 the Special Powers Act was avowedly temporary, and came up for renewal every year. An Act of 1928 renewed it for five years. But in 1933 it was prolonged indefinitely – 'until Parliament otherwise determines.' No doubt the alarm created by Mr de Valera's rule in Southern Ireland rendered this possible. But it cannot justify it; since any temporary disorders which might have been occasioned (but in fact were not) could still have been adequately dealt with under a temporary measure.

In point of fact the original measure of 1922, so far from

having been in any way relaxed, has been progressively stiffened and supplemented. This has been done through the power conferred on the Home Minister of the Northern Government to make new Regulations, which have the same validity as the thirty Regulations originally scheduled to the Act. The power has been used extensively, and down to recent dates. The legislature of Northern Ireland retained no right to disallow a Regulation; it can only *petition* that it be revoked, the actual decision resting with the executive. Thus it has effected an almost complete delegation of its law-making power to the executive, within a sphere defined as 'the preservation of peace and maintenance of order,' and the modification of the Regulations themselves. Can this be squared with the United Kingdom's Act of 1920, whereby the Parliament at Westminster devolved such powers as it did devolve in Northern Ireland upon the elected representatives of the people? The Commissioners, all of whose members save one were lawyers, regard the constitutional point as doubtful.

Meantime the Home Minister enjoys practically unlimited power to govern by decree. Next, he has unlimited power to delegate his authority. The arbitrary courses which he is entitled to take may equally be taken in his name by anyone whom he designates. They are in fact taken by departmental officials and by officers of the police. The Act and its supplements create a large number of offences additional to those under the ordinary law, and drastic penalties are provided, including in some cases death and flogging. Despite the number and variety of charges which may thus be brought, the Act contains an amazing provision against the unforeseeable. Section 2 (4) runs:

> 'If any person does any act of such a nature as to be calculated to be prejudicial to the preservation of the peace or maintenance of order in Northern Ireland and not specifically provided for in the regulations, he shall be deemed to be guilty of an offence against the regulations.'

On this the report very justly comments that it not only gives the executive *carte blanche* to prosecute anybody (however innocent of crime) whose activities it may dislike, but it violates the foundations of public law. 'In countries where the rule of law prevails it is recognised by all jurists that no man may be prosecuted and punished unless for the contravention of some specific provision of the criminal law.'

155

Besides being enabled to convict a prisoner without proving a specific offence, the Home Minister is given the right to detain or intern persons for an indefinite period without trial. In the view of the Commission, 'the effect of these Regulations is completely to abrogate the principles of Habeas Corpus,' and 'coupled with the disestablishment of the rule of laws in the Six Counties puts the executive in a position paralleled only by continental dictatorships.' Further, the police are given power to arrest without warrant upon suspicion, to search premises without warrant, to stop and search persons and vehicles anywhere, to stop and interrogate any person, and to seize property. When it is added that these and other drastic powers belong not to the Royal Ulster Constabulary only, but extend to the multitude of auxiliary lay police known as the B Specials and drawn from the Government's most fanatical partisans, some idea may be formed of how the whole system works out.

What does the coercion amount to in practice? The answer to that depends to some extent on the credibility of witnesses. The report gives details of stringent repression exercised by the Government against both political and economic movements. But the Acts carry their own condemnation in their text. Such legislation might be defended as a sort of martial law during a state of siege. As permanent mechanism for the Government of part of the United Kingdom it is beyond any defence at all.

29 May

IS MR THOMAS GUILTY?
[WILSON HARRIS]

The findings of what may conveniently be termed the Budget Tribunal have been received with some surprise and some uneasiness; with surprise, because it had been generally assumed by men of average intelligence who read the full reports of the evidence day by day that while the Tribunal would inevitably find proof of a leakage it could hardly be in a position definitely to incriminate any particular individual; with uneasiness, because no one is happy to see a man hanged on circumstantial evidence, and though Mr Thomas is not being hanged his public life is ended as completely as if he were, and that as the result of findings which are avowedly no more than inferential. Those findings are, none the less, categorically expressed. Twice in identical terms Mr Justice Porter and his colleagues affirm unequivocally that 'there was an unauthorised disclosure by Mr J. H. Thomas' in the one case to Mr Bates, in the other to Sir Alfred Butt, 'of information relating to the Budget for the present year,' and it is added that in each case the recipient of the information made use of the information for his private gain. If Mr Bates and Sir Alfred Butt had produced letters from Mr Thomas stating in black and white that income-tax was to be raised by threepence and tea-duty by twopence the verdict could not have been more uncompromising.

Yet so far from that, Mr Bates and Sir Alfred Butt swore that Mr Thomas made no disclosure to them, and though the Tribunal characterises them both as unreliable witnesses, it uses the evidence of both of them to incriminate Mr Thomas. Mr Thomas declared repeatedly on oath that he made no disclosure of any kind regarding the Budget to anyone, and pointed out with some force that he was well schooled in keeping Budget secrets, having heard the contents of nine Budgets disclosed to Cabinets of which he was a member. He can claim, moreover, that the moment he heard his name and his son's were being mentioned in connexion with a rumoured Budget leakage he went immediately, first to the Prime Minister and then to the Chancellor of the Exchequer, to insist on a searching investigation into the whole business. No evidence was adduced specifically alleging a disclosure by Mr Thomas, the only two approaches to that consisting of a piece of irresponsible hearsay and an unwarrantable inference which threw light on nothing but the state of mind of the witness from whom it emanated. In view of this has Mr Thomas, who since the issue of the report has reiterated his complete innocence, reason to complain of the Tribunal's findings?

The answer to that must depend on the weight attached to circumstantial evidence and the confidence reposed in the personnel of the Tribunal. As to circumstantial evidence, it is inevitable that, unsatisfactory as it is, nothing else is available in certain classes of case, particularly in the divorce-court, and if it were ruled out many manifestly guilty persons would escape punishment. If, in this case, Mr Thomas did in fact violate his Privy Councillor's oath and improperly disclose official information it is hardly to be assumed that he would treat the oath taken in the witness-box with greater respect. Other witnesses who by the findings of the Tribunal are credited with guilty knowledge which they used for their own gain were under much the same temptation to add perjury to their previous offence. As to the personnel of the Tribunal, there is no need to say more than that the members of the Court amply merit the universal admiration they have won by the ability and scrupulous justice with which they have conducted a singularly difficult enquiry, in which circumstances forced them at times almost into the attitude of prosecutor. Their report deserves equal commendation. The evidence could not have been more comprehensively reviewed or more skilfully marshalled. The Court not only heard the evidence – in that it had little advantage over the newspaper-reader, who was provided with what were almost verbatim reports daily – but also saw it given, and twice in the report occur the significant words 'we, having heard the witnesses and observed their demeanour ...' Undue importance can no doubt be attached to a witness's behaviour in the box, but an experienced judge and two able counsels are not in danger of overstressing this factor. We may confidently accept their valuation of the witnesses.

The processes of reasoning by which the Tribunal arrives at its findings are impressive. It had two questions to answer – whether there had been a Budget leakage, and if so by whom an unauthorised disclosure had been made. The evidence of the vice-chairman of Lloyd's and others left no room for doubt that a leakage had taken place. If so the delinquent must have been a Cabinet Minister or a civil servant. The Court was satisfied on the evidence that the Civil Service was blameless. Among Cabinet Ministers one alone was pointed at, though it is fair to Mr J. H. Thomas to remember that his name was first mentioned in connexion with the operations of his son, Mr Leslie Thomas, whom the report completely and expressly exonerates. But the Court shows that the series of insurances effected by Mr Bates and his various associates were all arranged immediately after the long week-end spent by Mr Bates in close contact with Mr Thomas at Ferring and elsewhere; and that the action taken by Sir Alfred Butt followed immediately on his brief interview with Mr Thomas at the Colonial Office on the morning of Budget-day; and it is satisfied, in spite of the strenuous denial of all the three persons concerned, that *post hoc* is in this case also *propter hoc*. That is not the kind of proof that fully satisfies in a case of this importance. It is not in the strict sense proof at all. Indeed, strong though the inference is, it is only the confidence this particular tribunal has inspired that secures general acceptance of its considered finding that there has been an unauthorised disclosure and that Mr Thomas was the person responsible. But it does secure it, and the courage of the Tribunal in stating its conclusions thus categorically adds further to the debt under which it has laid the whole nation. The promptitude with which the Tribunal was appointed, the wisdom shown in the selection of its members, and the ability and impartiality displayed by them, have all combined to relieve the concern which a singularly unhappy episode has inspired. Such incidents are rare in our public life and we have shown that we know how to deal with them when they do occur. What sympathy, if any, is due to Mr Thomas we unfortunately cannot tell. His 'unauthorised disclosure' may have been flagrant and deliberate, but it is far more likely to have taken the form of an indiscreet hint, manifestly culpable, but not to be judged too ruthlessly by critics who have most of them in their time been guilty of indiscretions great or small. The air has been cleared. The dust can now well be left to settle.

5 June

A SPECTATOR'S NOTEBOOK
JANUS

By Canon Dearmer's sudden death (not so completely unexpected to those who knew how serious his illness last summer was) the Church of England loses a distinctive and in its way a distinguished figure. Few men could speak with greater authority on Church art, Church music, and liturgical ritual. Of the vast number of volumes he produced on different subjects two will keep his name alive longest. *The English Hymnal*, of which he was joint editor with five colleagues, and *Songs of Praise*, for which he was personally responsible. Both volumes display an admirable catholicity; Dr Dearmer once observed to me how strange it was that some of the best modern hymns seemed to be by American Unitarians. He had particularly in mind Samuel Johnson's 'City of God, how broad and far' and F. L. Hosmer's 'Thy Kingdom come, on bended knee,' and of course, Oliver Wendell Holmes' 'Lord of all being, throned afar.'

5 June

ON THE DOLE
WALTER GREENWOOD

I write these lines in Glasgow. It is a cool Sunday evening, and I am standing in the middle of a smallish crowd of unemployed working men, most of whom are grey haired and all of whom are shabbily dressed. The open-air meeting has been organised by the N.U.W.M. (National Unemployed Workers' Movement), whose membership, in Glasgow, numbers 500 out of 96,000, which is the total figure of Glasgow's unemployed. I should add that this is the *official* figure given by the Labour Exchange.

This is one of the tragedies of the Means Test. It kills even the spirit of protest in its victims. These men of the audience stood staring stolidly, listening, without interruption, to the speakers' explanations of what the new Means Test scales would mean.

From the point of view of statistics we are told, by the returns for 1935 from the Unemployment Assistance Board (and the letters U.A.B., soon will be as familiar as the P.A.C. – Public Assistance Committee – particularly to the unemployed) – the returns from the U.A.B., for 1935 showed a total of 725,000 people applying for public assistance. Three quarters of a million able-bodied paupers who have exhausted their unemployment benefit and who now are 'on the rates.' The Board is making a deal of noise about the increases that it will grant to the 200,000 P.A.C. 'cases.' It does not stress what is to happen to the remaining 525,000 – except for the ominous remark: 'Where the regulations require reductions in the allowances, action will be taken gradually over a period of 18 months, in close consultation with the local advisory committee.' The Board continues: '... during the first four or five months, reductions in the existing allowances will be confined to cases of grossly excessive allowances, ... and to those cases of single persons under 25 years of age.'

It would be interesting to meet the person responsible for the phrase 'grossly excessive allowances': surely he ought to be writing leaders for one of the national dailies.

In case you are unaware, in the instructions for the guidance of Public Assistance Committees, the following scales are laid down: 10s for a man, 10s for his wife, and 2s for each dependent child. This, at the discretion of the Committee, can be increased, but not in excess of the amount the 'case' would receive from unemployment benefit. I actually know of towns where the Committee is so extravagant as to give 3s to each child each week!

Here is a typical example of a 'case' in Glasgow.

The family consists of a man, his wife, a son aged 24 earning 40s a week, and a daughter aged 17 earning 25s a week.

Under Transitional Benefit only 5s of the son's wages and 2s 6d of the daughter's would be deducted from the man's 26s, the sum he would be entitled to receive. In other words, he would get 18s 6d a week.

The New Means Test regulations will apply in the following manner:

The first 16s of the son's wage will be disregarded: 16s is subtracted from his wage of 40s which leaves 24s, a half of which (12s) will be deducted from his father's benefit. Now comes the daughter's wage which 'the Board must take into consideration.' The first 12s of her wage is ignored. 12s from 25s leaves 13s: a half of this sum, which is, of course, 6s 6d, will be deducted from her father's benefit. The Board, therefore, will take from the old man's pay 12s and 6s 6d, a total of 18s 6d. This sum deducted from his Transitional Benefit of 26s will leave him 7s 6d a week to bring home to the missis.

He, of course, and men like him, won't be the only ones to 'get it in the neck.' There are the single men and women under 25 who come under the control of the Board which, in its kindness, is to reduce their pay 'over a period of four or five months.' The torture is to be dragged out. Instead of a lad being able, at one blow, to say to his mother: 'They've taken so much from me because my father's working,' he'll have to do it two or three times.

How can a young man be a young man when he is treated as a 'case' or as a child? And not all working men and women can afford to be subsidising their adult children indefinitely even if the children can stand the indignity. Some of them *do* want to get married. But what can a young fellow do on 17s a week, which can be reduced to nothing when the Board have inquired into his and his parents' means? The army? You've got to be fit to join that: and a few months of the dole robs you of that.

What happens? Don't ask me, go and see for yourself. They're standing in groups at the street corners of most industrial towns; you'll find them in the cheap doss houses where they've taken up residence so that, being no longer with their parents, the latters' incomes can't 'be taken into consideration'; and thus the sons and daughters can be become qualified, as able-bodied paupers, to receive Public Assistance.

That's what we're doing in England. Young men who've 'served their time' to this or that trade; seven years' apprenticeship at boy's pay, discharged when their term of apprenticeship is completed because they are then entitled to man's pay.

What they've really served their apprenticeship to, it would seem, is able-bodied pauperdom at twenty-one years of age.

17 July

ANTI-SEMITISM IN THE EAST END
THE RT HON. GEORGE LANSBURY, M.P.

East London is one of the most interesting parts of our great metropolis. It stretches right away from Aldgate to West Ham, and from the river to Stoke Newington. The population, especially in Stepney, Poplar and Bethnal Green, is a very mixed one. Indeed, gathered within these boroughs you will find men and women who have come to us from all parts of the world; people who follow all kinds of religions and whose personal and social habits differ as night differs from day.

Jews form a very large part of this varied population. In Stepney they form the majority. In other boroughs they are in the minority. But many or few, they and their gentile fellow-citizens live together in peace and harmony. We East-Enders, no matter what our race or creed, are good citizens. The years since the creation of the County and Borough Councils have seen a great growth in the spirit and practice of civic duties and civic pride – pride in our boroughs although most of our streets are very drab and overcrowded; but the great main roads bring to us such fresh air and sunshine as is available in London, and our parks and open spaces, with Epping Forest close at hand, give all and sundry the opportunity of realising that God is in His heaven even if all is not right with the world.

We seldom fall out with each other about religion or what we mean by God and religion. We judge each other for what we are and not by our creeds. Consequently, the coming of the 'Blackshirts,' with their terrible doctrine of hatred of Jews as Jews, has aroused great indignation among all kinds of people. We have had our share of class-hatred, although in its most distressful days our hatred was nearly always confined to the system which created and perpetuated class distinctions and poverty of mind and body. But this present campaign of religious and social intolerance and persecution is something we neither understand nor tolerate. We long ago gave up the doctrine of 'original sin' as it used to be preached when I was very young.

We know that Jews do not choose either their race or their parents; but most of all we know that as a people they are just like the rest of us – good and bad, with goodness predominating. Because this is so, we view with shame and disgust the conduct of those who come from other parts of London and carry on propaganda of hatred, provocation and persecution against these our fellow citizens, whose only crime is that they are the children of their parents. Most of them are as English as we are. There is a large proportion who are naturalised, but many Jews are just as much English by birth as are Methodists, Anglicans or Roman Catholics. This wave of persecution would be stupid if it were not accompanied by what amounts to terrorism.

Words do not always hurt unless followed by deeds, and the organised propagandists of hate not only attack individual shop-keepers and others by name, but they also do their utmost to provoke disorder by marching through market-places where Jewish traders are carrying on business as costermongers, treading on the toes or heels of the men and women behind the stalls, using foul, obscene language about Jews, and by every means in their power striving to stir up a disturbance. Sometimes they succeed, and usually when the police arrive, those who attack manage to get away. Only the other day a quite young man, stung beyond endurance, rushed at his tormentors with a knife and was prosecuted. The Magistrate wisely discharged him, believing, I suppose, that he was not the guilty party.

In Poplar for many years past we allowed meetings to be advertised by chalking on the pavements. This practice, during times of excitement due to unemployment, was occasionally abused, but no serious harm was ever done. The gentlemen who invade us dressed as 'blackshirts' took advantage of this privilege to chalk outside the entrance to shops owned by Jews the most foul and disgusting attacks on those whose one crime was that they were Jews and were successful. So dangerous became this abuse that the Socialist borough council, much against its will, has been forced to pass a by-law making it illegal thus to chalk defamatory libels on the pavements, or, in fact, using this method of advertising at all. One would have thought the mere

163

fact of writing such incitements to violence would be illegal without a by-law. The Council were advised that this is not so.

Everybody in East London is in favour of free speech and freedom of meeting. It is often said that we are a disorderly crowd at election times. There is some truth in that statement. But our worst enemies will not deny that such disturbances only take place when feelings run high on some special question connected with poverty and unemployment. But disturbances arise now because an entirely new form of meeting is held. A force of stewards is imported, made up of men and women trained and drilled as 'chuckers out'; taught how to manhandle in a most brutal manner any person they think should be expelled. There is no chairman, and people are removed with the maximum of violence simply for interjecting a remark.

I have often been interrupted in East London, and on two occasions, together with my fellow Guardians, I have been locked in a board room all night. But none of us felt any hatred towards our persecutors because we knew they were suffering from a keen sense of social injustice. These men imported from outside our district come to us and preach racial and religious hatred, and do so in language which provokes protest. Free speech does not mean the right to malign and scandalise your opponents. The police for years attended meetings addressed by myself and others, and note-takers took down, as far as their limited skill would allow, reports of our speeches, and prosecutions often followed. This practice continues, I am told, so far as Communist meetings are concerned, and prosecutions occasionally follow. But at the open-air meetings organised by the 'blackshirts' no government reporters are regularly in attendance, and in view of the widespread opinion that speeches at these meetings are deliberately made for the express purpose of stirring up hatred and violence against individuals simply because of the accident of birth and creed, is it not the duty of the authorities to treat those responsible for such speeches as they treat ordinary working people who may be Socialists, trade unionists, or Communists?

There is a widespread opinion that in this matter of the drilling and marching of organised bands of men and women whose avowed object is to upset, if necessary by force, the whole constitution, is illegal and should be stopped. People remember Lord Carson and his rebel army, and how it grew because of toleration and support in high places. Public opinion in East London is quite certain that ordinary folk would never be permitted to make the speeches made by Fascists without being prosecuted, and ask why this should be? We want equitable and just treatment for all. It is true that some Jews are bad landlords, house-agents and employers, but so are some gentiles and Christians. The mass of us, Jew and gentile, are decent, clean-living people, and this Fascist propaganda is aimed at dividing us in the worst possible of ways, that is, according to our birth and what passes as religion. I believe we shall not succumb, but those whose duty it is to preserve order must have the courage to hold the balance fairly.

24 July

THIS DEGENERATE AGE
[GORONWY REES]

There is a certain monotony in the frequent attacks on the degeneracy of the age. Those who are not conscious of sin become somewhat irritated by having their vices enumerated; one day even an Oxford crew, easy-going though Oxford oarsmen are, will rebel against accusations of decadence. But the condemnations continue; on Monday, at the Royal Empire Society conference at Bristol, Professor Hearnshaw, of London University, took up the attack. It is interesting to notice how many critics of the age are historians and professors; in a book lately published, called *In the Shadow of Tomorrow*, Professor Huizinga, of Leyden, who is a historian of the greatest distinction, has made just the same charges as Professor Hearnshaw. The views of the professors are easily summarised. The age is on the decline; morals are loose; manners are bad; society is unstable; there is no respect for reason. And, like other critics, Professor Hearnshaw chooses among the artists examples with which to illustrate his case; his particular aversions are Bax, Stravinsky, Epstein, Joyce and the surréalistes. A connoisseur of such modern *indices expurgatorii* will miss in this list the name of D. H. Lawrence, who ought no more to be omitted than a fast bowler from a Test team; but Professor Hearnshaw makes up for the omission by the vigour with which he condemns those he has included. 'Bax and Stravinsky are positively and definitely ugly.' 'Epstein is definitely obscene.' It is a little alarming to those who have enjoyed, innocently as they thought, *Petruschka*, and even

165

Ulysses, to find their taste so professorially condemned; but perhaps not to be conscious of vice is worse than vice itself.

These examples, taken from the arts, may give a clue to the condemnations of the morality of the age. By Professor Hearnshaw's standards, these artists are all bad, and all equally bad, because they reflect contemporary conditions. It is inevitable that those who find modern conditions alarming, and novel, should find distasteful the works in which they are reflected; to them they must all be ugly. And to the professors of a certain school it is genuinely incomprehensible that anyone should find modern conditions natural and acceptable, and even hope to make something more out of them than a mere return to the comfortable stability of before the War. The professors forget that today Europe is largely inhabited by people who have never known society to be anything but insecure, and uneasy; for such people the only acceptable modern works are those which their professors and elders condemn. Yet for them, because there is no initial difficulty of understanding, it is possible to discriminate between modern artists, even though they all reflect the same conditions. They see as many differences between Bax and Stravinsky as the professors see between Dickens and Charles Kingsley. It is this inability to discriminate, it is the universality of their condemnation, which makes the attacks of the professors so unconvincing.

But in their moral condemnations there is the same lack of discrimination. The professors would have us believe the age degenerate because it does not observe the moral standards of 1910. To them, all deviations from those standards, because deviations, are to be condemned. Now it is certainly true that those standards are no longer generally observed; but there are so many differences, of goodness and badness, in the lack of observance, as there are between the various painters who do not paint like Royal Academicians. Those who have been lucky or unlucky enough to live when Victorian morality has broken down, who find it natural that it should have broken down, can have no nostalgia for the days of Victoria. Indeed, to have that morality restored would be intolerable. It would be possible only by restoring, by brute force if necessary, what Professor Hearnshaw calls the vanished domination of the Victorian middle-class, whose morality it was. For those who have to live today it is possible only to discriminate, just as they may discriminate in the arts, between the various ways of deviating from that

166

morality. Though all are deviations, not all need be degradations. Some indeed may be, or may have the germs of, a freer and humaner way of life. Professor Hearnshaw, for instance, deplores a lack of respect for fathers which, he says, would not have been possible in 1910; yet that lack of respect may be evidence of a happier relationship than the servility which, it seems to us now, fathers once demanded of their children. Equally there are those who deplore what is called the sexual freedom of the age; yet some forms of that freedom may give greater prospects of human happiness and goodness than the tyranny of a rigid and conventional morality. To condemn all manifestations of that freedom is to ignore the distinction between considered conviction and mere indulgence. To test all things and choose what honestly seems to be good is perhaps the only means still left of exercising what may be called the moral taste. It need not be denied that, in the absence of a generally accepted morality, men and women may be faced with evils from which before they were protected. It may be admitted that even in its best manifestations the moral freedom of the age has its dangers. But we can still say with Hölderlin:

> Wo aber Gefahr ist
> Wächst das Rettende auch.

31 July

WHAT SHOULD WE FIGHT FOR?
A. L. ROWSE

I have been asked as, I suppose, a young man of military age who is also a Labour candidate, to answer this question. It is a very difficult one; it is perhaps impossible to give a general answer, valid for all circumstances: the matter depends so much upon particular contingencies. There is, for example, the ambiguity in the question, 'what should *we* fight for?' Who are 'we'?

All we who are socialists are convinced that there is no hope of any international order which can secure peace in the world except through the victory of socialism; that all hope of peace is indissolubly bound up with socialism; that there can be no peace unless the forces of the Left are to win. I do not wish to argue this proposition here and now; this is not the place to do so, though I am always ready to defend it and have done so in various writings. But it is not a merely emotional conviction, it

167

is an intellectual one, based upon considerations of an economic and political order, no less than psychological and cultural. In fact, I may say in passing, that for myself I can hardly conceive the state of mind of those people (though I know only too well the considerations that move them) who cannot or will not see the plain evidence written across the face of Europe and indeed the world, since the War, that there is no hope whatever of peace so long as the existing economic and political order maintains its hold, so long as the rule of the upper classes last. The evidences are only too plain: 'Look at circumstantials,' said Cromwell: 'They hang so together!'

The relevance of all this is that to a socialist the answer is plain and easy: since we are convinced that socialism is the only hope (in a political sense) of a world worth living in, we are prepared to fight for what advances the cause of socialism. We have no difficulty or hesitation there.

But we are not living in a socialist world – though the forces of socialism have a very important part in it; nor is this country socialist. We are then here in a region not of certainty, nor of plain straightforward choices, but of checks and counter-balances, of the calculation of forces, of expediency; a region of probabilities, where obligations are a question of degree.

In a general way, the right line for a socialist is to take that course of action which most advances the cause of socialism. In contemporary Europe, and the world at large, the gravest danger to socialism, as to the hope of any secure peace, comes from the forces of Fascism, strong in most countries, entrenched in abso-lute power in some. Anybody ought to be able to see that, and to see further that the more the forces of reaction win, with every step we are precipitated nearer to war. It is the common interest both of socialists and of those who wish to maintain peace, therefore, to form such an overwhelming collective organ-isation in the world that the forces of disruption and nationalist-Fascist anarchy may not break through and render the world intolerable to live in with their ceaseless propagation of a war-mentality. And, if necessary, it is our duty to fight for it.

But on terms. The terms are that the proper objects of that collective organisation to maintain peace are not thwarted and frustrated at every turn by duplicity or incompetence, but are sincerely and straightforwardly held to. Take the case of the Labour Movement in this country. It will be generally agreed that no war can now be fought by this country unless it has the full participation and the agreed will of the Labour Movement behind it. In the great test of collective security which came last year over Abyssinia, the Labour Movement, which took a line which was in accordance with the interests both of this country and of the collective system, and was prepared to implement their obligations, was fraudulently 'sold' by the Government. That at any rate – I am not arguing it, I am merely stating it – is the opinion held throughout the Labour Movement.

It has meant a great growth of opinion in favour of a 'war-resistance' policy. It means, moreover, that nobody in the Labour Movement – the position has been stated in so many words by Mr Attlee – would be prepared to fight in a war which was conducted by the present Government as it now stands, *for whatever purposes*. Apart from the less important consideration, for it is not one of principle, that we have no confidence whatever in the ability of such a collection of crocks and incompetents to direct the policy of this country, let alone run a War – there has never been such an incompetent Government, so incapable of leadership, since the days of Addington or Goderich; apart from that, they cannot be trusted: they have gone back upon their obligations.

No doubt if a real crisis arises, and we are involved in a war, and the war is in pursuance of our obligation to maintain such a collective organisation that the disruptive forces of nationalist anarchy shall not break through successfully and remake the world to worse than before – no doubt in that day and to meet that need, a real government of the nation would arise in which Labour would claim at least an equal share in determining the objects for which this country fought and the conduct of the war. In that case circumstances would be assimilable to the first case that I put; and the answer whether we should fight or no, might be given with not less certainty.

31 July

THE MARCH FROM JARROW

Everyone agrees that the condition of Jarrow, like that of the depressed areas in general, demands immediate redress; whether the demand is most wisely presented by the 200 marchers who on November 3rd will present a petition to Parliament is more arguable. But whatever the march is it is, *pace* the Bishop of

Durham, in no way a 'revolutionary' act; the title to petition Parliament is an ancient, a valuable, a well-recognised right. The march itself is to be welcomed, like the King's visit to South Wales, as a means of concentrating public attention on a problem which should not for one moment be ignored until a solution for it has been found. It cannot be forgotten that some months ago a scheme which would have been of the greatest value to Jarrow, and was in itself economically justified, was defeated by a combination of private interests over which the Government has considerable influence; when that opportunity was lost, it might well seem that somewhat dramatic gestures were necessary to call attention to the needs of Jarrow. Miss Ellen Wilkinson has quoted a statement of the President of the Board of Trade that 'Jarrow must work out its own salvation.' That statement exemplifies an attitude which, rightly or wrongly, is widely believed to be that of the Government; and it is this belief which inspires marches which are much more pathetic than revolutionary – and which, let it be added, will soon lose their force if frequently repeated.

30 October

THE PRESERVATION OF ENGLAND
PROFESSOR G. M. TREVELYAN, O.M.

In the matter of the Preservation of the Beauty of Rural England, *what we need* is a State policy, the support of the Ministry, of Parliament, and of legislation. At present, with the exception of the admirable activities of the Ancient Monuments Department of the Office of Works, which are confined to the ruins of old houses and churches, the State washes its hands of the whole business, although its own system of taxation is one of the chief causes of the destruction of beauty.

In old days the refusal of the State to concern itself with questions of amenity did no harm, because the ordinary economic development of the country did little harm to beauty; and the citadels of rural beauty – parks, woods, country houses – scattered thickly over the land, were kept up by individual owners. Now the development of motor traction turns every 'beauty spot' into an 'eligible building site,' and the State by its taxation forces owners to sell, while at the same time it refuses to control the evil consequences of the sales of private property which its financial policy compels. The State is Socialist enough to destroy by taxation the classes that used to preserve rural amenity; but it is still too Conservative to interfere in the purposes to which land is put by speculators to whom the land is sold.

A characteristic performance of the State is the Ribbon Development Bill. The evil is well known and admitted by all. It is not only destructive of the beauty and dignity of the country, but it is socially undesirable that houses should be strung along the whole length of the country's roads, instead of being grouped in villages. But the State will neither forbid building in undesirable situations near the road without compensation, nor will it find the compensation money. It has simply, by its Bill, flung the problem at the head of the unfortunate local authorities, and washed its hands like Pilate. The local authorities in nine cases out of ten have not the money to compensate wayside owners, and without compensation cannot prevent undesirable building. Regional and town plans are made, often with great pains and ability, but cannot be carried out because there is not the compensation-money. Everywhere we see ribbon development going on, and on it will go till our roads are streets – unless the State will face the problem instead of playing with it.

Similarly, nothing is done about National Parks, because the Treasury and the politicians, by an old Victorian tradition, now wholly out of date, regard amenity as a thing on which public money ought not to be spent. National Parks in England would not, of course, mean the same thing as National Parks in America or Africa, where great wildernesses can be reserved as parks before mankind has settled in them at all. We are two thousand years too late for that policy in England. By turning, say, the Lake District into a National Park, ownership would be undisturbed, and agriculture and sheepfarming would continue as it does now. Indeed, the farms are part of the beauty of the landscape. Only the rights of owners to develop their properties would be limited by certain regulations, to ensure the preservation of the characteristic beauty of the Lake District, and compensation would be paid to the owners. Such a scheme would be of limited cost to the Treasury. The equivalent of the amount of money now annually spent on the upkeep of parks in great cities would go a long way to supply the nation with great playgrounds of natural beauty all over the island. As soon as people care enough about it to pay for it, it can be done.

I am not a fanatic in these matters. I fully realise that this is

171

a small island full of folk, and that the prime needs of industry, housing and defence have to be met, often at the expense of natural beauty. But in disputes and bargains between these rival interests, the interest of amenity is unduly handicapped. It is not officially represented in Government departments; it is only when a protest is raised in the newspapers that the departments occasionally throw it a bone.

Thus, in the matter of planting trees. In old days it paid best to plant hardwoods. Now it often pays best to plant conifers – at least, the return is quicker. Therefore, both individual owners and the State through the Forestry Commission plant very few hardwoods. In a hundred years' time, to a large extent in fifty years, the beauty of England would be only half what it is now from that cause alone. Look at any typical English landscape other than pure moorland, and see if its beauty is not mainly dependent on the hardwood trees. Well, they fall; and when they fall they are not now being replaced. Almost every new plantation one sees is confier. The only remedy is that both individuals and the State should deliberately plant more hardwoods. There is no use abusing the Forestry Commission, which makes about as many concessions to amenity as its commission from Government allows – for example, its recent agreement to keep out of the heart of the Lake District and to consult the C.P.R.E. in other places. What is wanted now is that Government should modify its policy and charge the Forestry Commission with the business of planting more hardwood and allow it to acquire land suitable for that purpose. At present it is much restricted by its orders from so doing. It is for the nation to decide what sort of forests it wants to plant.

But in any case the Forestry Commission can't maintain the small plantations and coppices and hedgerow timber. That can only be done by private owners, small and big. What we want is that they should feel it a duty to posterity to put in hardwood trees, even if it be only a few, to mitigate the inevitable deterioration of the English landscape in the future. 'When ye hae naething else to do, ye may be aye sticking in a tree; it will be growing, Jock, when ye're sleeping.'

Lay not that flattering unction to your souls that the National Trust is solving the problem of rural amenity. It has indeed made great headway in the last few years, but even now it owns only some 60,000 acres, with 10,000 more protected by its covenants. What are they among so many? Recently a patriotic

172

owner gave a strip of five miles of Cornish coastline to the Trust. That is good, and there are a few more such cases. But elsewhere, with appalling speed, the coastline of England is being desecrated and its majestic and lovely beauty is being destroyed for ever. Nothing but action by the State or local authorities can save the coastline on a large scale.

Yet in the meantime the C.P.R.E. and National Trust do what they can, and through them the patriot can do something at least to save the beauty of his country, until the State has been aroused to do its duty. A thousandth part of a loaf is better than no bread. I would particularly commend to your readers the practice, which recent legislation has rendered possible, of owners placing lands under covenant, either with local authorities or with the National Trust. By these covenants lands can be placed out of the shot of the jerry builder and exploiter for all time to come, into whatsoever hands the lands may pass. The owner does not, under this system, give up ownership or the rents. But he forgoes further development value and prevents himself and his heirs from selling it as building land. This arrangement is proving more and more attractive to owners who care for particularly beautiful pieces of the land they own.

20 November

OCCASIONAL BIOGRAPHIES: MR CHURCHILL
[WILSON HARRIS]

Mr Winston Churchill was sixty-two last Monday. It has been a crowded, an adventurous, and in its way a spectacular, life. And through the whole of it onlookers have been kept wondering. Mr Churchill is the son of his father (and, what is so far less important, the father of his son). Lord Randolph Churchill, founder, so much as any single individual was the founder, of the Fourth Party, made his reputation by sharp-shooting at his own Front Bench. As Chancellor of the Exchequer he discovered what 'those damned dots' meant; he might, if occasion had offered, have done the wrong thing about the gold standard. And he found to his undoing that no man is indispensable in politics; there is always a Goschen waiting forgotten in the background.

So heredity tells - or history repeats itself. And heredity in this case goes a long way back. John Churchill, first Duke of Marlborough, whose portrait his versatile descendant is painting

173

on a spacious canvas, was not primarily conspicuous for the permanence of his adhesions. And in the first couple of decades of this century the floor of the House of Commons was worn into a pattern by the constant passage of the latest Churchill across it instead of up it. That Churchill, elected as a Conservative in 1900, sat as Liberal from 1906 to 1922, quitting Mr Asquith for Mr Lloyd George in the 1916 crisis. When Mr Baldwin took office in 1924 it was found that Mr Churchill had caught the train as a Conservative once more, and ensconced himself comfortably (yet was he so comfortable?) as Chancellor of the Exchequer. In 1929 the Baldwin Government fell, and its Chancellor has been in the wilderness ever since. It must have taken some resolution on the part of successive Prime Ministers to keep him there, for one of the many reasons for including him in any Cabinet is that the most formidable critic the House has known for a generation is thereby muzzled.

Winston Churchill has filled in his time about half the executive offices. He has held four out of the six Secretaryships of State – for Home Affairs, War, Air, Colonies. He has been First Lord of the Admiralty and Chancellor of the Exchequer and President of the Board of Trade and Chancellor of the Duchy. He is essentially a man of action, whether as administrator or fighter; he is a great speaker, and when he chooses a great writer. His life of his father was the first proof of that, his book, *The World Crisis*, the second. Not all the credit for having the fleet at its war-stations in 1914 before the German ships could move was his – half of it belongs to the First Sea Lord, Prince Louis of Battenberg – but the despatch of the battle-squadrons into the fog of war was a typical Churchillian touch, and no one but Churchill could have written the unforgettable description of zero hour at the Admiralty on the night of August 4th.

Today, at 62, Mr Churchill is setting onlookers wondering again. He has been out of office for seven years, in five of which his own party has been in power. Throughout he has been their most dangerous critic, except when, as in the case of the India Bill, he has defeated himself by his own extravagance. Now comes a new crusade – for the defence of democracy against the menace of the dictatorships. Is it a crusade with a double object – to achieve its avowed purpose and at the same time carry its author back to office? Those who will can say so; there is no method known yet of reading men's minds. But the genuineness of Mr Churchill's belief in the need for a swift demonstration by this country that aggression from any quarter will be made disastrous to the aggressor is beyond doubt or question. He has preached that gospel tirelessly in the House of Commons, and in carrying it now to the public platform he is obviously more concerned that the country should be roused than that he himself should be enlisted to administer the policy he sponsors – though that is not to say that he would refuse appropriate office if it were offered.

But what would appropriate office be? He has been Secretary for War and Air and First Lord, and Minister of Munitions as well. On the face of it, if anyone is cut out for the post Sir Thomas Inskip holds it is Mr Churchill. But truth is not always written on the face of things. Delicacy is needed in that office as well as drive. The three services have their own Ministers, their own heads of departments, and their own Commanders-in-Chief. To conciliate the independence and experience which those varied personalities represent may be more effective than to put dynamite behind them. The same may be true of the Cabinet. Is the Member for Epping, assuming his diagnosis of the international sanction accurate, of more value as mere Member for Epping or as Minister of the Crown? As a Minister he must speak with Ministerial restraint, and restraint sits ill on those impetuous lips. As a popular leader he can preach preparedness and the defence of peace and freedom with liberty to lay hands on any instrument calculated to serve his purpose best. There is, of course, one post as yet beyond his grasp. If he held it, he might apply stimulus where stimulus is needed much more effectively than Mr Baldwin – and at the same time upset a great many apple-carts which the present Prime Minister keeps firmly planted on their wheels. As spear-head of a great popular movement for the defence at home and abroad of all that democracy cares for he may achieve what he never could if checked by the trammels that accompany the authority of office.

And he is capable of contenting himself with that great *rôle*. For on whichever side of the House he may sit he has always had the essential stuff of democracy in him. He cares about the people; he was responsible a quarter of a century ago for the Trades Boards and the Labour Exchanges. And he would be false to all his ancestry if he did not care intensely about the British people. That democracy in this country is looking for a leader and a voice is manifest. Has it found them? If so, how will the leader use his opportunity? There are obvious dangers to

175

avoid. A Churchill who showed himself as Teutophobe as he once was Russophobe would be doing peace no better service than Herr Hitler himself. There must be no *Delenda est Germania*, no playing into the hands of the forces in Europe that are working to divide the Continent into *blocs*. To do Mr Churchill justice, he is fully conscious of that danger. He has insisted in language at once conciliatory and vigorous that no nation is asking anything for itself that is not available on equal terms to a peaceful Germany. Subject to an ample freedom to criticise he has always supported the League of Nations. Conscious of the necessity to defend the ideals enshrined in the Covenant and the Kellogg Pact, he urges that public law in the world must be buttressed by the joint strength of the nations that accept it. Germany can be of that number or not as she chooses. Without her or with her – but at greater cost in the one case than the other – the world must and can enjoy security. Mr Churchill's native belligerence – for there is more than a streak of that in his make-up – could find no better outlet than in leadership of a crusade for what he calls 'well-guarded peace' – wherever it may take him.

4 December

Part Four: The Arts

Writers and Writing
PETER QUENNELL

Not long ago when I asked a good friend, a distinguished modern novelist who has published many books and had a wide experience of life, if he had ever happened to meet D. H. Lawrence, he answered, a little testily, I thought, that Lawrence, after all, had died in 1930, before he himself was nine years old. Though proclaiming one's seniority is a rather dismal privilege, age has certain obvious rewards. I have greatly enjoyed being able to look back as far as 1936 and see its landscape quite distinctly – that of an Age Before the Flood, not, alas, the 'Giant Age' that John Dryden once reverently remembered; a period, nevertheless, during which some admirable works were produced, and literature received much more public attention (since more readers, I believe, were interested in and could still afford to buy books) than serious writing often gets today.

True, we were conscious, now and then vaguely and over-cheerfully perhaps, of living on the verge of an unimaginable catastrophe; and articles *The Spectator* regularly printed – among them 'The Real Hitler' by R. H. S. Crossman and an editorial, 'Does Germany mean Peace?' – reflect a growing sense of strain. But only one imaginative writer assumed a resolutely optimistic pose, that extraordinary prophet and false prophet the indefatigable Wyndham Lewis, author of *Blast*, a brilliant novel, *Tarr*, *The Lion and the Fox* and *Time and Western Man*, who now dashed into the field with a pugnacious diatribe entitled *Left Wings over Europe; or, How to Make War about Nothing*, where he asserted that Hitler was essentially a man of good will, an opinion for which in *The Spectator* he was soundly castigated by E. H. Carr. Lewis, as an original writer, was no doubt a man of near-genius. But, Carr suggested, he was 'a whale of a publicist', glad to exercise his considerable gift of alarming and astonishing the minnows. He had, moreover, a paranoiac tendency that latterly disfigured almost everything he wrote.

Carr was a fine political journalist; and in 1936 *The Spectator*'s literary critics, too, exhibited a formidable array of talents. In the forefront, Graham Greene, whose *A Gun for Sale* appeared that same year, continued to turn out excellent reviews; and his notice of Beverley Nichols's latest picturesque effusion, *No Place Like Home*, must have been the unkindest blow that the vastly popular Nichols, though elsewhere manhandled by David Garnett, had ever taken on the chin. Headed 'Portrait of a Lady', it suggests that the victim's printed name was possibly the pseudonym adopted by an unmarried middle-aged woman – 'I picture her in rather old-fashioned mauve' with a stiff Edwardian collar – and observes that the lady's innocence is such that she is shocked by the glimpse she catches of a man in pyjamas. Here Greene may be wielding a tomahawk to attack a fairly inoffensive mouse; but his review of Walter de la Mare's new volume of stories, *The Wind Blows Over*, is evidently a work of love, and defends the sexagenarian writer against the foolish charge that his poetry and prose belongs to the so-called 'literature of escape'.

Among other critics who then enlivened *The Spectator*'s pages were Evelyn Waugh, William Plomer, V. S. Pritchett, Edmund Blunden, Seán O'Faoláin, Elizabeth Bowen and Rose Macaulay, each of whom – an extremely valuable asset – could discuss writing from a professional writer's point of view. But a particularly incisive full-page article opened Books of the Day on 20 November – it was an unsparing analysis of *The Oxford Book of Modern Verse*, which W. B. Yeats had recently edited, written by the crippled man-of-letters John Hayward. Yeats was seventy-one; and, since he had developed a romantic affection for Lady Gerald Wellesley, the close friend of another poetess Victoria Sackville-West, his literary judgement had begun to weaken. He chose no fewer than fifteen of her poems, as compared with twelve of T. S. Eliot's, nine of Sacheverell Sitwell's and six of Ezra Pound's. Lady Gerald's ally W. J. Turner also had a handsome showing. The pair were plainly the editor's personal favourites. He had read certain of their poems, he announced, 'with more than all the excitement that came upon me when, a very young man, I heard somebody read out in a London tavern the poems of Ernest Dowson'.

Hayward was a scholarly academic reviewer; and so, in their different fashions, were Maurice Bowra, John Sparrow and A. L. Rowse, who expressed their likes and dislikes with all the measured authority of an Oxford Senior Common Room. While both Bowra and Sparrow wrote of the late A. E. Housman, his crusty scholarship and strangely revealing lyrics, Rowse, already at the top of his form, discussed a new biography of Babington, the sixteenth-century conspirator, in which the authoress, he was prepared to admit, showed 'a great gift' for drawing historical portraits, but had given us a notably defective appreciation of the glorious Queen herself.

Although the critics it produces certainly illustrate the spirit of an age, at this point, no doubt, I should leave reviewers and reviewing, and turn to some of the more imaginative books we read and admired in 1936. Hemingway, of course, we knew well; Cyril Connolly was presently to acclaim him as a highly original modern stylist, 'the outstanding writer of the new vernacular'. He and Scott Fitzgerald – *The Great Gatsby* had reached us during the previous decade – were the American novelists we particularly valued, despite the fact that *The Green Hills of Africa*, with its glorification of masculine bravado and bloodthirsty big-game hunting, slightly lessened our esteem.

Meanwhile, at home, we reacted, some of us rather violently, against an English novel that delighted a multitude of middle-brow readers, and which the otherwise exacting French critics assured us was a twentieth-century masterpiece – *Sparkenbroke* by George Moore's protégé and pupil, Charles Morgan. I remember making heavy fun of the book and what I thought its bogus classicism, and hearing soon afterwards that the author had publicly declared that, were he ever to encounter me, he would immediately leave the room – a decision, I am glad to say, he seemed to have happily forgotten when I met him at his gifted daughter's wedding.

No major novel came from Evelyn Waugh that year; but he published a fascinating entertainment, *Mr Loveday's Little Outing, and other Sad Stories*, to which Maurice Bowra, again in *The Spectator*, paid the tribute it deserved: 'The world of Mr Waugh's imagination [he wrote] is intensely alive because every item ... has been chosen with a perfect literary tact and unfailing sense of its place in the complete structure. It may not be everybody's world, but it has its own laws and its own indubitable charm.'

Much less enthusiastically received was Cyril Connolly's first and only novel *The Rock Pool*. William Plomer, by no means a puritanical critic, would appear to have thoroughly disapproved of its characters and theme. The inhabitants of the rock pool, bohemian drunks and frustrated amorists, he protested, were quite unworthy of the novelist's attention: 'it is unfair, like keeping the zoo up late ...' Luckily, on the other side of the Atlantic, Edmund Wilson, an unusually perspicacious judge, took a better-balanced line. The story, he remarked, might 'owe something to *South Wind* and Compton Mackenzie's novels of Capri. Yet it differs from them through its acceleration, which, as in the wildly speeded-up burlesques, has something demoniacal about it.' Personally – and I must confess that I was the dedicatee – I have re-read a paperback reprint with a great deal of interest and pleasure; for it anticipates many of the novelist's later achievements and contains a preliminary hint of his more mature productions, *Enemies of Promise* and *The Unquiet Grave*.

In those days, prose and poetry often flourished cheek by jowl; some prose-writers tried their hands at verse, and poets ventured into fiction. Thus, all three members of the Sitwell family performed a double literary role. T. S. Eliot's *Collected Poems* (which included *Ash Wednesday* and ten choric passages from *The Rock*) were followed by Auden's volume *Look, Stranger!* and Edith and Sacheverell Sitwell's latest selections of their work; to which Sacheverell added *Deaths and Entrances*, one of the expansive prose-digressions, a blend of dreams and memories, fact and fantasy, that, in a light-hearted mood, I have heard him call his 'oratorios'.

1936 wasn't a dull period; and the bookish pre-war reader couldn't claim he lacked variety, so long as at least a dozen writers, many of them still young, for example the twenty-two-year-old Dylan Thomas, Wales's dionysiac prodigal son, were quickly building up their reputations. A survey of this kind, however, is bound to be fragmentary and incomplete; and, while I have attempted to give a general picture of the age, I have omitted numerous names and titles – Auden and Isherwood's joint poetic drama, *The Ascent of F.6*; Stephen Spender's short stories, *The Burning Cactus*, said by a conservative critic (not in *The Spectator*) to reveal the 'plight of a defeated generation'; two memorable travel books, Graham Greene's *Journey without Maps* and Freya Stark's account of her earliest odyssey, *The Southern Gates of Arabia*. Among literary biographies I appreciated at the time was Edward Sackville-West's sympathetic portrayal of De Quincey, *A Flame in Sunlight*; among collections of essays, E. M. Forster's *Abinger Harvest*.

I think I have said enough about its occupants to indicate that the literary scene in 1936 was an unusually active one; and most of the men and women who peopled it were themselves odd and interesting characters. Dylan Thomas's manic extravagances have all too often been described; but I alone can claim to have watched him at a nightclub drinking somebody else's wine, which he had suddenly removed from their table, out of his own dilapidated shoe. Dylan was not only a natural poet, a Celtic word-master, but had an inborn histrionic gift, and played the part of the Mad Genius – a combination of Rimbaud, Chatterton, John Clare and Christopher Smart, who, recollected Johnson, took healthy exercise by *walking* to the ale-house but was always *carried* home again – with indomitable self-assurance.

Another arresting figure, born in 1903 like his school friend Cyril Connolly, was Eric Blair, renamed George Orwell, who two years earlier had published *Down and Out in Paris and London*, a record of his experiences as a voluntary outcast – he had various economic safety-lines he felt too proud to use – and in 1936 produced a not very accomplished novel, *Keep the Aspidistra Flying*, through which he continued his protest against modern capitalist society. It was the Spanish Civil War and his bitter disillusionment with Communist dictatorship that enabled him to display his true gifts and inspired his Swiftian masterpiece *Animal Farm*. When I knew him at Cyril Connolly's parties, he sounded a friendly but incongruous note – a lonely Ancient Mariner, contemplating in a mildly reproachful way the crowd of thoughtless Wedding Guests. He also resembled Don Quixote or one of Cromwell's 'preaching generals'. Perhaps he had chosen the wrong Civil War. The devout yet philosophic seventeenth century might have given him an outlet for his native goodness.

MARGINAL COMMENTS
ROSE MACAULAY

Among the minor quarrels which are warming up the cold new year, there appears to be one on hand about whether or not young poets should be (*a*) angry, (*b*) unintelligible. (The two qualities would seem to have no connexion, unless it is held that poetic rage plays the devil with grammar and construction.) Should human beings express in verse the indignation which they have always, and very properly, felt against the exasperating actions of other human beings and the shocking world which we have all helped to make? I gather that Mr St John Ervine thinks no, Mr Geoffrey Grigson yes. Should we wait to compose verse in some moment (if any such should arrive to us) of comparative good humour, or should we fling on to paper in corrosive ink our numerous and harmonious rage? The answer could only be properly arrived at by lengthy examination into the effects of anger on poets, past and present.

How various poets have carried their anger is almost as important as how they have carried their love. The cause of their rage is also of some relevance; which of the particular aspects of the disgraceful world (as Mr Grigson very properly calls it) has inflamed them. All human beings sometimes, and poets very often (some, like Pope, continuously), are angry with the disgraceful treatment accorded them by their fellow creatures; others less personally, with some disgraceful deed or deeds they observe to be committed; others, like Shelley, with the disgraceful world at large. All three rages may produce fine, or extremely poor, poetry. When into *Lycidas* stalks the angry St Peter, shaking his mitred locks and delivering himself of his strong disapprobation of the state of the church, the result is a fine passage, and a memorable social indictment, but loveliness only returns, with Alpheus, when the dread voice is past. Yet Milton could be angry beautifully; so could most great poets who have vented their rage in numbers. The anger in love was carried by Shakespeare, and even by Donne, to heights that it has never, I think, touched again; on the other hand, Shakespeare's anger with the sorry scheme of things was less anger than a splendid philosophic pity. Dryden in angry satire was often tiresome; the incomparably more exquisite Marvell still more so.... But this vast theme cannot be discussed haphazard.

As to the other complaint about 'young poets,' that they write unintelligibly, there would seem to be only three things which should make anything written honestly, by someone in possession of his senses, unintelligible to a reader similarly endowed. The writer may refer, without adequate elucidation, to some undivulged fact, to which the reader has no access; or he may write on a subject outside the reader's intellectual ken; or he may use defective grammar and construction. Short of these, any verse can surely be grasped, if so desired, even through verbose wrappings (the great fault in much modern technique) and despite necessarily imperfect sympathies between the concrete and imagist method of expression, and the more traditional literary and abstract. The reader may feel often, 'Surely rather many words for a rather simple thought,' and that a poet of a terser age and a finer phase of the English language would have disposed of it more quickly and more memorably; but he will grasp it all right.

As to anger with the world, do modern young poets express more of this than did their predecessors? I have observed in them rather a certain complacency, an optimistic belief that the disgraceful world may be on the way to be saved after all. I cannot quite share this belief, but it is very respectable, and I hope the young poets will not lose it and become despairing cynics.

10 January

THE THEATRE
PETER FLEMING

Tonight at 8.30, Noël Coward. At the Phœnix

'I wonder what he's like on the tightrope?' pardonably mused the lady on my left. We were nearing the close of the second of the two alternating programmes of three short plays. Mr Noël Coward, in addition to being their author, had revealed himself as actor, producer, composer, and dancer with effortless success; there seemed to be a feeling abroad among his more insatiable admirers that he might have thrown in some more flamboyant proof of versatility – ventriloquism, perhaps, or snake-charming.

But Mr Coward had done what, in his programme manifesto, he had set out to do; he had, indubitably, 'provided a full and varied evening's entertainment.' Two of them, in fact. *Family*

185

Album – slight, repetitive, unoriginal, a shade too unmistakably Coward in texture – had nevertheless amused; the gravest criticism which can be levelled against this elaborate Victorian repudiation of the proverb *de mortuis nil nisi bonum* is that the family circle is little more than a geometrical expression, with the minor characters – which might have been the funniest of all – mere cyphers. It was followed by *The Astonished Heart*, a clipped but powerful domestic drama, whose spare and subtle dialogue exhibited to great advantage Mr Coward's gift for writing between the lines. As partners in a guilty passion Mr Coward and Miss Lawrence were taut and tortured and laconic, implying rather than expressing their emotions; as far as acting honours went, Miss Alison Leggatt outshone them with a beautifully-timed portrayal of the injured wife. The first programme ended with *Red Peppers*, wherein Mr Coward and Miss Lawrence showed us in cross-section the private and the public lives of two second-rate variety artists. As a 'turn' the sketch was brilliant; yet could it not have been something more than a turn? There were openings, in the hand-to-mouth existence of these resilient, sparrow-like creatures, which a Chaplin or a Clair might have exploited: a slightly deeper realism, a touch of pathos, might have raised to the status of drama an entertainment too strongly reminiscent, as it stands, of unusually inspired charades.

The second programme opens with *Hands Across the Sea*, a play in one scene which, to my great regret, I did not see. I understand it to be a brilliant essay in Mr Coward's most flippant manner. *Fumed Oak*, described for the first time in its long and honourable career as 'an unpleasant comedy,' reminds us that even a worm will turn. Mr Coward plays the suburban worm in an admirable make-up and an authentic accent. Miss Lawrence, though her own personality and the dialogue combine to make her more sympathetic than is altogether healthy for the balance of the play, transforms herself wonderfully into a nagging housewife; Miss Alison Leggatt does further injustice to mothers-in-law, and Miss Moya Nugent presents the awkward age in suitably repulsive effigy.

Shadow Play, which ends the second triple bill, is the least successful and the most interesting of the six pieces. Victoria Gayforth (Miss Lawrence) is – like almost all her creator's characters who qualify for super-tax – at the end of her emotional tether. She seeks relief from frayed nerves, and oblivion of impending divorce, in a sleeping draught which is just a little too potent. Half-dreaming, half-delirious, she and her husband recapture intermittently the lovely essence of their early love. As a technical experiment *Shadow Play* is a suggestive failure; rather more obvious treatment – a sharper definition of the boundaries between past and present, illusion and reality – might have made it a notable innovation in dramatic technique. As it stands, it is a puzzling, pleasing chiaroscuro, charmingly illumined by the grace and beauty of Miss Lawrence.

If one cannot but feel disappointment that no one of Mr Coward's six plays reveals to the full the possibilities either of his genius or of his medium, one cannot but admire whole-heart-edly his many-sided ability to entertain. Miss Lawrence supports him with wit and glamour; and the acting of Miss Alison Leggatt and Mr Alan Webb, and the décors of Mrs Calthrop, contribute to fulfil Mr Coward's wish 'that a good time be had by all.'

17 January

RUDYARD KIPLING

Mr Rudyard Kipling's death occurred too late for mention in last week's *Spectator*, and today it is inevitably overshadowed for the nation by a greater bereavement. But even now some estimate of the man entitled to be regarded as the doyen of English letters is due. Mr Kipling was not the oldest living author of distinction (Mr Shaw is nine years older), but the longest effectively before the public. *Plain Tales from the Hills*, that first book of short stories which carried his name at once throughout the English-speaking world, was published before he was 23; and the major part of his output, both for quantity and quality, fell within the ensuing eleven years before his grave illness in 1899. Had that illness proved fatal, as for many anxious days seemed likely, his name, as a dazzling and immeasurable 'might-have-been,' would have stood altogether higher in our literature than it will now.

In estimating the higher flight of his genius one must estimate the character of the age which fostered it. The Imperialism of the 'nineties was compounded of a few simple elements in the England which lay immediately behind it. One was that forthright form of Evangelicalism – 'fundamentalist' we might call it today – which ruled mid-Victorian England and caused people in all ranks of society to live with one eye fixed perpetually on the Last Judgement. Whatever be thought of this creed on the intellectual side, its efficiency value was incontestable. It caused Englishmen for two generations to display in industry, in world-enterprise, in exploration, and in such a task as the ruling and defence of India, qualities that the men of no other contemporary nation equalled. Kipling, who had the creed in his bones, was intensely conscious of its results; and for him Englishmen were the Lord's people, and foreigners 'lesser breeds without the law,' even at a time when the decay of faith was in truth sapping all his assumptions. Secondly, there was the undoubted fact that in colonising and exploring, in administering coloured peoples and in replacing their lawlessness by law, the mid-Victorian English had led the world. The Kiplingite deduction, that this had come about by nature, not accident, and was due to inherent superiorities in the English race, is hardly borne out by the world's subsequent developments; but it was more plausible at the time, and its pride in service (the 'white man's burden') was no mean pride. Last, and very closely interwoven with the rest, was the idea that the Englishman had a permanent lead in the development and use of machines; a lead attributable to the Evangelical honesty and vigilance ('They do not teach that their God will rouse them a little before the nuts work loose') which could alone match machinery's austere requirements. To this main idea Kipling has given in prose and verse more memorable expression than any other author; and though the nationalist British twists which he put on it seem today obvious anachronisms, they were not so unplausible at the time.

But he had grave limitations. The new idealism of the twentieth century found in him nothing but an uncomprehending foe. With the social reforming current which rejuvenated British society he could make no useful contacts at all. It was not merely that, while he knew so much about fighting lawlessness in India, he knew so little about the desperate wars against slumdom and drink, sweating and disease and destitution at home; it was that the whole this-worldly character of these modern betterments did not square with his other-worldly Last-Judgement outlook. And so he fell back on the safe minor themes of literature – on praising his adopted Sussex, his home sights, his dog, his garden; on archaeologising and boating; on reading the ancients and writing attractive fancies in prose and verse about the Romans and Greeks. It is no disparagement of these pieces, glorified as many of them are by the alembic of style, to say that in comparison with his promise they are but a notable aftermath.

A permanent place in literature is assured to him, but what place remains still uncertain. It is possible that his poetry will outlast his prose; already they date less. Nearly forty years ago a great man of letters characterised his early tale *William the Conqueror* as the 'almost perfect short story'; few would do so now. On the other hand his poems, while reaching the popular ear better than any other poet's, have yet perhaps to receive full justice from literary critics. An early poem like 'The First Chantey' is really astonishing in the originality of its conception and the clean fineness of its execution; and even in late books so obviously on his more modest level as *Puck of Pook's Hill* you may find a short piece as wonderful and as deeply felt as the Roman soldier's prayer to Mithra. Before the whole future of poetry and poetic appreciation in England there stands at present a formidable question-mark; but if it ever comes to count again, as it used to count, in the lives of the young *intelligentsia*, there is a substantial *corpus* of Kipling's verse that can scarcely be forgotten.

24 January

WINGS OVER WARDOUR STREET
GRAHAM GREENE

In a few months now it will be possible for us to sit in our own homes and watch a film by television. Neither sound nor the improved colour in *Becky Sharp* represented so revolutionary a change, for they left film production in the same hands, the hands of large-scale financiers able to spend hundreds of thousands of pounds on a single film, but forced for the same reason to get their money back from the public the easiest and quickest way, to take no risks. That is one aspect of the star system: a comparatively inexpensive insurance against fallible directors, fallible story-writers: the quality of the films may vary so long as the public taste is stabilised on the star.

But what is going to be the effect of television on these huge financial organisations? Their position on the face of it looks desperate. Mr Dallas Bower, who speaks with technical authority, for he has been a sound recordist, a film editor and a director, foresees the necessity of handing over to television all that at present we mean by Cinema and inventing a new style, even a new type of theatre, with which television cannot compete.* This is the very interesting subject of his book, though we have to reach it by way of some cheap and ingenuous social digressions. His post-television theatre is in the shape of an arena, with the screen, a cylindrical screen, in the centre, played on by four overlapping projectors. The screen is translucent; when the theatre is in darkness we shall see no screen, but solid figures moving in the round. The idea of 'solid cinema' seems less fantastic than the idea that the great companies will be prepared to scrap their present theatres and begin to build anew. That must depend,. of course, on the success of television as a creative, and not a merely reproductive, medium.

The film companies, at any rate in this country, may not be in immediate danger; they have the stars, and television will have to appeal on other than star terms. Nor has the B.B.C. in the past (we have only to remember the broadcast play) developed at all the creative side of broadcasting. The first cinemas to suffer will be the news cinemas, though even they may be allowed a breathing space, if the B.B.C. fails to realise that *direct* television of *any* kind is impracticable. (Even Mr Bower speaks of direct television for news events, political speeches, talks by distinguished people, &c. But you cannot televise news directly and get results which for clarity, excitement or even apparent authenticity can compete with a news film where half a dozen cameras have been employed, the best shots chosen and the film edited; and even if you wish to televise a talk with no more than the features of the speaker, the close-up should surely be arranged as carefully as were the close-ups in the B.B.C. film made by Mr Grierson's unit, and that, too, means film and film cutting.)

Mr John Grierson in a preface to Mr Rotha's *Documentary Film* states the case against the B.B.C.:†

> 'The B.B.C. has been conservative till now in the use of its instruments. Its producers have used the microphone very much as the early film makers used their camera. They have accepted it as an essentially immovable object to which all action or comment must be brought.... A few simple deviations there have been in the so-called "actuality" programmes (in this borrowing from our documentary example), but they have been so tentative and ill-equipped, that for all its years of work and national fields of

---

* *Plan for Cinema*, Dallas Bower. (Dent)
† *Documentary Film*, Paul Rotha. (Faber and Faber)

opportunity the B.B.C. has created no art of microphonic sound and, in its own technique, not a single artist.'

The B.B.C., of course, can reply that it is a department of public relations. From the broadcasting of a village fire-brigade to the Empire broadcast on Christmas Day its most important object is to teach one man how another man lives. We are not, the B.B.C. may argue, primarily concerned with art any more than with entertainment in the sense of dance orchestras and plays. But I think Mr Grierson and Mr Rotha, who, as producers of documentary films, are equally concerned with public relations, with 'making things known that need to be known,' would be justified in retorting that nothing equals the persuasiveness of art and that as makers of documentaries they have developed an art unattained in any other branch of cinema, that under the direction of Mr Cavalcanti the G.P.O. Film Unit is the first to realise the enormous possibilities in the editing and the invention of sound. Mr Grierson sees in television an even wider field for the documentary method, and surely one is not 'kill-joy' in believing that it is there that the main future of television must lie, with story films occupying no more important a part in the programmes than plays do now. (I say story films because there is obviously no future for the direct television of plays.) We cannot yet speak of the 'art' of broadcasting; if television enables one documentary film to be made of the quality of *Song of Ceylon*, of *Coal Face*, of, even with all its faults of simplification and sentimentality, Mr Rotha's *The Face of Britain*, it will have introduced into broadcasting a creative element which at present it entirely lacks. There is the real threat to Wardour Street, the gradual realisation by the public of the finer excitement to be got in their own homes with documentary than in the super-cinema with the stars. There will always be an audience for the spectacular story film, but a very big audience is needed to carry the costs.

Mr Rotha is rather afraid of the word Art in relation to documentary films. Good photography, a pretty picture, skyline poses in the Flaherty manner, certainly do not make a good documentary film; but neither, as he points out, does bare realism. The news-reel is the closest the cinema comes to realism, but a news-reel is certainly not documentary, for the object of documentary is more than mere communication of fact; it is interpretation, persuasion, and the creative element, the *art* of

191

documentary, lies there. The first part of Mr Rotha's book, so admirable when it reaches the actual making of documentaries, is rather tiresomely Marxist. He uses the word propaganda rather than persuasion because no object is so important to him as the political. But in that sense documentary has obviously little future in television under the present system. We fear our own vices, and it is interesting that Mr Rotha, whose films are seldom free from a certain prettiness and self-consciousness, should be so afraid of the word art which Mr Grierson, a producer almost aggressively free from style for style's sake, uses with admirable boldness. If propaganda, Mr Grierson writes, takes on its more political meaning, the sooner documentary is done with it the better. 'Art is wider than political doctrine and platform solution.... It may, like politics, realise the social ills, but it must also sympathise more widely.' To sympathise more widely.... I can think of no better distinction between art and propaganda, and with that object in view art may surely be allowed to find its way even into Broadcasting House. If it does, then indeed the wings are over Wardour Street.

24 January

AUNT EUDORA AND THE POETS
SIEGFRIED SASSOON

On New Year's Day I went to see my Aunt Eudora. In spite of having been born on the day of the outbreak of the Crimean War, she was looking remarkably well, and it soon became apparent that she was as vigorous and emphatic as ever in the expression of her opinions. Aunt Eudora is, among other things, a sound judge of poetry. Always a believer in keeping abreast of the times, she has watched many poetic fashions appear and pass away, while maintaining her own sturdily independent attitude toward them – an attitude based on a solid grounding in the best poetry from Chaucer onwards and sustained by the possession of what she calls 'a nose like a hound for anything first-rate.'

On January 1st, 1936, however, she wasn't in the best of tempers. In her hand was a small book bound in orange-vermilion cloth,* and what it contained had evidently distressed her.

'I can't make head nor tail of the Poetry of the year 1935!'

* *The Year's Poetry*, 1935. (Bodley Head)

she exclaimed, almost angrily, though she is by nature a good-natured old lady.

'Whatever made you buy it?' I asked.

Her tenaciously retentive memory enabled her to reply, *'It is unique as the anthology which, year by year, can give a really adequate idea of the poetry that is being written in our time.* That's what one of those Radical weeklies said about the book, so I sent for it.' As an afterthought she added, 'It won't be long before I'm in the next world and I want to have something new to tell dear Mr William Morris when I get there!'

Aunt Eudora had, from her girlhood, been faithful to pre-Raphaelitism, which was, she maintained, 'a Movement and not a Fashion, in spite of all those mawkish artistic females who went about swathed in garments of dim green arras spouting Dante Rossetti's poems. I always stuck up for Christina,' she said, 'and nobody denies now that she was the best of them.'

Suppressing a strong desire to keep her talking about the great Victorians – she had once been in a cab accident with Robert Browning and George Meredith had enphrased her as 'handmaid to Creative Spirit on tip-toe' – I persuasively removed *The Year's Poetry* from her lace-mittened old-ivory hand, passed her the filigreed smelling-salt bottle, and suggested that we should investigate the up-to-date volume in cerebral collaboration.

'We'll just dodge about and see what we can make of it,' I remarked. 'The poets are arranged in order of age. The first dozen or so are either safely established or past praying for, so we'll leave them alone. But before we start, just repeat a few lines you're fond of, so that we can begin by reminding ourselves what poetry used to be like before 1935.'

> 'They have no song, the sedges dry,
>   And still they sing.
> It is within my breast they sing,
>   As I pass by.
> Within my breast they touch a string,
>   They wake a sigh.
> There is but sound of sedges dry;
>   In me they sing.'

'That's by Mr Meredith, and it's good enough for an old stick like me.' She spoke bluntly, but there had been a catch in her voice while she quoted. And I wondered to myself – and not for the first time either – whether any poetry matters except the poetry that springs direct from the heart.

A little reluctantly, perhaps, I opened the book, and gave her the opening stanza of 'In the Square,' by W. H. Auden.

'O for doors to be open and an invite with gilded edges
To dine with Lord Lobcock and Count Asthma on the
 platinum benches,
With the somersaults and fireworks, the roast and the
 smacking kisses . . .
 Cried the six cripples to the silent statue,
 The six beggared cripples.'

'Good gracious, darling, how perfectly extraordinary! I don't like it at all!' exclaimed Aunt Eudora, resorting to her smelling-salts.

'It does sound a bit odd,' I admitted, adding, 'A lot of people think highly of Auden, you know. The younger generation regard him as a very live wire indeed.'

'I'm sure they're right. He certainly gave me a shock. Try someone else now, dear.'

'Well, here's one called "Doctrinal Point" by William Empson:

"The god approached dissolves into the air.

Magnolias, for instance, when in bud,
Are right in doing anything they can think of;
Free by predestination in the blood,
Saved by their own sap, shed for themselves,
Their texture can impose their architecture;
Their sapient matter is already informed."'

'Stop!' cried Aunt Eudora. 'What sort of poetry is that?'

'It's metaphysical. And the more you know about things, the more you know what it means.'

'Metafiddlesticks! I never heard such flat lines in my life.'

Seeing that I'd failed again, I embarked on 'To a Chinese Girl,' by Ronald Bottrall.

'Your grapnel eyes dredging my body through
Haul up the uncharted silt, efface
The mud flats of impeding residue.

Thus trenching you rive up my yesterdays:
Exposed to sun, your eastern sun, not mine,
Compromise shrivels in Confucian rays.

Fitly proportioned pigments will combine
In deeper values, but vague ampersands
Choke the lacunae of our strict design.'

Again she checked me with a protesting hand. (The word 'am-persands' had puzzled her.) 'Really, Aunt Eudora, you must let me finish the poem. One shouldn't judge these things by frag-ments.'

'No dear, I'd much rather hear what the Chinese girl said to him. In my day that sort of stuff was called pretentious verbiage. It may be clever. If so, I'm stupid. Try reading the *last* stanza of a poem, please.'

With deepening dismay, I obliged her with the last lines of an Ode by R. E. Warner:

> 'Twining of serpents! Halitosis of lions!
> be backward from the body.
> Be speed from the wind and lightness in the air,
> following no sandy path from Italy,
> but moth-soft, palpitating, where
> by wind's plume silver splashed
> the untroubling negro water
> Shrives with the light, O whitely blushes.'

'What is the subject of the Ode?' she enquired. Her eyes were closed, and she was beginning to look all her age.

'Well, it seems to be about the author returning to England from Egypt. . . .'

No doubt it was extremely unfair to the anthology, but I simply hadn't the heart to read Aunt Eudora any more extracts. It was obvious that she would never catch up with the poetry of 1935. So I asked her to recite me something old-fashioned again before I said good-bye. And, oddly enough, she repeated some early lines by Gerard Manley Hopkins, that great Victorian whose later and much more elaborate idiom has been applauded and imitated by the present 'younger generation' of poets:

> 'I have desired to go
> Where springs not fail,
> To fields where flies no sharp and sided hail
> And a few lilies blow.
>
> And I have asked to be
> Where storms not come,
> Where the green swell is in the havens dumb,
> And out of the swing of the sea.'

How lovely it sounded! And how I wished that the young poets of 1935 would try to express themselves less artificially!

31 January

RUDYARD KIPLING ET LA FRANCE
ANDRÉ MAUROIS

L'une des plus belles histoires de Kipling a pour titre: *Le Miracle de Purun Bhagat*. Elle se trouve dans le *Second Livre de la Jungle*. On y apprend comment Purun Bhagat, ministre d'un état indigène des Indes, homme de vaste culture, honoré par les Anglais pour ses merveilleuses qualités d'administrateur, décoré par eux de tours leurs ordres, docteur de toutes leurs Universités, décide en pleine maturité de quitter son palais et ses titres pour devenir un ermite et un saint. Pendant vingt ans, celui qui a gouverné un peuple vit d'aumônes, près d'un village des collines. Puis, un jour de terrible catastrophe naturelle (le glissement d'une montagne), le saint se souvient qu'il a été un chef et, retrouvant sans effort ses qualités de conducteur de peuples, sauve les villageois qui l'ont fait vivre.

Cette histoire pourrait être un symbole assez exact de la vie de Kipling lui-même. Il a commencé la vie en homme d'action. Il a vécu parmi ceux qui travaillent et luttent. Il a appris d'eux à vénérer le Dieu des Choses Telles qu'Elles Sont, à mépriser les bavards et les menteurs, à respecter l'Univers et les lois, les dures lois de la Jungle. Puis, à trente ans, ayant déjà dit l'essentiel de ce qu'il avait à dire, ayant composé en dix ans plus de chefs-d'oeuvres qu'aucun homme de ce temps en la plus longue des vies, ayant conquis une gloire telle qu'une grave maladie de sa trentième année fut dès lors considérée comme un malheur universel, le sage alla vivre en ermite dans les campagnes anglaises.

C'est en vain qu'on a voulu le peindre comme un partisan politique. Qu'importait à Kipling, qui vivait hors du temps, la victoire de tel ou tel petit homme? Ce qu'il voulait, c'était que son pays conservât les vertus qui lui avaient permis de conquérir et de gouverner un immense Empire; c'était que l'humanité n'oubliât pas les belles et terribles Lois de la Jungle, hors desquelles il n'y a que désordre, anarchie et misère pour tous. De temps à autre, quand la montagne menaçait de s'écrouler sur les siens, l'ermite sortait de sa retraite et criait aux siens: 'N'oubliez pas! ...' Par ses poèmes, il créait un lien vivant entre tous les peuples de l'Empire; en temps de guerre, il rappelait les conditions de la victoire; en temps de paix, les conditions de la sécurité; en tous temps le respect dû par tous au Dieu des Choses Telles qu'Elles Sont.

Kipling enseignait une morale éternelle, héroïque et dure. Mais non point doctrine théorique. Sa morale était faite d'images et de portraits. Un jeune lieutenant, un administrateur civil qui sauve un district, un planteur de coton, un mécanicien, tels étaient ses héros. 'Ils meurent, ou se tuent de travail, ou brisent leur santé pour que l'Empire soit protégé de la mort et de la maladie, de la famine et de la guerre, et un jour capable de se gouverner lui-même.' Kipling, qui, de ses yeux si vifs sous les sourcils broussailleux, avait bien observé les actions des hommes, était sans illusions. Il ne haïssait ni ne méprisait l'humanité. Au contraire il la jugeait capable de grandeur, mais il savait que l'homme, même quand il se croit civilisé, vit sur une frange étroite audelà de laquelle il n'y a plus que le chaos. Et l'ermite veillait sur ses villageois.

En particulier nous, Français, lui devons une reconnaissance émue, durable, pour avoir fait de nous à l'Angleterre une peinture si généreuse. Il aurait pu, en un temps de rivalité franco-anglaise, avoir des préjugés; il en avait eu dans sa jeunesse; mais son grand respect pour les choses telles qu'elles sont ne lui permettait pas d'accepter sans contrôle ces images déformées des peuples que créent polémiques et passions. Kipling ne recevait pas ses images des autres. Il allait voir, et enregistrait avec une merveilleuse exactitude ce qu'il voyait. Inlassablement, pendant des années, il courut les routes de France. Il connaissait leurs noms, leurs gîtes d'étape, les paysages qu'elles traversent; il avait parlé avec les paysans de toutes nos provinces; il savait que 'la poussière est blanche à Angoulême, que le soleil est chaud à Blaye et qu'en passant près de Langon on commence à sentir l'odeur de la résine et des pins'; il savait que 'la vraie force de la France, c'est le sol' et il reconnaissait en chaque paysan français un frère infiniment estimable qui, comme lui, avait compris les Lois de la Jungle et les respectait à sa manière.

Je voudrais que chaque Français pût lire ce petit livre: les *Souvenirs de France*. Il y verrait comment le génie permet de franchir les hautes barrières de l'histoire et des moeurs pour aller droit au coeur d'une civilisation étrangère; il y trouverait la précieuse confirmation des raisons qu'il a lui-même de croire en la force et en l'avenir de son pays.

'Un pays où les hommes, les femmes, les enfants et les chiens tiennent le travail pour une part normale de l'existence est un pays qu'on n'a pas comme on veut, écrit Kipling ... Cette vertu de labeur s'accompagne d'une habitude d'économie en toutes choses qui fait que le reste ne coûte plus rien ... "Monsieur, vous oubliez un sou!" Ce n'est pas la somme qui importe, c'est le principe ...

Et cette habitude de se priver, cette acceptation d'une vie dure fortifie le tissu moral.'

Au hasard de ses promenades françaises, Kipling parle avec des gendarmes, avec des maçons, avec un vétéran de 70 qui, sur la route du Canigou, discourt sur le ton d'Anatole France, avec un facteur rural qui a été à Madagascar, avec un marmot du Béarn, avec un camionneur de Digne, avec le vieux Clemenceau ... De tous il tire des faits, des images précises, des 'choses telles qu'elles sont.' J'aime son ton d'interrogation pressante qui va directement au problème essentiel. A Poincaré, après le sauvetage du franc en 1926, il demande quelle a été la répercussion *humaine* des mesures prises; à Clemenceau il dit: 'Voyons, après ce qu'ils vous ont fait, que pensez-vous des hommes?' Et Clemenceau, le cynique et pessimiste Clemenceau, alors tout proche de la mort, répond:

> 'Les hommes? Ils ne sont pas si méchants ... Qu'est-ce qu'ils m'ont fait? Rien du tout ... Les hommes, allez! ... Au bout du compte, ils valent mieux qu'on ne croit.'

'Et voilà,' conclut Kipling, 'quelques-unes de mes raisons d'aimer la France.' Et voilà, dirons-nous à notre tour, quelques-unes de nos raisons d'aimer Kipling. Il voyait clair et il voyait grand. Il savait embrasser d'un même regard le passé et le présent. Il peignait mieux que personne les luttes qui avaient, au cours des siècles, opposé son pays au nôtre. Mais c'était, parce qu'il avait l'âme noble, pour y trouver des raisons de louer un adversaire digne d'estime. 'Pardonnons-nous les vieilles fatalités que n'effacera nul pardon ... O France chère à toute âme éprise du genre humain.'

O Kipling cher à toute âme éprise d'héroïsme et de dure vérité, demeure pour ton peuple comme pour le nôtre le sage, le saint que l'on va consulter quand la folie des hommes ou la fureur des choses ont mis les villages en péril. La vie est trop courte pour que chaque joueur puisse, lui-même, retrouver les lois de la défaite et de la victoire; toi seul avais su enseigner à tes 'louveteaux' comment 'le grand jeu de la vie a été joué par les meilleurs joueurs.' Toi seul, en un temps d'orgueil et de mensonge, avais compris que la civilisation, notre bien unique, est un très fragile édifice qui repose sur quelques règles précises et impitoyables. Toi seul avais su incarner ces règles qui, abstraites, eussent été inefficaces, en des légendes et des poèmes qui demeureront éternellement vivants. Longtemps encore, parce que de jeunes hommes, chez toi comme chez nous, te liront, s'accomplira dans les âmes des hommes le Miracle de Rudyard Kipling.

7 February

THE THEATRE
DEREK VERSCHOYLE

The Dog Beneath the Skin, W.H. Auden and Christopher Isherwood. At the Westminster

The Dog Beneath the Skin is in every respect a much more impressive work than Mr Auden's earlier play, *The Dance of Death*. It is more precise, and therefore more pointed, in its choice of subject-matter, more consistent and (for the most part) more mature in its satire, and, apart from its rather embarrassing conclusion, much less naïvely evangelistic in its political attitude. It takes its form from musical comedy and revue, and differs from everyday revue (which it occasionally challenges on its own ground) chiefly in its assumption of a comprehensive moral outlook. The choruses, in which the authors underline the purport of their satire, are eloquent and often moving, the dialogue has a competence of wit, and the prose scenes, which range from the burlesque to the gravely ironic, bear the mark of a genuine dramatic talent. Nevertheless it is far from being a completely satisfactory play.

The *Dog Beneath the Skin* has it in common with its predecessor that it is a satirical study of a society which has surrendered to unreason and attempts to conceal from itself the symptoms of its own decadence. The examination of this society is made inclusive by a device borrowed from everyday musical comedy. Alan, the hero, is an unsophisticated village youth who is chosen by lot to conduct a search for the lost heir of the local landlord, the promised reward for success being the hand of Sir Francis's sister. He is accompanied on his journey by a woolly dog, an animal of remarkable intelligence but with a regrettable habit of lapping whisky incontinently from a bowl, who more than once manages to extricate him from a dangerous situation. The moral indignation of the authors directs the pair through the representative institutions of a decaying continent. The countries which have succumbed to Fascism are shown as giant lunatic asylums, a decrepit monarchy as a gilded brothel, and England as a feckless suburb in which the population attempts to escape from reality through athleticism, aestheticism, eroticism, hypochondria, or intellectual suicide in a herd. In the last scene the lost heir, who has emerged from his hiding-place under the dog's skin, delivers a sermon on the iniquities of contemporary society to the massed inhabitants of his native village, who have been mobilised into a patriotic organisation by the vicar and a choleric colonel, and is promptly shot for his pains.

It seems to have become a commonplace of criticism that an author who exposes social evils is under no obligation to suggest a remedy. But the validity of this assumption surely depends on the amount of novelty in the exposure. So far from being new, many of Mr Auden's targets – the press, the pulpit, the armament-manufacturer, the party-politician and the rest – have been familiar objects of intellectual ridicule for a decade. One has no objection to his attack on them on this occasion, beyond being rather bored by so assiduous, and sometimes so feeble, a pelting of already battered Aunt Sallies. But one rather expects that, by way of compensation for the lack of novelty in his attack, Mr Auden will make some attempt to prescribe a constructive substitute. It is a grave fault in the play, as much considered purely dramatically as in its capacity of social analysis, that it provides no more to this point than a vague and doctrinaire outline of a priggish and watery Utopia.

There is no space in which to discuss the Group Theatre's production in detail. As a whole, it showed almost as great an improvement on the production of *The Dance of Death* as the play itself showed on its predecessor. Mr Rupert Doone appears to have learned that it is not the most effective method of staging a revue to be ironically apologetic about that unexalted but expressive dramatic form, and his direction is much more balanced and less inclined to force after freakishly nervous effects. The best performances came from Mr John Moody as the hero, and from Mr John Glyn-Jones and Mr Desmond Ellis as two journalists who accompany and complicate his search; the worst from Mr Gyles Isham, who declaimed the choruses with a painfully gentlemanly air. Mr Auden's speech contributed greatly to the gaiety of the evening.

7 February

THE CINEMA
GRAHAM GREENE

Modern Times. At the Tivoli

I am too much an admirer of Mr Chaplin to believe that the most important thing about his new film is that for a few minutes we are allowed to hear his agreeable and rather husky voice in a song. The little man has at last definitely entered the contemporary scene; there had always before been a hint of 'period' about his courage and misfortunes; he carried about with him more than the mere custard pie of Karno's day, its manners, its curious clothes, its sense of pathos and its dated poverty. There were occasions, in his encounters with blind flower girls or his adventures in mean streets or in the odd little pitchpine mission halls where he carried round the bag or preached in pantomime on a subject so near his own experience as the tale of David and Goliath, when he seemed to go back almost as far as Dickens. The change is evident in his choice of heroine: fair and featureless with the smudged effect of an amateur water-colour which has run, they never appeared again in leading parts, for they were quite characterless. But Miss Paulette Goddard, dark, grimy, with her amusing urban and plebeian face, is a promise that the little man will no longer linger at the edge of mawkish situation, the unfair pathos of the blind girl and the orphan child. One feels about her as Hyacinth felt about Millicent in *The Princess Casamassima*: 'she laughed with the laugh of the people, and if you hit her hard enough would cry with their tears.' For the first time the little man does not go off alone, flaunting his cane and battered bowler along the endless road out of the screen. He goes in company looking for what may turn up.

What *had* turned up was first a job in a huge factory twisting screws tighter as little pieces of nameless machinery passed him on a moving belt, under the televised eye of the manager, an eye that followed him even into the lavatory when he snatched an illicit smoke. The experiment of an automatic feeding machine, which will enable a man to be fed while he works, drives him crazy (the running amok of this machine, with its hygienic mouth-wiper, at the moment when it has reached the Indian corn course, is horrifyingly funny; it is the best scene, I think, that Mr Chaplin has ever invented). When he leaves hospital he is arrested as a communist leader (he has picked up a red street flag which has fallen off a lorry) and released again after foiling a prison hold-up. Unemployment and prison punctuate his life, starvation and lucky breaks, and somewhere in its course he attaches to himself the other piece of human refuse.

The Marxists, I suppose, will claim this as *their* film, but it is a good deal less and a good deal more than socialist in intention. No real political passion has gone into it: the police batter the little man at one moment and feed him with buns the next: and there is no warm maternal optimism, in the Mitchison manner, about the character of the workers: when the police are brutes, the men are cowards; the little man is always left in the lurch. Nor do we find him wondering 'what a socialist man should do,' but dreaming of a steady job and the most bourgeois home. Mr Chaplin, whatever his political convictions may be, is an artist and not a propagandist. He doesn't try to explain, but presents with vivid fantasy what seems to him a crazy comic tragic world without a plan, but his sketch of the inhuman factory does not lead us to suppose that his little man would be more at home at Dneipostroi. He presents, he doesn't offer, political solutions.

The little man politely giving up his seat to the girl in the crowded Black Maria: the little man when the dinner-bell sounds tenderly sticking a spray of celery into the mouth of the old mechanic whose head has been caught between the cog-wheels: the little man littering the path of the pursuing detectives with overturned chairs to save his girl: Mr Chaplin has, like Conrad, 'a few simple ideas'; they could be expressed in much the same phrases: courage, loyalty, labour: against the same nihilistic background of purposeless suffering. 'Mistah Kurtz – he dead.' These ideas are not enough for a reformer, but they have proved amply sufficient for an artist.

14 February

AUNT EUDORA AND THE POETS
(To the Editor of *The Spectator*)

Sir, – It seems sensible to offer you my reactions to Mr Sassoon's article of January 31st, against various recent poets, as I am one of the four quoted. I can see that the scraps from me and R. E. Warner go pretty flat, anyway from that angle. I can understand that many Aunt Eudoras can't enjoy the verse from Auden, or a great deal of Shakespeare either. But the lines from Bottrall

seem to me so direct and so obviously good that Aunt Eudora, snarling, in her underdog way, about how she 'may be stupid,' and would rather hear gossip about Bottrall, becomes a figure of low comedy. Anyway Mr Sassoon has played fair: it is a real difference of judgement; if I had respected his Aunt Eudora I might have tried those two bits on her myself. – Yours sincerely, *W. Empson*
71 Marchmont Street, W.C.1.

14 February

UP THE GARDEN PATH
NICHOLAS BLAKE

The A.B.C. Murders, Agatha Christie. (Crime Club)
Murder isn't Easy, Richard Hull. (Faber and Faber)
Scandal at School, G.D.H. and M. Cole (Crime Club)
A Word of Six Letters, Herbert Adams. (Crime Club)
Who Killed Gatton?, E. Charles Vivian. (Ward, Lock)
Vultures in the Sky, Todd Downing. (Methuen)
The Nursing Home Murder, Ngaio Marsh and Dr Jellett. (Bles)

> 'I think I'll go and meet her,' said Alice. . . .
>   'You can't possibly do that,' said the Rose: '*I* should advise you to walk the other way.'
>   This sounded nonsense to Alice, so she said nothing, but set off at once towards the Red Queen. To her surprise, she lost sight of her in a moment, and found herself walking in at the front-door again.'

The Garden-of-Live-Flowers incident in the Alice-mythos anticipates the method of the modern detection-fan. To find the Red Queen he has learnt to go in the most unlikely direction. So now the hard-pressed writer is inclined to try a double bluff and make his criminal the obvious suspect throughout. It would give away her whole plot to tell which of these bluffs Mrs Christie employs in her new book: one can only chalk up yet another defeat at her hands and admit sadly that she has led one up the garden path with her usual blend of duplicity and fairness. This is all the more riling, as she conveys throughout the book a subtle suggestion that she is not playing fair; I, at any rate, was convinced – until the final chapter – that at last I had caught her out putting across a fast one over her public. Moreover she deceives us, not by irrelevant red herrings, but by the identical trick the A.B.C. murderer uses to deceive the police. The murderer writes to Poirot, giving him full warning of his intentions. Then a Mrs Ascher is killed at Andover, Betty Barnard at Bexhill, and so on. In each case an A.B.C. railway guide is found beside the body. What more ingenious devilry could a homicidal maniac devise? The characters, particularly that of the murderer, are rather too perfunctorily sketched. Apart from this, one can have nothing but praise for *The A.B.C. Murders*, which is really a little masterpiece of construction.

Mr Hull, on the other hand, as we realised in his first book, *Murder of My Aunt*, has a great gift for character; and here again he gives it full scope by recording events in the first person. The three partners in the NeO-aD advertising firm have got on each others' nerves, and distrust each others' business abilities – not without reason, as we soon come to see. Things finally get to the pitch when two of them say, 'There's a limit to the extent to which the folly of any man can be allowed to ruin a business.' They take steps, and are found simultaneously poisoned with a preparation which the firm is advertising; one of them has a black eye thrown in. Neat, without being gaudy. Though the construction of *Murder Isn't Easy* is not so clean as that of *Murder of My Aunt*, it holds the interest throughout and presents a more credible situation. It demonstrates effectively, too, the truth of the old adages – (1) that the only reason why business-men succeed in business is that they have only business-men to compete with, (2) that it is self-deception which makes the world go round.

In *Scandal at School* the Coles have paid much more attention to character than in some of their earlier books. The dialogue is consistently lifelike. The setting, too, is well done – Santley House, one of those advanced schools where the headmaster addresses an invocation to the Sun by way of grace-before-meat, the children are compelled to make their own rules out of the sheer boredom of having nothing to rebel against, the staff is a nicely graded mixture of dim hacks and lush yearners, and a general ultra-violet atmosphere (or Twilight of the Educational Shibboleths) pervades the scene. Or so the critics of such establishments would have us believe. The Coles, at any rate, make it quite convincing. Less convincing is the character of the victim, a small girl who is found poisoned by dial in the sanatorium. She is already a hardened blackmailer; and, while such activities are all in the day's work at Narkover, I doubt if they would have survived so long at Santley House. This weakens the motive; grown-ups are not likely to be driven to desperate expedients by the threats of a child. The plot, also, rather resembles a clockwork mouse; erratic in direction, and requiring too frequent winding-up.

Mr Adams presents a very much more conventional situation. A disagreeable rich old man, Barty Blount, has invited his equally disagreeable relatives to celebrate his 70th birthday. After tea he goes riding, and is discovered later with a broken neck. The young local doctor, for no reason except that he is in love with the old man's neice, Ella, suspects 'foul play' (Mr Adams' phrase, not mine) and finds a quantity of sulphonal in the body. Ella was not present at this party; but later, when she is discovered to be Blount's heiress, somebody starts being dastardly again. She narrowly escapes three fatal accidents, aided by luck and the young doctor. This part of the book is quite exciting, and the solution – though obvious – is adequate. But *A Word of Six Letters* must be criticised on the following counts. (1) Supineness of police. (2) Padding: there is too much superfluous eating and drinking; this is only permissible when the author (*cf.* Mr H.C. Bailey *passim*), and therefore the reader, gets a kick out of it. (3) Title: crosswords play a very subordinate part in the plot. (4) Archness: *e.g.*:

> 'Romp it was. There can be some merry doings in searching pretty girls for an elusive slipper.'

Crumbs!

In *Who Killed Gatton?* we turn from the arch to the heroic-on-stilts style:

> 'Head entered, and stood before the tall, slender, normally lovely but now furious girl – or woman.
> ' "The reason for this insult, officer?" she demanded.'

The book also contains a great deal of cap-lifting whenever England, the dead, &c., are mentioned, a magnificent 1890 vintage proposal-of-marriage scene, and a ditto never-set-foot-in-my-house-again one. Those who, like myself, revel in this sort of thing, will be rewarded as well by an exciting and cleverly worked-out tale. A young aviator, in order to visit his lady-love, uses an experimental plane which he is trying out for his company. Later he is found shot, and it is soon evident that he had died trying to protect the secrets embodied in this plane from foreign agents. Two questions to Mr Vivian. Would any coroner, even under the present rules, bully a witness so scandalously? Isn't it now established that 'anything you may say ... may be used as evidence *against you*' is not the correct formula?

I have not read *The Cat Screams*, but if it is as good as Mr Downing's new book it is very good indeed. He has that command of tempo without which a detection writer can never rise into the first class. He avoids the American tendency to overwrite the trivial, yet can write up to the dramatic situation when it comes. He has the *sotto-voce*, ungesticulating way of leading one up to the edge of a precipice which makes a walk with Dr M.R. James so deliciously uncomfortable. Not that there is anything supernatural about *Vultures in the Sky*. In a train going through Mexico a man is found poisoned by an injection of nicotin; other deaths follow: the climax comes when, in a Pullman deliberately uncoupled and left standing in the middle of a desert, four men by the light of matches discover that their clothes are smeared with blood. A kidnapper and a revolutionary travelling on this train add to the complications. These are admirably worked out, though the movements are so involved that they ought to have been tabulated at some point. My only other criticisms are (1) that hypodermic syringes are exceedingly fragile at one end, (2) that nicotin alkaloid is colourless, not – as Mr Downing says – 'almost as black as ink.' This book puts him into the Van Dine-Ellery Queen class; I do not expect to read a better detective novel for a long time.

Little space is left for *The Nursing Home Murder*. The Home Secretary receives a fatal dose of hyoscine. There are several people with sound motives – the operating surgeon, a Communist nurse, the anaesthetist, and the statesman's discarded mistress. These, plus a charming detective, local colour obviously put on by a professional hand, a pretty wit, and a perfectly reasonable solution, form the ingredients of a mix-up that can be unreservedly recommended and will elicit loud cries for 'more!' from all who taste it.

14 February

AUNT EUDORA AND THE POETS
(To the Editor of *The Spectator*)

Sir, – The bitterness which enters into nearly all discussions of modern poetry is very notable. Powerful prejudices are involved and the majority of older readers seem to approach modern poetry, if they approach it at all, in a spirit of hostility, expecting trouble and prepared to make it. It is surprising to find Mr Sassoon, whose work once met the same hostility and deliberate misunderstanding, now taking the side of the poet-baiters, many of whom rail at the younger poets without being able to name them or quote from their works at all.

Since such strong feelings are involved, it would surely be worth while to try to discover the roots of the trouble. It is useless to put all the blame either on the poets or the readers. Both sides are at fault, but the difficulty is to find precisely where the fault lies. If some modern poets do not write lyrics on rural topics without bringing in politics and morality and heaven knows what, it is because they cannot honestly keep these topics out: to give an accurate and spontaneous account of his feeling on looking at a buttercup the poet may be compelled to mention, say, the unnecessary suffering in the world. This makes the poem rather nasty for people who don't want to be reminded of such things. Again, the majority of modern poets have had an ordinary grammar-school or public-school education, and, because a certain amount of chemistry and physics is as familiar to them as the main stories of Greek mythology, they find it natural to refer to ideas which are ingrained in their thought but foreign to readers brought up on a different curriculum.

There is no doubt that some of the work of the younger poets is more tortuous than it need be: in attempting to express thoughts as well as feelings they use abstract statements less exact and less moving than the images which the poem really needs. Again, they expect the reader to be willing at all times to enjoy a certain amount of lively thought, and the difficulty is to know where to draw the line, and at what point the labour of thinking makes the reader become insensible to the imagery and rhythm of the poem. A person who was puzzled for a single instant by Janus's problem last week about the pound note isn't likely to be able to read Mr Empson's poems without losing sight of the sensuous elements altogether. Mr Empson would admit, I think, that some of his poems have been too tightly knotted to please any large number of readers.

But something more than this is involved: it does not account for the deliberate reluctance of readers to enjoy the poetry first and understand it afterwards, as they willingly do on reading Shakespeare. I do not think that this reluctance is wholly due to the number of critics who have done their best to convince the public that all the young poets are deliberately incomprehensible, nor can the turgid verbiage and large claims of the other critics whom Mr Sassoon quotes have much to do with it. For one thing, few people read them; and for another, Shelley made claims for poetry quite as ambitious as those which Mr Sassoon considers 'a pretty tough proposition.' To talk of resolving 'psychological, ethical and logical conflicts' may well alarm some readers, but hardly enough to make them dislike the poetry at sight. Readers of *Kubla Khan* are not put off by the jaw-cracking terminology which Coleridge used in his criticism. Surely a poet may tackle something harder than the problems of a simple descriptive poem without becoming, as Mr Sassoon seems to imply, a prig. Probably the poet will solve the 'problem' when he is not worrying about it, and the reader will not think of it as a problem at all. After all, some of the problems are pretty easy, and the 'solutions' neat and enjoyable.

What, then, is the real source of the hostility? Is there today a divergence between young people and their elders so profound that the older people instinctively dislike and ridicule the most articulate of their juniors? It seems unlikely, but if it really exists it ought to be remedied. This is a job for some critic to tackle, and for which Mr Sassoon is well equipped. The issue is important, because, while the squabble is going on, people are turning away from poetry altogether, and a language without a living poetry is poor and crude. If people cannot appreciate the rhythms and sensuous significance of words, they can no longer use speech to tidy their thoughts and phantasies and feelings. For that reason, those of us who are opposed to the tendency to treat poetry as a silliness of school girls should thrash out our differences patiently and honestly until they disappear or assume their true importance in the light of graver issues. We don't want to appear like a pack of Edinburgh Reviewers debasing criticism to the level of buffoonery or gang-warfare.

Presumably, Mr Sassoon was trying to be critical in his review of *The Year's Poetry:* 1935; but his essay leaves me unenlightened. Obviously he dislikes the poems of his juniors, and obviously he thinks that those of us who like them are in some way his inferiors, but instead of trying to show us our shortcomings, he ridicules the poems, or rather, he shirks the responsibility of ridiculing them by pretending to hide behind the opinions of an aunt who prefers poems about snowdrops. (Why, knowing her tastes, did Mr Sassoon not read to her Mr Dyment's *Switch Cut in April?*) Finally, Mr Sassoon contrasts the complexity of the 'flat lines' of a stanza from the most complicated poem Mr Empson has written with the simplicity of one of the very few simple poems ever written by Hopkins, obscuring the fact that Hopkins is, on an average, far more difficult, and does far greater violence to the English language, than Mr Empson or any other young poet.

If I reviewed Mr de la Mare's poems and happened to dislike them (I don't) and, after quoting the line 'Sacred of old was the dyed baboon' as a fair example, reported the comments of an imaginary nephew who preferred poems about cowboys, I am sure that Mr Sassoon would think, quite rightly, that I was being silly. Clearly, Mr Sassoon is not in the habit of being silly, and he has himself written poems which are more often enjoyed by the people who like the poems he condemns than by the Aunt Eudoras. Perhaps he will take us into his confidence and explain what he really thinks about the poetry he was invited to review, and explain in what way those of us are at fault who find that our enjoyment of Empson's *Doctrinal Point*, MacNeice's *Perseus*, or Spender's *North* differs from our enjoyment of Shakespeare, or Donne, or Shelley, in degree but not in kind. – I am, Sir, &c.,
Michael Roberts
Newcastle-upon-Tyne

21 February

AUNT EUDORA AND THE POETS
(To the Editor of *The Spectator*)

Sir, – Mr Michael Roberts has written you an epistolary article, of 1150 words, in which he deplores my unfairness to the younger poets and my behaviour in 'pretending to hide behind the opinions of an aunt who prefers poems about snowdrops.' I am therefore compelled to confess that when reporting my conversations with Aunt Eudora I had two objects in view. Firstly, I wanted to write something amusing to *The Spectator*. (I felt that the dear old lady needed a tonic.) And secondly, I wanted to give the younger poets a chance to be amusing at my expense. Whether Aunt Eudora has amused your readers can only be conjectured. Whether the younger poets have replied amusingly is also conjectural, but to me their remonstrances have been a disappointment. I suppose they took me too seriously.

A. C. Boyd wrote that 'Aunt Eudora must have overlooked the metaphysical verse of the seventeenth century, and this gap in her reading might partly account for her difficulties with the poetry of 1935.' It might. A. E. Housman, in his lecture on *The Name and Nature of Poetry*, described the metaphysical poets of the seventeenth century as follows. 'There was a whole age of English in which the place of poetry was usurped by something very different which possessed the proper and specific name of wit: wit not in its modern sense, but as defined by Johnson, "a combination of dissimilar images, or discovery of occult resemblances in things apparently unlike." Such discoveries are no more poetical than anagrams; such pleasure as they give is purely intellectual and intellectually frivolous; but this was the pleasure principally sought and found in poems by the intelligentsia of fifty years or more of the seventeenth century.'

I am, of course, aware that Poetry is undergoing an anti-romantic revival – or ordeal. There is also the superficially 'new' visual mechanism caused by the cinema. There is also the tendency to over-exploit the discoveries of modern psychologists. Nevertheless I feel that Professor Housman's lecture contains wisdom which most of us can afford to assimilate with our chemistry, physics, and the rest of the 'curriculum of contemporaneity.'

Mr Michael Roberts concludes his letter by asking me to explain my failure to share his enjoyment of three poems, which he specifies. Mr Empson's *Doctrinal Point* may be good metaphysical verse, but I cannot agree that the following lines, when printed as prose, are anything else. 'Professor Eddington with the same insolence called all physics one tautology; if you describe things with the right tensors all law becomes the fact that they can be described with them; this is the assumption of the description. The duality of choice thus becomes the singularity of existence; the effort of virtue the unconsciousness of foreknowledge.'

Then there is Mr Spender's *The North*. I do not wish to heckle

Mr Spender, any more than I wish to discourage Mr Empson.
Both of them are trying very hard to produce something original
and significant. But I feel that they are trying a little *too* hard.

As descriptive semi-prose *The North* is interesting. But consider this:

> 'Return, return, you warn. We do. There is
> A network of railways, money, words, words, words.
> Meals, papers, exchanges, debates,
> Cinema, wireless; the worst is in Marriage.'

Was Mr Spender writing poetry when he wrote that? If so, the
art of Poetry must find a new name.

Mr MacNeice's *Perseus* is carefully contrived and highly artificial. It is without emotional vitality:

> 'Shut your eyes
> There are suns beneath your lids
> Or look in the looking-glass in the end room
> You will find it full of eyes
> The ancient smiles of men cut out with scissors and
> Kept in mirrors.'

Mr Roberts states that his enjoyment of these three poems is
comparable, in degree but not in kind, to his enjoyment of
Shakespeare, Donne, and Shelley. Without the least desire to be
offensive, I differ from him. A clever, self-conscious arrangement
of words is an unsatisfactory substitute for the real thing. (Mr
Spender *has* occasionally produced the real thing, or something
very like it.) My advice to our younger poets is that they should
control their imagery and study simple and direct utterance.
Also their rhythms worry me, and seem to lack impetus. But
I am a pre-machine-age poet, and therefore hopelessly old-
fashioned. Schubert-minded, I crave tunefulness! I also crave the
forgiveness of the younger poets for lecturing them like this. –
Yours truly,
Siegfried Sassoon

[The administration of a tonic to *The Spectator* was a kindly
thought on Mr Sassoon's part. Actually our circulation and re-
venue figures are serving that purpose quite adequately. – ED.
The Spectator.]

28 February

ABINGER HARVEST
ELIZABETH BOWEN

Abinger Harvest, E. M. Forster. (Arnold)

In an age when novelists hum like factories, keeping up to date
with themselves, Mr E. M. Forster's output has been, in bulk,
small. The novels which, with their 'new standard of truth,'
create an absolute world are five, only, in number. It is over
thirty years now since the first: *Where Angels Fear to Tread* was
short, and contained in embryo all the other books. The authority with which the novels are written, the power they have to
expand inside the mind account, perhaps, for the patience with
which his silences are received – he has never been mistrusted
and never declined. An artist does not rank somewhere between
entertainer and tradesman for nothing; he is expected to ring up
the curtain again promptly, punctually to deliver the goods.
Silence is undue, and makes the public suspicious. But a quality
in all Mr Forster's work makes peremptoriness of this kind
impossible. The books are so clearly more than efforts of his
intelligence; when they do come they have so clearly imposed
themselves that it is impossible to demand them when they
do not come.

Actually, he has not been so silent. Two collections of stories,
Pharos and Pharillon, Anonymity, Aspects of the Novel, the Lowes
Dickinson biography have been landmarks down the last twenty
years. And the eighty or so 'articles, essays, reviews, poems, &c.,'
reprinted in *Abinger Harvest* have been appearing since 1904. If
they were nothing more – and they are much more – they would
be notes on his so-called silences: the absorption and rapture of
travel, the exploration of books. That he has been prevailed
upon to assemble and republish them is a matter for gratitude.

Too often, collections are to be dreaded. They are the severest
test a writer can face. Tricks of mind, prejudices, an overworking
of privilege, an iota too much of accomplishment in the writing
stick out in the short essay, the *tour de force*: cumulatively, the
effect may be desolating, show up unsuspected weakness in other
work. Too many collections are scrapheaps from well-known
workshops – shavings no doubt of excellent wood, but the dismal
topicality of decades ago sits on them like dust, or a journalistic
smartness tarnishes them. Too few writers are right in throwing
nothing away. Mr Forster is one great exception: *Abinger*

Harvest comes with harvest richness and timeliness.

The essays have been assembled in four groups – The Present, Books, The Past, The East – and the scenario, which is beautiful, of the Abinger Pageant stands alone at the end. The order is vital and should, I feel, be followed – though it is tempting to keep darting backwards and forwards, attracted by titles or opening paragraphs. The collector's desire to be read in this order is more than a whim; it gives the book a form, unity and intention rare in its kind. The dates, startlingly various, of the essays play no part in their arrangement, and should not: there has never been any question of Mr Forster's *development*; there never seems to have been any early work. The age factor with him must have stayed outside and arbitrary; his maturity is innate. That so many of the essays should be so short, too short, seems less a fault in them than in circumstance. (Many appeared in weeklies.) This tantalising briefness, whatever its first object, is the one trying element in the book – the Greek beauty-box, the physician Cardan, the Doll Souse, the Emperor Babur, the rational Indian wedding, Cnidus in the rain, the Jodhpur dragon, the Scallies pass for moments into the light and disappear too soon. But, for all one's own regrets and disruptions, the book has its own, an extraordinary continuousness. Perhaps because Mr Forster has changed so little, perhaps because his mind does not flick on and off – it must impregnate not only his writing but all his conscious moments; its abeyances, even, must have their colour. What is remarkable, in these essays as in the novels, is his power of having access to the whole of himself, to what he has called 'the lower personality': the obscure, the involuntary, the general that is in us all the stuff of dreams and art, the source of perception, the arbiter of memory. Few intellects so active are less isolated from the whole of the being. Mr Forster does not make a doctrine of spontaneity; 'intuition,' he even says, 'makes dancing dervishes of us.' He must have come to terms with his intuition: happen to him what may, he remains, or appears to remain, at once the most active and the governing factor in his own experience. If the perfectly adjusted person does not suffer, Mr Forster is not the perfectly adjusted person: the perfectly adjusted writer I feel he is. With him, intellect not so much controls susceptibility as balances it; many of us have not the wits to feel. Given this highly sensitive equanimity, the effect of this quick succession of essays is, his not so much pitching upon a series of subjects as momentarily enclosing and then releasing them, added to.

To criticism he brings the make-up of the artist. He perceives in another man's work what he himself knows – which accords with his theory of the deep down, giant part of us being general. In his own novels the sense of conscious life's being built up over a somehow august vault of horror, that rings under the foot, that exhales coldly through cracks, is constantly palpable. Of *The Waste Land* he says: 'the horror is so intense that the poet has an inhibition and cannot state it openly.' And, later in the same essay: 'In respect of the horror that they find in life men may be divided into three classes' ... He finds the romantic in Ibsen, in Proust the adventurer. If he is hard on a writer it is in the manner of one accustomed to being hard on himself; he has none of the critic's godlike non-participation. He detects the finest fatal crack in the bowl. He sees Conrad's 'central obscurity.' 'The secret casket of his genius contains a vapour rather than a jewel.' Love for Jane Austen steels him against Miss Austen, who forgot the nobility of Anne, the wise wit of Elizabeth, when she wrote letters. In some of the critical essays his own image more nearly appears than elsewhere; they are the least, in his own sense, anonymous of his work.

The prose throughout *Abinger Harvest* is the prose of the novels; not a word he uses ever obstructs the mind – prose which makes objects appears brighter than themselves, as in very clear morning light, instead of darkening behind a mesh of words. Like Flaubert's, though so unlike, here is a style made perfect by being subject to purpose, and beautiful with vitality. Its rhythm is so inherent in its content that one cannot detect it without analysis. The least frigid of writing, it is the most impersonal; he is enemy to all those lovable little tricks. 'Literature,' he says elsewhere, 'tries to be unsigned,' and as far as manner goes he approaches anonymity. But in prose the point of view is inevitable; every sentence must bear, however lightly, the stamp of the mind, its governing quality. Behind his irony, his impersonality, his gentleness, Mr Forster is passionately civilised. The novels are manifestos, these essays ring with a note that is startling because it is rare. Passion will out, however much, however wisely irony may temper it. Beliefs that root in the nature cannot be silenced: this give him an unmistakable touch on a page. That he has written little that could be wrongly attributed is not as he would wish, but too few people are like him.

20 March

MR ELIOT'S POETRY

EDWIN MUIR

Collected Poems 1909-1935, T. S. Eliot. (Faber and Faber)

The first eighty pages in this volume are taken up by the poems which have already appeared in *Poems 1909-1935*; the remaining hundred pages contain Mr Eliot's poetic production for the last ten years, except for *Murder in the Cathedral*, which is not included. This second part begins with *Ash-Wednesday*, embraces two unfinished poems, *Sweeney Agonistes* and *Coriolan*, ten choruses from *The Rock*, four *Ariel Poems*, thirteen *Minor Poems*, and ends with *Burnt Norton*, which is in some ways different from any of Mr Eliot's other poems, and is one of the most remarkable, I think, that he has yet written.

It will be seen from this that Mr Eliot has been considerably more productive during the last ten years than during the sixteen years before; but it is very difficult to judge whether he has been productive on the same level, firstly because a writer of such individuality as his changes the taste of his readers, and they come to his later work with a different mind, and secondly because his style has altered. The alteration has been towards a greater explicitness of statement; *Ash-Wednesday* is far more explicit than any poetry that Mr Eliot wrote before it, and it represents, I think, a turning point in his development. *The Waste Land* is no doubt his greatest work, but there is in it, compared with his later work, a certain blindness both in the despair it expresses and in turning away from despair at the end. Since *The Hollow Men*, where that despair reached its lowest depths, Mr Eliot has never expressed it again; he has taken it as a theme, certainly, in *Sweeney Agonistes* and other poems; but though he is still in the midst of it, he is no longer within it. That is to say that he is not so firmly under the influence of his time and is more deliberately concerned with permanent things. The difference may be seen by setting side by side:

'These fragments I have shored against my ruins'

from *The Waste Land*, and

'Redeem the time, redeem the dream
The token of the word unheard, unspoken'

from *Ash-Wednesday*. This difference, the difference between

215

despair and faith, is so great that it is very hard to compare the two kinds of poetry that derive from it. A good deal of the second kind is obscure, like the first, but with a different obscurity: not the obscurity of deep darkness, but rather that of darkness against light. It is consequently less heavily charged and more easy to understand, more finally comprehensible. This must be admitted to be in its favour, unless we are to regard obscurity in itself, deep and total obscurity, as a poetic virtue.

The second half of the volume is nevertheless more unequal than the first. *Sweeney Agonistes*, brilliant as it is, is definitely in a lower class of poetry than the rest, and doubtless is intended to be. The choruses from *The Rock* are first of all choruses, that is compositions intended to be spoken and to be comprehensible as soon as spoken. They contain some beautiful poetry, they are original in form, but they naturally lack the condensation which Mr Eliot's poetry has at its best. On the other hand, almost all the shorter poems have intense concentration and perfect clarity at the same time; *Ash-Wednesday* and the four *Ariel Poems* are works of great beauty; and *Burnt Norton* is surely one of the best poems that Mr Eliot has ever written. Its subject is Time and its main text a quotation from Herakleitos to the effect that the road upwards and downwards is one and the same road. This poem is different from the others inasmuch as it is not at all dramatic, being a pure intellectual enquiry into the nature and forms of Time. It alternates between the most close argument and the most vivid imagery expressing the contradiction of Time, a contradiction implicit in the recurring phrase, 'At the still point of the turning world.' It contains lines of great beauty:

> 'We move above the moving tree
> In light upon the figured leaf
> And hear upon the sodden floor
> Below, the boarhound and the boar
> Pursue their pattern as before.'

That is a far more rarefied poetry than

> 'In the juvescence of the year
> Came Christ the tiger
> In depraved May, dogwood and chestnut, flowering judas,'

but it has something in common with it, a sense of the fabulous; the difference is that the second kind is very much more figured and patterned (to use words that recur frequently in it), which means that it is more thoroughly worked out. Imagery which is thoroughly worked out often becomes mechanical and lifeless; but in this poem both the thought and the imagery are intensely concentrated, and gain immensely from the development. Whether this poem owes anything to Dante I do not know, but one might chance the guess that Mr Eliot's later development as a poet has been away from the Elizabethans, by whom he was so much influenced at the beginning, towards Dante.

Mr Eliot's position as a poet is established, and his work has been more thoroughly discussed than that of any of his contemporaries. His influence on poetry has been decisive. That influence was due chiefly to his genius for poetry, but it was due also to certain qualities which he held in common with some other men in his age. He has had an influence on the form and on the attitude of poetry. By this I do not mean that he has encouraged a kind of poetry in which all sorts of poetical quotations and reminiscences alternate with realistic descriptions of contemporary life. This method was employed very effectively in *The Waste Land* because it was a natural part of the scheme; it has not been employed successfully by any of Mr Eliot's imitators, and as a set poetic method it is obviously ridiculous. Mr Eliot's dramatic approach has influenced the form of poetry away from the purely lyrical, and his exercise of the historical sense has influenced the attitude of poetry. The first influence has been entirely salutary; it has led to a necessary reform of poetic language and a spirit of objectivity which had been buried in the degeneration of Romanticism. The reliance on the historical sense Mr Eliot himself seems to have lost in his later work; it does not go with religious poetry; it cannot survive the vision of 'the still point of the turning world.' But even in *The Waste Land* he used it conditionally, for there too, if less explicitly, he was concerned with permanent things, which are not affected by history. When the historical sense is employed without reference to these permanent things it leads to a shallowness of the imaginative faculty, for it robs the individual existence of meaning and can in itself give no meaning to society, since society is still in becoming, and by the laws of history will always be. Where the historical sense has been used in this way, the responsibility is not Mr Eliot's; but it partly explains why his influence should be so great with poets who do not hold his beliefs.

3 April

VINDICATING THE VICTORIANS
ARTHUR WAUGH

As I Remember, E. E. Kellett. (Victor Gollancz)

Every generation has to endure the challenge of its immediate successor; and, having endured it, recedes into its proper place in the pageant of history. So, by slow but sure degrees, the Victorian age is passing into its own; and a book, like this of Mr Kellett's, so serene in temper, so penetrating in analysis, and so wide in range, offers an effective rebuke to the young Absaloms of criticism who wage rebellious war against the authority of their fathers' house.

The rebuke is the more convincing for its deliberate moderation. 'Having spent many of my best and happiest years,' says Mr Kellett, 'in the Victorian age, I do not like to hear it disparaged. I do not agree that those years were one long nightmare of priggishness, narrow-mindedness, self-complacency, hypocrisy, and goody-goodiness.' But he is far too wise a critic to waste words in abusing the plaintiff's attorney. He faces rhetoric with facts; and presents a varied and lively panorama of Victorianism, based partly on his own memory, and partly on the testimony of his forbears, animated by extensive knowledge of men and manners, of contemporary history, literature, religion, politics and sport, and everywhere irradiated with a quiet judgement which is not afraid of weakening its argument by facing both sides of the question fairly and squarely. Though saturated with personality, the book is not a collection of personal reminiscences. It is the map of a period, not the portrait of an individual. And, though its aim is atmosphere, the atmosphere is composed of a medley of elements. It abounds in sketches of character, in descriptions, and in anecdotes. Not all the anecdotes are new, and some of them have been better told perhaps elsewhere. But in their fresh setting they cluster together, and combine in an attractive pattern. The Victorians are vindicated by evidence, and the evidence is handled with equanimity and force.

Mr Kellett is by circumstance a Liberal Nonconformist, bred in a strictly religious, almost a theological community. His boyhood was not immune from the mental sufferings of a generation subjected to every Puritan test of faith and works; and he would be the first to admit that much that he was taught was terrible. Nevertheless, he has a kindly indulgence for those forms of superstition which sprang from a sincere conviction of the reality of the spiritual world, and of the secret processes of Providence in the ways of human life. Was all this confidence hypocrisy? Some of it, perhaps; since the Victorians were often as vicious as Pagans; but certainly not all – perhaps not even the greater part. Mr Kellett lingers gently, but not sentimentally, in contemplation of the Victorian home, where the day began and ended in family prayer, the hearth was the centre of the universe, and the concerns of the household were of paramount interest. If these people were hypocrites, their hypocrisy was of the kind common to all humanity. 'Can we uncompromisingly assert that there is anywhere a single person entirely free from this most subtle and elusive vice? We all practise it, and our purest and most candid actions are touched with it.'

But their hypocrisy was sentimental, rejoins the Devil's Advocate. Well, says Mr Kellett in effect, not all sentimentality is to be despised. Victorian Literature (and the author's acquaintance with the *infusoria* of the libraries seems inexhaustible) – especially the favourite fiction of the day was bathed in tears, palpitating with the emotion of the death-bed. But the men and women who wept for Little Nell, for the boy-hero of *Misunderstood*, and the lonely orphan of Eliza Cook's *Old Arm Chair*, were, in their fashion, fulfilling the Aristotelian doctrine of purging their sentiments in sincere example. This generation had not learnt to bottle up its feelings, or confront calamity with a sneer. Still, it produced a national character which, when it issued in action, was susceptible to great movements and capable of revolutionary reforms. It was an age of sympathy, which did not stop short at protestation.

The chapters on Politics, School, and Games are among the best in the volume, covering wide spaces with shrewd, interpretative insight. Particularly illuminating is the study of the growth of Imperialism, with the dawning suspicion, even in the heart of its acclaimed Laureate, that the commercial spirit of the race was stealthily infecting its idealism, and that the dust that builds on dust was fatally threatened by the winds of the world. The history of the period builds itself up under Mr Kellett's constructive touch; and behind the fabric of history, the character of a race emerges, working out its own salvation. That is the author's constant conviction. History may be made by tyrants and schemers; but the future is fed from the character of the crowd. And the Victorian crowd was sound at heart. The value of its legacy begins to be appreciated now, and will be more fully recognised in the perspective of years to come.

3 April

VERY CLEVER HISTORY
JOHN BETJEMAN

Little Arthur's History of England, Lady Callcott. Century Edition revised to the Accession of King Edward VIII. (Murray)

The late King's Silver Jubilee coincided with the hundredth birthday of Little Arthur's History and the one hundred and fiftieth of its authoress, the wife, by her second marriage, of Callcott the Academician. The book has been through 70 editions and has sold 800,000 copies. There is no reason why it should not go on selling now that Mr C. E. Lawrence has continued it to the present day.

He has retained the naïve and knowledgeable style of the original, even using some of Lady Callcott's adjectives and phrases:

> 'And lastly, we must not forget to mention the marvellous discovery, by a clever Italian called Marconi, of wireless telegraphy.'

And in a bald and moving account of the Great War he says:

> 'Greece pretended to help us, but did not.'

Unluckily there is a danger that the reissue of this child's history book will be accepted as one more titillating contribution to the Victorian Revival which has filtered through to contemporary literature *via* interior decorators. Certainly Little Arthur is taught Protestant and Imperialist principles. The latest editor says in his introduction that the book 'arouses a right interest in the story of the growth in power, responsibility and honourable glory of our race'; and he describes the Boer War with a grace that Lady Callcott herself would have admired. This is not a book to please left-wing intellectuals, though it can hardly fail to interest them. All the same, children, Communist, Evangelical, Nudist, or ordinary will delight in this way of telling history and find their 'almost boundless inquiries' satisfied, as the authoress desired. For history to young children is not a matter of tendencies, influences, franchise and constitutions but of battles, kings, murders and personalities. Little Arthur has history divided up for him into kings and picturesque figures like

220

Lady Jane Grey and Sir Thomas More. Even the most unimportant kings are mentioned. The character of George I for instance is summed up thus: 'yet still, upon the whole, he was a useful king.' Poor Queen Anne does not seem to have been all she might have been:

> 'Queen Anne was kind and good-natured, but not very clever. She was rather lazy, and allowed the Duchess of Marlborough to govern her for several years.'

Do not suppose, on the strength of its baldness of statement, that Little Arthur's History is a useless book. Little Arthur could put his history, coupled with a list of dates, to good use in the School Certificate. The authoress clears up the troubles of the Commonwealth and even clarifies the Wars of the Roses. Given a working knowledge of his book, Little Arthur, if he is a good bluffer, could progress further still down the futile path of the examinee. With a nice sixth-form essay style of prose and a few vague abstract clauses, he might even carry off the usual third in the History School at one of the Universities.

Think what verbiage can be made out of this simple sentence at the beginning of one of the Chapters on wicked Henry VIII:

> 'In several parts of our history we have read of the Pope, that is, the Bishop of Rome.'

this can be spun into at least two paragraphs:

> 'The power of the papacy, which, for the last hundred years had, &c., &c., &c., ... now found itself face to face with a monarch on the English throne who &c., &c., &c. ...'
>   'Regarded from the standpoint of the rising tide of Protestantism, the Papacy was no longer arrayed in the costly vestiture of supreme dominion in Christendom, but appeared in the less awe-inspiring habiliments of a perfectly ordinary Continental bishopric, albeit an important one, which was at once open to contradiction and subject to human frailties.'

Possibly neither Lady Callcott, Mr C. E. Lawrence nor Little Arthur read so much into the simple words. But we can congratulate the authors on a useful and very clever history book which, unlike other school histories, is good reading for its own sake. And we can congratulate Little Arthur on being taught palatable history.

The old romantic wood engravings survive and photographs have been added to the modern chapters.

10 April

SHORT STORIES
GRAHAM GREENE

From Death to Morning, Thomas Wolfe. (Heinemann)
The Marchesa, K. Swinstead-Smith. (Hogarth Press)
The Cosy Room, Arthur Machen. (Rich and Cowan)
Cosmopolitans, W. Somerset Maugham. (Heinemann)

It sometimes amuses me, if I have a volume of rather inferior
short stories to read, to look first at the end of each story; it can
tell so much. There is, for example, the popular pompous ending,
the great Wurlitzer organ playing its deepest, most heartfelt
notes to show that the entertainment is definitely over. That is
Mr Wolfe's way:

> 'The history of old Catawba is the history of millions of men
> who have lived their brief lives in silence [at this point one feels
> for one's hat] upon the everlasting earth, who have listened to the
> earth and known her million tongues, whose lives ['excuse me,
> please, excuse me'] were given to the earth, whose bones ['I'm so
> sorry, do you mind – '] and flesh are recompacted with the earth
> [out into the gangway as the lips meet], the immense and terrible
> earth that makes no answer.'

Mr Wolfe is considered in the United States, and even by some
of our own more impressionable reviewers, a Considerable
Writer. Listen to a few of his titles; they give you the atmosphere: 'Death the Proud Brother,' 'Dark in the Forest, Strange
as Time,' 'Only the Dead Know Brooklyn.' If I had been reading
for pleasure I might have read no more of Mr Wolfe than his
titles and endings, and that would have been hasty. For the
organ note has sometimes been used by good writers. 'He stood
lonely in the searching sunshine; and he looked beyond the great
light of a cloudless day, into the darkness of a world of illusions.'
That is a Conrad ending: a quieter organ, more meaning in the
music, but it has a relationship with Mr Wolfe's.

Yes, almost everything about Mr Wolfe is silly, but not quite
everything. He is as conceited and romantic as Mr Saroyan: he
thinks it grand to have big emotions: all through his book he is
competing in emotions with the reader, like Coriolanus's opponents who capitalised their scars. 'He carried all within himself,
the slow gluttony and lust of the unsated swine, as well as
strange and powerful music of the soul.' (That first phrase would
be just as accurate, but not so resounding, if Mr Wolfe wrote:
'the gluttony and lust of the unsatisfied pig.') America has built

the tallest building in the world; and Mr Wolfe is determined that she shall feel the biggest emotions: Empire State emotions. Nevertheless, under his fake poetry, his booming commonplaces, Mr Wolfe has got buried an ear for popular dialogue a good deal more true than Mr Hemingway's, and he has written one very good 'period' story of a ride at dawn round and round Central Park in an early motor-car, the recollection of something silly and happy and drunk and reckless at twenty-five miles an hour. But even that story has too much explicit poetry about it.

Miss Swinstead-Smith is a new writer; she hasn't yet got a personal idiom, and it would be unfair to judge *The Marchesa* by this ending, though it does represent one trend in her work:

> 'Very far down her body lay in the bed of a tiny rivulet, her scarred cheek hidden. Curled up, she looked as if she was sleeping, her net veil spread out in the water – a sleeping Princess waiting for the kiss of the Prince to awake her from her trance.'

This is just one of her contradictory qualities. Several of her stories are set in Calabria, and as one might expect she is least good when she is dealing with Calabrian characters: sentimental and melodramatic. One is never convinced that she *knows* these people (she makes a pious Catholic refer to the children of Our Lady), but out of Calabria there is an agreeable strain of cruelty in her work, a little melodramatic in 'Night in a Train,' but quite beautifully conveyed in a Gibraltar sketch called 'Heat.' If she develops along these lines, her next book will be of great interest; if she doesn't follow the other trend, of the sleeping Princess, of a feminine tenderness for her own creations. The sense of pity is essential to a writer, but it should be an attitude of mind; it shouldn't dictate the style.

Mr Machen's endings, too, are various. There is an 'occasional' air about his collection which has been written any time since 1890. There are two patriotic stories inspired by the War (one of them is called 'Drake's Drum') which it was unwise to reprint: there is an excellent sketch of child sadism (1897), a murder story inspired by Crippen's crime called 'The Islington Mystery' (1927), and there is a ghostly fantasy about Stoke Newington (1935). Mr Machen's feeling for London, the suburbs as well as the Strand, is his most attractive quality. It is this which makes his earliest stories so agreeable. They have the Baker Street air with their exaggerated ironies, their four-wheeler daring. 'My wife and I met quite by accident; in fact, I was enabled to render her some assistance in a dispute with an insolent cab-driver; and the acquaintance ripened into affection.' One of Holmes's clients might be speaking. The date is 1890. This is a London of 'little trips to Hampton and Richmond; of jingling hansoms and St John's Wood moons,' recorded at the time. One hears 'the popping of champagne corks and certain strains of French songs of a *fin de siècle* character.' There is a strong scent of patchouli. One notices of the man-about-town that 'though there had not been rain for many weeks his trouser-ends were duly turned up.' 'By Jove,' he exclaims, and sometimes more strongly, 'Hang it.' He drinks with a sense of devilishness in little Soho restaurants. 'We'll have some of that Italian wine – stuff in salad oil flasks – you know what I mean.' Whatever the literary quality of these tales one is grateful to Mr Machen for disinterring from the ruin of war a world of such innocence.

> ' "They're good boys, both of them. (An old Englishwoman, keeper of a hotel in Asia Minor, is speaking.) They've never given me a moment's trouble from the day they was born and they're the very image of Signor Niccolini."
> "I must say no one would think they had an English mother."
> "I'm not exactly their mother, sir. ... They're the sons that Signor Niccolini 'ad by a Greek girl that used to work in the 'otel, and 'aving no children of me own I adopted them."
> I sought for some remark to make.
> "I 'ope you don't think that there's any blame attaches to Signor Niccolini," she said, drawing herself up a little. "I shouldn't like you to think that, sir." She folded her hands again and with a mixture of pride, primness and satisfaction added the final word: "Signor Niccolini was a very full-blooded man." '

That ending is unmistakable. These stories of Mr Maugham may have been made-to-measure, they certainly do not rank with his best work, but with the exception of half a dozen tired perfunctory anecdotes, they have his supreme competence, the dry amusing reserve of a man who has the highest admiration for the interest, rather than the goodness, of human nature. They are splendidly objective, but they catch no echo of the general life. They mean what they say (which is more than can be said of most writers) but nothing more. That is what separates Mr Maugham from his master, Maupassant; he conveys no sense of the world outside the liner routes and the leisured quarters. His poor are nearly always the picturesque poor: the beachcomber, the adventurer, 'German Harry' or 'French Joe,' and one cannot really believe in their existence, for they have no background, they have emerged from nowhere. They are seen at their most pictorial on a tropical beach or in a hospital bed. They have no relationship with the huge class which has produced them – or rather, Mr Maugham has no intuitive or empirical knowledge of their class, as Maupassant had of the Normandy peasants. Mr Maugham's adventurers are tourist stuff. They are like the cheap, bright, bogus goods brought out when the mail boat is sighted.

17 April

LEGEND
GRAHAM GREENE

The Burning Cactus, Stephen Spender. (Faber and Faber)
Flowering Judas, Katherine Anne Porter. (Cape)
To Tea on Sunday, Leslie Halward. (Methuen)

Mr Spender, we have it in his own words, intends the five stories in his book to be neither 'anecdotes nor incidents. Each story attempts rather to create a legend.' This intention distinguishes him from Mr Halward. Mr Halward is a documentary writer of the very best kind; his tales are incidents told with remarkable accuracy and tact: each small tale, whether of the sudden death at tea of a working man, of a dreary, mismated, adolescent pair walking out, of a boy's first public boxing match, contains just the right quantity of emotional undertone and no more. They are 'slices of life,' but not in the usual grim Zolaesque sense, which excludes humour, brevity, the unexpected. Mr Halward does not need the curiously irrelevant championship of Mr E. J. O'Brien, who writes (after remarking of Mr Spender among others: 'some shyness, some fear, some sense of isolation prevents them, we feel, from walking along the road for an hour in happy conversation with a tramp or a sailor'): 'these social barriers, these inhibitions evidently do not exist for Mr Halward.' This odd hiking scale of values is quite inapposite as Mr Halward is obviously writing only of the class with which he is most familiar.

Mr Spender, and Miss Porter too, have a more poetic intention. When Henry James was accused of having falsified the capering, acquisitive type of young American woman in the person of Daisy Miller, he defended himself by saying that Daisy was 'pure poetry.' Daisy Miller in other words is a legendary figure as

Mr Halward's characters are not, as Maupassant's or Mr Maugham's, Boule de Suif or Ashenden, are not, just as Madame Bovary *is* legend, and in her lesser way María Concepción who in Miss Porter's magnificent story murders the loose village woman and discovers how the other village women rally to protect her from the police. ('They were around her, speaking for her, defending her; the forces of life were ranged invincibly with her against the beaten dead.') Legend, figures which will dramatise the deepest personal fantasy and the deepest moral consciousness of a man's time: this, if one is not to be an anecdotist or a documentary writer, is the only thing worth attempting.

Miss Porter is twice brilliantly successful, though brilliant is a misleading word to use for the magnificent deep sobriety of her style. These seem to me the best short stories that have come out of America since the early Hemingways, and there is more promise of future life in them, the sense of a consciousness open to any wind, a style adaptable to any subject.

Mr Spender's volume is more uneasy, less accomplished. The legend, except in the fine title story, has been insufficiently dramatised; the umbilical cord has not been cut. Some of the prose is really bad: Sitwell prose: 'As a seamstress, sewing a tapestry, would jab a needle amongst many leaves and branches of her work, to put in a tiger, so he, seeing a tiger amongst the pattern of leaves, would shout at it': similes used for the sake of decoration, without urgency. The style wanders all the way from: 'He was short and there was a certain violence in his supple movements like those of a caged animal, as in his muzzled expression imposed on the dark cornelian eyes, the curling-back black hair, upward curving mouth, high cheekbones and pointed ears of a faun' to such a passionately realised image as 'the weight of his body was inanimate and cruel as though the weight of a wheel pressed against her in a street accident.' The dipsomaniac boy remains an abstraction, has no independent objective life, perhaps because it is a *political* legend Mr Spender is trying to create: 'In him is incarnated the moment when a civilisation really begins to lose grip, when violence becomes an end in itself.' (Such explicitness about a legend ought not to be necessary.) But experience seems to show that the real legendary figure is never political. The political idea is arguable; legend must be passionately and instinctively accepted. The faun figure with cornelian eyes and a 'lurid' grin appeals to the unconscious mind no more than Dorian Gray. It is in the figure of the suffering posing hysterical homosexual of the title story that a profound social awareness of things as they are combines with a poet's personal fantasy to create a work of art.

24 April

WINTER LANDSCAPE
BERNARD SPENCER

The spiky distance was the town; spires,
Factories, gasworks, shrunken in the telescope of blue.
If there was any sound
Across that giant nerveless palm of ground
– Work from the rail – its action was long done,
And it came limping late on lame feet
Past the tiny horses among the steel floods.
Brush over the sky with endless weeping clouds
Ascending towards us from those thorns; the town.

Near the bridge an aeroplane was perched.
I saw the pilot square in his padded coat
Smoking, chatting to friends.
He mounted, waved to the three waving friends;
Turned the plane, jolting, on to even ground:
Then she ran up wind with an excitement of engines,
Poised her bird's tail, was in air now, sweeped about
As a sower throws, a waker stretches, and
Strong up some sky-scent followed, glad as a hound.

24 April

FICTION
WILLIAM PLOMER

Keep the Aspidistra Flying, George Orwell. (Gollancz)

Mr George Orwell's new book, bitter almost throughout and often crude, is ... all about money. He opens it with a long quotation from the Epistle to the Corinthians in which he has seen fit to substitute the word 'money' for 'charity.' His version ends: 'And now abideth faith, hope, money, these three; but the greatest of these is money.' The scene is London, the time is the present, and the hero is Gordon Comstock, a seedy young man of thirty who works in a seedy bookseller's shop. Gordon would like to be famous and to be loved. He has vague aspirations in regard to the writing of poetry, and tender feelings towards a certain Rosemary. His heredity and upbringing have been against him. His exceedingly depressing and depressed lower-middle-class family have set, he considers, undue store by money, of which they have seen little. Reacting against their standards, he refuses the chance of becoming 'a Big Pot one of these days' in a red lead firm, deliberately throws away his good prospects in a publicity company, and embraces squalor. The embrace is protracted for some three hundred pages, and Mr Orwell, who is the author of a book called *Down and Out in London and Paris*, spares us none of the horrors of sordid loneliness and a hypertrophied inferiority complex expressing itself in physical grubbiness and stupid debauchery. In the end, after various contretemps, described with what may be called painful realism, Rosemary comes to the rescue and persuades him to return to publicity and bread-and-butter, which is just as well, for there is an unknown child to be considered. Turning over the pages of a magazine he takes a straight look at the world to which he is returning:

> 'Adorable – until she smiles. The food that is shot out of a gun. Do you let foot-fag affect your personality? ... Only a *penetrating* face-cream will reach that under-surface diet. Pink toothbrush is *her* trouble. ... Only a drummer and yet he quoted Dante. ... How a woman of thirty-two stole her young man from a girl of twenty. ... Now I'm schoolgirl complexion all over. Hike all day on a slab of Vitamalt!'

His rebellion against money has brought him 'not only misery, but also a frightful emptiness, an inescapable sense of futility.' Yet in the conclusion his bitterness is softened by the reflection that although 'our civilisation is founded on greed and fear, in the lives of common men the greed and fear are mysteriously transmuted into something nobler.' He therefore marries and settles down with Rosemary – and an aspidistra, which has to be 'kept flying,' for perhaps it is 'the tree of life.'

24 April

THE JOURNEY

EDWIN MUIR

First in the North: The black sea-tangle beaches,
Brine-bitter stillness, tablet strewn morass,
Shawled women against the sky with heads covered,
The witch's house below the black-toothed mountain,
Sea-echo in the roofless chapel,
The dead castle on the swamp-green mound,
Darkness at noonday, wheel of fire at midnight,
The level sun and the wild shooting shadows.

How long ago? Then sailing up to summer
Over the cant of the world, black hill of water,
Rivers of running gold. The sun! The sun!
Then the free summer isles.
But the ship hastened on and brought him to
The towering walls of life and the great kingdom.

Where long he wandered seeking that which sought him
Through all the little hills and shallow valleys
Of the green world. That whose form and features,
Race and speech he knew not, faceless, tongueless,
Known to him only by the impotent heart,
And whether on earth the place of meeting,
Beyond all knowing. Only the little hills,
Head-high, and the twisting valleys
Twisting, returning, until there grew a pattern,
And it was held. And there stood each in his station
With the hills between them. And that was the vision,
The meaning, the consummation. And not a meeting.

Though often through the wavering light and shadow
He thought he saw it a moment, watching
The red deer walking by still waters
At evening, when the bells were ringing,
And the bright stream leapt silent from the mountain
High in the sunset. But as he looked, nothing
Was there but lights and shadows.

                            And then the vision
Of the conclusion without consummation,
The plain like glass beneath him
And in the crystal grave that which had sought him,
Glittering in death. And all the dead scattered
Like nether stars, gathered like leaves hanging

From the sad boughs of the heavy tree of Adam
Planted far down in Eden's plot. Conclusion
Without consummation. And on the mountains
The gods reclined and conversed with each other
From summit to summit.

Conclusion
Without consummation. Thence the dream rose upward,
The living dream sprung from the dying vision,
Overarching all. Beneath its branches
He builds in faith and doubt his shaking house.

15 May

LONG LIVE LIBERIA
PETER FLEMING

Journey Without Maps, Graham Greene. (Heinemann)

Readers of *The Spectator* need no introduction to Mr Graham
Greene. Tart, discriminating, brilliantly selective, its underlying
melancholy tempered by a genuine inner acrid merriment (he
himself would have put it better; but commas would have been
as scarce), the texture of his prose and the working of his imagination promise in every second line something a good deal
better than brilliance. This, his latest book, brings him no nearer
to that something; but none will deny its brilliance.

Only the other day Liberia was promoted to the position of
being the only part of Africa where white men do not rule; one
country at least has cause, however infinitely oblique and academic, to thank Mussolini for enhancing its prestige. 'The love
of liberty brought us here' is the motto of this much less than
half-baked Republic; it was founded by released American slaves
in 1847 and it has been a flop. But a Republic which flops on
the West Coast of Africa attracts far less attention than an
aviatrix who lands at the Cape; and Liberia has survived to
allure Mr Graham Greene by her seediness and her uncharted
obscurity. He marched for 350 miles from the Sierra Leone border across – few of her citizens would be offended by hearing it
thus described – the top left-hand corner of the Republic,
through a salient of French Guinea, and at last – considerations
of health, supplies, and finance enforcing a curtailment of more
ambitious plans – south to the Coast, pell-mell.

The journey, though short by African standards, was arduous. The lack of maps – no mere titular braggadocio – was a grave handicap; there were plenty of paths, but few certain destinations. Mr Greene's attempts to impart a European urgency to the progress of his caravan of carriers made life, when it was not boring, irksome. Disdaining a hammock, he walked the greater part of the way: a twentieth-century Mungo Park, differing from the original chiefly in that his aloofness and his curiosity were more sophisticated and in that he had before him no glamorous and uncertain goal, to be reached at any price. His journey was full of a squalid discomfort rather than of the hardships in which men – even when driven involuntarily to submit to them – sometimes are able to exult: rats, cockroaches, jiggers, dirt and heat and the threat of many horrible diseases. Mungo Park fared worse; but his desperation-point was lower, he had no whisky and mosquito-nets and epsom salts, and he probably therefore minded less.

From its start – from the English restaurant car where 'we sat before the little pieces of damp white fish' – the whole journey is described with imaginative sincerity – with that touch of something a good deal better than brilliance which illumines a page or sometimes a chapter without ever quite spreading its refulgence to the whole book. The writing is essentially subjective; Greene thoughts in a Greene shade. But the author is a master of atmosphere. He can catch and convey the atmosphere (as he felt it) or the meaning (to him) of a trail or a hut or a village, and the contemptuous, unillusioned honesty which stamps all his impressions is a trade-mark good enough for the reader. The validity of this picture or of that may be undermined by the writer's ignorance or the writer's indigestion; but though we may suspect this we do not care, for the picture is an honest one.

The book challenges – and emerges creditably from – comparison with the recently published *Green Hills of Africa*. Mr Hemingway and Mr Greene were both fugitives from western civilisation, lured in the one case by kudu and in the other by curiosity. Mr Hemingway chose a conventional *safari*, Mr Greene (who dislikes the sight of blood) an unorthodox and rather hazardous scramble. Both were new to the country. Both, afterwards, wrote books about their experiences. Both have a highly individual style and a highly personal attack. Mr Hemingway – vigorous, staccato, cut-the-commas-and-come-to-the-cusses – failed signally to get away with it; in spite of some good descriptive passages, his book was soaked in an egotism at once petty and portentous, and he himself capered too insistently between the reader and the African scene. This is not so with Mr Greene. That note of disgust which pervades all his writings sounds, it is true, all the time in our ears; but, though his style is nearly as obtrusively his own as Mr Hemingway's and though his recurrent lapses into introspective anecdotage are even less relevant to his theme than Mr Hemingway's camp-fire literary debates, we feel in his descriptions of the interior that we are looking (as with profit and enjoyment we may) through his eyes; whereas in the other book we are always being forced to look *into* Mr Hemingway's.

My only serious criticism of Mr Greene is that he had one travelling companion (his cousin) and that he tells us absolutely nothing about her. His own reactions to everything are described – even the characters of his carriers sketched – in detail and with fidelity; but of the person who shared his journey we are told nothing. The more fascinating his narrative becomes – the more deeply interested we are in his own hunger or fatigue or whisky-drinking or the background to these things – the more disproportionate and unreasonable seems his studied neglect of the only other *dramatis persona* with a white skin. But this is a minor criticism, and I recommend this book to every class of reader except those of Liberian nationality.

15 May

THE DIE-HARD'S DILEMMA
E. H. CARR

Left Wings over Europe: or How to make a War about Nothing, Wyndham Lewis. (Cape)

Mr Wyndham Lewis is a whale of a publicist. It is therefore small wonder that he is ill at ease in the muddy little duck-pond of international affairs and that, when he lashes out with his tail, the minnows scatter in all directions. It is small wonder too that he finds it difficult to distinguish between the minnows, that he thinks Mr Baldwin and Sir Walter Citrine interchangeable, and can see nothing between *The Spectator* and one of its more radical weekly contemporaries but 'a dead level of liberal-pink orthodoxy.' The whale cannot be expected to have an eye for these finer gradations among different categories of minnow. Mr Lewis honestly does his best. He even apologises in one place to the reader for feeding him with 'facts requiring more time than I can give him for assimilation.' Graciousness from a whale can, one feels, go no further.

It is not surprising that, in the embarrassing position in which he finds himself, Mr Lewis's snortings and lashings should become a little incoherent. You will quickly perceive that he is indignant; for the noise is almost deafening. There is no mystery about the objects of his indignation; for he is indignant with nearly everybody from Miss Ellen Wilkinson to Mr Churchill and from Mr Eden to Mr A. P. Herbert. But the question what, if anything, he is driving at is more difficult to answer. *Facit indignatio versum*, but what next? What is Mr Lewis's philosophy, parts of which, as he assures us in his preface, he shares with Lady Houston, Mr Maxton, Sir Stafford Cripps and Sir Oswald Mosley? By way of relief from Mr Lewis's own flights of rhetoric, I will try to analyse it as prosily as I can.

Once upon a time there was a Good Die-Hard. Being a British Die-Hard, he was a stout conservative; for the British Die-Hard, unlike Die-Hards of some other brands, is so satisfied with what he has already got that he cannot imagine any change which could possibly be worth dying – or even stirring from his armchair – for. He hated Democracy, and the League of Nations, and the Huns, and coloured men and Bolsheviks. He loved Dictatorships, and Signor Mussolini, and (if he had ever heard of Poland) Marshal Pilsudski, and France; for France, though regrettably republican, was unimpeachably conservative and, though deplorably weak about coloured men, hated Huns and Bolsheviks as much as he did, and would have nothing to do with all this nonsense about disarmament. He stoutly continued, from 1922 to 1933, to propound these views in the columns of the *Morning Post* or in other choirs and places where Good British Die-Hards sing together in unison.

But in 1933 something dreadful happened – something so dreadful that the Good Die-Hard was obliged, for the first time for fifteen years, to think for himself – or at any rate to get somebody to do a spot of thinking for him. There was a revolution in Germany; and Germany acquired that envy of all true Die-Hards – a Dictatorship. Worse still, Germany came to the true way of thinking about coloured men, even including in that category (the Good British Die-Hard would not have gone so far

233

himself, but it showed the right spirit) the Jews. Worst of all, Germany shook off the dust of Geneva from her feet, denounced the League of Nations in purest Die-Hardese, and attacked disarmament in the most practical of all ways by rearming and conscripting her population. In other words Germany, which had for so long been merely a territory inhabited by Huns, now suddenly became a White Man's Paradise, a land fit for Die-Hards to live in, and was helping manfully to make the world safe for Dictatorship. It was all very bewildering to the Good British Die-Hard, who did not like changing either his arm-chair or his opinions.

Nor have the years since 1933 done anything to save him from the dreadful fate of having to think for himself. Monsieur Litvinov floated to Geneva on the stream of a Franco-Soviet alliance. Love me, love my dog; and the Good Die-Hard seemed now to be faced with the choice of embracing the Bolsheviks or ceasing to embrace the French. Moreover, things were seriously complicated by the apparently final and irreparable quarrel between Herr Hitler and Signor Mussolini about Austria. When dictators fall out, and the most conservative country in Europe takes Monsieur Litvinov to its arms, what can a poor British Die-Hard do with his divided loyalties?

This somewhat tedious analysis of the Die-Hard's dilemma is necessary to the understanding of Mr Lewis's convulsive tail-lashings. Stirred from his comfortable arm-chair, the Good British Die-Hard (who was once Mr Lewis's Fairy Godfather) has shuffled off after Mr Churchill and the will-o'-the-wisp of collective security, leaving Mr Lewis, alone like Casabianca, to defend the 'Black Principle' against the 'Red Menace.' So much does the modern Die-Hard (Mr Lewis always excepted) detest the Hun that he is prepared to embrace what Mr Churchill used to call the 'bloody baboonery' of Bolshevism and bless an alliance, in Mr Lewis's words, 'between the Scarlet Woman of Moscow and the smug Pickwicks (or must we say Pecksniffs?) of the western world.' So much does Mr Churchill hate Herr Hitler that he is even prepared, in a spirit of solidarity, to hate Signor Mussolini and to hamper him in his efforts to fulfil the White Man's mission to the coloured races. And knowing his Die-Hards, Mr Lewis is genuinely frightened that they (and not the comparatively harmless Mr Baldwin) will land this country in 'the war about nothing,' of which he speaks in his sub-title, at the nefarious dictation of Geneva and Moscow.

It will be seen that Mr Lewis is concerned, when indignation does not choke his utterance altogether, with the two most vital problems of British foreign policy at the present time; the feasibility of keeping the peace by a system of collective sanctions, and the possibility of coming to terms with Herr Hitler. He writes in what is politely termed a provocative style, and may suggest fresh trains of thought to readers in search of light on these problems. But they will be under little temptation to accept his views as they stand; and it is to be hoped that they will be equally cautious in their attitude to his facts. It was not, on any long-term view, 'England who effected the exodus of Germany from the League.' It is certainly not true that the 'Bankers' Olympus' wants war with Germany. The events of the last year seem to have disposed of the rather antiquated charge that 'English democracy' is exclusively interested in 'the problem of bread-and-butter, procreation, crimes of violence and ball-games.' Finally, what shall we say of the statement that the Italian campaign in Abyssinia was 'not a sanguinary and merciless war like, say, the Boer War,' but that 'the well-known bloodthirsty propensities of the Abyssinians were bound in the end to turn this exhibition of engineering skill on the part of the peaceable Italian "invaders" into a most unsuitable brawl'? Evidently Mr Lewis in his lighter moments is not above the gentle art of pulling our leg. It will be the reader's own fault if he does not get plenty of amusement out of *Left Wings Over Europe*, as well as some instruction.

12 June

SUPERREALISM IN LONDON
ANTHONY BLUNT

Take Blake's anti-rationalism, add Lamartine's belief in the individual, stir in some of Coleridge's faith in inspiration, lard with Vigny's ivory-tower doctrines, flavour with Rimbaud's nostalgia, cover the whole with a thick Freudian sauce, serve cold, stone-cold (dead, stone-dead), and you will have before you roughly the Superrealist dish, varieties of which are now thrilling, horrifying, puzzling, scandalising or just boring London in the exhibition of Superrealism at the New Burlington Galleries. For Superrealism is only an extreme assertion of the romantic principle in art, as Mr Herbert Read says in his preface to the

235

catalogue, though he thinks fit to double this with the astonishingly unhistorical statement that all classical art is 'dusty and dead, and for ever unappreciated.'

The fundamental claim in the Superrealist doctrine is for complete freedom of the imagination in the artist. Imagination is not responsible to anything else. It recognises no standards outside itself. It refuses all control, and in particular it rejects the control of reason. The original definition of Superrealism given by Breton includes the statement that it is 'the dictation of thought, free from all control exercised by reason and remote from all aesthetic or moral considerations.' And elsewhere the same writer says that he 'can abandon himself to imagination without fear of making a mistake.' To these views comes as a corollary the next important principle of Superrealism: 'the astonishing (*le merveilleux*) is always beautiful, anything astonishing is beautiful, in fact nothing but the astonishing is beautiful.' This is really only a deduction from the belief in the supremacy of the imagination, since it is the unexpected, the peculiar, the supernormal and the exceptional that appeal to the imagination, whereas the reason delights more in the general, the usual, the typical. It is perhaps this emphasis on the element of surprise which is most striking in the present exhibition of Superrealist works, in which human beings grow into animals, legs join on to heads, cups and saucers are made of fur, and funguses grow out of high-heeled shoes.

Considered from another point of view the aim of the Superrealists is simply to let loose the forces which exist in the subconscious and to express repressed desires by means of symbols in works of art. This attitude again is only an extreme statement of a common Romantic doctrine, that the poet writes in order to express himself. For the poet then writes because he has something to say and not because he wants to convey something to an audience (which would be the classical point of view). That is to say, the poet writes to get something off his chest, simply because he can't help it. Or, to put it in terms of psychology, he writes in an attempt to bring some repressed desire to the level of consciousness and so dispose of it.

So the Superrealists rely entirely on the subconscious. They have turned their eyes entirely away from the external world and directed them inwards on themselves, on their own processes of thought, and particularly on the mysterious dreams and phantoms which emerge from their subconscious. They claim for these a reality at least equal to that of the outside world, from the depiction of which painting has been forced by the invention of photography. Not being able to compete with the latter in accuracy of representation painting has had 'to entrench itself behind the necessity of expressing internal perception visually.' Artists, therefore, instead of exploring the outside world and establishing relations between it and themselves, have dug further and further into themselves, reaching deeper and deeper layers of their subconscious selves.

These appear to be the main tenets of the Superrealists, and those whose liking is in general for the Romantics will probably find their works sympathetic and stimulating. But certain implications of their theories are worthy of notice and development.

Superrealism is simply the last stage of an individualistic and subjective attitude towards art. It is subjective in that it demands the complete submission of the artist to whatever impressions may come into his mind, which he must in no way tamper with, control or alter. The recipe for writing a Superrealist poem begins: 'Put yourself into the most passive or receptive state possible,' and later gives careful directions for excluding any intrusion of the conscious mind into the direct flow of words from the subconscious. The system is intensely and wholeheartedly individualistic, since it cuts the artist off completely from the outside world, makes him believe that the only events that matter are those that take place inside his mind, and in particular those which spring most immediately from his subconscious. The Superrealist can admit of no standard outside himself. Provided his work achieves its particular and private aim of purging his subconscious, it is a good work.

This limitation of the purpose of art to bringing repression to the level of consciousness means that Superrealists have really moved from the field of art into the field of psychology. What they produce is not works of art, but works of medicine. For their products, apart from their immediate private effect on the artist himself, may have a secondary effect in helping, by their organisation of symbols, to clarify the subconscious of the spectator. How far they have gone away from art into psychiatry is shown by the inclusion in the present exhibition of 'found objects' (freak branches or stones) which in their natural state happen to perform the therapeutic function which the Superrealists demand from their paintings.

Further, it is hard to defend the view put forward by Breton that the mechanical perfection of photography has forced the painter back on the inner vision. Even if this explanation applied to the case of painting, it would hardly account for the exactly parallel developments which have taken place in literature. But it is not even relevant in painting. Photography may have killed a particular kind of painting like Impressionism, which sought just those chance visual effects that the camera can most easily render, but it is certainly not yet fully enough developed in subtlety to kill the kind of realistic painting which involves making elaborate statements about the outside world. Even if it is ultimately so developed, the conclusion will be not that art must take to the inner vision, but that painting ceases to be important as an art and is replaced as an art by photography. When that stage is reached painting can safely go Superrealist. At present it has more important things to do.

19 June

THE CINEMA
GRAHAM GREENE

Dangerous. At the Regal

Miss Bette Davis won some kind of a gold medal for her acting in *Dangerous*: the cinema is a shady business and one would like to know more about that medal, who gave it, how many carats, who the judges were; but at least it indicates that the publicity hounds have recognised her disturbing talent. Her performance in *Of Human Bondage* was wickedly good – up to a point, the point when passion got a little tattered, and even the most inconsiderable films – *Border Town* and others of which I have forgotten even the names – seemed temporarily better than they were because of that precise nervy voice, the pale ash-blonde hair, the popping neurotic eyes, a kind of corrupt and phosphorescent prettiness. *Dangerous*, like the others, is a picture to see for her sake, although the story is poor, the ending atrociously sentimental (*Dangerous* and *Show Boat* tie for the worst endings of the week), and although alas! Miss Margaret Lindsay is also in the cast, as if to reassure people that, whatever the censor may say, this film is U.

Hollywood has never forgotten its startling discovery that raffishness – the wild parties, the drugs and bathing belles and suicides and Fatty Arbuckle – was bad business. There is nothing now it takes to its heart so firmly as gentility: so that Miss Kay Francis is advertised as a woman who can wear the best clothes; Mr Aubrey Smith, that amiable and bushy Wellington, is made to remind us, even in *The Crusaders*, of the straight bat of his cricketing past, and Miss Lindsay is starred less as an actress than as a nice eligible girl, comradely and refined, who can pour out tea as if she really belonged to a tea-drinking nation. Miss Lindsay as the deserted but understanding *fiancée* provides the antidote to Miss Davis as the great actress who has become a drunken and friendless failure because of her intense selfishness which ruins every play she acts in or any man she likes. A highly-coloured situation, this, which does little justice to Miss Davis's talent for vivid realism; we are aware all the time that she is acting, acting for the highest honours, for the questionable carats, acting with immense virtuosity, from the moment when the successful young architect (Mr Franchot Tone) spots her in the speak-easy. For Hollywood has a way of refining even Miss Davis: another performance so horrifyingly natural as her mean greedy little waitress in *Of Human Bondage* and her film career would have been ruined; and so with great ingenuity Hollywood adopts the homeopathic method, doubles the gin, multiplies the drink stains, intensifies the squalor, until you can safely cease to believe, until Miss Davis's latest picture becomes as curious, absurd and period as 'Sell No More Drink to My Father.'

19 June

G.K.C.
E. C. BENTLEY

A giant of English letters, and a man in whose personal society admiration seldom failed to grow to a far deeper feeling, has been taken from us with the death of Gilbert Keith Chesterton. As a friend of his from boyhood, I cannot at this moment, even if I would, think of passing a judgement upon his work and his influence; it is enough, or too much, under such a sense of loss to try to present something of the truth of that exuberantly joyous and love-compelling personality. Nor can that be done otherwise than in a formless and haphazard way while the effect of the news is still fresh.

There are many who did not share his convictions; but there is no question, at least, of the richness and the variety of his gifts. The volume of what he produced in half a dozen fields of

239

literary work is astonishing in itself; and the least friendly critic would allow, I think, that nothing ever came from his pen – even the least considered of trifles – that had the air of being perfunctory, or had not in it the stuff of thought and conviction. If you did not agree with him, you still could not help reading him. The colour of poetry and eloquence in that overwhelming style, its potency of humour and wit, could not be resisted. And it was true of him, if it ever was of anyone, that the style was the man. It was utterly unstudied writing; it came from him as naturally and fluently as his talk, which, leisurely and measured though it always was, had no hesitation and no thought of effect.

I do not mean that he was given to monologue in company. No talker was ever more conscious of the duty of courtesy; indeed, it was hardly a duty, for when he talked to you he was as interested in you as in his subject, be you as unimportant, as ignorant or as simple as you might. He never seemed to be busy or preoccupied in the presence of others; yet there the record of forty years' unflagging industry stands – great poems, the lightest of light verse, floods of it, works of biography, long excursions into history, novels, detective stories, a few plays that surprised everyone by their natural sense of 'theatre,' countless essays of a quality such as might have made a reputation by themselves alone, and with all this an immense body of testimony to the reality and power of the Christian faith that was the deepest interest of his life, both before and after his 'going over to Rome' fourteen years ago.

To him all men were brothers, not because he held it as an opinion, but because he felt it as a fact in his own case. That was for him the sole and all-sufficient basis of democracy, which he held to have for its one foundation the dogma of the divine origin of man. He was a Liberal because he believed in freedom and hated regimentation and imposed uniformity; for the same reason, not a Socialist.

This friend of all men and respecter of every honest opinion had among his foremost qualities an enormous intellectual pugnacity; for the love of his kind involved, for him, the intolerance of wrong, of error, of the abuse of power or influence. It began, it is true, in a pleasure in abstract argumentation. The Clerk of Oxenforde, in that age in which Chesterton's imagination delighted so much, was obliged to dispute in the schools once a week; which would have seemed a starvation allowance to G.K.C. at the Clerk's time of life. It says something for that old Oxonian rule that the gymnastic quality of Chesterton's intellect, its readiness, tenacity and lucidity, were due largely to that habit. Anyone who shares my memory of 11 Warwick Gardens in his boyhood will agree that vigorous and long-sustained arguments with anyone who would take up the cudgels were the most keenly felt of pleasures for G.K.C. – sweeter even than the joy in books, or that collaboration in the producing of oceans of nonsense with pencil and paper which was the favourite amusement in that schoolboy circle. And if there was no friend of like disposition at hand, there was always present one antagonist who was spoiling for a fight – his brother Cecil, a man whose death as a soldier in the War was the end of extraordinary talents which had already begun to make their mark, and between whom and G.K.C. there existed the deepest of brotherly attachments. Family affection, indeed, was the cradle of that immense benevolence that lived in him. I have never met with parental devotion or conjugal sympathy more strong than they were in the exceptional woman who was his mother; or with greater kindliness – to say nothing of other sterling qualities – than that of his father, the business man whose feeling for literature and all beautiful things worked so much upon his sons in childhood. The parents made their home a place of happiness for their two boys' many friends, a place that none of them can ever have forgotten.

Whenever I think of that juvenile love of intellectual combat in G.K.C., I recall how, many years later, he fell upon the most famous intellectual gladiator of his time, F. E. Smith, who in a platform speech had alluded to the Welsh Disestablishment Bill as a measure which had 'shocked the conscience of every Christian community in Europe.' That was quite an ordinary piece of political fustian; but it happened to rasp a tender spot in G.K.C., who instantly 'went for' the formidable F. E. with as little hesitation as a terrier would feel about chasing a cat. The resulting verses, in which the peasants of Brittany and Russia, the persecuted Christians in Turkey, were pictured as following the Parliamentary fortunes of the Bill with shuddering dismay, ended with the sufficiently provocative lines:

'It would greatly, I must own,
  Sooth me, Smith,
If you left this theme alone,
  Holy Smith!'

241

For your legal cause or civil
  You fight well and get your fee.
For your God or dream or devil
  You will answer, not to me.
Talk about the pews and steeples
  And the Cash that goes therewith!
But the souls of Christian peoples . . .
  Chuck it, Smith!

There was, however, no come-back from F. E.; for what, indeed, was there for him to say? I remember that, for long after, Mr Asquith was accustomed to refer privately to his then most merciless opponent as 'Chuck-it Smith.'

A word ought to be said of Chesterton's friendship of nearly forty years with Hilaire Belloc, whose first words to him (as G.K.C. once told me) were, 'Chesterton, you write well.' It was the supreme intellectual association of his life, as natural, and almost as much a part of him, as that devotion between himself and his wife that continued and deepened the happiness of his early years. If in that friendship he was more influenced than influencing, there is this too to be said: that his thought had always been moving steadily in the direction of that body of ideas which was already formed and clean-cut in the other man's mind when they met, and that their very different natures seemed as if meant for one another.

And now I can say no more, but that with Gilbert Chesterton gone the world can never be the same again.

19 June

FICTION
WILLIAM PLOMER

The Weather in the Streets, Rosamond Lehmann. (Collins)
A Gun For Sale, Graham Greene. (Heinemann)
Their Ways Divide, Dennis Kincaid. (Chatto and Windus)

It would be dangerous to speak without qualification of a book as 'essentially feminine,' for this might easily be taken as a term of abuse, since the fallen women of today are those who from sheer ignorance, economic pressure, or a bad home influence, are busy at their desks, writing novels in which they offer their naked and essentially feminine souls, with the shameless abetment of publishers, to the circulating libraries. On the other hand, there are occasions when one can think of no higher praise, and the novels of Miss Rosamond Lehmann owe their charm and value, and perhaps also their success – they are best-sellers in America and France as well as in this country – largely to the fact that no man could have written them. What is more, no other woman could have written them, for probably no other woman writer with an equal knowledge of the feminine heart in relation to modern moneyed society would be able to go on being so kind. If only because they show no touch of scornfulness, Miss Lehmann's writings must be specially comforting to all those of her readers who doubtless feel that she would understand their troubles without laughing at them. It would be absurd to try and make out that Miss Lehmann writes like a sort of solemn and maternal confidante, but how can one help calling her sympathetic? Who else would have dreamt of writing 'An enemy's death is simply awful'? Who else has shown, in a succession of books, so much concern with the fate of the woman who 'has little and expects so much,' or has much and expects a great deal more? *The Weather in the Streets*, a sequel to *Invitation to the Waltz*, is an elaborate study of a woman in love, a married woman in love with a married man. As a picture of certain aspects of contemporary life it could scarcely be bettered, for Miss Lehmann knows, as they say, her stuff, and knows it through and through. She is just as strong on family life as on the circumstances surrounding adultery and abortion, and in one conversation piece after another shows us every stage in the progress of an affair which does not run altogether smoothly. The sureness of touch which leads to comments like 'Kate, bless her, had slipped with no trouble into a suitable marriage within easy motoring distance' and to things as brilliant as the account of Olivia's visit to a respectable abortionist goes with a strong sense of the irony of situation. 'I don't really see,' says Olivia's husband Ivor, from whom she is living apart:

> 'I don't really see any reason why we shouldn't occasionally see each other, do you? As a matter of fact, I've often felt I'd like to ring you up, or drop in ... I didn't quite like to.'

If there is a fault to be found, it is that Miss Lehmann here in places has abandoned the neatness of, for instance, *A Note in Music*, for diffusiveness, continually pressing into service our old acquaintances, the Three Dots.... She seems to be one of those writers who feels that the complexity of our lives and the relation between what happens inside and outside us cannot be faithfully rendered by sticking to any rigid or narrow form or convention, even a newly-invented one. They may be right, but perhaps they allow themselves too much freedom. Nature Miss Lehmann obviously loves, 'and next to Nature, Art,' but she is at her very best where she shows no favouritism and loves them equally.

Of Mr Graham Greene, who needs no introduction to readers of *The Spectator*, one would say that more than most writers of his generation he has from the first been technically indebted to the cinema. As a film-critic (fortunately not swayed by a boisterous enthusiasm) he has no doubt found out more thoroughly than ever how the wonderful means at the disposal of the film-makers are often applied to contemptible ends, and the result is really remarkable, for in *A Gun for Sale* he has beaten both the scenario-writers and the ordinary writers of adventure stories at their own game. He has written an exciting thriller which reads very much as a quick-firing gangster film looks and sounds, and whereas successful English writers of action stories tend to equip their heroes with the standards of an old-fashioned public school and with ideas (if they can be called ideas) far removed from present-day needs and facts, Mr Greene, shrinking from uplift, provides a topical satire on the seediness and callousness of social and political life. We know that in the present century assassination is deliberately used as a political method and that wars have been deliberately fomented by the agents of armament manufacturers; we know too well that a single incident of a violent nature, a murder for instance, might be enough to destroy the world we know. Allowing a few accepted facts of this sort to cast their menacing shadows across his pages, Mr Greene at once produces an air of tension and foreboding, and then follows, with quick camera-work and skilful sound-effects, the closely linked fortunes of a variety of individuals. The strength of the modern hero, from amateur gunman to dictator, is as the strength of ten because his heart is warped, and this decidedly applies to the harelipped hero of *A Gun for Sale*. There is not a clean limb in the story, and Aunt Sallies, from rich thugs to wearers of old school ties, fall in heaps in the course of a personally conducted lightning tour of the seamy side. Mr Greene describes all this as an entertainment. He is right. It is. Try it and see.

Their Ways Divide is Mr Dennis Kincaid's fourth novel about India. If the earlier ones are as good as this they must be very good. First of all we are shown a pleasant meeting in the nursery of a collector's bungalow between Edward Holme, the collector's little son, and Naru, a little Brahman; then, in alternate chapters, their growth and education. Edward goes to England and Naru stays in India. 'You are going to school soon,' remarks Edward's aunt, 'and English schoolboys are very brave and self-controlled and they tease anyone who is a milk-sop.' Meanwhile a pandit comes every morning to teach Naru Sanskrit, and wearing a white *dhoti* he strolls under flowering trees. Edward moves on to a public school, and Naru, having gone through the thread-girding ceremony, which makes a true Brahman of him, to the Gothic cloisters of the Rajwada College in Poona. 'I am sorry to notice,' says Edward's housemaster, 'that at the house-match on Saturday several boys – several I repeat – showed so little interest, so little *esprit de corps*, that, instead of watching the match properly, they were talking and laughing together.' And Naru presently comes under paternal correction for flirting with advanced ideas. The next thing is that Edward, now grown up, returns to India as an official, and at a Bombay cocktail party meets Naru again. Mr Kincaid's descriptions of Bombay seem particularly good, and while he is amusing us he is busy showing us modern India. A Mr Hashimbhai, for instance, said at the party that he thought Poona 'rather awful'; it made him feel 'quite *désorienté*.' The ways of Edward and Naru now converge. Edward is amiable but hopelessly unimaginative; and Naru, emotional and adoring, awaits an understanding of which his English friend is incapable. Their ways divide, and the end is disastrous and dramatic. There can be few novels that state more clearly the difference between the Englishman and the Indian, and the fatal results of education – Edward facing the world with sealed eyes and sealed lips, and Naru vainly imagining that violence may help.

17 July

A DECLARATION OF INDEPENDENCE
ALISTAIR COOKE

The American Language: An Inquiry into the Development of English in the United States, H. L. Mencken. Fourth Edition. Enlarged and Rewritten. (Kegan Paul)

Two hundred years ago Richard Owen Cambridge, an Englishman, remarked that since the flow of American words into English was already so rapid, a glossary of them would soon be in order. The suggestion has been renewed with decreasing seriousness ever since. The only charming idea left in the history of the opposition is the recollection that of all innocents it should have been John Wesley who, by using the American word *bluff* for the English *bank* in his diary in December, 1737, set the Great English Wrath ablaze. Nowadays this educated anger crackles away regularly in the Sunday newspapers, and only a fortnight ago a correspondent coming recently on Dr Heinrich Spies' German translation of Mr Mencken's third edition apostrophised as a titbit of irony a distinction between an American usage and one 'of British English,' though it is a distinction made by all good writers on language and is indeed essential in those continental and Japanese universities where two courses are offered, one in each dialect. It seems that in language, as in other fields, where there is no educated opinion already formed, educated people tend to pick up the illiterate opinion that happens to be lying around.

But Americans need to know that our ancient prejudice is not entirely due to our natural stubbornness and condescension. It has been confirmed and abetted by at least two sorts of Americans.

There are what Mr Mencken calls the Anglomaniacs, who have deceived many an Englishman into thinking he had come to terms, at the cost of little effort, with America and Americans. On one page or another Mr Mencken routs them all, from Washington Irving to Henry James (here impaled in the bleakest anecdote a man could wish to have forgotten), though he somehow omits the latest, greatest of the expatriates, of whom the present Professor of American History at Harvard superbly said that he had 'retraced the spiritual progress of his ancestors.'

And there is the Loyalist party, which was originally encouraged in its aloofness and suspicion of the new way of life by Webster's absurdly self-conscious plans for a Federal English. In the party today there are strange bedfellows: school-marms, passionate for elocution, still reviving Better Speech Week; New Englanders flattered by the British rationalisation of their geography – the north Atlantic seaboard is America (because, of course, it's nearest to the British Isles) and the rest of the continent 'the provinces'; Hollywood, more than we dare ever dream a partisan of our island prejudice, spreading among what Mr Mencken once called the booboisie the gospel that British voices are right for 'straight' parts and American for 'character.'

246

But left to itself, without this colonial aid, what are the symptoms of the British prejudice, which in the face of all linguistic history and other sorts of history as well yet takes offence at the idiom, the pronunciation and vocabulary of another nation's tongue?

First, is the rooted belief that what was transplanted was a medley of provincial dialects. Although Sheldon and Whitney have pretty well disproved this, their findings have not been noised abroad much outside the publication *Dialect Notes*, and there is still much of the controversy in doubt. Secondly is the most beloved doctrine of layman and pedant – the aesthetic approach to innately 'beautiful sounds.' There is too the very natural projection, at this peak of our history, of British ideas on to a puzzling continent: our inability to appreciate a society in which regional accents imply no loss, but rather a more honest assurance, of social status; our unwillingness to admit that the Anglo-Saxon is now a negative minority influence; our distaste for 'the melting pot.' And when these instinctive ideas are applied to language, there is the greatest difficulty of all in clarifying linguistics for the layman: the fact that he is unaware that in such things there is a professional opinion.

So when Mr Mencken's first edition of the present work was published in this country in 1919, even reputable philologists greeted it as if it were the first professional textbook and not the first popular one. Now the idea is gaining currency that that language is no private invention of Mr Mencken (like Ethnic or Mr Ogden's Basic, or even Mr Dooley's 'English language run over by a musical comedy') but an historical fact. We begin to admit that a language is not made as we thought they pretended, by a few vaudeville comedians taking thought, but by a whole nation taking in new experience, a new landscape, three or four climates, the first idea of essential economy, the later idea of lavish natural rewards (it would be possible to tell the history of the Grass Lands through merely the ebullient, and lately tragic, idioms they have directly inspired).

Mr Mencken begins his huge labour with the fairest kind of shock tactics, by showing how in the eighteenth century simple English utility words changed their meaning, so that an Englishman today has to learn again what an American is thinking of when he talks or writes about a creek, a shoe, lumber, corn, a rock, a partridge, a barn. He then proceeds to an historical account of the British attack. The second section is an attempt

247

to define fairly and finally 'an Americanism.' There follows a hundred-page history of the growth of the language; another hundred pages of patient and detailed equation of American and British English; separate and tireless sections on pronunciation, spelling, the materials of the common speech; a section on proper names in America; another on American slang; an enormous appendix on the contribution to American of 33 non-English dialects. And Mr Mencken's final chapter expounds the thesis that American is already gaining on the parent language, will overtake it, and that probably English will not very distantly become a dialect of American.

English readers will probably continue, even in the face of this magnificent compilation of the great authorities, to be sceptical and sad. For this feeling too there is already palpable justification. For the impact of American on English has been at least as bad as it has been good. In the last hundred years it has given us endless words and idioms we should now hotly protest as Briticisms. But the neglect of the study of American in this country has been at a price. Mr Mencken constantly notes that the British cannot distinguish slang from educated usage and good from bad slang (and it is merely wish-thinking to say we have taken only the best of American). It is not remarkable, then, that for every group of writers, like the editors of *London Week*, who manage to take over with fair success a style (from the *New Yorker*'s inimitable 'Talk of The Town') they well understand, there will always be the *Daily Express* to take over (from *Time*) a style it profoundly misunderstands. The significant example of P. G. Wodehouse, who has declined steadily in proportion to his absorption of American, points to our still vast ignorance of the feel, the character, what Sapir calls 'the slope,' of this new and ripening language. It is on this score that English readers may complain of Mr Mencken – that we could have done with some exposition of the varieties of American style. But of course, this is selfish. Mr Mencken is talking, in 800 beautifully documented pages, about the materials of the language, not its resources. How vast those materials are may be gathered from the fact that in 600 years of a unified English language there has been no survey of a living language which can compare with the truly gigantic prospect of the *American Linguistic Atlas*, a survey of a language 200 years old, a project which hopes to complete – in 25 years – many thousand maps specifying every variety of locution, vocabularies, dispersion of words, meanings, intonations, inflexions, idioms, constructions and so on over the entire north-American continent.

It is a proud reflection that Mr Mencken, whose literary career has been most remarkable for a gift of invective and for a frequent sneering at the researches of scholarship, should here magnanimously play fair by his gift and produce in his maturity a great work of scholarship. Let no reader be deterred by that word scholarship. A reading of the section giving a full account of the Englishman's magic incapacity to write American English when creating American characters in fiction – this alone is extremely funny, awarding as it does the booby prize to Galsworthy and Conan Doyle, with Wells, Kipling, Miss Rose Macaulay, and Edgar Wallace in hot pursuit for the title. And for readers who never touch learned works of any kind, there are the pleasures of geography, crossword puzzles, social history, hundreds of anecdotes, all the pleasures of a journey to America without the hangover.

31 July

UNDISCOVERED ASIA
EVELYN WAUGH

News from Tartary, Peter Fleming. (Cape)

News from Tartary is one of the rare books about which one can legitimately use the phrase 'eagerly awaited.' When, early last summer, a brief note in the Press told us that Mr Fleming had appeared at Kashgar after seven months of unexplained absence, we could be pretty certain that he had done something interesting. Later, when his articles appeared in *The Times*, we realised how sensational his and his companion's achievement had been, but newspaper articles are far from being the best means of communicating a narrative of this kind; they suggest, it is true, the main structure of a journey; they place in all too great a prominence the dramatic incidents; but they necessarily omit the day to day routine; the delays and uncertainties, the minor vexations – whole drab, uneventful patches of sheer hard work and discomfort which form the very stuff of travel, of which Mr Fleming's style and attitude make him the most felicitous of chroniclers.

Here at last we have the journey 'in book form,' and let me at once congratulate the publishers on that form. It is one of the

249

best produced books, and certainly one of the cheapest that I have had the pleasure to handle. The photographs with which it is extravagantly scattered are all admirable, many of them of very great beauty. There is even a comprehensive and, I think, quite superfluous index.

Superfluous because this is not a book that anyone will read as a definitive, scholarly treatise. Mr Fleming is the first to admit that. 'The world's stock of knowledge – geographical, ethnological, meteorological, what you will – ' he says, 'gained nothing from our journey.' There are far easier paths by which to reach India than Mr Fleming's route; there are, in fact, none harder. Just as mountaineers will risk their lives to seek a peak ascended on the other side by funicular railway, Mr Fleming undertook his stupendous journey for its own sake. Getting across country, overcoming difficulties that he has deliberately courted, ticking off the mileage stage by stage – these are clearly Mr Fleming's primary interests; there are other secondary interests of which he takes full advantage – some sport of a haphazard kind, some enchanting encounters with odd people on the road, the provision of intelligence which the Foreign Offices of more than one nation greatly coveted about the condition of a totally isolated province. This last was what Mr Fleming's editor wanted; it was what gave political importance to the trip; but reading Mr Fleming's narrative we cannot avoid the conviction that probably to him, certainly to his companion, it was a secondary aim.

The figures are startling. Mr Fleming covered over three thousand miles, for the most part across ground that was both physically and politically unmapped; he took seven months; he spent £150. He and his Swiss heroine formed the sole constant constituent of the expedition. They changed animals and guides repeatedly; they seldom had anything with them that could legitimately be called either a guard or a servant; they 'lived on the country' in a way which will seem incredible to all ordinary travellers; they were grotesquely under-equipped by all normal standards. When I read Mr Fleming's catalogue of his outfit, I thought of the immense crates of foodstuffs, medicine and ammunition, telescopes and camp furniture and tropical underwear which, shortly afterwards, were to be disembarked at Djibouti to support the special correspondents in the hotels of Addis Ababa and Harar. I cannot help thinking that Mr Fleming was recklessly ascetic. He got through, as we all know, but by a series of happy coincidences, the failure of any one of which might have been fatal. Another two pack animals, another two men, another £100 would have been reasonable. He certainly had good reason at the outset to avoid attention; if the Chinese authorities had guessed his ultimate destination he would never have been allowed to leave Lanchow, but later he found that his impoverished appearance told against him. More ingenuity in embarking stores would seem to me to bring the expedition nearer the requirements of theologically justifiable risk.

It is a radical disadvantage of a book of this kind, which no literary skill can possibly disguise, that the reader knows it ended happily. It was the unique quality of Mr Fleming's *Brazilian Adventure* that the reader did not know until the last pages who was going to win. Mr Fleming assures us that he did not expect to get through; we believe him but with the clear evidence of his success before us it is hard to share his anxiety. It is only after one has finished reading, and begins counting up his chances that one sees how preternaturally consistent was his good luck. Nothing ever went seriously wrong. But Mr Fleming had no reason to expect it.

There is no need at this stage of his career to comment on Mr Fleming's literary style. It is as well known as any English writer's. He lacks poetry and aesthetic interest and he wisely never attempts to counterfeit them. It is rather better to be Doughty than Fleming, but it is a great deal better to be Fleming than a sham Doughty. He never allows himself a shoddy phrase; he often achieves one of memorable wit and pungency. He has great clarity in analysing a political situation. The situation in Sinkiang was so obscure before Mr Fleming went there that most well-educated Englishmen failed to realise that there was any mystery. What Mr Fleming found I leave to readers of his book. To me at least it was quite new and quite thrilling to learn that imperialistic expansion and the gas-bombing of savage peoples can be carried on by a Marxian as well as by a Fascist or Democratic State. I hope some of the English Socialists who can read, will read Mr Fleming's chapters about Soviet penetration in Sinkiang.

I have only one complaint about Mr Fleming's writing, and that a small one. I detect a note which at times rings rather pharisaical in Mr Fleming's repeated protestations of honesty. Not once but again and again he pauses to remind us that a less austere and objective writer might have let himself go in an insincere purple patch. We who know and admire Mr Fleming's work need no such reminder and I for one slightly resented it.

7 August

FICTION

V. S. PRITCHETT

The Rock Pool, Cyril Connolly. (Paris: The Obelisk Press)

... Sharing with Mr Connolly an un-English preference for unpleasant characters in fiction and feeling often like busting up the whole simpering and mumbling tea party, I expected to find in *The Rock Pool* some scabrous abominations. They were not, however, so much abominable as futile; and being futile had nothing to say; and having nothing to say were boring. Perhaps it is not the duty of the futile to say anything; perhaps they should be either disastrous or ridiculous. But under Mr Connolly's direction, his collection of artists left behind in the Mediterranean after the slump, are dingy, the victims of Mr Connolly's excessive intelligence. That seems to me the trouble: Mr Connolly is too intelligent, too drastically lucid a floodlight to play upon the promiscuities, bedroom quarrels, studio drunks of the surviving crustaceans. It is unfair, like keeping the zoo up late on Thursday nights. Of course there is some stinging farce and Mr Connolly is expert in all the slashing intellectual savagings of self-defence: Naylor, the virgin Wykehamist, the mean, swindled, snobbish would-be lecherous biographer of Samuel Rogers, sits at the end of the decade, the last of the expatriates, reflecting:

> 'And what was more, he liked the troglodytes, these fierce, un-fashionable expatriates. What was fine in them, their refusal to conform, their independence, their moral courage, was their own; what was weak, their instability, their hopelessness and predatory friendships was the result of a system: of the clumsy capitalist world that exalts money making, and poisons leisure, that suppresses talents, starves its artists and persecutes its sexual dissenters, that denies opportunity, infects charity and encourages only the vulgarity of competition, the triumphs, the suspicion, the heartbreaks of the acquisitive.'

This passionate outburst looks like an afterthought, for where in this book have we seen the fineness of the refusal to conform? We have seen only the dinginess of it. The lens adjusted with brilliant critical concision to a scene, invective, withering ex-aggeration, the superb fusillade against publishers and public which appears in the dedication to this novel, seem to be Mr Connolly's strong points; not people. He does not like himself enough to make them interesting.

7 August

PORTRAIT OF A LADY
GRAHAM GREENE

No Place Like Home, Beverley Nichols. (Cape)

I found myself thinking of Guy Walsingham, the author of *Obsessions*. Readers of *The Death of the Lion* will remember how Mr Morrow, of *The Tatler*, interviewed her. For Guy Walsingham was a woman, just as Don Forbes, author of *The Other Way Round*, was a man. 'A mere pseudonym' – that was how Mr Morrow put it – 'convenient, you know, for a lady who goes in for the larger latitude.'

A confusing literary habit, which led me to wonder a little about the author of *No Place Like Home*. For all I know Mr Nichols may be another Mr Walsingham. A middle-aged and maiden lady, so I picture the author, connected in some way with the Church: I would hazard a guess that she housekeeps for her brother, who may be a canon or perhaps a rural dean. In that connexion she may have met the distinguished ecclesiastics who have noticed a previous book so kindly. ('The chapter on Sex,' writes a Dean, 'is the best sermon on the subject I have ever read.') She is not married, that I am sure, for she finds the sight of men's sleeping apparel oddly disturbing: 'it was almost indecent, the way he took out pyjamas and shook them,' and on her foreign holiday, described in this book, she hints – quite innocently – at a Man. 'His knowledge was encyclopaedic. His name was Paul. He was about forty-five. We had better leave it at that.'

It is impossible not to grow a little fond of this sentimental, whimsical and poetic lady. She conforms so beautifully to type (I picture her in rather old-fashioned mauve with a whale-bone collar). A Christian, but only in the broadest sense, emotional, uninstructed and a little absurd, as when she writes of the Garden of Gethsemane: 'Here I had the greatest shock of all. *For the garden was not even weeded!*' She is serious about Art ('try a little experiment. Hold up your hand in front of your eyes so that you bisect the picture horizontally'), a little playful ('Dürers so great

253

that you feel you must walk up to them on tiptoe'). She loves dumb animals, and hates to see even a field mouse killed ('one mustn't let oneself wonder if perhaps the mice were building a house, which has now been wrecked, if perhaps Mrs Field Mouse was going to have babies, which will be fatherless'), and in *their* cause she shows considerable courage. ('On more than one occasion I have created useless and undignified scenes at theatres in a vain protest against the cruelty of dragging terrified and bewildered animals to the footlights for the delectation of the crowd.') This almost masculine aggressiveness is quite admirable when you consider the author's natural timidity, how nervous she is in aeroplanes ('It is with the greatest difficulty that I refrain from asking the pilot if he is sure about the tail. Is it on? Is it on *straight*? What will happen if it falls off?') and how on one occasion, climbing a pyramid, she very nearly had what she calls 'a swooning sickness.'

But what engaging company on these foreign cruises and excursions a maiden lady of her kind must have been, exhilarated as she was by her freedom from parish activities ('All that matters is that we are alone and free, *free*. Nobody can telephone to us. Nobody can ask us to lecture on the Victorian novelists. It is beyond the realms of possibility that anybody, for at least twenty-four hours, will ask us to open a chrysanthemum exhibition'), and hilarious with the unaccustomed wine ('We are, beyond a shadow of a doubt, Abroad. And not only Abroad but At Large. And not only at large but in a delicious haze of irresponsibility and white wine'). Her emotions are so revealing: she weeps, literally weeps, over Athens, she disapproves of women who don't grow old gracefully ('I also thought how very much nicer and younger the average woman of forty-five would look, in this simple uniform, than in the stolen garments of her daughter'), she feels tenderly towards young people ('the silver treble of youth that is sweeter because it is sexless'), her literary preferences are quite beautifully commonplace: 'What a grand play Galsworthy would have written round the theme of Naboth's Vineyard.' Excitable, sound at heart, genuinely tied to her brother and the vicarage: 'the old dear,' one exclaims with real affection, and I was overjoyed that she got safely home to her own garden before – but I must not spoil her closing paragraphs:

'There they were, dancing under the elm, exactly as I had planned them.
'I was in time for the daffodils.'

28 August

IN THE NIGHT
WILLIAM PLOMER

When the pillowed head instead of sleeping ponders
The night is given shape by noises half expected
And freed from untrue light imagination wanders
To find the shape of life in violence recollected.

The tower clock in striking tells not of time so clearly
When on the air we breathe impinge those bronze vibrations
As of the lives we lead and ways we cherish dearly
Shaken by sudden fears and wounding revelations;

As of those shocks of pleasure, a phrase, an act forbidden,
That an infant hoarded up, his secret and his treasure,
Guides to later conduct, clues to wisdom hidden,
Truer than clocks or calendars as rules by which to measure.

Startling here a folded thought, an impulse uninvited,
Streets away an engine screams, starting for the west,
At the tremor nerves respond, as a bulb when lighted
Suddenly reveals a room whose existence was unguessed.

By a parting, by a journey, by adventure yet unknown
Though already understood by a shadow cast ahead
We discern in part the pattern of the lives we lead alone
Faithful to designs bequeathed us by the dead.

Eternity's blue flesh seen through a cloud in tatters,
Voices in a villa garden, and an open door,
For a moment seem familiar, then the vision scatters,
Memory seems to seize on something somehow known before.

And the future *is* the past in the head upon the pillow,
The eye rests on a landscape where the heart will throb,
A house by a canal, a white wall, and a willow,
Remembering what has not happened . . . Do you hear a sob?

We bleed from others' wounds; for our own the styptic
Is not time, no healer for the heart that grieves,
But resistance to surprise and acceptance of the cryptic:
And now the night wind sighs abruptly in the leaves.

25 September

THE DARK ENEMY
GRAHAM GREENE

The Wind Blows Over, Walter de la Mare. (Faber and Faber)

It has become fashionable to regard the poetry and prose of Mr de la Mare as belonging to 'the literature of escape,' a vague term which, in these days, is meant to convey a kind of moral reproof, as if the artist had been caught asleep on sentry-go in the front trench. But the reproof is peculiarly inapplicable to a poet in whom we can trace two predominating motives: an almost sensual delight in the visible, audible, tangible world and an inquisitive, inquiring horror of what may follow death. Death is more inevitable than social change and causes hourly more misery than poverty, and we should welcome one artist who is less concerned with politics than with human fate. Our awareness of life bears a direct relation to our awareness of its end, and to those of us who haven't felt the immediate fear of extinction, who have pushed the future into the background, the injustices, miseries, inequalities lying over life must be the most present reality. But that will not alter the fact that it is *we* who are escaping, who are not listening to the deepest human instinct, the instinct of self-preservation, who are deceiving ourselves by thinking death less important than a change of government.

The first of Mr de la Mare's new stories, the dream of a woman under an anaesthetic, deals directly with the shadow. As the woman is carried through the dark countryside in the silent steel-twisted motor-coach, the vividness and authenticity of the images strike us: the jagged hole in the glass windscreen like a huge black star, the stained, wrenched seat, the silent conductor sitting face cupped in hands like Rodin's *Le Penseur*. The same vivid details fill the little ante-room of the Wigston public hall, to which Professor Monk has followed the chairman after his academic lecture, punctuated by the sound of slag falling from the foundries, on the life and works of Edgar Allan Poe. Every detail is true of this world, but the shadow is there; like the objects in a surrealist *collage*, the broken scissors, screws and eggshell and torn news scrap, they add up to a less conscious sum.

> 'In a few minutes, the Hall already nearly empty, he had followed his chairman down the five well-worn, red-drugeted steps into the ante-chamber. There he was welcomed by a row of

empty wooden chairs, a solid grained table, a copper-plate engraving in a large black frame over the chimney-piece of a gentleman in side-whiskers, whose name, owing to the foxed condition of the print, he had been unable to decipher, and the ashes of a fire in the grate. It had been feebly alight when he arrived. It was now dead out.'

One is reminded of the grim, choked railway fire in the waiting room at Crewe in Mr de la Mare's earlier tale. How can one talk of escape when the imagination functions so persistently under that shadow?

If the imagination struck one as less profound, then the artist's preoccupation with death would have as little importance as Jules Verne's trifling with imaginary continents beneath the sea. But in Mr de la Mare's case it is worth remembering Henry James's reply to Sir Walter Besant, who had declared that a novelist should only write from personal experience and that 'a young lady brought up in a quiet country village should avoid descriptions of garrison life.'

> 'Experience (James wrote) is never limited, and it is never complete; it is an immense sensibility, a kind of huge spider web of the finest silken threads, suspended in the chamber of consciousness, and catching every air-born particle in its tissue. It is the very atmosphere of the mind, and when the mind is imaginative – much more when it happens to be that of a man of genius – it takes to itself the very faintest hints of life, it converts the very pulse of the air into revelations.'

And so, disquieting thought, Mr de la Mare's 'fictions' may be as much material for the psychical laboratory as a piece of ectoplasm, his hints from the unknown garrison as true as the experienced life he makes us so vividly see: 'cold, kitchen solitude, hushed mice, day-secreted cockroaches' no more accurate an impression than the 'dark lean meditative' manservant in funereal morning coat who leads the anaesthetised woman across the paved passages and rooms of the strange house.

No reason to call *this* the literature of escape, but there is a point in many of these stories where Mr de la Mare does flinch, fall back into an embarrassing whimsicality, a curious spinsterish femininity, as though he were remembering his own warning against the exploration of the region 'where human pathways end. And the dark enemy spreads his maddening net.' A disciple of James, he has not the same firm grasp of his subjects: he sometimes sets out on journeys he hasn't, when it comes to the

257

point, the heart to finish. In his latest collection perhaps only *A Froward Child*, a dreadful little picture of fear and corruption on a cold Christmas railway journey, is quite worthy of the author of *The Return*.

2 October

A. E. HOUSMAN
JOHN SPARROW

More Poems, A. E. Housman. (Cape)
A. E. Housman, A Sketch with Indexes of his Classical Writings,
   A. S. F. Gow. (Cambridge University Press)

More Poems should give pleasure to all Housman's many readers: to his detractors, because it contains several pieces to which they will be pleased to point, quite justly, as almost parodies of himself; to his uncritical admirers simply because they will find in it, beyond expectation, a further and not unworthy instalment of *A Shropshire Lad;* to those whose worship stops short this side idolatry, because it will afford them the opportunity of comparing Housman's less successful with his more successful efforts, and of speculating which pieces he excluded from his earlier books and why he did so; and because it contains not only several poems in which Housman is at once at his best and his most characteristic, but also a few which are more intimate than, and in a way quite different from, anything published by him in his lifetime.

Almost all the new poems are entirely characteristic, full of the peculiar quality which invests everything that Housman published; for even his few failures are unmistakably his, and carry a charm which reconciles the reader to words, images, and turns of phrase not easily defended against the objections of an unsympathetic critic. It is this charm which captures the unliterary as well as the literary, and makes them admire all his work with equal fervour; it is a charm not unlike the charm of Fitzgerald's *Rubaiyat*.

What is its secret? Like all charm, it cannot be analysed; it is part of the man, and is not wholly explained by considering the mechanism of his verse or by recalling its themes – the passions and the moods that it expresses. To feel its force, one must read his poems at length: one likes them, or one does not; there is no more to say.

But it is possible to discuss, and should be possible to explain, the difference between the good and the less good; and it is interesting to read Housman's poems carefully, with an eye on his technique (he studied the craft of verse-writing very minutely, as appears from a note in *The Name and Nature of Poetry*), and to notice when his failures are due to mere exploitation of a knack or repetition of a formula – to a feeling too easily expressed – and when they are due to something not felt, or felt too easily.

A review does not afford space to do more than indicate the lines which such criticism might take: Housman's poetic genius cannot be illustrated by selections (he was quite right not to allow his poems to appear in anthologies), for an isolated stanza or two does not do him justice; nothing, on the other hand, is easier than by such a selection to exaggerate his weakness and to make what is in keeping in its context appear affected or ridiculous by isolation.

Some indication of the quality of the new book may be gathered, however, from the following:

> 'Bells in tower at evening toll,
> And the day forsakes the soul;
> Soon will evening's self be gone
> And the whispering night come on.
>
> Blame not thou the blinded light
> Nor the whisper of the night:
> Though the whispering night were still,
> Yet the heart would counsel ill.'

This is not outstanding in merit, but it is a good example of how economically and effectively Housman can convey a mood. We hear in the reduplicated 't' the measured toll of the bell, and the thin long 'a's' in the second line contrast with the deeper vowel-sounds that precede them, and suggest the dreary forsakenness which the line describes (substitute 'desert' for 'forsake' and see what is lost). Between stanzas 1 and 2 there is, as it were, a whole stanza in which nothing is said, but in which the word 'whisper' has acquired a sinister meaning. The strong alliteration in line 5 masks and makes more effective that in line 6; the last line is weak, for the last two syllables are cacophonous, and it may be that this cacophony led Housman to reject the poem.

This may be taken to represent the average of the poems:

259

sometimes a poem falls below it because the artifice seems too easy –

> 'But now their coins are tarnished
> Their towers decayed away,
> Their kingdoms swept and garnished
> For haler kings than they – '

sometimes because the verse itself does not convince us of the genuineness of the mood, so that an attitude seems merely a pose:

> 'Then came I crying, and today,
> With heavier cause to plain,
> Depart I into death away,
> Not to be born again.'

Surrender to the music and accept the idiom, and the verse gives nothing but pleasure; but by a severer standard it is condemned, and Housman no doubt rejected such poems because he had done the same thing, and had done it more successfully, already. We should not, however, be ungrateful to his brother for now printing them, since, in this separate volume, they do not spoil his other work, and they afford material for an interesting comparison.

It is easy to illustrate these fallings away from Housman's supremely high standard, but harder to illustrate his successes by quotation. The opening poem deserves to be quoted, however, for it is one of several in which there sounds a note not familiar from his earlier work; it is called *Easter Hymn*, and this is the first verse:

> 'If in that Syrian garden, ages slain,
> You sleep, and know not you are dead in vain,
> Nor even in dreams behold how dark and bright
> Ascends in smoke and fire by day and night
> The hate you died to quench and could but fan,
> Sleep well and see no morning, son of man.'

It seems here as if the poet were speaking in a more directly personal tone, the rhythm and form are less epigrammatic, less lapidary than usual; the cloak of convention has been cast aside. This abandonment of convention shows most strikingly in the personal poems in this volume: in several of these we hear Housman speaking undisguisedly in the first person and not through the mouth of Terence; and the effect of these poems – for stance, XL ('Farewell to a name and a number'), LXII (headed with the initials 'A.J.J.'), XLIV (addressed to 'Andrea') – is not to show that the Terence poems, with their 'my lads,' their red-coats, their death in battle and their prison-yards, are unreal, but to demonstrate the depth and nature of the emotion which needed that imaginary setting and those half-real characters for its poetic expression.

These poems reveal pretty clearly (and those who care most for Housman will find the revelation least surprising) the spring of Housman's personal emotions. Light on his way of life, on the side of his nature which he showed to his colleagues and ac-quaintances, comes from Mr Gow's biography. This is more than a mere record of the few events of Housman's career, it is an exceedingly sympathetic account of his character, and it explains clearly the two motives which drove him to the life of a scholar and a recluse – the passion for truth and the shrinking from personal contacts which he feared might hurt him more deeply than he could bear. Mr Gow knew his colleague probably as well as any man during the last twenty-five years of his life; he has said all that needed to be said, and it could not have been said better. It is not too much to say that it is worthy of its subject, and Mr Gow will not ask for higher praise than that.

30 October

MR YEATS'S BOOK OF MODERN VERSE
JOHN HAYWARD

The Oxford Book of Modern Verse, 1892-1935, chosen by W.B Yeats. (Oxford: The Clarendon Press)

The Oxford Book of Modern Verse will surprise and bewilder a great many people. It will, I believe, shock some of its editor's friends, admirers and disciples, particularly the youngest of them, and it will certainly be, to the envy of more commercially minded publishers, 'one of the most widely discussed books of the year.' This is all to the good. Poetry draws strength and encouragement from debate, and the debate promises to be a lively one, since the selection Mr Yeats has made is unlikely to meet with approval from experienced critics. But before going any further it is important that the ordinary reader, or, more precisely, the reader who finds all the poetry he needs in the

Oxford Books of Verse, should understand clearly that *The Oxford Book of Modern Verse*, though it has been chosen by Mr Yeats, assumes, by virtue of its title, an authority it would not possess if it had been called, as I think it should have been, *Mr Yeats's Book of Modern Verse*. For the implication is that the Delegates of the Clarendon Press, having given their imprint to the book, and having included it in a series which, for better or for worse, is commonly accepted as authoritative, and permanent, offer it as a definitive anthology of modern poetry. This it most certainly is not.

No one is going to deny the attraction of Mr Yeats's name on the title page; no one can fail to be curious about the attitude to contemporary poetry of its most eminent living exponent. But, in selecting him to edit the last of the Oxford Books for many years to come, the Delegates of the Clarendon Press may not unreasonably be accused of opportunism of a kind that tempts newspaper editors to print the opinions of the Church on the Modern Novel and of Modern Novelists on the Church. Mr Yeats is a poet. It does not follow, it very rarely follows that the creator is also a critic. (Dryden implied as much when he observed that 'the corruption of a poet is the generation of a critic.') It is the nature of an artist that he cannot, as a critic can, be detached and impersonal in his relations with art. No better confirmation of this could be found than in the extremely personal introduction Mr Yeats has written to introduce his extremely personal choice of modern verse by poets 'who have lived or died from three years before the death of Tennyson to the present moment.'

Some statistics may help the reader to realise the scope of his anthology. Ninety-five poets are represented by 438 poems – figures which justify, at least arithmetically, Mr Yeats's contention that 'England has had more good poets since 1900 to the present day than during any period of the same length since the early seventeenth century.' Pride of place (estimated in pages) is given to Miss Sitwell (18), followed by Herbert Read (17) and W. J. Turner (16); Binyon and Lady Gerald Wellesley (15); Eliot, Yeats, Gogarty (12); Sturge Moore (10); O'Connor, Arthur Waley, Sacheverell Sitwell (9); Wilde, Francis Thompson, Abercrombie, MacNeice (8); Hopkins, Bridges, Monro, Robert Nichols, Day Lewis (7); Dowson, Synge, Blunden, Higgins, Masefield, A. E., Pound (6); Blunt, Davies, Lawrence, De la Mare (5); Stephens, Housman, Tagore, Lady Gregory, Flecker, Auden (4);

Hardy, Margot Ruddock, Henley, George Barker (3). Twenty-two poets are represented by a single short poem apiece. Apart from Eliot and Pound, no American poets are included; on the other hand, 41 of the poems are translations, chiefly from the Irish. Robert Graves and the executors of Sir William Watson refused permission to print. Kipling and Pound are poorly represented because the Clarendon Press would not pay for their work. The following omissions will probably be regretted, and perhaps resented, in some quarters: Wilfred Owen, T. E. Hulme, Charles Sorley, Edwin Muir, Isaac Rosenberg, and Dylan Thomas.

Unfortunately, Mr Yeats's fragmentary introduction throws very little light on his method of selection. It is a curious, tantalising and unintegrated piece of work, too perfunctory and shapeless to satisfy the reader who expects a critical survey of modern verse and not sufficiently conclusive to explain or justify Mr Yeats's predilections. There are, however, hints and implications. Thus, the disproportionate amount of space given to Herbert Read's long poem 'The End of a War,' can be accounted for by Mr Yeats's 'distaste' for war poems and his decision to print, as an example, one that has not found its way into anthologies and was, in fact, written long after the armistice. Yet I cannot agree that Mr Yeats's contention that 'passive suffering is not a theme for poetry' – surely a very questionable assertion – is a reason for excluding from his anthology Wilfred Owen, who, technically at least, has been an influence, second only to Hopkins, on the young poets of today whom Mr Yeats pretends to admire.

I find it far more difficult to understand Mr Yeats's abounding admiration for the verse of Lady Gerald Wellesley and W. J. Turner. 'I have read,' he says, 'certain poems by them with more than all the excitement that came upon me when, a very young man, I heard somebody read out in a London tavern the poems of Ernest Dowson.' And later he adds the puzzling remark that he would 'but for a failure of talent have been in [the school] of Turner and Dorothy Wellesley.' I am at a loss to understand what the author of 'The Tower' and 'The Winding Stair' implies by 'a failure of talent' or why, a major poet, he should aspire to be of the 'school' of two minor poets. It would be more reasonable, I feel, to attribute his pleasure in Lady Gerald Wellesley's verses, which were unknown to him 'until a few months ago,' to the fact that at their best they echo his own.

263

The preponderance of poems by Irish writers, like Gogarty, Higgins and O'Connor, and of poems which can be classed as ballads, songs and folk-legend is not unexpected, though many of them would be more appropriate to an Oxford Book of Irish Verse than to the present volume. This Irish bias, I suspect, accounts for Mr Yeats's preference for Louis MacNiece amongst the youngest of the moderns. Auden and Spender, oddly enough, are very weakly represented. Still, many people will probably feel that it is premature to include in an Oxford Book poets born little more than twenty years ago who have only just begun to find their pens.

The scope, however, of Mr Yeats's anthology was, presumably, fixed by its sponsors, so that the Delegates of the Clarendon Press will have only themselves to blame if they find that their new book is in part unrepresentative, in part out of date, in a few years time. Meanwhile they and their technical staff, whom I had always supposed and have, indeed, claimed to be accurate beyond reproach, must find somebody to blame for slovenly proof-reading. The misprints, omissions and inconsistencies in the indexes are an insult to the reputation of a great press.

20 November

MR AUDEN'S POEMS
EDWIN MUIR

Look, Stranger!, poems by W. H. Auden. (Faber and Faber)

This volume brings out more clearly than anything else he has written the variety and originality of Mr Auden's genius. Both his thought and his imagination have clarified and now speak for themselves. The main outward difference between these poems and his first ones is an increased mastery of form. His theme is still the same, but it is stated more objectively, without the willed emotion which sometimes intruded into his work. His realisation of the plight of the world, one feels, has grown too deep for mere exhortation; and here the poetry itself works far more strongly on us than exhortation could. He leaves nothing out of these poems that he took into his former ones; but he uses his properties more truly and poetically. This poetry is like a natural language which can be used for any purpose.

It is impossible to enumerate all the virtues of these poems, or decide whether their variety or their formal perfection is more striking. The second song for Benjamin Britten enchants one by its mere shape:

> 'Underneath the abject willow,
>   Lover, sulk no more;
> Act from thought should quickly follow;
>   What is thinking for?
> Your unique and moping station
>   Proves you cold;
>   Stand up and fold
> Your map of desolation.'

That lightness, considering the urgent, compulsive quality of the poetry, is an extraordinary feat. It is seen even better in the opening verse of the twenty-seventh poem:

> 'Fish in the unruffled lakes
> The swarming colours wear,
> Swans in the winter air
> A white perfection have,
> And the great lion walks
> Through his innocent grove;
> Lion, fish, and swan
> Act, and are gone
> Upon Time's toppling wave.'

In achieving this perfection Mr Auden has not lost his power to strike out sudden visionary lines:

> 'Through the blue irises the heaven of failures,
> The mirror world where logic is reversed,
> Where age becomes the handsome child at last,
> The glass sea parted for the country sailors.'

These lines seem to me to give the very flavour of Mr Auden's poetry, though in saying that I am perhaps forgetting its variety; they have a quality which used to be called magical, though the magic is not that of romantic poetry. There is nothing else like it; it is new and unique. It is quite distinct from

> 'But deaf to prophecy or China's drum
> The blood moves strangely in its moving home,'

though that is also filled with Mr Auden's quality. It is a sort of magic with new associations.

One of the most exhilarating things about these poems is the vast landscapes they suddenly suggest, the feeling they give of surveying the world from a height. This is probably a result of their inclusive temper. 'China's drum' is an instance, but these sudden broadening flashes return again and again, in such parentheses as

> 'Though sombre the sixteen skies of Europe
> And the Danube flood,'

and in set pictures. The compression of Mr Auden's style has always been striking, but now it is intensified by a powerful lucidity. His thought has increased its range, while remaining as closely knit as before. There is hardly any of the inequality which marked his first book. How far Mr Auden may yet go, it would be vain to speculate, but this volume by itself is sufficient to establish his name as a poet.

4 December

A SANCTIFIED VOLTAIRE
A. J. AYER

Voltaire, Alfred Noyes. (Sheed and Ward)

'If thou wouldst view one more than man and less, made up of great and mean, and foul and fair' – these words of Macaulay's, which Mr Alfred Noyes quotes in the first chapter of his biography of Voltaire, prescribe a rule which every portrait of Voltaire must be judged. We require of the biographer of Voltaire that he should recognise the contradictions in that extraordinarily complex character, and that he should strive to make them intelligible to us; but not by ignoring or explaining away whatever does not fit into some pre-established framework. This, an essential condition of the adequate portrayal of Voltaire, is one which none of his English biographers has yet been able to satisfy. Lord Morley did not satisfy it. It is inconceivable that his militant rationalist should have prostrated himself, as Voltaire did, before the God revealed in the sunrise or felt the terror that Voltaire felt of having his body thrown into the sewers after death. Lytton Strachey did not satisfy it. One cannot recognise in his grinning monkey the benefactor of Marie Corneille or the defender of Calas. Mr Alfred Noyes has not satisfied it. In cor-

266

recting the bias of Lytton Strachey he has gone to the other extreme. He gives us a Voltaire wholly 'more than man,' a white-chokered Voltaire, sanctified and de-humanised.

This Voltaire is never vain or petty or mean or spiteful or ridiculous. He emerges from Mr Noyes's account of the squabble with Frederick, the Hirsch lawsuit, the wooing of Benedict XIV, the cornering of Desfort's lottery, with his character unblemished and his dignity unimpaired. Mr Noyes does not mention the ludicrous affair of the Président de Brosses and his fourteen loads of wood, which must prove a stumbling-block to anyone who wishes to think of Voltaire as being neither vindictive nor avaricious. If he had mentioned it, he would no doubt have made his hero behave very soberly under great provocation. For this is a uniformly softened portrait. The strident hypochondria of Voltaire is toned down to an 'occasionally humorous exaggeration of his ailments.' His obscenity has vanished altogether. The humour of *La Pucelle* becomes under Mr Noyes's analysis as gay and healthy as that of Father Ronald Knox. Its author himself is made improbably virginal. Not even Madame du Châtelet is allowed to have been his mistress. This does not accord very well with the memoirs of Longchamps or the letters of Madame de Grafigny. But then Longchamps was a discharged valet and Madame de Grafigny a malicious and unprincipled sponger; and so, argues Mr Noyes, their evidence is not always to be trusted. He has not, however, succeeded in giving any very cogent reason for disbelieving them in this instance.

Mr Noyes is anxious to rehabilitate Voltaire not only as a man but also as a writer. He is able to admire the tragedies in which Lytton Strachey could see only 'a procession of pompous commonplaces.' I agree that this condemnation is far too summary. It can, I think, reasonably be argued that Voltaire had a good sense of the theatre. Perhaps a performance of *Brutus* or *Mérope* could still be made moving. But not every play that can be made moving on the stage is a literary masterpiece; and Voltaire's surely are not. Their plots, except when he is drawing on a classical model, are crudely melodramatic. They contain, so far as I can see, no outstanding feats of characterisation. And the style in which they are written tends to make the worst of two worlds. It has neither the naturalness which is required in the modern theatre nor the majesty and beauty for which we value Racine. If it was Mr Noyes's intention to make us look upon Voltaire as a great writer he would have been wise, I suggest, to

267

devote less space to the tragedies and more to the letters and prose stories. For it is as a writer of prose and not, in spite of one or two charming lyrics, as a poet or a dramatist that Voltaire holds his place in the history of literature.

The admiration which Mr Noyes feels for Voltaire does not extend to the other *philosophes*. He is particularly contemptuous of D'Alembert, whom he accuses of having a 'quick, shallow and sometimes repulsively leering mind.' Yet the contributions of D'Alembert to the theory of probability are far more acute and original than anything that is to be found in the philosophical writings of Voltaire. What prevents Mr Noyes from doing justice to D'Alembert is the fact that 'he had never felt the faintest stirrings of any kind of religion.' Voltaire, on the other hand, is regarded by Mr Noyes as having been a profoundly religious man.

How much truth is there in this characterisation of Voltaire? It is clear enough that he was not an atheist. Like other pre-Kantian philosophers, he accepted the argument from design. He saw no fallacy in assuming that it was valid to speak of the world as of a house which pre-supposed an architect. We may allow also that he felt at least an intermittent impulse to worship the God of whose existence he was intellectually convinced. Whether he believed in a personal and benevolent God is more doubtful. The most that can fairly be said, I think, is that he felt that such a God was required to redress the balance of evil in the world over good, and that, with his great sense of justice, he could not bear the thought that it might after all go unredressed. I agree with Mr Noyes in regarding the lines in the poem on the Lisbon earthquake *Un jour, tout sera bien, voilà notre espérance; Tout est bien aujourd'hui, voilà l'illusion* as truly expressive of Voltaire's attitude. But it must be stressed that this religious optimism was in him no more than a hope. As for the divinity of Christ, the evidence is markedly against his having believed in it. I cannot sum up his attitude on this point better than he does himself. *Dieu puissant! Je crois! Quant à Monsieur le Fils, et à Madame sa mère, c'est une autre affaire.*

Mr Noyes's book is very long but it is nearly always interesting. Whatever else may be said against it, it is not a shallow work. I have given reasons for thinking that it gives only a one-sided and, to some extent, distorted picture of Voltaire. But it remains a contribution to an exceedingly complex subject, of which subsequent biographers will do well to take account.

11 December

BOOKS FOR CHRISTMAS
EVELYN WAUGH

For the logical mind the Teutonic observance of Christmas is a highly puzzling business. Even in the nursery, where one was beset by unlimited, acquisitive impulses dependent solely upon adult caprice for their satisfaction, I remember moments of extreme vexation against benevolent elders who had too casually interpreted the detailed appeals to Santa Claus, which we used to put up the chimney. Why would they not give the money and let me choose for myself? But at least in those happy days no return was expected more valuable than a hand-painted Christmas card.

But Nordic man, ever wistfully and whimsically in pursuit of his own childhood, encouraged by shopkeepers of every faith and race, has insisted on perpetuating the custom. It is in accordance with Christian charity that the rich should send gifts to the poor; it is dignified and fitting that the Ambassadors of different races should present examples of their culture to the monarchs to whom they are sent. (In 1930 the Prince of Udine gave an aeroplane to the Emperor Haile Selassie.) But it is hard to see what useful end is served by the annual exchange of objects of identical value between people of identical income.

It may be supposed that we all have certain desires that the limits of our income render unsatisfied. Few but ourselves know of them; none know them exactly. The probability of a friend hitting upon them by chance is very remote. The best he can do is to give us something which we should have to buy for ourselves – a box of the cigars we habitually smoke, razor-blades, a dozen hair-cuts – thus setting free a part of our income, previously earmarked, for less prosaic ends. This is highly desirable, though very rare, for particular occasions such as weddings. But how much simpler for him to send us a cheque. And how foolish we should look at Christmas if we all, with expressions of love and good wishes, exchanged cheques of the same value; and how painful it would be to receive a cheque for a guinea from someone to whom we had sent only a pound. If, on the other hand, we are to receive objects which we should not have bought for ourselves, and do not particularly want, in exchange for objects sent to our friends of precisely similar character, we are all so much the worse off: neither clergy nor poor have gained anything. It is an odd way to celebrate a religious festival.

269

This logical absurdity is slightly relieved by the giving of books. In the first place there is no need for delicacy about their cost. There is no hope that our present looks more expensive, no fear that it looks less than it is. The prices are clearly printed upon the wrapper, and if we remove that, we are open to the suspicion of having sent a second-hand or complimentary copy (since some papers have the nasty habit of labelling the books they send out for review). Moreover, in our choice, we are able to point morals and criticise our relatives in a way which, more directly done, would be grossly offensive. There is no question of our giving a book which we think the recipient would like; we give what we think will do her good, and in this connexion one may pause to condemn a singularly futile scheme that was lately launched by the book trade. This was a system of 'vouchers' by which one gave a receipt for the value of a certain sum to be spent on books; the most ignominious present to receive, approximating to the admonition offered the tramp 'Now spend this on nourishing food, my good man, not in beer,' having the disadvantages, suggested above, of the ordinary banker's cheque, and none of the advantages.

But in choosing the books ourselves we can wipe out many an old score. Someone has taken a snobbish line towards us; we send the biography of one of our ancestors. We have had a political argument, and feel that we did not make the best of our case; we can send the work from which we drew our own garbled version. We have disagreed on a point of history; here is the moment to prove ourselves right. We have long been distressed by the prose style of a literary acquaintance; Fowler's *Modern English Usage* for him. A book of our own is about to be re-maindered; give it to everybody. We wish to convert someone to a crank notion of our own; inundate him with tendentious literature. We find someone's food unpalatable; a case for cookery books. They do not know how to bring up their children; a treatise on discipline. It is not difficult in the spate of contemporary fiction, to find types to which our relatives approximate in their less companionable moments. It is possible sometimes with industry, to find illustrations which caricature their features. And we can send these missiles in the happy assurance that in the dyspeptic gloom of Boxing Day, any hit which we score will be doubly painful.

18 December

Part Five: Life and Leisure

Part Five Life and Poetics

MARGINAL COMMENTS
ROSE MACAULAY

1936 is opening, even more noticeably than most years, in an atmosphere of mutual international distastes. One is not surprised to be told that this has been a remarkably home-keeping Christmas; for abroad is just now, for most nations, a somewhat perilous pleasure-ground, and the winter resorts of other days have assumed, for one reason or another, an intimidating, even a menacing, air. Yes; even our adored Balearics ... while as for the Italian Riviera ... One can still cruise, you say, about the high seas? But doubtfully, warily, looking up at the heavens, looking for all the fire-folk seated in the sky....

To set against these imperfect sympathies, each nation would appear to be taking increasing pleasure in its own qualities and exploits. One boasts itself a democracy, which can write letters to its representatives telling them where they get off, thus changing history; another delights to be a corporate State, obeying orders in unison; another to be a great republic, thinking with resolution and continuity of its own security; one is proud to be marching, Roman civilisation in hand, into uncultured lands; one to be outside European imbroglios, soothing the troubled waters and the raging flames with oil. There is always some cause for national self-love; and for my part I find it a pretty and engaging spectacle, in a world of nations whom there are all too few to love. For this reason I enjoy the broadcast European Interchanges, and regret the cancelling last week of that between an Englishman and a Russian. I always like to hear the Briton posing the alien with the time-honoured British question, asked by English tourists abroad for many centuries, 'How do you like having no freedom?' and to hear the foreigner vehemently explaining that he has as much as, or more than, his questioner. I should like to have heard, and hope still to hear, the repartee of the representative of the U.S.S.R. 'In Russia we say that it is you capitalist States who have no freedom.' Or, 'Freedom is of no importance. What matters is social welfare.' Or, 'Well, you see, Russians have never had any freedom, so don't miss it.' I should enjoy him on capitalist vice and soviet virtue, and the Englishman on the reverse. It would be, surely, an agreeable entertainment, and to cancel it because inaccuracies, or asperities, or both (in fact, human nature) would keep breaking in was a timid and a tedious act. 'The free range and fair balance of give-and-take argument could not be secured,' the B.B.C. is reported to have said. But who wants it, when we might have instead the free range and unfair lack of balance of human and naional vanity, beside which fair argument is but a dull and prosy affair? Give us free human nature to divert us, and we will not ask for fairness. Alice, a dull little prig, was shocked by the unfairness of the 'nice knock-down arguments' used by Humpty-Dumpty and the other beings she encountered; had she been wiser, she would have listened to them with delight. 'How unfair they are both being!' That is what we say when we hear these international back-chats: doubtless we should have said it again had we been permitted to hear the Anglo-Russian dialogue; but should we have turned if off for that? A thousand times no. No one wants people to be fair or balanced about the places they live in; a fine and maniac frenzy should possess them (and does) when they describe their no doubt deplorable homes. For one must remember this: if we do not belaud our own places of residence and national habits, these may lack altogether a trumpeter, and become melancholy affairs indeed.

Give us, then, our Anglo-Russian air-chat, for we shall enjoy it greatly.

3 January

THE SUBURB WIFE
FRANCIS GOWER

What happens to the further education of the girl who leaves a secondary school at eighteen, puts in a few years at secretarial or other work, then marries a husband with an income of something between £300 and £500 a year in a suburban flat or villa? The income is enough to live on in a simple way. Lack of means is not the trouble, unless an attempt is made to set standards that the income will not justify. The question is not how to lay out money, but how to lay out time. It is probably a no-maid house, with daily help more or less adequate. The husband goes off by the 9.17 and gets home by the 6.59. Before the children begin to come, at any rate, everything necessary about the house is done by lunchtime. When luncheon is cleared away – no formidable matter – five solid hours remain before the business of getting supper is put in hand.

How are they to be employed? How, in fact, are they employed today? Is there any link between them and the formal school education that ended half a dozen years before? Can they be used, are they used, to enrich life with something that will compensate for the inevitable toil and drudgery to which so many hours of the married woman's life must be devoted? It is no use pretending that drudgery does not bulk large in such a life. It does, and it must. No one can contend that there is anything inspiring or enlarging to the mind in making beds or darning socks or cleaning silver or planning meals. They are all useful and necessary pieces of service, but life contains higher possibilities than that. A life in which the waking hours of the average day was filled with duties such as these would be a static, barren, undeveloping affair. The more we are cumbered about with doing, the more imperative it is to give thought to being.

This is a social problem of real importance, and it deserves to be seriously discussed, as it is being in some quarters. I noticed a remark made the other day by the Editor of *The Spectator*, to the effect that 'age could not wither Cleopatra nor custom stale her infinite variety, but a one-maid villa in a London suburb would do it in eighteen months,' which – quoted, I gather, without any of the reservations with which it was hedged round – enabled enterprising reporters to elicit admirably indignant comments from various inhabitants of the local-government area in question. Yet – with the reservations – it is obviously true. The line of least resistance is very nearly the strongest thing on earth. To drift through life is ten times easier than to cultivate life. It needs an effort to grasp an opportunity; it needs none at all to let a dozen slip. Of course there is no case for sweeping generalisations. I have the profoundest admiration for the young men and women, married or unmarried, who buy or borrow books worth reading and read them, who stand hours to get into the gallery at a theatre or concert, for whom the radio means more than jazz and the cinema more than meretricious romance. They, at least, are getting something a great deal better into their lives than ever Cleopatra did.

But are they the majority? And even if they are, which I doubt, is not the minority so large as to justify some concern? I am not for a moment blaming; I am only wondering, and at most regretting. I am conscious enough how easy it would be for me, if I were a woman left alone with an afternoon on my hands five days a week, to let the walls of life insensibly close in on me, and find myself (or, worse still, fail to find myself) growing petty and superficial. For the married woman in the suburban villa has little external stimulus. She is likely enough to be a stranger to the neighbourhood. Organisations like the Workers' Educational Association, or the Association for Adult Education, or the Women's Institutes, are for the most part not for her; the wage-earner and the salary-earner do not always mix. Nor, certainly, are the admirable lectures and classes organised in many centres for the unemployed. She is not, like her husband, brought daily in contact with another and a larger world. Just where she is there is a gap, and too often she falls into it.

So far as this is true it is clearly to be deplored. And something, just as clearly, should be done about it. To put it on no other ground, it is desirable that citizens should be good citizens, and voters intelligent voters. It is important, to begin with, that the good citizen, in this case a feminine citizen living on a modest household income and with some hours of leisure daily on her hands, should keep herself reasonably conversant with the life of the nation and the world. She must, in a word, read a daily paper – which is sometimes difficult if the husband carries it off every morning to read in the train. And it must be read critically, not, as too often, with blind credulity. That argues the possession of some 'background,' which every girl reasonably educated should have acquired by the time she leaves school at the age of eighteen, and *ought* to have gone on developing since. We have just witnessed an astonishing popular manifestation of opinion on a vital question of foreign policy, but from precisely what strata of the population it emanated it is difficult to know. How many, for example, of the suburban wife class had views on the peace-plan, and expressed them by writing to their M.P., or supporting some resolution at a local meeting? It would be interesting and valuable, but probably impossible, to discover.

Even if all this, or much of it, is true, what, it may reasonably be asked, can be done to keep lives from narrowing? Two things at least. More agents and instruments for the broadening of life must be provided, and the girl must be sent from school into the world resolved that she will not let her tastes degenerate or her interests grows cramped when they ought to be continually expanding. That is a task for the teachers, who have enough tasks, and difficult enough, as it is. Somehow they have to equip girls not merely to earn a living, but to live. Only on a sound foundation can a sound superstructure rise. If there is an inner demand for worthy sustenance for the mind and spirit, it will not be content to go unsatisfied.

But externals are essential too. To read about the events of the day with no one to discuss them with (till after 7.15 p.m.) is dull work. The Churches used to make contacts far more than they do today, for the simple reason that far more people were associated with churches then than now. Societies, political, social, religious, for the most part meet in the evening, in the hope of securing husband as well as wife; actually they more often succeed in getting neither. It is with the B.B.C. pre-eminently that the opportunity lies. Perhaps Sir John Reith and his colleagues realise it. Perhaps they are trying to provide in the afternoon hours programmes which are neither dull nor highbrow, but which will extend the knowledge of the young wife of modest means, and keep her interest in literature and art and music, and all that gives life eternal values, fresh. They may be trying, but after some study of afternoon programmes, I rather hope they are not. For they are obviously not succeeding, and I should like to think it was still open to them to try and to succeed. A field lies fallow that both demands and deserves cultivation.

10 January

WINTER SEASIDE
JAN STRUTHER

Literature, that assiduous foster-mother of fallacies, has long kept alive in us the belief that we are a sea-faring, or at any rate a sea-loving, nation. We must continually (or so we would have the foreigner believe) go down to the sea again; and all we ask is a tall ship and a telescope to look at her through. In sober fact, however, the sea, for most of us, comes but once a year – in August. For the rest of the time it might just as well not exist: indeed, on the rare occasions in the past when some emergency has taken me to its borders during the intervening months, I have been apt to look at it a little queerly and say 'Good Lord – it's still there!' as though I had expected someone to roll it up and put it away under the band-stand along with the deck-chairs and all the other paraphernalia of summer.

But a year ago I fell into the clutches of an ex-coastguard cottage, intending to use it only in the summer holidays. Since

277

then I have spent almost every week-end by the sea: and curiously enough it is the winter ones which I have enjoyed the most.

A town, a seaside resort, is a different matter. There, the deserted pier, the derelict bathing huts, the forlorn and shuttered kiosks, stand as melancholy reminders of suspended activity: it is like a ballroom in dust-sheets. But here, though the beach is thronged in summer by the overflow from the bungalow village a mile to the east, there is, in winter, nothing to remind one of the invaders, except a small wooden hut which clings precariously to a jutting ridge of shingle. In one of the recent gales it failed to cling, and through its upside-down windows one could see a litter of thick white cups and saucers. When the owners righted it and repaired the damaged side they put back one of the planks the wrong way up; so that the legend on its east wall now reads as follows:

BEACH
TRAYS

Except for this hut, and a couple of tarred shacks where the fishermen keep their gear, there is little to break the horizontal lines which make sea and marshland so much more restful to the townsman's eye, ceaselessly fretted by perpendiculars, than all the enchantments of woodland or mountain scenery. To the west lie the saltings of the estuary, their pools lapis, their herbage astonishing jade; and beyond them the river, deepened and narrowed by its restraining walls, swirls out savagely at six knots. To the east, beyond the bungalow outcrop, eight miles of unspoiled coastline stretch between here and the lighthouse on the Ness. Ironically enough its peacefulness is due to war: for if it were not for the artillery practice-ranges which lie behind it, it would long ago have been exploited. Disarmament will spell its doom.

To the south lies the sea itself, a couple of hundred yards away at high-water, but at the low springs nearly a mile. It comes in across the flat sand not, perhaps, 'faster than a horse can gallop,' but certainly faster than a human being can wade in gumboots: as I discovered one bitterly cold December day when I walked out (half-way to France, it seemed) to buy shrimps from an old man with gold ear-rings. He had caught no shrimps that day: but he mentioned *en passant* that he had seen his grandfather ploughing them sands with a pair of horses by moonlight to find bars of gold which had been cast up from the wreck of a French brig. Which, even if it was really silver, and by daylight, and somebody else's grandfather, and only one horse, was worth getting wet to hear. And if, like him, I had been wearing thigh-boots, I should have stayed for a great deal more.

Bar-gold is rare, but the sands hold other treasures: indeed, one of the reasons why I prefer the winter is the superior quality and richer variety of its flotsam. The morning after a gale yields the best results, and if the wind has been southerly most of the tins and bottles have French names on them: a detail which has somehow put France on the map for me as no amount of geography lessons had ever done.

The items in my year's list may be divided into animal, vegetable and hardware. The hardware includes tea-chests, sugar-boxes, logs, spars and other potential firewood; bed-springs, mattresses, motor-tyres, bathing shoes, rope, saucepans, frying-pans, and kettles; a green glass net-float (falsely reputed unbreakable), a window-frame, several hatch-covers, a life-jacket, a pound of candles (salt-caked), two netting-shuttles, a panama hat, a topee, and three beautiful and luxurious wicker-covered flasks, invaluable for picnics. The animal section tells a sadder tale, for it consists almost entirely of dead birds, black duck for the most part, who have died of disease or starvation, their feathers clogged with fuel-oil. Larger corpses have been mercifully lacking, with the exception of two sheep who made the shingle spit unvisitable for a couple of weeks before they were solemnly interred in quicklime by the local police. As for the vegetable section, it would stock a greengrocer's. I have found oranges, lemons, grape-fruit, apples and greengages; carrots, onions, cabbages, radishes and potatoes; and after one particularly rough night the beach was improbably strewn with excellent cobnuts. Strangest of all, there is an intermittent but hitherto lavish supply of coconut husks, which, dried, burn very sweetly with a white ash and a faint ropy smell. The collecting of them, in sacks, enables much good *Man of Aran* stuff to be put over on guests who are in need of exercise.

I have kept to the last – since it will not be believed anyway – my crowning, my red-letter day, when I found, on a single tide, an unbroken electric light bulb, a stuffed olive, an arum lily and a moth-ball.

As the water ebbs it reveals another beauty which in summer is quickly trampled and obscured but which in winter lies almost untouched from tide to tide: namely, the curious and lovely patterns traced in sand by the complicated cross-rhythms of wind and water. Only an experienced needlewoman could do justice in words to such a variety of rimplings and crinklings, of pleatings and puckerings, of gaugings, rufflings, gofferings, and pin-tuckings as it is possible to find; though somebody with a knowledge of heraldry could perhaps convey a few of the designs in such terms as nebuly, raguly or dancetty (semée, he might add, of starfish proper). If the wind has been strong and steady, the ridges are as deep and regular as corduroy; if it has blown gustily, they may look like a cardiographic record of a man in the last stages of heart-disease; while if the day has been windless the gentle laminations of the ebb will have left nothing but a delicate surface embroidery, a pattern of interlinked chevrons damascened on the smooth sand in a fine nacreous dust of powdered shells.

As for the weather, until a year ago I imagined that the seaside, from October to April, was an unremitting hell of cold, wind and wet. Well, there is certainly cold, but it is not the sodden cold of weald or marsh, and it has been more than worth while for the sake of two new experiences: the sight of a thousand upturned shells frozen into the rimed sand, each filled with a precise individual helping of snow; and the curious, half-crisp, half-soapy texture of frozen foam when crushed between the fingers. But even in a district whose low rainfall is made up for by the speed, strength and frequency of its winds, there is a surprising number of days when it is possible to sit on the beach and enjoy all the advantages of summer without its two crowning drawbacks – the presence of other people, and an uneasy feeling that you ought to be immersing yourself in the sea.

England – which is why her climate is so often abused by people with tidy minds – wears her seasons haphazard, dining in tweeds if she feels inclined and flaunting a ball-dress for breakfast when the mood takes her. You may find a patch of purest winter in July (like 'Part of Flint' on an old map), while the pieces of summer which are scattered recklessly throughout the year would, if put end to end, make a total of which any country might be proud. If this is true of her countryside, it is even more true of her sea-coast: for here there is not even a skeleton tree or a bare hedgerow to point inexorably to the calendar, shattering our make-believe; here the splendid insignia of summer, never worn, cannot be missed; and the year, like the human heart, is as young as it feels.

10 January

COUNTRY LIFE
H. E. BATES

SWAN FOR DINNER

At least one distinguished novelist has eaten an unusual Christmas dinner – a swan. The bird – whether a cob (male) or pen (female) I do not know – was very large and from all accounts very good. The flesh seems to have been like goose, but lighter, more delicate. After having seemed a little fishy while cooking it later turned out, roasted and stuffed with chestnuts, to be well worthy of Chaucer's famous praise of the bird. All of which recalls a very different episode related in masterly fashion by Hudson. It concerns the cooking of a heron, Hudson having met the two daughters of a man who had cherished a lifelong ambition to taste that bird. For years his daughters had put him off, but finally Hudson relates how he procured a bird and ordered it, tyrannically, in spite of all protests, to be cooked. And cooked it was, with ghastly results. The flesh turned out to be hideously black, fishy and uneatable, the daughters were almost poisoned, the countryside was fouled by a stench as of many diabolically ancient fishshops, and at least one person was cured for ever of a desire to eat fish-loving birds. Swans are, I think, presumed to be the property of the King and of certain Companies such as the Dyers and Vintners Company, the royal swans being marked with five nicks, two lengthwise and three crosswise, on the bill. Peacocks are another matter; and there is on record the charming story of a girl who, while shooting, innocently mistook one for a pheasant. But it was a shallow excuse, since neither peacock nor pheasant was hers to shoot anyway.

* * * *

GRASS DRYING

Something like a revolution is going to take place in English grassland farming if the problems of drying grass for winter fodder are finally and successfully solved. It has been known for some time that grass cut at the height of a few inches and dried by hot air or particular gases will retain far higher nutritive values than hay, the dried grass retaining almost the qualities of fresh grass. Experiments have already shown that a drier introducing gases at 250 degrees C does no harm to the grass, that the grass keeps its colour well, and that there is a singular decline in the feeding value of grass from May to the end of June, albuminoids and fats declining by about a third. Even the layman must see what this means: that a grazier may, on good land, by judicious cutting and feeding, obtain a production of highly nutritive young grass throughout the summer instead of a single crop at a time when the feeding values of the material have greatly fallen. Such a yield might very well double the value of land. Estimates made by a committee of the Agricultural Research Council put the production cost of a ton of raw material at about 40s, and the value of a ton of dried grass, as compared with current prices of other foodstuffs, at about £6 10s. What now seems to be needed most of all is a cheap small-scale plant to do the job. If it comes, and if grass-drying in this country proves a success, we may very well see summer fields like lawns and hear the clack of the grass-cutter from June till September.

* * * *

WILLOWS AND OSIERS

The total area of willows and osiers under cultivation in England has declined by half in ten years, and stands now at something like 3,000 acres, of which more than half are in Somerset. The introduction of all sorts of substitutes, Chinese sea-grass, cane in split or pulp form, fibre and so on, has been largely responsible for it, but the competition of foreign rods, in spite of a decline in imports since 1930, has also helped. There has been a large decrease in importation from Holland and Belgium, but a large increase from an unexpected country, the Argentine, one-year-old Argentine rods apparently attaining a greater length, without a corresponding increase in diameter at the butt, than those grown elsewhere. Polish and Silesian rods have also increased. The four chief varieties grown here, *Salix triandra*, *S. Amygdalina*, *S. viminalis* and *S. Purpurea*, have produced some attracting named varieties: Black Hollanders, Glib Skins, Pomeranians, Spaniards, Brown Merrins, Dicky Meadows, Long Skins and Dark Dicks, which read rather more like the characters out of piratical romance. As to cultivation and cutting, this is another case where, as with sweet chestnut, everything looks very pretty, but is in reality very expert. Cultivation is something more than the mere planting of sets in marshy ground, and cutting far more than the mere hacking off of leafless rods. The time of cutting depends entirely on the treatment which rods are

282

subsequently to undergo: so that rods for 'buffing,' or buff colour, are cut as soon as the leaf has fallen, rods for 'brown' not until the whole leaf crop has fallen and rods for 'white' not until early spring. Standing osiers and willows have always seemed to me among the best of trees in winter. But it was not until December that I saw such a plantation of bloody orange as flamed up by the side of a small Kentish mill: in the late afternoon the rods seemed to be covered with a kind of fiery varnish, so rich that they seemed to give out a tawny blood-shining light in the falling darkness.

*   *   *   *

A CENSUS OF BIRDS' NESTS

Looking up an old number of *The Countryman* I find one of those obvious, simple queries which occur to all of us when someone else has thought of them first. 'How many of us know within 10 per cent the number of nests in any given acreage of English countryside?' The writer is suggesting a census of nests, his purpose being to test a statement by a firm of bird-seed suppliers that the mortality among young wild birds every year is 80 per cent, a figure which he doubts. He goes on to detail a bird-map, made for his purpose, of a garden of ten acres, the site containing 67 nests. One at once sees the value of such a record, since nothing fades more quickly than last year's spring and the detail of its nests unless it is last year's summer and the detail of its flowers. If we make and keep plans for herbaceous borders why not plans for fields and the nests in them? A plan might resolve itself into a five-year plan: so that the increase or decrease of birds might be tested, the partiality of birds for certain sites, the incoming or disappearance of rarer birds, the use by certain species of almost the same site over and over again. I cannot remember, for the life of me, how many nests I discovered last spring. It would vary from twenty to forty, perhaps, every afternoon I went out. The species have got mixed up. I know there were a great many chaffinches. Many odd wrens. A particular cirl-bunting's. I could mark, perhaps, fifteen or twenty sites. The rest are forgotten. A map – it would be a delightful pastime for all children – would not only have recorded them all but would have formed a working plan for the coming spring, the excitement of which would no doubt have been doubled in consequence. In short, the idea of a census of bird's nests seems to me just as worth carrying out as the recent census of starlings. Perhaps more.

* * * *

POACHING: OLD AND NEW

Civilisation threatens many rural figures, but not the poacher. He survives and flourishes in a world which has long since annihilated the smuggler. I may be pardoned, I hope, for a profound admiration for the true poacher, a survivor of a wilder life, the sole remaining example in these islands of the hunter who is also hunted. He carries on a craft which needs insuperable courage and cunning and which is often pretty poor in its rewards and harsh in its penalties. I am not so sure of the modern poaching upstart, the gent who now brings his lorry to country lanes and picks up, by the hundred, poached game for the town. This new type of mechanised poaching is now quite common, and the possibilities of turning it into a racket, gangster fashion, seem to me considerable. The snag would come with the intimidation of solitary poachers, and I like to speculate on its chances of success with an old poaching acquaintance, who has just died. He used to take his wife with him. She seems to have been a lean little woman, like a ferret, tough as hawthorn, and she went wherever he went, which might be twenty or thirty or even forty miles, by night, in winter, and was ready, like him, for anything. He himself was a man of fifteen stone, a bruiser, and it must have been a good sight to see them working together, he so big, she no bigger beside him than a dog. And she deserves, I think, the record of his verdict: 'A good gal. And as good a hand as I ever worked wi'.'

10 January

TATTOOING
WILLIAM PLOMER

'The universality of this practice,' said Captain Cook of tattooing, 'is a curious subject of speculation.' It is indeed, and from time to time it has engaged the attention of anthropologists and other learned persons. Lombroso put it down to atavism, and it has intermittently been regarded, from ancient times until the present day, as a barbarous thing to wear pictures on one's skin by choice, and an ignominious thing to wear them by compul-

284

sion, for tattooing has sometimes been used as a method of branding criminals, and cases have been known where they have been sentenced to proceed on their life's journey wearing satirical verses about their own misdemeanours.

It has often been and still is in many places a matter of tribal custom, sometimes crudely and to our tastes repulsively executed, especially where it results in deformation of the surface of the body, but among various races it has been done with great skill, as among the Maoris, who covered their faces with formal curves and spirals, or with a curious neatness, as among the Gilbert Islanders, some of whom go about covered from head to foot with a quiet herring-bone pattern in navy blue. The Japanese, who excel at applied arts, attained a wonderful technique in this one, but tended to go in for drearily elaborate conventional designs resembling those on some of their cheap printed stuffs at the present day, which produce the effect of a too heavily flowered cretonne. In the extreme north of Japan one can still see Ainu women who have assumed on marriage not a wedding-ring but a tattooed blue moustache of the arrogant shape once favoured by the ex-Kaiser.

It would be a mistake to suppose that tattooing is only to the taste of primitive people or that it has been confined in Europe to criminals, prostitutes, soldiers, sailors and workmen, for towards the end of the last century, in the heyday of prosperity and imperialism, it became popular amongst people of wealth and position, and there is reason to believe that some very important individuals still carry on their persons the jingoistic emblems which enthusiasm for the Boer War induced them to select, to say nothing of snakes, daggers, butterflies, dragons, roses, mermaids, curly monograms and so forth, at prices varying from five shillings to ten pounds. In 1903 there was an article in the *Tatler* entitled 'The Gentle Art of Tattooing: The Fashionable Craze of Today,' and in the Spanish monograph on the subject by R. Salillas (1908) we learn of a Mr Macdonald that *'en su estudio de Jermyn-Street ha recibido la visita de individuos de la más alta aristocracia, de príncipes de la sangre y de duques.'*

Often people have tattooed or been tattooed for no particular reason, because they have had nothing better to do, or have been confined in a narrow space, exiled, isolated, or driven in upon themselves, or have been bored and in need of amusement. This partly accounts for the frequency of tattooing, especially in the past, upon sailors, soldiers, legionaries and various sorts of

285

vagabonds, prisoners and criminals. Custom, fashion, imitative-
ness, or some herd or group instinct have often been reasons for
tattooing, and so has vanity, as in a recorded case of a master
mariner who had his official certificate reproduced in bold letter-
ing on his façade. But the most interesting motives of all are
emotional or psychological ones, and the most interesting tattoo-
ings are those which express in a symbolical form some strong
feeling, religious, patriotic, or personal, and which reflect the
private thoughts, moral sentiments, or images most dear to the
wearers. Thus Lacassagne and Vervaeck, two authorities on the
subject, give us examples of religious men being marked not only
with such emblems as crosses, hearts and anchors, but with elaborate crucifixion scenes with attendant angels, or altars bearing
the sacramental vessels.

Patriotic enthusiasm is expressed not only in national flags,
trophies and heraldic emblems, but has been known to trace
itself in portraits of various celebrities from Joan of Arc to Gari-
baldi, and reached a climax in the indelible likeness of Bismarck
with which a French soldier once chose to decorate his posterior.
Another managed to combine a sentiment of loyalty to his country with a hint at his tastes as a gourmet in the phrase, '*Vive
la France et les pommes de terre frites.*' Political passion gives us
such mottoes as '*Mort aux bourgeois,*' '*Vive l'anarchie,*' and other
equivalents of 'Up the rebels.' A lawless man proclaims the fact
in the words '*Ni dieu ni maître,*' or in some hint of vengeance,
and a travelled and adventurous German is known to have chosen a baroque composition called 'Lowenabenteuer in Palmen-
landscaft.' Another German, more hedonistic, was tattooed with
the couplet:

'Wer nicht liebt Wein, Weib, Gesang,
Der bleibt ein Narr sein Leben lang.'

Sometimes an impulse towards autobiography finds an outlet, as
in '*Enfant de la gaieté*' or '*Le passé m'a trompé, le présent me tour-
mente, l'avenir mépouvante,*' and there is on record the case of a
French murderer on whose forearm was written '*Né sous mauvaise
étoile*': this slogan so impressed one of his intended victims that
she was able to identify him by it, a circumstance which helped
to convict him. It may also be recalled that the question of
tattooed markings played some part in the Tichborne case.

As an instance of tattooing being used to express a personal
taste, I know of an English sportsman of the upper classes who

had his torso covered with pheasants, grouse, partridges, shot-guns and sporting dogs. In Belgium a drunkard was tattooed with a picture of a man sitting on an enormous bottle of gin, and gamblers have chosen dice, playing cards, fighting cocks, or the numbers of lottery tickets. Sometimes the wearer's trade or profession is indicated: for soldiers, bugles, lances, military badges, or the heads of horses; for sailors, mermaids, lighthouses, anchors, ships, or coils of rope; keys for a locksmith; a lyre for a musician; a pick and shovel for a miner; a tree for a gardener; a boot for a shoemaker; or a hammer and anvil for a blacksmith. But nowadays, when people have mechanised jobs or no jobs at all, or change their jobs frequently, such occupational signs are getting rare.

It is natural that love, lust, or vague amorous leanings should be among the most frequent feelings recorded by the tattooer's needle. Thus we get portraits, names, or initials of persons be-loved, clasped hands, hearts pierced by arrows, and symbolic flowers like roses or pansies, with suitable mottoes, 'True love,' and so on. Filial love is shown by a single word like 'Mother,' or by clasped hands holding a flower and surrounded by the initials of the bearer and both parents, or by crosses bearing the initials of the dead. For simple wish-fulfilments a dove or swallow will do, carrying in its beak a letter, perhaps marked 'Good News'; or else alluring figures of ballet-dancers, circus-riders or acrobats; and sometimes, of course, the wearer's most personal inclinations are advertised suggestively or with frank pornography. One of the most celebrated examples of purely ornamental tattooing was that of George Constantine, a well-built Greek who took part in a French expedition to Cochin-China, got himself finely and elab-orately tattooed in Burma, and afterwards travelled with Barnum's circus. The work, which took nearly three months to do and consisted of nearly four hundred designs, covered almost the entire surface of his body: on his chest alone he exhibited two sphinxes, two serpents, two elephants, two swans, and a horned owl.

The aesthetic merits of tattooing are debatable, but it should not be condemned out of hand as a debased practice. It is no more barbarous than other processes that lead to personal adorn-ment, such as painting the nails and mouth red, or catching wild animals in cruel traps for the sake of their fur. At its worst it reveals a lack of taste, a fault which is very common and often far more blatantly and publicly expressed; at its best it may

287

have a decorative or sentimental value, it may be a clue to character, and it may have even more than the poetical significance of the words and pictures written up by prisoners on the walls of cells, for it is inscribed on the outer wall of the prison that contains the soul.

17 January

COUNTRY LIFE
H. E. BATES

COUNTRY CUSTOMS

When I wrote, a fortnight ago, of 'the category of vanishing country festivals' it did not occur to me that I could fill this page, and another, with even brief descriptions of the feast and festival days, now obsolete, which must have been commonly kept in the childhood of our grandparents. Since then I have been able to gather some notes on about thirty customs. Unfortunately not all are complete enough to be included here, and some, such as Pancake Day and Oak Apple Day, need no description by me. But what of Clipping Posies, Duck under the Water, Largess, Lowbelling, Valentining, Possessioning, Booting, Dyzemas Day, Mop, Riding and Stattis? These read like the quips of an Elizabethan clown, and to most of us will mean about as much. Yet in the last century they must have been a fixed and cherished part of country life. And many of them, if they are completely dead at all, must have died out quite recently. The distribution of largess is commonly remembered. Possessioning survives under its better-known name, Beating the Bounds. Of the rest Valentining and Mop are certainly observed; Valentining in the Eastern counties, where children still beg for coppers on Valentine's Day with a song:

> 'Holly and ivy and tickle my toe,
> Give me red apple and let me go.'

And Mop, or Mop Fair, certainly survives, particularly at Boston, in Lincolnshire, and is still a great day there. Mop is roughly synonymous with Stattis, a corruption of Statute, in turn an abbreviation of Statute Sessions, established by Edward III in 1351. Both Stattis and Mop came eventually to mean an annual fair or gathering for the hiring out of servants to new masters, the difference being that Stattis comes before Michaelmas and

288

Mop after. Every Hundred in England originally had a Stattis, with attendance of magistrates, to solve the servant problems. Later the attendance of magistrates ceased and the fair grew up, an occasion of rejoicing and a chance to buy a new rig-out. My own grandfather regularly attended a great Stattis at Kimbolton, in Huntingdonshire. Today, at Boston, servants are still said to buy new clothes on Mop Fair day. But what no longer survives, and what must have once coloured the whole Stattis scene delightfully, is the wearing of emblems of service, the shepherd carrying his lock of wool, the cow-man his tuft of cow-hair, the carter his whip. And whether the rest of these odd customs survive at all or not, they go to prove at least one thing: that country life in the past was not quite so dull as this age is apt to think it. Nor quite so circumspect. Take the ceremony known as Riding. The wife who wore the trousers got no change out of Riding, in which two men, one dressed as a woman, rode in a cart to the house where the husband was henpecked and went through a satirical mimicry of female persecution, the woman walloping the man with a basting ladle. And discontented married couples could hardly have been sweetened by the custom known as Lowbelling, where a crowd of neighbours turned out, rattled ironical tin cans for their benefit, and gave them the contemporary equivalent of the raspberry.

* * * *

THE VILLAGE HALL

Village life, indeed, can hardly ever have been so stereotyped and in that sense so dull as it is today. Of the three great pillars of pre-War village life, two – the church and the big house – have been badly shaken. The pub, alone, thanks as much to the townsman as anyone, keeps its place. It is a place that must, however, have been challenged, if only a little, by the post-War rise of the village hall, an erection which, incidentally, has often outdone the corrugated-iron chapel in its depressing ugliness. That there is no need for this unimaginative village jerry-building – which has, I expect, too often been the result of the notion that village folk 'wouldn't appreciate anything better even if it were put up' – was emphatically proved by an admirable article by Mr J. W. Robertson Scott in the *News Chronicle* recently, in which he described an almost Utopian village hall just completed in the Cotswolds, a fine building in local style and stone, with bath-rooms, sports changing-rooms, concert hall and so on. Now comes the news that the National Council of Social Service is prepared to grant financial assistance to villages which desire to build halls. The scheme embodies a free grant of one-sixth of the total cost of erection, with a maximum of £350, together with a loan of not more than one-third of the total cost, with a maximum of £500. This means that if both loan and grant are approved the village itself must raise, in cash, one-half the total cost of erection; if the grant only is made, the village must raise the whole of the balance. Loans are made free of interest, and special loans, also free of interest, are available for the improvement of existing village halls. This is the mere outline of a scheme which ought to give a great many villages something to think about, and full details can be obtained from the National Council of Social Service, 26 Bedford Square, W.C.1.

* * * *

PRESERVING THE COAST

In their love of country the English are occasionally responsible for some crazy paradoxes. Thus, for centuries much has been sung, written and otherwise declaimed in praise of the English coast and sea, from the patriotic lyricism of poets down to the bombast of politicians. Yet, according to a qualified authority, only a fraction of the coastline of these islands is owned by the National Trust and preserved for the nation in its natural beauty, and the very part of the country which ought to be a national heritage and pride is in fact at the mercy of the speculating jerry-builder. Already parts of the Sussex coast and the unique coast-line of Romney Marsh from Hythe to Winchelsea have long been ruined by atrocious vandalism. Parts of the Essex coast are a disgrace to a civilisation whose language contains the words 'preservation' and 'beauty.' Neither the Essex nor the marsh coast is remarkable for cliff scenery and magnificence of views, and it is the cliff coast and its preservation which has been interesting Dr Vaughan Cornish, whose excellent paper *The Cliff Scenery of England and the Preservation of its Amenities* has just been issued in pamphlet form. On the assumption that out of a total coastline of 1,800 miles about 500 miles is cliff of not less than 100 feet, Dr Cornish estimates that the total cost of preserving the English cliff coastline for the nation, on a basis of £100 an acre, would be only £2,000,000, a moderate enough sum, and even more moderate in comparison with the proposed L.C.C.

expenditure of £35,000,000 on slum clearance. And what, one may well ask, has the preservation of cliff scenery to do with slum clearance? To which Dr Cornish replies: 'The project for slum clearance and that for national parks ought to be envisaged together as complementary parts of one great movement for saving England from what is mildly termed undue urbanization, a condition that is to say in which the towns are not fit to live in and the countryside not fit to look at.' I do not need, I think, to comment on this spirited passage, except to repeat that the English are, sometimes, masters of the art of destroying what they most profess to love.

* * * *

THE VIRTUES OF WALNUT

There is a shortage of walnut; and since the wood is excellent for gun-stocks, Mussolini, apparently, is responsible. It is hardly likely that the Duce will see these notes, but it is interesting, nevertheless, to reflect that the tree has some other and not inappropriate virtues. According to Culpepper: 'if they (the leaves) be taken with onions, salt and honey, they help the biting of a mad dog, or infectious poison of any beast.' And according to a nineteenth-century herbalist: 'The green rind in decoction is administered with great advantage to patients who labour under imbecility.' But neither these virtues nor Mussolini himself have any place in the sober little pamphlet of half-a-dozen pages just issued by East Malling. This is an account of the result of walnut research there, and it reveals the depressing fact that out of a large collection of nuts from widely different English sources less than 1 per cent were of a satisfactory standard of quality. This is largely due to the prevalent planting of seedling rather than named varieties, and all varieties in this country are apparently hopelessly mixed. But no doubt Italian trees, having a nobler destiny, are better disciplined.

17 January

NATURE'S TRIUMPH
J. S. COLLIS

It always holds my attention – a certain spot on the Maidstone Road. The floor of this earthly site is not made of soil. Bolts, screws, nails, nuts, broken bits from tools meet the eye; look closer and still no earth can be seen – only tiny screws and nails, washers, miniature nuts, pieces of metal, ends of wire, all crushed together into a smooth dark surface. Such is the ground. Part of the area is filled by a public house in the middle, backed by every sort of shed. Two bungalows crouch down on each side, as if born diseased and blighted. The space between each bungalow and the pub, is heaped high with the wreckage of machinery – for the inhabitants are car-breakers. The nose of a Morris Cowley wipes the dust; the chassis of another sits open to the sky; inextricable tangles of wire and de-gutted machinery defeat the endeavour of two sides and four wheels to suggest a living car; the back of a saloon sits wheelless on the ground; old tyres lie about; half a hood shields a back-axle; three or four outwardly whole cars, now for ever stationary, wedged in dying embrace, and clothed snow-deep in rust, provide one bungalow's barrier against the East wind and rain.

The human settlers here are a queer lot. These men of machines are as creative as the men of horses from whom they are descended, and as happy. They spend their days overcoming the machines. Their faces are not weather-worn or tanned or elementary sage; their hands are not dirty with the dust of the earth, they are thickly grimed with every sort of oily blackness; their eyes never look upwards into the sky, nor across any field. The derelict scene around moves them like the sight of flowers, it is their garden and their warming sun. But this spot is Nature's triumph. Hers actually is the glory and the final force. These men never stay there. They remain for six months, then pass on. Then for another six months the place is empty. It is worth visiting during these empty periods.

I went there again the other day to see one of the mechanics. He had left – some months ago, I gathered. I walked round the premises. The inhabitants of both the bungalows had gone. All was silently desolate. I had been inside one of the dwellings – a scene more chaotic and dirty than outside, more extraordinary indeed in the dilapidation of the furniture and annihilation of comfort, than anything in a dream. On this occasion I stood outside the other one. It held my attention. The half-broken windows were filled-in with rags, the top of the door patched like a pair of trousers – the whole, you might say, painted with dirt and smudged with youthful decay. Two pails full of rubbish stood immediately outside the door; there was a tea-pot on the ground beside a ruined kettle; a few yards out, all by itself, a water-cock rose from the earth like an erect snake. Old tyres, piles of machinery entanglement, bonnets of cars, pieces of rubber, wrecked hoods, lay about.

They commanded attention. But what held me more was the triumph of nature and time over all this. Everything here was *temporary* save mother earth and father time. Marvellous to see how the hard unbending iron was melting into powder under the motion of the air! Before my eyes the strong machinery was sinking down into the earth from which it came. Overthrown were the hulking vessels by the movement of a root, by the pressure of a leaf. Steadily and without pause the slender green shoots were quietly covering the unresistant metal. It would not be long before the same strange power of gentleness removed the bungalows from mortal sight. So, in this graveyard of mechanism, I attended at the resurrection of everlasting life.

3 April

THE INTELLIGENCE OF CATS
MICHAEL JOSEPH

In most arguments about animal intelligence cat-lovers are an eloquent minority. A comparison between cats and dogs is inevitably made, nearly always to the cat's disadvantage. The dog has all the virtues which gratify his master's sense of proprietorship. He is useful, loyal, good-tempered, demonstrative and always ready to adapt himself to his owner's mood. The cat is independent, fastidious, disobedient, and master of his own destiny. It is because the cat is relatively unpopular that his intelligence is in danger of under-estimation. Unpopular animals are rarely credited with their good qualities.

Sentiment and tradition are largely responsible for popular fallacies about animals. The lion is universally hailed as the king of beasts, whereas he is in fact inferior in courage, strength and skill to other animals. But he looks the part. The intelligence of the horse is overrated, because he is a handsome and willing creature. The dog is by tradition the friend of man, and I will not deny that he deserves his popularity, although I suspect he is often credited with more intelligence than he really has. The squirrel is a pretty little thing, but does far more damge than the rat and is infinitely more cruel and destructive to bird life

293

than the cat. Yet the cat is more unpopular. The very qualities which excite the admiration of his friends cause him to be disliked by others. Few people will take the trouble to insinuate themselves into friendship with a cat. Why should they? If all they want is an affectionate, uncritical, obedient companion, there is always a dog to be had. It is only the true cat-lover who can understand the subtlety of the cat's character.

The intelligence of animals is a favourite subject with the present-day biologist. Scientists claim that they can assess the intelligence of any living creature by applying a series of laboratory tests. An American authority on animal psychology recently rated animal intelligence in this order: chimpanzee, orang-outang, elephant, gorilla, dog, beaver, horse, sea-lion, bear – with the cat tenth on the list.

It is easy to dispute an individual assessment of intelligence. Consider the notorious fallibility of examinations. Every schoolmaster knows that the student who excels in the examination room is not necessarily superior to others who are mentally or temperamentally unable to do themselves justice in written papers. I wonder whether the scientists are on the right track. Can the cat be classified by scientific experiments? Remember that cats are peculiarly sensitive and temperamental creatures. You can learn nothing about them unless you first establish friendly relations, and that takes time, sympathy and patience. They are easily frightened and cannot be intimidated. Everyone who has studied them closely knows how cats will isolate themselves if there is any attempt at arbitrary procedure. For this reason it is rarely possible to teach a cat even the elementary repetitive tricks which monkeys, dogs, and some other animals learn with ease and sometimes with relish. To my mind, this merely proves that the cat is unwilling to obey. The assumption that he does not *understand* what is required of him seems to me quite untenable.

The nature of the scientific tests from which the cat emerges so discreditably in the eyes of the professors is worth examination. A favourite method is the maze. A cat (or other animal) is put in the maze and left to find his way out. Usually a reward of food is placed at the exit. The maze can be fairly simple, with only one blind alley, or more intricate with many turnings. Another instrument is the puzzle-box. This is a kind of cage from which the imprisoned animal can only escape by manipulating latches and similar contrivances. The victim's intelligence is

294

measured by the speed with which it overcomes mechanical obstacles and the faculty it shows for recognising and memorising
such artificial devices as a white card placed over the correct exit
from a maze.

To test an animal's 'intelligence' by such methods as these is
absurd. A maze is chiefly a test of sense of direction. Fish can
manage mazes with four or five turnings; monkeys and even rats
can negotiate a labyrinth. Cats and dogs, however, make wild
and 'unscientific' attempts to extricate themselves. Such experiments are presumably based on the assumption that the captive
wishes to escape or eat as quickly as possible. The food placed
at the exit may be a magnet for some animals, but to try to
induce a cat to perform any sort of evolution for the sake of food
betrays a complete misunderstanding of feline nature. Fear has
a stronger influence over cats than hunger; and every cat-lover
knows that a frightened or even an offended cat cannot be
tempted by food. The fallacy underlying these 'scientific' experiments is quite plain, except to the scientists. Their idea appears
to be to test animals by human standards. Up to a point such a
test probably is illuminating, provided it is only applied to animals like the chimpanzee, who are physically capable of imitat-
ing human actions and to whom such imitations are plainly congenial. Nothing could be more uncongenial to a cat, on the other
hand, than imitations of human beings.

I like to imagine a new Gulliver in Cat-Land, put through his
paces by inquisitive cats. What an unhappy and unsuccessful
time this Gulliver would have! In Cat-Land he would cut a sorry
figure. He would be made to jump 'blind,' to judge distance to
the fraction of an inch, to climb, to move adroitly, to fend for
himself in primitive surroundings, to catch fish with his hands.
to defend himself against the aggression of menacing creatures
much heavier and stronger than himself. By cat-standards poor
Gulliver would fail as miserably as the cat in the hands of the
human investigators.

It is impossible to understand cats on the strength of superficial acquaintance. They are shy, unobtrusive creatures who prefer solitude to uncongenial company. Unlike dogs, they are not
anxious to make a good impression. In the cat's personality there
is aloofness, pride and a profound dignity. Even the most ordinary cat has a touch of the aristocrat. The cat does not ask to
be understood. The blandishments of other more sociable animals are not in his line. If human beings are so foolish as to

295

regard him as the social inferior of the dog, as a convenient mousetrap and nothing else, the cat's philosophy is proof against such injustice. He goes his own way, blandly indifferent to human folly. It is not his business to correct it. Above all, the cat is independent. If he chooses he will follow you around, play with you, demonstrate his affection; but try to exact obedience from a cat and you will immediately find it is not forthcoming. Even Siamese cats, who are more responsive than other breeds, will refuse to do what they are told. If I say to my dog, 'Come here,' he comes. I have not the slightest doubt that my cat understands me, but, unless he feels like it, I can summon him in vain.

This reluctance to obey – call it perversity if you will – is responsible for the common lack of appreciation of the cat. His disregard of us and our wishes is disagreeably unflattering. The trouble is that we human beings are so vain that we look upon the habits of any domestic animal (of course, the cat is not truly domesticated) as being specially developed for our benefit. The dog or monkey who will learn mechancial tricks for the reward of a pat on the head or a piece of sugar is acclaimed for his skill. And this ability to understand *and obey* is applauded as a sign of intelligence.

The cat, on the other hand, applies his skill and intelligence to his own purposes. There is truth in Bernard Shaw's remark that footballers' brains are in their feet. The cat reveals his braininess by incredibly skilful feats of jumping and balancing, but it is useless commanding him to perform. The rarity of performing cats is significant. Anyone who has an intimate experience of cats will agree that the cat is temperamentally incapable of obedience.

Because I think that intelligence is something more than the ability to understand and to obey, I offer this definition of animal intelligence: *an animal's ability to reason and act for itself, in any situation which may arise in its experience, without human interference.* Judged by this standard, the cat passes with distinction. If there is an opportunist in the animal world, it is the cat. He is independent and resourceful; and innumerable stories have been told, by such expert observers as the late W.H. Hudson, which confirm the view that the cat is a highly intelligent animal. There can be no doubt that animals exhibit activities which are obviously not mechancial, and that the cat is one of the animals which can learn and profit by experience. The extent of the cat's intelligence can only be gauged, in my opinion, by close observation allied to a peculiar sympathy with the cat's character. That is where the scientists go wrong. A detached and objective attitude towards cats is likely to yield very misleading results; and although allowance must be made for the excessive enthusiasm of the cat-lover, I am convinced that the cat can only be understood and appreciated by his friends.

10 April

THE DISASTROUS RAT
S. L. BENSUSAN

It is matter for surprise that while experts estimate the damage done by the brown rat in England and Wales at £1 per head per annum of the population, references to rat infestation, whether made in the House of Commons or at Rural District Council meetings, arouse little more than laughter. This is very disquieting, because as scientific investigation proceeds to study the causes of certain epidemics, it tends steadily to refer more and more of them to the rat.

Of late the Weil's disease popularly known as infective jaundice has been traced to rats; this trouble accounted for the closing down of a coal-mine in Scotland a few years ago, because the miners in considerable numbers were contracting the complaint. Twenty years ago the Corporation of the City of London made a grant to Professor Foulerton to investigate in the Valley of the Wye the evidence connecting Weil's disease with rats. For some time past the infection due to the *spirochaete ichterogenes* has been known in Germany, and considerable research work has been carried out on it in Japan. The virus reaches rats through abrasions in the skin and is readily contracted by human beings. Bathing-pools to which rats can gain access are a source of grave danger. Only a few years have passed since some of the frequenters of a well-known pool in Holland developed infective jaundice; it was found that the area around the water was infested by rats; they were destroyed and the infection ceased.

Last year in London a sewerman contracted Weil's disease in the course of his work, and the attack proving fatal, the widow received an award under the Workmen's Compensation Act. Cases of infective jaundice have been reported as near to London as Hertfordshire and as far away as Shropshire. At Newcastle last month a colliery shifter claimed and received compensation following alleged infection from rats; it was proved that the seam in which he worked was wet and rat-infested, and that one of his mates had died from infective jaundice. During the investigation it was shown that ten other cases had occurred between 1933 and 1934; some had been treated at the Infirmary in Newcastle. Experiments by a pathologist at the Sunderland Infirmary showed that virus from a rat killed a guinea-pig in eleven days, and blood tests from ten men working in the coal-mine showed positive results in nine cases. The disease apparently is carried by a parasite which lodges in the kidney of rats, but human beings can also be carriers. The bacteriologist at the Wellcome Bureau of Scientific Research in London, Major H. C. Brown, who is regarded as an expert on Weil's disease, says that about one-third of the rats in the British Isles harbour the parasite, and that anybody bathing in rat-infested waters is liable to get infection through the mouth.

In connexion with this charge against the brown rat it is worth remarking that further and other serious charges have been established. Rats act as primary host of the tapeworm, which is often conveyed to the pig, and from the pig to the human, causing trichinosis. They spread equine influenza, mange, ringworm and distemper; they are beginning to be recognised as carriers of tuberculosis from farm to farm. When the late Sir Arthur Shipley, Master of Christ's College, Cambridge, declared in his book *Some Minor Horrors* that the rat was a carrier of foot-and-mouth disease, his statement was regarded as unfounded; indeed several men of science who discussed the question with the writer dismissed it as not worth consideration. Since then the belief has been fully justified. Experiments in Denmark, apart from those conducted in this country, have shown that rats disperse the virus of 'foot-and-mouth' and that before a farm on which an outbreak has occurred is disinfected, it is absolutely necessary to exterminate the rats. So much for *rattus norvegicus*, but his work as a disseminator of disease and contaminator of food does not tell the full tale of the nation's trouble. In the past thirty years, since concrete has been so freely used in building, the brown rat has been greatly discouraged in the City of London and the black (alexandrine) rat has taken his place. Experts say that while there were no alexandrine rats in England thirty years ago, today the population of black to brown in the City of London is as ten to one. The black or alexandrine rat (*rattus alexandrinus*) is a far more pleasant animal than his brown cousin. He is cleaner, friendly, lives in the house-tops instead of the cellars, but unhappily keeps bad company, acting as host of the plague flea – *xenopsylla cheopsis* – and was certainly responsible for the great plague of London in 1665 and 1666, and possibly for the Black Death which devastated Europe some centuries earlier.

Bubonic plague has certain centres in which it is endemic and from which it spreads periodically. The East and Western Himalayas, the Altai Mountains, the country round Lake Tana in Abyssinia and certain parts of the highlands of Brazil are centres; from them the disease always tends to move westward. It is checked by a system of sanitary cordons, but today bubonic plague is latent in Persia, Asia Minor, parts of European Russia and South Eastern Europe. The Metropolis has long been saved from trouble by the extraordinary vigilance of the Port of London Authority, but it may be remarked that black rats carrying plague fleas did break the cordon at another port – Liverpool – not long ago. There two rats infected with bubonic plague were found – one in a grain warehouse. The facts were stated in *The Times* of January 21st. If they could penetrate London, the fleas would find an infinite number of black rats waiting to receive them.

We have in this country a Rats and Mice (Destruction) Act which is nearly a dead letter. Local Authorities will not be troubled to administer it. Some County Councils suggest that they cannot afford the services of whole-time Rat Officers. It follows that the rat, whose rate of increase is astonishing, is costing this country an incredible sum of money every year, and meanwhile exposing citizens to the risk of deadly diseases.

17 April

THE INTELLIGENCE OF CATS
(To the Editor of *The Spectator*)

Sir, – I heartily agree with Mr Joseph's defence of the cat's intelligence. I am a victim to the cat, but though fascinated I am not blinded. She is a bad lot, but of her intelligence there can be no question.

I have long heard a theory that the proverb as to her nine lives is misunderstood, and that her 'nine lives' are her nine ways of getting a living. Maybe she has more, but nine are easily tabulated. She can (1) lie in wait, (2) stalk, (3) pounce, (4) sprint,

(5) climb, (6) fish, (7) fight, (8) cajole, (9) steal. The dog can but run in a straight line, with loud outcry, until he, or his prey, can run no more.

If intelligence be to know your own interest and follow it exclusively, by force, fraud, or flattery, using the strong hand or the velvet glove, killing without mercy, thieving without shame, and accepting favours so prettily that you seem to confer a favour, why then it seems to me that the poor silly dog has but his virtue to keep him warm.

It is on the dog's virtues that his friends must concentrate. He has the elements of Religion in him, as Anatole France has pointed out. He knows reverence and he knows shame – the cat knows neither. The dog is not clever. No. But he is good. The cat is not good. But she does belong to the intelligentsia. – I am, Sir, yours obediently,
Wilfrid S. Jackson
Cliffe Hill, Lewes

24 April

'... BEHOLD THE HEBRIDES'
JAN STRUTHER

That the Scots run England is a time-hallowed music-hall joke, and, like most music-hall jokes, largely true. Nobody, at any rate, attempts to deny it. The Scots do not deny it because they have far too great a respect for tradition. And the English do not deny it because they find it such a convenient belief; for if anything goes wrong with the running of England they can always blame it on the Scots.

It is not surprising, really. The Scots as a race combine an almost terrifying talent for organisation with a marked distaste for being organised: the English, on the other hand, have no great passion for organising themselves but are too good-humoured and too orderly-minded to object to somebody else doing it for them. The arrangement works admirably.

But what is surprising, at first sight, is that the natives of such a beautiful country as Scotland can so readily exile themselves from it. All over the world lusty Scottish voices (for our musical tastes incline more towards the sing-song than the concert-hall can be heard uplifted in praise of their homeland's natural beauties, from the Banks of Loch Lomond to the Braes of Bonnie

Doon, from the Birks of Aberfeldy to the Bush aboon Traquair. But the owners of the voices do not seem to go back there, even when they can; or at any rate they go only for a brief holiday – a Hogmanay reunion, perhaps, or a family funeral. Their feet are no sooner set upon their native heath than they are itching restlessly once more for the pavements of London or the engine-room floors of remote tramp-steamers. 'My heart's in the highlands,' the exiled Scot declares: but the rest of his body (which is perhaps why he is sometimes accused of heartlessness) remains firmly ensconced in London, Montreal or Buenos Aires. 'Oh, gin I were where Gadie rins!' he trolls over a stiff sundowner with a perfectly genuine lump in the throat: but he takes mighty good care that the river which runs past his windows or his port-holes shall be the Thames, the Hudson, the Ganges, the Amazon or the Yangtse-Kiang.

The truth is that the Scots are born exiles, and Scotland the perfect country to be exiled from. Do not imagine that I am running down Scotland. Far from it. When I go back there myself I never want to come away again: but then, I am half English. No: what I mean is that Scotland's beauties, though undeniable, are obvious ones, easy to carry in the heart, easy even to describe to the benighted members of less fortunate races. Lakes, islands and mountains, heather and rowan, broad straths and narrow glens – these are jewels easily worn in the memory, easily captured in verse or prose even by the most inarticulate people in the world. It would require far more technique to be an exile from, say, the Essex marshes, where atmosphere counts for more than outline, where mutable clouds must do duty for mountains and where transient effects of light and shade are the incidents which capture the heart. These beauties are difficult to take about with one; all that sticks in the mind is the memory of many lovely moments, and the sense of something lost – a mood more than a picture. Nor can they be passed on to anybody who has never known them, either by words or by the dexterous whipping-out of snapshots.

The midlands, too, would present a difficult problem to exiles. Their comfortable, cultivated charm could so easily be made to sound merely smug and prosperous. Perhaps that is why they possess little or no nostalgic literature: or perhaps the real reason is that so few people are fools enough to leave them.

The southern counties, though scarcely more spectacular in appearance, have (partly owing to a greater density of population) been the home of more poets than the midlands, and they are therefore far better equipped with those memorable rhythmic tags which are both the fruit and the food of nostalgia. Sussex-by-the-sea, for instance, is now a most satisfactory place to be exiled from, so persistently have the poets of the Georgian school over-dramatised her homely beauties and woven facile jingles out of her place-names; while Devon, of course has stolen a march on the whole lot by means of a mere accident of rhyme. I do not deny that it is a very lovely county: but it is interesting to speculate how the poets and song-writers would behave if Devon and Norfolk, say, were to exchange names. I suspect that they would tumble over each other to catch the 3.40 from Liverpool Street, and that Mousehold Heath would soon become as famous as Dartmoor.

The exile from London – and perhaps this applies to any large city – has neither romantic nor literary status. Music-hall songs are his only living folk-music. He may long as passionately as the rest, but those who do not share his longing seem to think that there is something slightly comic and more than a little immoral about London nostalgia. Leicester Square, Piccadilly, the Old Kent Road: a bit of fun, or stewed eels – they all know that's what *he's* after. He yearns, and they read a wink into his gaze. He has no means of explaining to them the complex charm of what he is missing, for like a subtle and expensive scent it is compounded of many ingredients which, taken by themselves, would seem to repel. Fogs, slums, dirt, pneumatic drills – there is more than a touch of civet in the spiritual exhalation of London: but occasionally, to one who is banished from it, there comes an ache no less intolerable than that which assails the mountain-dweller in the plains. And what he longs for is not a sight or a sound or a touch or a scent but a bit of all four and something more besides – hot asphalt, shouting paper-boys, fluttering plane-leaves, the comfortable contact of unknown but friendly humanity; or street-lamps shining on wet pavements and a barrel organ playing in the rain; or something more indefinite still – a mere memory of a ghost of a mood that he once had while walking down a quiet side-street at dusk.

Beside these vague regrets, these shapeless rags and tags of homesickness, the sentimental equipment of the exile from Scotland seems as neat and manageable as a well-packed suitcase. There is a place for everything and everything in its place. In his mind's eye are the snowy crags and cool corries of the

Grampians, in his ears the skirl of the pipes or the lapping of loch-water against heathery headlands; whether he comes from Mamore or the Mearns, from Cape Wrath or the banks of Yarrow, his lips need never lack a poignant ballad, nor his throat a beautiful sad air, in which to convey, and thereby assuage, his melancholy. Nostalgia suits him: it suits the timbre of his voice, the stern set of his jaw, the far-away look in his blue, blue eyes. It is fortunate, and not to be wondered at, that the Scotsman so seldom goes home: for he is never so attractive as when, five hundred or five thousand miles away from them, he is agreeably engaged in beholding the Hebrides.

29 May

THE PRESS AND THE LAW OF LIBEL

The draft Bill for the amendment of the law of libel prepared by a committee of the Empire Press Union is a document of great importance. That libel laws are needed admits of no dispute. Men of repute – and every honest man has some kind of reputation to lose – must have legal protection against scurrilous attacks in irresponsible journals. But between restraining an offender and enabling the victim to derive financial benefit from a journal's often unwitting offence there is a fundamental difference. In an action for slander damages are (with certain limited exceptions) awarded only when it can be shown that actual financial damage has resulted. The Empire Press Union Bill proposes to assimilate the law of libel with the law of slander, and the case for the reform is overwhelming. Some recent decisions, involving what most people would regard as inordinate penalties, have made the libel question acute. There exists, notoriously, a certain class of lawyer perpetually on the alert for the opportunity of instigating proceedings for libel on the principle of 'no damages, no expense to the litigant.' Juries moreover have a habit in doubtful cases of acting on the assumption (usually quite erroneous) that after all papers can afford to pay. To offer the chance of damages as an incentive to litigation is open to the gravest objection.

12 June

A SPECTATOR'S NOTEBOOK
JANUS

The great railways of this country receive deserved eulogies for their handling of long-distance traffic, but very different language is called for when their treatment of the millions of suburban workers whom they carry to and from work is in question. One evening this week I was carried by the Southern Railway from Waterloo to Dorking – which is reputed to suffer from a worse train service than any other town of its size within a 25-mile radius of London. We left Waterloo with 17 in the compartment. At Clapham Junction we were increased by two. At Wimbledon we effected some exchanges and got away with 18. At Raynes Park still 18. Motspur Park 18 still. Stonebridge Park presumably has attractions (certainly not visible from the line), and there we actually got down to below 10. This was an ordinary train on an ordinary evening, and I was paying 1½d a mile. The railways may contend that this is what rush-hour means, but they know when rush-hour is coming, and if the directors can't cope with it the railways had better be nationalised and run on Post Office lines.

12 June

SPEECH-DAY APHORISMS
[GORONWY REES]

Once more the term is nearly over and schools like empires are breaking up. Schoolboys and schoolgirls are subjected to a last and stupefying dose of advice. Before they are set free they must hear once again the wisdom distilled from the experience of their elders: no doubt the orators at speech day hope that their victims will ponder their advice in the idle hours of the holidays. But even if the pupils have not been asleep and if they remember what has been said, they will not always have learned much that will help them in later life. They will have heard, once again, that the School is the World in small, a microcosm – and nothing could be less true; that games are the foundation of character, if played not to win but for the sake of the team. The boys who have won no prizes are told that prizes are of no importance. Those who have not worked hard are told they will be all the healthier for it and find idleness in school an added incentive to work hard later on. Those who have worked hard with no success are told that one's job is to work hard without thinking of success; those who have worked hard and successfully, that it only shows where hard work will get you. But for those who have succeeded without doing any work at all there is no future. They have shirked at games and at work; they have seduced boys into the pleasures of idleness; they have set a bad example; and even though they smile at the reproofs now administered from the platform they will find that mere brains without character will bring them to a bad end.

These are the platitudes of speech-day oratory, and they are even less true than most platitudes. Generals, admirals, civil servants, colonial governors descend upon the schools on speech-day to offer advice which they would never think of accepting themselves; and boys and girls who desire to be released from school are led to believe that the world outside is even more unpleasant and less rational than school itself. To hear sense spoken on speech-days is as surprising as hearing it at a Nazi meeting at Nuremberg; in the last orgy of speech-day oratory last week-end Mr Ormsby-Gore was one of the few who distinguished himself by speaking at Shrewsbury of the world as schoolboys may really find it today. He did not pretend that mere character is sufficient for all evils, that honesty and good nature will carry one as safely through the world as it does through school, or that the world today has the stability of school life. 'There are threats of gigantic changes and new forces of a formidable character. You will see in this country inevitable struggles between clashing sets of ideas.' That is an accurate description of the world as the young can expect to find it; to speak otherwise is to mislead them. There are many possible attitudes to adopt towards such struggles, and Mr Ormsby-Gore did not presume to indicate the right one. But he did suggest, most justly, that one of education's chief functions is to equip men and women to maintain successfully whatever attitude they do choose. And far from assuming that the whole duty of boys and girls at school is to learn how to serve preconceived and perhaps discredited ideals, he said that he hoped they would in the wider world live dangerously and take risks. Depressing though the world's condition is, it is something at least, for the young, that it offers immense possibilities for intellectual, physical and even moral adventure, and it is for such possibilities

305

that they must be equipped if education is to be of any use.

But unfortunately there are few speech-day orators who are even aware of such possibilities. They are for the most part concerned to impress on their audience the necessity of preserving what their elders have created; and it does not occur to them that the young may wish not to preserve but disown the achievements of their parents. Yet even they cannot quite ignore the world as it is. 'There is a demand from many quarters that we should bring our education into line with modern life.' The demand is natural but not, apparently, to be conceded. It is the modern world that must learn from the school and not the school from the world. 'What is lacking in the modern world is not information but reason, not knowledge but wisdom, not policy but principle, not efficiency but morality,' and the school is prepared to supply the deficiency. There are other masters who take what is perhaps a more advanced view of the functions. 'The handicraft side,' said the Headmaster of Wellington, 'is being developed in sympathy with modern tendencies – tendencies which would make the future weapon of the officer the spanner rather than the sword.' Beating swords into spanners is indeed an advanced handicraft; and the training of officers is the proper concern of Wellington. But it is disconcerting to find that elsewhere also our educationists are showing a profound concern with military developments. 'To parents I would say,' said Lord Lloyd at Malvern, 'encourage your son to play his part in national defence if you do not want conscription to be upon us very soon.' We must all join up quickly to avoid being conscripted.

Such logic is no good example for schoolboys, and it may be doubted whether the needs of national defence are really the most urgent concern of education. It may be doubted also whether the speech-day orators of today have the right to speak with complacency of the duties and responsibilities of the young. They have not done so good a job that a little humility before the young would be out of place. 'We older men,' said Admiral Sir William Goodenough at Giggleswick, 'rely on you to take our places and see that you don't fail us.' It would, perhaps, be of greater value if the 'older men' would admit that they had failed themselves and tried to explain the reasons for their failure, so that the young might learn to avoid them. To speak of duty, of character, of service is of little use when no one knows of what kind they must be: until we know, it would be wiser to speak, like Mr Ormsby-Gore, of the dangers and the struggles and the adventures the young will have to meet, and try to prepare them for a world of whose future no man can be certain.

26 June

A SPECTATOR'S NOTEBOOK
JANUS

The permission given by King Edward to the Yeomen of the Guard to shave their beards is interesting, as coming from the first clean-shaven king this country has known for nearly a hundred years. I have been investigating this grave matter, with the assistance offered by the National Portrait Gallery. Bearded monarchs in our recent history are rare. There were, of course, King Edward's father and grandfather, and his great-grand-father, the Prince Consort, wore a moustache and side-whiskers. But all the first four Georges and William IV were clean-shaven. So, I think, were their predecessors back to Charles I. King Edward, therefore, is strictly in the royal tradition.

3 July

COUNTRY LIFE
W. BEACH THOMAS

A Dog's Inference

Everyone who owns both knows the fondness of a dog for a motor-car. Its speed and the succession of smells give him Para-disiacal conditions. Dogs love a car but are subject on occasion to car sickness, and are often delighted when the journey is over. More than that, they know when the end is approaching, by sight and smell and, in the case of one puppy at any rate, by sound. The turn up to the dog's home is abrupt and steep. It is therefore necessary to put the car into its lowest gear when turning in. The law of the association of ideas always works strongly in the dog's mind; and this puppy (of eight months old) so associates the noise of the low gear with the arrival home that his master is quite afraid of using the gear on other occasions. The dog is so firmly convinced that he is at home that his excitement becomes uncontrollable.

3 July

MODERN GLADIATORS

J. S. COLLIS

Scene: Blackfriars Ring on a Thursday evening. For some time I had meant to look in and see what all-in wrestling was really like. I was prepared to watch something rather primitive; and, on going at last, I was not disappointed. I may add that I have seldom seen anything more revolting, more consciously sadistic, or more significant of the long night of barbarisation that lies before mankind.

Entering the 'theatre,' I found myself in a packed crowd, the members of which were watching the ring with over-normal excitement. Two strikingly powerful men were engaged in the extremities of combat. One of them was unaesthetically fat; the other was not fat – merely gigantic. As I came in I saw the fat man's opponent toss him head-over-heels into a corner and then jump on his stomach with both feet. However, the latter speedily rose and exchanged a similar courtesy. Followed a slashing blow in the face which again floored the first, who again rose, and this time knocked his opponent so violently against the ropes that the latter's foot got caught in them, and he hung upside down helplessly while the foot was seized upon and savagely twisted. But as the ankle did not belong to an ordinary man, and as the referee seized the twister by both ears and dragged him backwards, the other was able to break free, to regain his perpendicular, and to fetch the opposing tonnage of flesh such a blow that it crashed through the ropes out of the ring. The latter, on re-entering, evidently answered with a foul, for boos broke from the crowd, and the victim of the foul managed to twist the fat man's arm in such a way that he lay exposed on the ground while his opponent, as a gesture of contempt, plucked hair off his chest.

As an unknowledgeable spectator I found the rules of the game difficult to follow. It did not appear that there were many rules. All one could safely assume was that the man who was killed first, or had a limb broken or was otherwise laid out would be the loser. Yet I saw no limb broken nor actual death. That's the queer thing: no one was killed outright in the course of the evening. It is hard to understand; I have never been a hundred per cent footballer, but I used to play occasionally with internationals, and I'm quite sure from what I know of them that if a Cove-Smith or my brother, W. R. Collis, spent five seconds in the ring with one of these gladiators, each would return to his respective hospital, not as a doctor but as a patient.

For these men belong to a different species. After receiving a blow or a fall that would finish off a normal man, these wrestlers immediately rise to their feet and carry on with measurably increased violence. However, besides the somewhat obscure rules of the game, three things safeguard each fighter from the extremities of foul ferocity. First, there is the weight of public opinion: it is demoralising to have the crowd booing at you. Second, it is inadvisable to so outrage your opponent that a worse fate may be visited upon yourself. Third, the business of the referee is not to see that the rules are observed, since there are few rules, but to come to the rescue of a man who seems in most need of it. The presence of the referee is not suffered gladly by the wrestlers and he is frequently knocked down himself or thrown bodily over the ropes out of the ring. But if he is good he attends to his business ceaselessly, and when one man having floored his opponent is about to bite off an ear, break an ankle, or execute something less mild, the referee, seizing him by the hair, hurls him backwards.

The first match over (I forget which of them won), another pair appeared who performed similar prodigies of ferocity. Twice an arm was broken, twice it mended itself again. Three times one man was killed, three times he rose from the dead. Following these came two light-weights – one of them having an extraordinarily goodlooking body. They played clean from first to last. This was scarcely appreciated by the audience, who, feeling let down, shouted at them satirically, 'Mind the Old School Tie!' However, this unfortunate lapse was fully compensated by the performance of the fourth contest.

This last pair were the most interesting, and I was convinced that this sport was certainly the best method by which such men could satisfy their emotional and physical needs. Two giants strolled into the ring: one red-haired and very long, the other dark-haired and immensely well built and in fine trim. Before the fight began the latter – an out-and-out exhibitionist – took the stage, quarrelling and shouting at everyone. He playfully seized the referee and threw him across the ring; he went up to his opponent to shake hands but knocked him down instead; he raised his arm, Hitlerwise, addressing the audience, but what he said I don't know, for the uproar was terrific. At length the fight began. The two of them were locked in a deadly embrace, then suddenly the red-haired one threw the other over his shoulder and half out of the ring. The latter retaliated by taking his opponent by the nose, then clinched him in a corner, got him on the ground, and was about to execute something exceptional when the referee seized him by the hair and threw him backwards. In a second the pair were at it again, exchanging blows that would have felled a hippopotamus, tossing each other into the air like tennis balls, seizing each other's ankles and exerting every effort to remove the foot from the leg. But exhaustion was evidently foreign to the dark-haired man, for when the bell sounded for an interval he still had sufficient energy to knock down his second and to address the crowd with pronounced disapproval.

It was an interesting evening and these moderns held attention. But the memory which I carried away with me was less of them than of the referee. He approached the sublime. He was a slim, medium-sized man with black hair and a strikingly intelligent face. Becomingly dressed in a long-sleeved silk shirt and long trousers and grey rubber shoes on his extremely small feet, he stood in the centre of the fray, flashing with electricity. He also was an out-and-out exhibitionist, intensely enjoying himself. Not that he was to be envied his pleasure. It was difficult to see how he remained alive. His job, as I have said, was to divert mortal blows into other channels. In doing so he was dealing with wild animals and would be occasionally flung out of the ring into the crowd. But in a second he would emerge from there, like Proteus from the Deep, and be back again in time to prevent one of the fighters from biting off an ear or breaking a limb. Sometimes these offices were so little appreciated that he himself would engage the full attention of the most violent of the combatants. On one occasion the dark-haired man rushed at him like a rhinoceros; but the referee, ducking with a flash, dived through his legs and came out the other side unscathed: again he was rushed at, and again he took the plunge to safety. When the match was over and the dark-haired man had lost (what constituted victory, heaven knows) he again leapt towards the referee, but the latter, springing to a post, put his back to it and holding the ropes with his hands raised both his legs up horizontally and met the oncoming figure with such a smack that he bounced backwards across the ring and fell to the ground. That referee was a flash of lightning, a genius.

11 September

THE DOOM OF THE COSTER
JAMES CURTIS

The shocking proposal to close the Caledonian Market and erect blocks of flats in its place is being bitterly received in all the poorer quarters of London. It is just another example of a tendency which is growing too pronounced, and which may result in the final extinction of the typical Londoner – the stall merchant.

Modern conditions make it increasingly difficult for a man to earn a living; unskilled labour will soon find its only outlet in illegal transactions of some sort or another. It almost seems as if the various authorities that control London of today have decided to get together and make things as difficult as they can for those who, with no trade at their fingers' ends, have found a livelihood as street-traders and barrow-merchants.

The first blow fell, of course, when Rag Fair was closed down. Rag Fair, Notting Dale, had been, for the past eighty years at any rate, the outlet for all the waste-paper and rag-and-bone trade in London. Many fortunes have been founded in Notting Dale, and a humble barrow has been the basis of not a few flourishing businesses. Certain abuses had no doubt grown up, and the houses of the adjoining streets had fallen into a grotesque state of disrepair while their inhabitants had earned a lurid reputation as roughs and toughs. Bangor Street had won a name for ferocity only equalled by that of Nile Street, Hoxton, and so the L.C.C. and the Royal Borough of Kensington made, several years back, a concerted drive on the market. The occupants put up a fight for it, but authority won. The stalls have all gone and the goods are sold today from the doorsteps instead. Rag Fair is but a shadow of its former self, and the 'totting' trade has received a staggering blow. Business is increasingly passing into the hands of big firms; the small barrow merchant, calling from house to house, seems to be doomed.

All over London the same thing has been going on. Little street markets have been closed down, and sometimes, as at Fulham and Euston, enormous market-halls have been built in their place. The result is, of course, that trade is cut in half, for who would bother to go into one of these gloomy, echoing, cavernous vaults when the bright lights and breezy back-chat of the streets are open to them? In some places the markets have vanished and not even a covered hall has been built to replace them.

Bad though the halls are, they at least provide a *locale* where the trader is allowed to work in peace.

The street trader proper, the costermonger, has been finding that each year makes his lot a little harder than before. Regulations get more and more severe. An appreciable proportion of his exiguous profits have to go towards paying fines for 'obstruction,' and the police are becoming progressively stricter in their interpretation of the word. A technique has, therefore, been developed by which a man can serve from a barrow which his mate is still pushing. Stories are told of a man appearing three times in the same day – paying a fine, going out to earn some money to replace it, and being promptly re-arrested. Each appearance was due to the same alleged offence – obstruction – and the penalties were strictly in accordance with the laws of geometrical progression. The usual amount of the fine varies, and has been known to swallow up a month's profits.

The recent edict from the Ministry of Transport closes to the costermonger all the principal West End streets – naturally his most profitable selling-centre. Ostensibly this is merely a step towards the straightening-out of London's practically inextricable traffic tangle, but in many a humble home it is a ukase received with consternation, mingled with bitterness and suspicion. It would almost seem – as is the very prevalent belief – that the authorities, both National and Local, are anxious to drive street traders out of business altogether in favour of the larger stores in which their members are often directly or indirectly interested. However this may be, that is the effect their actions have.

For the banned selling balloons or toys in the gutter is the only alternative. That may sound feasible enough, but all the best pitches have long ago been annexed, and it is a hard experience to change from being a small, independent trader into something very similar to a beggar.

Most street-traders, in fact practically all, have been brought up in the street-trading tradition. Their fathers and elder brothers have either pushed barrows or sold from stalls. Everybody in their district has made his living that way from time immemorial. So a coster or a 'totter' has never bothered to learn a trade. Increasing supervision and interference have already made him regard the policeman as his enemy. He considers he is not getting a square deal and has a grudge against authority. He has an active brain and a traditionally nimble wit; it will be small wonder if wholesale recruiting into the army of crime does take place.

The Islington Borough Council, the L.C.C. and the whole body politic would have far more reason to be proud of themselves if, instead of closing down Caledonian Market, which amuses the bourgeois as much as it benefits humbler citizens, they pulled down the neighbouring gaol at Pentonville and built their flats on that site. Better housing and ample facilities for a poor, but enterprising, man to earn an honest living are signs of a healthy social system – which will make the reduction of London's prison accommodation perfectly practical.

2 October

Part Six: The Drama of the Throne

The Abdication and the Press
WILLIAM DEEDES

On 27 October 1936 at the Ipswich Assizes Mrs Wallis Simpson was granted a decree *nisi* by Mr Justice Hawke on grounds of adultery by her husband, Mr Ernest Simpson. The act of adultery had been committed with a woman at the Hotel de Paris, Bray, in the preceding July. The suit was undefended. Mr Norman Birkett, KC, was in court on behalf of Mrs Simpson.

The christian name of the lady at the Hotel de Paris, though this does not appear in history books, was Marigold. I never met her, but I heard enough about her from colleagues attending the case to form an impression. I have always visualised Marigold as a figure straight out of A. P. Herbert's satire on divorce in those days, *Holy Deadlock*. I see her, even now, sitting fully clothed and knitting in the room of the gentleman concerned while the lurking detectives took appropriate notes.

Be that as it may, and it may well be too charitable, the extraordinary feature of the case that day in Ipswich was not Marigold, nor even the flash of lightning it cast over events to come, but the way in which our newspapers reported it. *The Times* carried twelve lines, the *Morning Post* a 10-point paragraph, the *Daily Telegraph* ran to twenty-two lines but on an away news page, sandwiched between 'Colonel accused in private' and 'Boy with a mania for silk stockings'.

Three questions arise. Was not the restrained reporting of this divorce (the significance of which was fully understood at the time) symbolic of the way the national press handled the affair between King Edward VIII and Mrs Simpson – until the Bishop of Bradford spoke on 1 December? The answer to that must be yes. The second question, more difficult to answer, is – why? The third is this: might the Abdication have taken a different course had the press, from the outset, reported the affair openly – as they most certainly would do now? The answer to that, as I shall argue, is that the course of the crisis would have altered but the outcome would have been the same.

My first connection with the Abdication came in the summer of 1936. As a reporter on the *Morning Post* I was asked to procure samples of what the press overseas was saying about the

King and Mrs Simpson. Mr H. A. Gwynne, my editor, wanted to show them to the Prime Minister, Stanley Baldwin. There was, I think, nothing particularly exclusive about my mission. A number of people were at the Prime Minister's elbow with evidence of what the world was surmising and we were not.

Gwynne, who had been editor since 1911, was close to Baldwin (notwithstanding disagreements over our India policy). Which of them initiated the request for cuttings I was not told and have never known. The slips were not difficult to gather. I worked through Hachette, the international booksellers and distributors. Some periodicals – including, I seem to recall, *Time* magazine – had been cut or blacked before I could lay hands on them. (This was not, as some will readily surmise, the work of ministers, but a precaution taken by distributors against possible writs for defamation.)

I submitted the bundle. Word came back: the Prime Minister tells Gwynne that he must have more time. History confirms that this was his tone at the period.

I became so impressed by the extraordinary situation, in which all the world knew about the King's affair except ourselves, that I tried a hand of my own. In September, with the help of a colleague, I drafted some words for the *Morning Post* to publish. Gwynne politely acknowledged this but said that, on learning of the possibility of the *Morning Post'*s entering even a subdued opinion, the Prime Minister had pleaded again, and successfully, for more time. We killed the draft.

Within a month of this, my marginal connection with King Edward's affairs took a different turn. On 18 and 19 November the King paid a visit to South Wales. I did not cover the tour but I heard about it, partly from journalists who went, partly from an uncle, Sir Wyndham Deedes, in whose house I resided. He was working with Lionel Ellis at the National Council of Social Service. Ellis was one of the party with the King. It was brought home to me how much the King was under strain.

On 18 November the King visited Merthyr Tydfil and the derelict steel plant nearby at Dowlais which had put most of the local community out of work. What he actually said was this: 'These steel works brought the men here. Something must be done to see that they stay here – working.' The words which echoed like a thunderclap round the kingdom and over the heads of hapless ministers were: 'Something must be done!'

Absurdly, those words were later brought into the Abdication crisis. Ministers, resentful of this royal reproach (so it was said), determined that the King must go.

For me they had another consequence. 'Something must be done.' Very well then, let us make a contribution, however modest. The *Morning Post* resolved that every child of unemployed parents throughout the so-called Distressed Areas (South Wales, NW Cumberland and the North-east) should receive *on* Christmas Day *by* post and anonymously a gift worth 2s 6d (today £2.50). I was told to get on with it.

Poignantly, the King contrived to interest himself in this small endeavour. He sent through Alec Hardinge what must have been one of the last cheques of his reign. Though long-forgotten, the fund carried one of the King's last imprints. A year later, and again in 1938, Lord Camrose asked me to carry on the idea for the *Daily Telegraph* after he had acquired the *Morning Post*. Most of the royal family subscribed and Queen Mary came to the office to cheer us on. I felt I understood why.

But this is some way removed from answering that second difficult question: why was this affair kept so dark by the British press until Dr A. W. F. Blunt, Bishop of Bradford, delivered his by no means sensational reflections of Tuesday, 1 December. For those unfamiliar with them, the gist of his remarks related to the forthcoming Coronation. The sting of them lay in three sentences: '... improper for me to say anything except to commend him, and to ask you to commend him, to God's grace, which he will so abundantly need ... if he is to fulfil his duty faithfully. We hope that he is aware of his need. Some of us wish that he gave more positive signs of such awareness.' The *Daily Telegraph* gave the story half a column on a subsidiary news page. Other newspapers were more generous. The cat was out of the bag.

There were at least two events during the summer which might have had the same effect. The lesser event was on 27 May, when the Court Circular showed that among royal guests for a dinner party were Mr and Mrs Ernest Simpson. The second occurred in August, when the King took a holiday cruise in the Mediterranean in the yacht *Nahlin*. Pictures of the King (in shorts only) and of Mrs Simpson (in a bathing dress) circulated freely. They increased speculation, but press comment in Britain remained muted.

Dr Blunt's speech on 1 December was therefore the culmination of several episodes, any one of which might have brought matters to a head – and most certainly would have done so today.

Was there a conspiracy of silence among the press lords? The *prima facie* evidence suggests that there must have been. My own experience of those times persuades me that there was not. For one thing, the press leaders did not get on very well with each other. Lords Beaverbrook and Rothermere hunted together. Neither Lord Camrose of the *Daily Telegraph* nor H. A. Gwynne of the *Morning Post* was likely to enter into arrangements with them. Nor was Geoffrey Dawson of *The Times*.

Like Gwynne, Dawson saw the Prime Minister fairly regularly. But he did not consort with other editors. Indeed, *The Times* historians Oliver Woods and James Bishop make this point about Dawson: 'But in other respects he was out of touch. He appears to have been in ignorance of the activities at the time of the King and Lord Beaverbook, directed at muzzling the popular press.'* Now it is undeniable that the King was troubled by what the press might say and through his own limited channels – mainly Beaverbrook and Sir Walter Monckton, KC – sought to influence this but it was not a very formidable obstacle.

Woods and Bishop say that Dawson saw Gwynne on the morning of 16 November. Gwynne (they say), seeking guidance, wanted simultaneous publication by all the newspapers at government discretion. Dawson's diary adds: 'The main point to me was that the *Morning Post* was not going to do anything without a lead.' That does not altogether square with my impression, which was that Gwynne was taking his pace from Baldwin, not from his colleagues on other newspapers; but Dawson kept a diary and I did not.

The only consultation between senior figures in Fleet Street which I know of came on the day that Bishop Blunt spoke. Lord Camrose of the *Daily Telegraph*, Gwynne of the *Morning Post* and Dawson of *The Times* consulted and agreed that editorial comment on the speech should be deferred until the following day. They reckoned, rightly, that Beaverbrook and Rothermere would be taking the same course.

This really does not add up to a conspiracy to suppress news about the affair. We have to look deeper for an explanation of the long silence of that summer and autumn. A passage in *The Times* account is suggestive:

* Oliver Woods and James Bishop, *The Story of The Times*, Michael Joseph, 1983.

> The Crown in England touches atavistic, often subconscious, springs of human emotion. The leaders of opinion, when they saw the Crown threatened, spontaneously coalesced to contain the explosion and ensure that it did as little damage as possible.

Too grandiloquent? I am not so sure. The factor we have to enter, and the hardest one now to accept, is how much our society has changed between that year and this; how dramatically the style of our news media has changed. Our attitudes to authority have changed. Our view of majesty has changed. Our beliefs have changed. No call to moralise about it. But it is so.

Lord Hartwell has reminded me of a feature which appeared at about this time in an American newspaper. It carried five portraits: Mrs Simpson's two previous husbands, the King, the Archbishop of Canterbury and the Prime Minister. The caption ran: 'First mate, second mate, third mate, Primate, Checkmate'. Such a feature in any of our own newspapers in 1936 was unthinkable. It is not unthinkable in these enlightened times.

So, finally, had we been then what we have become, had we in newspapers been ready to do what we unhesitatingly would do now, might the outcome have been different? I think not.

For it was not, as some later historians would have us think, determined by the 'establishment' – a Prime Minister, an Archbishop, the Dominions, or even by readers of the *Morning Post*. At one critical point after the crisis had broken, Stanley Baldwin faced a difficult meeting of his own party in private. Members were divided. He made one of his appeals. He told them to forgo some of their weekend engagements, to get into the pubs and working men's clubs and to talk to people. They would meet again on Monday. When they met, the message was clear. So it came about. In any case, the King's mind was made up. Our progressive, impulsive, intrusive, intensive media of today would have changed the timing, not his decision.

On the Friday night on which it ended, I had a private engagement, a dance for my eldest sister's coming of age at a hotel in Folkestone. During the afternoon a trusted source called me to say that in all likelihood the King would be leaving the country that night in an aircraft from Lympne airport. Lympne was adjacent to Port Lympne, home of Sir Philip Sassoon, a long-standing friend of the King. It sounded possible.

I reached a compromise with my newspaper. Lympne was about ten miles from Folkestone. They would supply a car. During the evening, dressed in a white tie, I would keep an eye on the airport. I made three journeys there. On the third visit, for some mysterious reason, all the lights were ablaze. It was a mirage. The navy was looking after the King.

While the dance was on, we stood on the floor to hear the final broadcast. 'At long last, I can say a few words of my own ...' As dancing was resumed, I took the floor with a girl I liked and who had stood beside me during the broadcast. During our dance neither of us could think of a word to say to each other.

THE PRICE OF KINGSHIP
[WILSON HARRIS]

No question, as every experienced journalist knows, is more difficult for a responsible journal to decide than the point at which a loyal reticence becomes a conspiracy of silence. The question has for months past been under anxious consideration in every newspaper-office in this country in a particular connexion. During that period the newspapers of the United States and of some of the Dominions have been printing millions of words on a subject on which the British Press has maintained an unbroken silence. Now silence is possible no longer. A sentence in the address of the Bishop of Bradford to his Diocesan Conference on Tuesday is unmistakable in its implications. Speaking, in reference to the Coronation ceremony, of the King's need for God's grace, Dr Blunt, having manifestly weighed his words, expressed the hope that King Edward was aware of the need, and added 'some of us wish that he gave more positive signs of his awareness.'

To those who have lived through the reign of King George V that is surprising and disturbing language, and if the Bishop of Bradford had not specific grounds for his criticism of King George's son condemnation of his temerity would be universal. As things are the Bishop will be generally held to have rendered a public service. That it did not become him in particular to render it may no doubt be argued. There are higher dignitaries in the Church and State to which the task more properly belongs. But no one who has read the leading articles, admirable alike in their firmness and their discretion, which the Bishop's address has inspired in some of the great provincial papers – most notably the *Yorkshire Post* can long retain any doubts of the advantage of elevating discussion of the King's affairs, if discussion there must be, from the chatter of railway-carriages and drawing-rooms and clubs to the responsible columns of serious organs of opinion.

For whatever comment is so expressed will be reluctant, respectful and profoundly sympathetic. The King of Great Britain and the Dominions is the servant of his people. His life is not his own but theirs. It is ceaselessly spread before their gaze, and 'the fierce light that beats upon a throne' is pitiless. In his self-sacrificing devotion to public duty King Edward upholds the highest traditions of his father, and with no such support and stay as his father drew from an ideal marriage. Set on his lonely eminence the King has a double claim on the affection and loyalty of his people. That claim, it is fair to add, has been honoured to the full. Never did a ruler of these realms ascend the throne more richly dowered. He succeeded to the privileges and obligations of a father who had been the very mould and pattern of a constitutional king, and a king whose unexampled hold on the loyalty and devotion of his subjects sprang before all things from their admiration of a family life which the highest and the lowest of his people could with advantage take as model.

It is to that tradition that King Edward is called on to be scrupulously true. The life of an unmarried king must necessarily in a measure be a life of solitude. None would dream of grudging him the fullest measure of such friendships as lesser men and women find part of the indispensable substance of a rounded life. None would willingly intrude for a moment into such privacy as the exigencies of his high station leave him. But the King, after all, has obligations that his subjects have not. In transferring to him unabated the confidence and affection bestowed on his father the people of these realms counted, and had a right to count, on that fulfilment of a spiritual and unwritten contract in which King George never faltered nor was capable of faltering. *Noblesse oblige*. Even in kingship there must be sacrifice. Both as prince and monarch King Edward has shown himself conscious to the full of that – never more than in the last few weeks, when his visit to his storm-tossed fleet and his tireless investigation of conditions in South Wales have identified him as never before with every section of his people.

But something still further is asked of the King. Nothing more is charged against him than a friendship carried to the point of unwisdom with a lady who, till the decree granted in her favour six weeks ago is made absolute, is still a married woman. Nothing need be said of that in itself. If it could be regarded as the King's concern alone every paper that has preserved silence so far would preserve it thankfully still. But what would be a private matter for a private citizen may have grave reactions when it involves a king. The person and personality of the sovereign is a factor of inestimable importance in the British Commonwealth of Nations. He is the supreme link between the Dominions and this country. In India above all, knowledge of the ground for any breath of criticism of the King-Emperor would have disastrous consequences.

Demands almost terrible in their rigour are made on the sovereign of these Dominions. They are not made lightly. There is no stint of generous sympathy with a King called on to observe standards set remorselessly high, which any of his subjects can transgress with relative impunity. But he is not asked for an unrequited sacrifice. If he so sets his course, and orders his associations, as to retain the homage and loyalty which the people of Britain and her Dominions bestowed in their amplitude on his father, he has a reward such as no other living man, and few in any age, could enjoy.

There may be something on which he sets an even higher price than that. If so, his decision would be received on public grounds with deep regret. On private grounds it could command nothing but sympathy and respect. Times change. The creation of new precedents causes no consternation. Restraints on a sovereign's choice of consort become increasingly distasteful. But that the question can be regarded as one for himself alone, in which his Ministers and his people have no part, is more than can be conceded. That is the price of kingship. The personality of the Queen and the mother of the King's children and heirs is a matter of supreme public concern.

4 December

A SPECTATOR'S NOTEBOOK

The relief in a thousand newspaper offices in this country at the breaking of the silence that has been so scrupulously and so loyally observed for months regarding the King will be immense. The tradition that at all ordinary times and in all ordinary cases puts the Royal Family beyond the range of public criticism is wholly sound (though a survey of some of the papers of a hundred years ago casts a startling light on the practice prevalent then) but a journalist's conviction that all news that is news should find a place in a responsible paper's columns is sound as well, and when every paper in the United States was printing columns daily about the King's friendship for Mrs Ernest Simpson, and the subject was a staple theme of conversation everywhere in London – though by no means to the same extent in the provinces – there was something professionally galling in the reticence that has been uniformly observed, without a shred of authority to enforce it, month after month by every paper in this country, from *The Times* to the *Daily Worker*. But their reticence has been infinitely to their credit.

4 December

THE COUNTRY AND THE KING
[WILSON HARRIS]

As the constitutional crisis moves towards a climax that may well come in the brief interval between the printing of these words and their publication there must be claimed for them such indulgence as may be considered due to an article written in circumstances so difficult. And in circumstances, it may be added, so melancholy, for however this unhappy affair may end it cannot end well. King Edward can only retain his throne with impaired prestige or bequeath to his brother a sovereignty brought for the first time in a hundred years under serious criticism. The harm was done when the King first allowed himself to set his affections on a married woman, and refused to recognise the inevitable outcome of failure to end an impossible relationship while it could be ended with a tithe of the pain that renunciation must cost today. No one has the right, and very few the inclination, to adopt the attitude of censor in this matter. The country has shown itself patient and generous and astonishingly united – and there was never greater need for the preservation of that unity than today. Kingship, as an institution, means much in this land. It has justified itself abundantly, and left small temptation to anyone to call himself republican. Deep as was the reverence and affection King George inspired, the loyalty he commanded was transferred unimpaired to his eldest son, and it will not weaken under the strain of another transfer, if another there must be, even in conditions so abnormal.

But it is not so much our loyalty that is under test as our self-discipline. The King's Government must be carried on whatever King is on the throne. These are days of anxiety and peril, and the most deplorable feature of the situation so suddenly created is that such a moment should have been chosen to lay an unprecedented burden on Ministers who were bearing responsibilities that almost over-taxed their capacity already. Thanks largely to the wisdom and self-sacrifice of the Prime Minister, who possesses ideal qualities for coping with such an emergency as this, they have proved equal to every demand made on them.

There has been no hint of Cabinet divisions. There has been no suggestion in the House of an attempt in any quarter to make party capital – personal capital may be another matter – out of a situation which every Member unfeignedly deplores but every Member is resolved to keep in its proper perspective and proportion in relation to the problems of the world and of the nation. As little has there been hint or sign of division or doubt among the Dominions. In the literal sense of the classic phrase, their unanimity is wonderful. Insidious suggestions have been made that the Government may not have put the issue to the Dominions fairly. Dominion statesmen and the Dominion public are not illiterate. They can read their newspapers. They do not depend on coded cables from Whitehall for material for their decision in such a case as this. The issue is clear and their judgement has been unhesitating and sure.

That judgement, neither in the case of the people of this country nor of the peoples of the great Dominions, takes the form of self-righteous condemnation. It was said here last week that any comments on the course the King has taken would be reluctant, respectful and profoundly sympathetic. That has been proved amply true. The King was wrong. He allowed an impossible situation to grow up and he proposed an impossible way of escape from his difficulties. To believe that a lady whom he recognised as unfitted to be Queen of England could be accepted as fit wife for the King of England betrayed a strange and disturbing misunderstanding of the mind of the Cabinet, Parliament and the people. Whatever way of escape there may be, that road at least is barred. Of the only two roads left, renunciation of Mrs Simpson and renunciation of his throne, King Edward, it seems, has chosen the latter. It is his right, and it may well, in all the circumstances, be the path of wisdom. It is an untrodden path for an English King, but he will take it sustained in the future as in the past by the sympathy and affection of his people. They would gladly forget the cause of his departure; they will never forget the life of service he has spent among them and the devotion with which he has discharged unfalteringly every duty attaching to his office as Prince or King. If today the involuntary comment must be 'the pity of it,' the King will know that, wherever the lines may fall for him, he need never forfeit his hold on the hearts of his countrymen.

If tomorrow the country is called on to pledge its allegiance to a new King, taking up his vast responsibilities in circumstances

327

that give the burden a doubled weight, it will pledge it without reserve or stint. Even where there was division about King Edward, there will be none about the duty to sustain his successor to the utmost. Nor will there be any question of forced confidence. The Duke of York has, through a lifetime only eighteen months less, been as familiar a figure in this country, though not in the Dominions, as his elder brother. Each lacks some qualities the other possesses and possesses some that the other lacks. In the younger there are more unconcealed reserves. In many ways he is more his father's son than any of his brothers. King George was mourned and honoured at his death for capacities unsuspected when he ascended the throne twenty-five years earlier; so it may well be with his second son. That son, too, like his father, can depend at all times on the support and sympathy and counsel of a wife as capable of sharing his public as his private life. The transition is painful. All partings bring sorrow, and this far more than most. But good may well come out of evil, even out of evil not apparent but real. Democracy has in these last days borne itself well, with dignity, with patience, with resolve. All those qualities, and more, will be needed still. Behind a new King must be an undivided people, and the world must be shown that plainly. We must be about our business. The formalities of transfer will go through smoothly. The appointed date of the Coronation, it may be hoped, will remain. The ship of State will vary neither its speed nor its direction. If the King departs, long live the King.

11 December

KING GEORGE'S SECOND SON
[ROBERT BERNAYS]

Prince Albert Frederick Arthur George, Duke of York, on whom the eyes of all the Empire have been set in these last days, has in common with his father the fact that he is a second son and reached manhood without the prospect of his one day becoming king being ever anything but remote. Latterly, of course, it has hung on the possibility of his surviving a brother who is only eighteen months older than himself. Like King George V, therefore, he grew to manhood without the shadow of prospective sovereignty overhanging him, and made his own place according to his own bent, so far as the demands of public duty permitted, in that field of public service in which all King George's sons have so selflessly laboured. Like his father again, he was trained for the navy, at Osborne and Dartmouth, and served as a sub-lieutenant at the battle of Jutland. Later he took to the air, qualified as a pilot and became wing-commander. A period of study at Trinity College, Cambridge, completed what may be regarded as preparation for life, as distinct from the sterner business of life itself.

Of that life one feature is of special relevance at this moment. The greatest of all the services King George V rendered to his people was his unfailing maintenance of the traditions of family life as this country has known it at its best. Here again King George's second son, taking the bride of his choice (once more like his father) from one of the oldest of Scottish houses, built up in an unpretentious house in Piccadilly a home reminiscent in spirit of that in which his own boyhood was most fortunately spent. Outside his home he has developed two main interests, a study of the industrial life of this country, and the annual seaside camp, bearing his name, where boys from public schools and poor homes meet on equal terms.

The interest of members of the Royal Family in the details of industry is too much taken for granted. In fact it by no means always existed. The part played by the Prince Consort in organising the Great Exhibition of 1851 was something quite different. Actually records show that in the first four years of King George V's reign not more than twenty factories were visited in the course of formal industrial tours by members of the Royal Family. Now hardly a week passes without a visit to some factory or mine or dock by the King or one of his brothers. Public interest in the structure and management of industry has been aroused, and the life and labour of the working population lifted into a position of dignity and importance. It cannot be denied that this change of view and the growing interest shown are due largely to the influence of the Duke of York in associating himself with all those questions which relate to industrial relationship and the well-being of the industrial worker.

Some of those who had been occupied during the War at the Ministry of Munitions in dealing with matters affecting the health and welfare of the munition workers, were struck by the absence of recognition given to industry by members of the Royal House. King George, of course, had constantly visited munition-factories and shipyards during the War, but these visits were of necessity of a somewhat formal nature. When towards the end of the War a voluntary body, the Industrial Welfare Society, was formed for the purpose of carrying on the work then begun, Prince Albert was invited, and readily consented, to become its President and expressed a keen desire to study industry at first hand without any show or formality.

It was this deep personal interest in the ordinary man and woman that decided him shortly afterwards, when he went to Cambridge, to study economics, and in those early days he was often referred to as 'the Industrial Prince,' a title to which he could lay good claim. Since then he has never faltered in his application to the task to which he set his hand, and, having regard to the numerous works he has visited, of every kind and in every part of the country, it may be questioned whether there is any other man in any rank or office who has had so unusual an opportunity of investigating at first hand so many manufacturing processes and the conditions under which they are carried on. He has descended coal mines; clambered up scaffolding; driven locomotives as well as petrol runabouts – once it was a tramcar, through the crowded Gallowgate in Glasgow, to the consternation of those who were responsible for his safety; poured molten metal from crucibles; blasted, by pressing a button, several hundreds of thousands of tons of rock – all in a desire to learn at first hand how things are done and how the working man's days are spent.

He possesses an uncanny gift of sensing the staged effect, and it is no ordinary employer who can deceive him by exhibiting a false picture of his relationship with his workpeople or conditions prevailing in his factory. Often the Duke will disturb the tour as planned by expressing a wish to see the rest-rooms, the canteens, the first-aid rooms, or some shop not included in the official itinerary. Sometimes he will get absorbed in the details of the canteen service and settle down to discuss the menu and prices with the cook, or cross-examine the nurse in the ambulance-room about her cases, the risks and hazards to which the workers are exposed and methods of dealing with them. Once, when visiting a soap works, he learned that associated with the plant was a glue department, at best a somewhat noisome place. When he wanted to see it he was told that the process was disgusting and the smell unbearable. He retorted that if the place was good enough for the people who worked there, it was good enough for him to see, and into the glue-works he went.

Any vicissitudes expected or unexpected – once he got to a factory ten minutes too soon and was kept waiting on the pavement by an inexorable gate-man, who had been instructed to let no strangers in – he takes in complete good humour, and here again discloses personal traits not always appreciated by those who have only had opportunities of seeing him on more formal occasions. His lack of the more superficial, spectacular gifts merely serves to emphasise the qualities, valuable and firm-based, that are part of his essential make-up. On any kind of occasion, and particularly at his now famous camp, whenever he forms one of a little group of persons gathered together to discuss some topic of interest, he casts off his seeming diffidence and shyness and reveals himself in a way that often creates surprise. As one of the camp boys with whom he had been chatting once observed, 'He is just like one of us.' If there is any fun or mild ragging on foot and he is within range, he can be counted on to take a part. None the less, if occasion arises, he can maintain his dignity to the discomfiture of anyone who attempts to take advantage of this free and easy attitude. A gesture or quiet retort, softened by a disarming smile, is usually enough to check the impatience of a speaker who misunderstands. Always he is ready to discuss affairs with all and sundry, though like most people he prefers a serious talk to a hurried interchange.

His tastes are simple, but when he has turned his attention to a hobby or recreation he is intent on mastering its technique, which largely accounts for the legends that have gained currency, much to his own amusement, about the wonderful workshop he maintains. His simple and delightful home life, already referred to, has played a great part in his development and constitutes his abiding background.

Overshadowed throughout his life by two or three outstanding personalities, he has had few opportunities of revealing his depth of character to any but those who have been brought into intimate and continuous contact with him, but given new responsibilities, and a greater freedom to go his way, there is no doubt that his quiet dignity and his deep sense of duty will enable him to face whatever may await him without faltering or failing, and steadily establish an enduring hold on the respect and regard of his people both at home and throughout the Empire.

11 December

NEWS OF THE WEEK

The climax of the drama of the Throne was reached after the last issue of *The Spectator* went to Press, but nothing of such comment as we based on the material then available needs to be modified or withdrawn. The swiftness and smoothness of the transition from King Edward to King George is still hard to appreciate to the full. On Friday morning King Edward was sovereign; by Monday the nation had settled down with complete calm and confidence to the beginning of what all pray will be the long and prosperous reign of a new King George, whose guiding principle, as he has already shown by several significant decisions, will be the traditions his father set. Acceptance of King George VI is universal, unhesitating and unqualified; papers and persons who aimed at another solution of the crisis have united with those who had concluded with reluctant conviction that this was the only way to keep the unity of the nation in the new reign unbroken. The crisis has taught us many things, and taught the world at the same time what a democracy in its best moments can be. Incidentally it has shown how limited the real influence of the popular Press in great matters is. Of the four large-circulation daily papers in London three pressed insistently for the morganatic marriage, but the instinctive soundness of judgement of the people was completely unaffected. It is just to add that it was fortified by a series of admirable leading articles in the *Daily Herald*, which from the first saw the issues clearly and gripped them firmly.

18 December

Epilogue

AS 1936 ENDS
[WILSON HARRIS]

In his review of the international situation before the House of Commons adjourned last Friday, Mr Eden felt justified in striking a note of cautious optimism. It amounted to little more than saying that the position of this country in the world was less unfavourable than it had been a year ago, but that is better at least than saying it was less favourable. When the Versailles settlement began to crumble 1935 was always looked on as the year of crisis. The world got through 1935 without a European war. It has got through 1936 without a war. Even the Spanish civil war has so far been confined to Spain, in spite of the perils springing from the active partisanship of Germany, Italy and Russia. Apart from Spain the world that enters 1937 is still a world at peace.

What is more, over large sections of the world the peace is stable and deep-rooted. It is going very little too far to say that war has been banished from the whole of the Westen Hemisphere. Even in Europe, where the embers of potential conflict smoulder unextinguished, the peaceful States are increasingly tenacious of peace and increasingly determined to deter aggressors in advance, even though it involves them in disastrous expenditure on armaments for which there ought to be no need and no excuse. From the Pyrenees through two-thirds of a circle right round through Scandinavia to the Turkish shores of the Mediterranean lies a ring of States – France, Britain, the Low Countries, the Scandinavian States, the Baltic republics, Soviet Russia, Turkey from none of which is any aggressive move to be looked for. None of them seeks territorial expansion. None of them desires anything but to develop its internal economy in peace.

Throughout by far the greater part of the Continent the main purpose is the consolidation of peace. The relations between this country and France have never been more cordial nor the understanding more complete. That, more than any other single factor, has been responsible for the successful localisation of the Spanish civil war. The understanding extends to Belgium and Holland, and makes the relations between the four Western States everything that the relations between States should be. In the East the same process is in operation. Russia has no external ambitions and is feared by no one, not even by Germany, which is actively developing trade relations with the Soviet Union in spite of the fulminations Herr Hitler and his Ministers find it necessary to deliver against the Bolshevism which Russia is steadily abandoning. A collision between Russia and Germany is made increasingly improbable by the close understanding developed between the buffer States of Poland and Rumania, now in cordial alliance, with plans for military co-operation fully concerted between them. Under Colonel Beck Poland's foreign policy has been equivocal – her geographical situation gives considerable excuse for that – but the Foreign Minister's declarations of last week evince a very proper determination to maintain the country's independence of both Germany and Russia, and lend no support to either country against the other. Poland is as much opposed to a war of ideologies as Britain.

In the south Italy is manifestly anxious to return to normal relations with this country. It was she who made them abnormal, and it is not to be pretended that there will be any condonation by British public opinion of Italy's breaches of treaty and her rape of Abyssinia. But correct diplomatic relations are possible, and to be desired. Antagonism in the Mediterranean will help neither country. Both have to use that highway, and it profits neither to deny it to the other. Here, again, the position is definitely better than a year ago, when open antagonism existed between Britain and Italy, and we could count only on reluctant and uncertain backing from the French. Since then the unlimited support of France has been pledged to this country in the case of any unprovoked aggression. There is, in fact, one quarter only in Europe from which the danger of war is apprehended. That, of course, is Germany, and no good purpose is served by disguising the fact. Germany today is a country organised for war. Every country is re-arming, but nowhere is rearmament and the potential mobilisation of the whole population made the predominant purpose as it is in Germany. Everything is being sacrificed to that. A military writer has disclosed that the whole Four Years plan is really designed to serve military ends. The people are told that guns are better than butter, and they are being deprived of a great deal besides butter in order that Germany may be made the greatest military Power in Europe. Why? Germany is threatened by no one. No State has ambitions to be satisfied at her expense. What ambitions does she aim at satisfying herself?

That is the unanswered question on which the preservation of the peace of Europe depends. It may be that it will be answered satisfactorily, for Germany's self-imposed isolation, the disquiet caused by her military intervention in Spain, the suspicions aroused by her agreement with Japan, the universal lack of enthusiasm for her anti-Bolshevik campaign, are producing visible uneasiness in Germany itself. But the *régime* is abnormal and periodical *coups d'état* seem essential to its existence. None is to be expected in the West, but the organised and completely unwarranted attacks on Czechoslovakia by the controlled German Press are a symptom not to be made light of. There is a considerable German-speaking (formerly Austrian, never German) population in Czechoslovakia, but it is by no means wholly Nazi and the Government is right to reject the claim of the majority, the Sudetendeutsch, to speak exclusively for majority and minority combined. None of the new States of Europe is more genuinely democratic than Czechoslovakia, under the distinguished Presidents, Masaryk and Benes, and although the Germans of the country may still have some grievances that deserve attention there would be no trouble of any kind but for encouragement from outside. It may be hoped that the fact that the eyes of Europe are on Czechoslovakia as a possible object of German aggression direct or indirect will in itself check any such intention if it exists. Germany's attitude towards the long-discussed conference of the Locarno Powers is still undisclosed; it is believed that Herr Ribbentrop has gone to Berchtesgaden for conversations on that point with Herr Hitler. If Germany is now ready to enter on that conference with an open mind she will be taking the best course to secure fair consideration of any grievances she may wish to put forward, and doing something substantial to make 1937 a better year than 1936 for herself and the rest of Europe.

25 December